Springer Proceedings in Business and Economics

More information about this series at http://www.springer.com/series/11960

Hadrian Geri Djajadikerta • Zhaoyong Zhang
Editors

A New Paradigm for International Business

Proceedings of the Conference on Free Trade Agreements and Regional Integration in East Asia

Springer

Editors
Hadrian Geri Djajadikerta
Edith Cowan University
Perth, WA, Australia

Zhaoyong Zhang
Edith Cowan University
Perth, WA, Australia

ISSN 2198-7246 ISSN 2198-7254 (electronic)
Springer Proceedings in Business and Economics
ISBN 978-981-10-1309-6 ISBN 978-981-287-499-3 (eBook)
DOI 10.1007/978-981-287-499-3

Springer Singapore Heidelberg New York Dordrecht London

Softcover reprint of the hardcover 1st edition 2015

Printed on acid-free paper

Springer Science+Business Media Singapore Pte Ltd. is part of Springer Science+Business Media (www.springer.com)

Preface

This book is a collection of studies on regional integration and dynamic business environment in East Asia. Papers included were presented at the 2014 Asia Pacific Business Conference on "Free Trade Agreements and Regional Integration in East Asia". The Conference was held at the Perth Convention and Exhibition Centre in Australia, and it was jointly organised by the Asian Business and Organisational Research Group (ABORG) at Edith Cowan University in Australia and the Centre for Economic and Social Studies in Asia (CESSA) at Yokohama National University in Japan. This Conference brought together academics, researchers, industry groups and policymakers from Asia, Australia and Europe to discuss ongoing research into regional integration in East Asia.

The Conference was organised in a timely manner just after the G20 Leaders' Summit in Brisbane, Australia. Western Australian Premier, the Hon Colin Barnett MEc MLA, delivered an opening keynote address and discussed the opportunities for growth in trade with East Asia. The Chinese Consulate General in Perth, Dr Huang Qinguo, delivered the other opening keynote address and discussed the importance of China's relationship with Australia.

Two industry keynote speakers contributed to the Conference. The Department of Foreign Affairs and Trade's Chief Free Trade Agreements (FTA) negotiator, Mr Graham Fletcher, spoke about the challenges and implications of FTA negotiations, while Bankwest's Chief Economist, Mr Alan Langford, discussed the challenges for Australia's economy in the global market. The Conference had also academic keynote speeches from two of the world's leading economists, Professor Paul De Grauwe from the London School of Economics and Professor Filip Abraham from Catholic University of Leuven. Both scholars discussed how Asia could learn from the monetary and financial integration in the European Union.

A total of 36 presentations were made by the keynote speakers, invited speakers and contributing presenters during the 3-day event. All academic papers submitted to the 2014 APBC by contributing authors have gone through a peer-reviewed process, and a total of 19 papers have been accepted for publication in this book. They address diverse areas related to regional integration, financial markets, investment, trade and capital flow, sustainability, accounting and auditing issues, exchange rates, strategies and business environment in East Asia.

We are happy that this first APBC has achieved its main objective of promoting collaboration with wide-ranging stakeholders in this growing area of importance: Asian business research. We believe that the Conference has built a solid platform for broader engagement and paved the way for many future conferences of this kind.

We would like to acknowledge the support of our sponsors: Edith Cowan University (ECU) and the Australian Department of Foreign Affairs and Trade. We would also like to thank the keynote and invited speakers, contributing authors and presenters, attendees, the Office of the Premier of Western Australia, the Consulate General of China in Perth, the Western Australia State Office of the Department of Foreign Affairs and Trade, ECU's Office of Research and Innovation, ECU's Marketing and Communications Services Centre (Corporate Events, Corporate Communications and Web Business), ECU's Faculty of Business and Law, ECU's School of Business, the Japan Society for the Promotion of Science, Yokohama National University and members of the Programme Committee for your highly appreciated contribution in enabling the success of this first APBC.

Perth, Australia Hadrian Geri Djajadikerta
Perth, Australia Zhaoyong Zhang

Contents

Chapter 1
What Makes for an Effective Free Trade Agreement? Examination of Theory and Evidence

Dess Pearson

Abstract Surprisingly, little research has been done on what factors make for an effective free trade agreement. By examining the theory and evidence, the author considers it may be possible to construct a model that sheds light on these factors. An index model, based on trade theory and evidence comprising 112 bilateral country trade pairs (including FTAs), has been developed to predict change in a nation's 5-year growth of bilateral trade relative to the growth in world trade. The use of an index model allows inclusion of those variables considered to have an important influence on the dependent variable – bilateral trade growth (BTG ratio) without requiring significant amounts of quantitative data to estimate model coefficients. The 24 variables in the model are binary, and the variable weights (model coefficients) are determined judgmentally from trade theory. An out of sample test of forecast accuracy was conducted on around half of the country pairs in the sample, and the result of a positive correlation between the dependent variable and the growth index was found. This adds weight to the validity of the author's model using the index method and confirms the view, supported by the literature, that growth in bilateral trade is driven by the variables such as GDP of the partner country, shipping costs, trustworthy institutions and strength of the FTA. If this research has unearthed a set of causal variables that can be used for prediction purposes by trade policymakers at minimal cost, then the resources devoted to this paper will not have been in vain.

1.1 Introduction

The central purpose of this paper is to pose and attempt to answer the question of what factors make for an effective free trade agreement. The author contends that by examining the theory and evidence, it is possible to construct a model that sheds light on this question, which, surprisingly, has not been adequately researched. By being able to isolate the drivers of a successful trade agreement, it should make it

D. Pearson (✉)
University of South Australia, Adelaide, SA, Australia
e-mail: dess.pearson@unisa.edu.au

H.G. Djajadikerta, Z. Zhang (eds.), *A New Paradigm for International Business*,
Springer Proceedings in Business and Economics, DOI 10.1007/978-981-287-499-3_1

possible to undertake preliminary and relatively inexpensive research prior to a country delving into a detailed and expensive benefit/cost, econometric and/or input–output study as to whether another country is a suitable partner for a free trade agreement (FTA).

FTAs are headline news in Australia and have been for the best part of this year which makes this research highly topical. Australian Prime Minister Tony Abbott recently signed two free trade agreements with Japan and Korea (Media Release, Department of Foreign Affairs and Trade, 8 July 2014 and 9 April 2014). And following the G20 meeting in Brisbane in mid-November, the Australian Prime Minister and the Chinese President signed the Australia–China FTA (Australian Financial Review 18 November 2014). Australia now has an FTA with its biggest trade partner.

Countries around the world are increasingly entering into FTA arrangements with chosen partners as a way of enhancing market access at a time when there is much uncertainty about the preferred way of settling access issues efficiently – multilaterally via the World Trade Organisation (WTO) negotiating rounds. As many countries, including Australia, have found, the WTO method to better market access is a long and arduous process involving around 160 countries and dealing with a host of issues (market access, industrial tariffs, agriculture, subsidies, intellectual property, trade-related investment, antidumping, trade and labour, trade and competition and trade and the environment). What this has meant in reality is that countries are looking for faster ways to achieve enhanced access to other countries' markets, and free trade agreements are a possible solution to this. Indeed, the WTO has commented 'the ever-growing number of regional trade agreements and preferential trade arrangements is a prominent feature of international trade' (www.wto.org).

Broadly, a successful trade agreement is where the benefits, in terms of economic welfare generated to citizens, outweigh its costs such as reduced output and subsequent unemployment in import-competing industries as well as possible loss of skills and erosion of human capital in affected sectors.

One of the main reasons for the recent proliferation of free trade agreements around the world is that with the current WTO Doha Round of multilateral trade negotiations in abeyance, countries are under increasing pressure to deliver market access outcomes by alternative means, such as through FTAs. Since some FTAs have been more effective in delivering trade outcomes than others (Eicher et al. 2012), policymakers around the world need to have an idea as to whether a given country makes for an ideal FTA partner. Some FTAs have shown themselves to be trade creating, where the benefits have outweighed the costs, whilst others have diverted trade by artificially lowering the prices of FTA partner countries vis-a-vis more efficient non-FTA suppliers (because of lower tariffs), and in these cases, the costs have often outweighed the benefits (Ghosh and Yamark 2004).

What this means is that policymakers need to have a reasonable idea before a detailed feasibility study is launched, on whether or not a particular country is a suitable FTA partner. In other words, there needs to be a checklist developed that policymakers could use to 'test' a country's FTA suitability. And if a country passes this preliminary test, that country could be then earmarked for further investigation as a potential FTA partner, meaning that a publicly funded detailed benefit/cost study would then be justified.

A key underpinning of why FTAs are entered into in the first place is the nexus between trade liberalisation and economic growth. And this has important implications for policy. If trade leads to higher growth, which is documented in the literature where, for example, world GDP growth is strongly correlated with merchandise exports (www.wto.org), and if FTAs produce greater trade, then it stands to reason that policymakers should favour FTAs – especially where it can be shown that their benefits outweigh the costs. There is much evidence to show that countries that liberalise their trade regimes experience average annual growth higher than before liberalisation. For example, Wacziarg and Welch (2008), writing for the World Bank, show that increases in economic growth caused by trade liberalisation can be as high as 1.5 percentage points and investment growth can be in excess of 2 percentage points higher than would otherwise have been the case. These differences are not insignificant and point to the view that if countries entered into successful and trade-creating FTAs, it would lead to higher economic growth – which in turn would have community welfare and employment-enhancing benefits.

Against this background, the author considers that the topic of what makes for an effective free trade agreement is important to the field of international trade theory and to public policy. It is therefore worth pursuing for the following reasons:

- First, based on an extensive literature search conducted, there appears to be a paucity of information and material on the topic of what the main drivers of successful free trade agreements are. Many journals and articles come close to the topic (Rose 2005, 2007), but very few specifically address it. Therefore, filling a gap in the literature is an important justification for this study.
- Second, having a sense of the factors that drive successful trade agreements will be of enormous benefit to trade policymakers around the world; determining whether a particular country is likely to be an effective FTA partner will be easier if the successful causal factors can be identified and documented. In addition, finding an appropriate FTA partner will be an easier exercise for governments, a lot less fraught with risk since entering into an FTA with an 'unsuitable' trade partner could be counterproductive.
- Third, being able to identify the causal variables should pave the way for more detailed benefit/cost analyses to be undertaken so that the value of an FTA over the longer term – that is, the benefits minus the costs – can be determined. Again, what this study aims for is a useful framework for policymakers to adopt as it would enable them to produce a list of likely countries where future trade agreements can be entered into.

Thus, the purpose of this research is to examine the factors that make for a successful trade agreement. The author contends that this research will not only contribute to knowledge, since there is a dearth of material in this particular area, but importantly it will assist policymakers by being able to quickly determine whether or not it is worth pursuing a particular trade agreement, thereby saving public resources in the process. The evidence for this research will be based on a sample of over 100 country pairs of trade partners (most of them FTAs) which will examine their trade performance (i.e. trade growth) pre- and post-FTA against world trade and will attempt to explain several causal variables. It will also test this model against a published trade model to draw comparisons.

In the next section, a detailed literature review will be undertaken. The review will cover whether or not FTAs cause more trade, what the case for them is and the results of FTA or trade policy modelling studies. This will then be followed by a description of the model employed, the data used and the choice of methodology. The model's results will then be discussed against the backdrop of an established trade model. Following this, a brief discussion of the implications of the research results for trade policy will be undertaken. Some concluding remarks will then be provided.

1.2 Literature Review

1.2.1 Do FTAs Cause More Trade?

A useful article for the purposes of this paper in estimating the effects of FTAs on international trade flows is by Scott Baier and Jeffrey Bergstrand (2008). In this paper, the authors provide long-run treatment effects of free trade agreements on members' bilateral international trade flows using (nonparametric) matching econometrics. Their most critical finding is that FTAs increased members' trade by an 'economically and statistically significant amount' in each of the 9 years of their sample (Baier and Bergstrand 2008). Their study provides some evidence that FTAs can lead to higher trade flows of member countries. The study was based on the ex post analyses of the partial effects of FTAs on trade flows, which were conducted using log-linear ordinary least squares (OLS) regression. Using a standard equation that trade flows (TF) were a function of GDP, distance (of FTA trade partner), whether or not the country pairs share a land border, common language and FTA membership, the authors found that country pairs with FTAs on average trade more than those without FTAs. For example, Baier and Bergstrand had determined that between 1995 and 2000, the log sum of trade for country pairs with an FTA was 14.57, whilst the log sum of trade for pairs without an FTA was 10.5, a sizable difference of 4.07.

The authors (Baier and Bergstrand 2008) note that 'conventional wisdom leads one to argue that trade between a pair of countries should increase when two countries enter into an FTA'. First, trade should increase due to trade creation as the pair benefits from lower costs. Second, trade between a pair could result from the 'diversion' of imports from previously lower-cost suppliers (which now accrue to the FTA partner due to lower relative tariff rates even though the partner country may be a higher-cost supplier than the country that has been displaced). For both these reasons, trade between FTA pairs should increase.

At the same time, the authors Baier and Bergstrand caution that their statistics do not necessarily imply that FTAs *cause* more trade. Clearly, there are many factors that drive bilateral trade such as GDP, size of market, common language and business culture and so on; one of these is FTAs.

1.2.2 Case for FTAs: Political and Economic

Apart from the Baier and Bergstrand article noted above, there was little in the literature on *factors that make for successful FTAs* (especially ex post analysis); accordingly, the primary focus in this section will be on the recent proliferation of FTAs, increasing political support for such trade agreements especially as many in the political space appear to have lost confidence in WTO processes and more generally academics' support for FTAs as a means to enhance market access and promote economic growth.

The rise of regionalism in recent years and the subsequent proliferation of FTAs (e.g. NAFTA in 1995, Singapore–Australia FTA in 2003, China–New Zealand in 2008, Australia–NZ–ASEAN FTA in 2009, Canada–Korea FTA in 2014) need examination in the context of what makes for an effective FTA. At the same time, it is recognised in the economic profession that free trade agreements, because they can cause trade to be diverted at the expense of efficient (lower-cost) producing countries, can have an adverse impact on welfare and are therefore something to be avoided (Bhagawati 1993). Economists such as Bhagawati consider that the multilateral approach to liberalisation, rather than bilateralism or regionalism, is more efficient. Nevertheless, because of the slow pace of multilateral negotiations in the WTO, many countries have had to look elsewhere for trade policy gains, hence the growing political support for FTAs. An obvious trade policy choice was thus bilateral or regional agreements.

Somewhat paradoxically therefore, a strong case for FTAs is that regionalism reflects the success of multilateralism rather than its failure. WJ Ethier (1998) argued this point. Ethier contended that the 1980s and 1990s spate of FTAs (or the so-called new regionalism) was motivated by a desire to facilitate entrance into a much more developed multilateral system; in other words, FTAs strengthened the multilateral system rather than weakened it. Ethier (1998) also considered that the undertaking of economic reforms was a necessary precursor to entering into FTAs; taking this a step further, it stands to reason that a phase of microeconomic reform in a country would be an explanatory variable to an effective FTA with that country; it is therefore one of the explanatory variables considered in this study.

In their article entitled 'The Politics of Free Trade Agreements', Grossman and Helpman (1995) analysed some of the political pressures brought to bear on a government as it decides whether or not to enter into an FTA. They ask questions like 'will an FTA between two countries be politically viable?' And if so, what form would it take? Grossman and Helpman address these questions through the use of a political economy framework that emphasises interactions between industry special interest groups and government. In their model, lobby groups offer policy-contingent campaign contributions to politicians who in turn make decisions that serve their own political objectives. In this setting, a country's policy stance reflects the relative political power of its organised special interests and also the extent of the government's concern for the plight of the average voter (who presumably is better off with free trade since he or she gets the benefit of lower product prices).

Grossman and Helpman (1995) found that, according to their political economy model, if an FTA was to completely liberalise trade amongst partner countries, a government might endorse an agreement in two situations:

- First, when an FTA would generate substantial welfare gains for the average voter (say through lower product prices)
- Second, when the FTA creates gains for exporters that are in excess of the losses that would be suffered by import-competing industries, plus the political cost of any welfare fallout

That is to say, the 'winners' from the FTA must, in theory, be able to compensate the 'losers' of the FTA for their economic losses, for example, loss of wages caused through unemployment in the import-competing industries.

Baldwin (1995) also contended that political forces could work towards entry into regional trade agreements. In his article, Baldwin posed the question of why countries were eager to open markets regionally but reluctant to do so multilaterally. Baldwin argues that a deeper integration of an existing regional bloc (e.g. the EU) can trigger membership requests from countries that were previously happy to be non-members. The logic, he contends, is simple. The stance of a country's government concerning membership is the result of a political equilibrium that balances anti-membership and pro-membership forces, and amongst the pro-integration forces are firms that export to the regional bloc. And since closer integration within a bloc is detrimental to the interests of non-member businesses, they will push politically for their country to join the bloc. This additional political activity may be greater at the margin than political action from the potential 'losers' of joining the firms in the import-competing industries and may tip the political balance in favour of joining.

These authors – Grossman and Helpman and Baldwin – show there was a growing groundswell of opinion politically for FTAs which, to a degree, explain their proliferation in recent years.

With respect to the economic case for FTAs, Eicher and Henn (2011) argue that preferential trade agreements[1] promote trade to a greater degree than WTO membership does, though with the caveat that trade growth is often uneven. The authors

[1] FTAs are also called preferential trade agreements (PTAs), since according to some trade economists, bilateral or regional trade agreements offer tariff and other non-tariff preferences to its members.

produce a model that essentially extends the gravity framework (the gravity model being that trade is a function of economic size and distance) by measuring the effects of WTO membership on trade flows amongst PTA countries and the effects of WTO membership on non-PTA countries. And they test this model through the use of multiple linear regression analysis. Eicher and Henn (2011) produce one consistent result: 'WTO effects on trade flows are not statistically significant, while PTAs produce strong but uneven trade growth effects across individual agreements'. This adds further weight to the economic case for FTAs.

To further support the case for PTAs, Foster and Stehrer (2011) examined the impact of membership in PTAs on trade between PTA members. Once again, the gravity model is the basis and the authors examine a large sample of countries over the period 1962–2000. They find that membership in a PTA is associated with an increase in the extent of intra-industry trade. Intra-industry trade refers to the extent of trade in similar products belonging to the same industry (e.g. different makers and models of cars that are exported and imported by the same country). Not surprisingly, the authors' results indicate that the trade growth effect for PTAs is greater when these agreements are formed between developed countries, with the effects of intra-industry trade between poorer countries found to be smaller. This is not surprising. Trade-in like goods reflects choice and variety, both of which are highly sensitive to income.

It is evident from the literature that there is a good case for FTAs; however, more detailed research needs to be undertaken to examine more specifically the factors that make for a successful trade agreement, as this is more relevant to policymakers. Accordingly, the next section examines the results of FTA modelling studies.

1.2.3 FTA Modelling Studies

In his article entitled 'Australia-China free Trade Agreement[2]: Causal Empirics and Political Economy', Tran Van Hoa (2008) assessed the potential benefits of a possible Australia–China FTA (ChAFTA) from an empirical perspective using aggregate economic modelling and historical data. Hoa undertook this analysis to contribute to the debate on ChAFTA's costs and benefits and for policy use. In his model, Hoa specified that growth in bilateral (China–Australia) trade was a function of several factors including openness/GDP, services trade/GDP, foreign investment/GDP, Chinese reforms, the Asia crisis and WTO membership.

Hoa obtained China's trade data from the International Centre for the Study of East Asian Development (ICSEAD) and Australia's trade data from the Australian

[2] The Australia–China FTA was signed by the Chinese President and Australian Prime Minister Abbott on the 17th of November 2014, and at the time of writing this article, negotiations were very much in the embryonic phase.

Bureau of Statistics. He estimated the equation using ordinary least squares (OLS) and two-stage least squares (2SLS). Hoa found the following:

- Both estimated growth models incorporating trade in goods, services and foreign direct investment (FDI) between Australia and China were statistically significant using the F-test.
- The estimated models appear free from autocorrelation.
- Trade as defined by total trade/GDP between Australia and China has a positive but weak impact on China's growth, though it has a strong positive effect on Australia's economic performance (which goes a long way to explain why the Australian Government was a lot keener to conclude an FTA with China than China was with Australia).
- Whilst China's goods and services flows have a small, beneficial and statistically weak effect on China's growth, FDI is found to have a positive and significant effect impact on this growth (this explains why China has been pushing so hard for higher liberalisation investment thresholds before they are referred to Australia's Foreign Investment Board for decision).

Overall, Hoa's analysis provides valuable guidance as to the selection of causal variables that explain the effectiveness of FTAs, especially ones like FDI/GDP and the role of economic reforms in further opening up a market.

In another study, modelling the future impacts of a Korea–US (KORUS) FTA , Yaylaci and Shikher (2014) find, using a general equilibrium computable model of trade (input–output analysis), that bringing KORUS into force would increase US manufacturing exports to Korea by a significant 56 %, whilst Korean manufacturing exports to the USA would increase by 19 %. It would also increase manufacturing employment by 26,500 jobs in Korea and 34,200 jobs in the USA. In other words, KORUS would generate a significant increase in intra-industry trade and, in doing so, change the patterns of trade and production in both countries. In sum, KORUS would increase economic welfare by 0.27 % in Korea and 0.013 % in the USA.

The welfare gains noted above were confirmed in another study by Lee and Song (2008) who found that the Korean GDP would expand by 0.32 %, indicating the substantial welfare gains possible from having an FTA with the 'right' partner.

From these studies on KORUS, it is clear to the author that one of the causal variables in predicting an effective FTA is the extent of intra-industry trade and that welfare gains can be substantial.

1.2.4 The Gravity Theory

In a paper by Andrew Rose (entitled 'Which International Institutions Promote International Trade?'), he estimates the effect of the WTO, IMF and OECD on export and import flows (Rose 2005). Rose used a standard gravity trade model of bilateral merchandise trade with a large dataset covering 50 years and over 175 countries. Rose notes the 'gravity model has a long track record of success in that it provides economically and statistically significant effects while explaining most variation in trade'.

Somewhat surprisingly, Rose finds that membership in either the WTO/GATT or the IMF is not associated with deeper trade. Consistent with other researchers, Rose finds that WTO membership in itself does not lead to greater trade growth. However, he found that the effect of OECD membership on trade was strong and positive. On this finding, Rose hypothesises that because one of the key criteria of OCED membership is evidence of economic reform, it is this which might help explain trade growth. In other words, a more liberalised economy is more conducive to greater trade flows. Accordingly, for the model specified in this paper, economic reform has been included in the list of causal variables.

As an aside, whilst economic reforms are, according to the literature surveyed, a necessary precursor to entering into FTAs (and which also make countries that undertake such reforms a desirable FTA partner), it could also be argued that countries seek bilateral and regional trade agreements as a means to lock in domestic reform policy, making it more difficult to subsequently reverse. Whalley (1998) makes a good case. Whalley argues that whilst smaller countries see bilateral and regional trade agreements with larger partners as a way of obtaining more security for their access to larger markets (e.g. Canada–US FTA, Australia–US FTA, New Zealand–China FTA), a strong justification was the need to underpin domestic policy reforms (e.g. Mexico in NAFTA).

Interestingly and consistent with other researchers in the field, Rose finds that the effect of FTA and regional trade agreement membership (e.g. EU, NAFTA, Mercosur) has a strong and positive impact on bilateral trade flows. Rose finds that the FTA/RTA impact on bilateral trade was even greater than that found in the literature he had surveyed in his paper (Rose 2005).

Though somewhat dated, Bergstrand (1989) provides evidence of both interindustry and intra-industry trade as driving variables of exports and imports. Bergstrand uses the analytical framework of the gravity model (trade growth is a function of size and distance) and extends it to include interindustry and intra-industry trade. Based on his general equilibrium model of world trade, he finds that both interindustry and intra-industry trade explains between 40 % and 80 % of the variation in trade flows. Bergstrand determined that exporter and importer income coefficients matched those from the gravity equations estimated for aggregate trade flows.

More recently, Antras and Staiger (2012) find that trade in intermediate inputs or 'offshoring' where production of intermediate parts is outsourced to lower-cost partner was an increasing feature of modern free trade agreements. Such trade flows are also a feature of intra-industry trade. The authors note that 'as a share of world trade, intermediate inputs appear to have increased significantly in recent years'. Interindustry trade is therefore a plausible causal variable for what makes an effective free trade agreement.

1.2.5 Economic Freedom and Trustworthy Institutions

More fundamentally, it must be kept in mind that some of the so-called 'softer' elements such as economic freedom and trustworthy institutions cannot always be taken for granted. These factors do impact positively on growth and trade, and hence, other things being equal, one would expect governments (and more likely policymakers) to take these into account when entering into FTAs or seeking suitable FTA partners.

One can look at the performance of countries by using an index designed by a Canadian think-tank – the Fraser Institute – called the Economic Freedom of the World Index (EFW). The EFW is a useful measure of the consistency of institutions and policies with economic freedom for countries and territories. The EFW covers 152 countries and territories, which makes it possible for scholars and policy practitioners to analyse the impact of cross-country differences in economic freedom. The index assesses countries on a scale of 1–10. The closer the metric is to 10, the greater the economic freedom, and the closer it is to 0, the lesser the economic freedoms. As a general guide, a metric over 7 signifies a country with a high degree of functioning economic and political institutions and high economic freedoms. Before entering into FTAs, policymakers can assess the EFW index of countries to see if they 'qualify' as a possible FTA partner. Economic freedom would therefore be a worthy variable to include in a model that looks at what drives bilateral trade growth.

With regard to trustworthy institutions, economic institutions are important as they have an impact on the structure of economic incentives in society; so one would expect that countries that have such institutions in place would be more sought after as an FTA partner. If property rights are unclear or uncertain, individuals will not have the right incentives to invest in physical or human capital or adopt more efficient technologies. Economic institutions are clearly crucial for long-run growth as they assist in allocating resources to their most efficient uses, which in turn helps determine who obtains profits and rights of control. When economic institutions are weak, or market signals ignored (as they were in the formerly centrally planned economies of Eastern Europe), resources are misallocated. Hence, it is countries that have robust economic institutions which facilitate and encourage accumulation of capital, innovation and efficient resource allocation that are a lot more likely to make for an effective FTA partner.

Acemoglu, Johnson and Robinson (2005) provide evidence for their hypothesis that institutions matter. That is to say, institutions do carry weight as an explanatory variable. The authors correlate the cross-country bivariate relationship between the log of per capita GDP and a measure of property rights calculated by an index that assesses and calculates risk that investments will be expropriated in different countries. The authors acknowledge that this measure may not be a perfect indicator of an economic institution and therefore insist that caution must be applied in drawing conclusions. Their findings – based on a scatter plot of log GDP per capita against the risk of expropriation – show that countries with more secure property rights, that is, better economic institutions, have higher incomes on average.

Despite the problems with data and causality, Acemoglu, Johnson and Robinson demonstrate that better economic institutions are the most likely determining factor of sustained economic prosperity. It is this that makes them ideal FTA trade partners.

The literature surveyed thus far reveals three elements that have important implications for this paper:

- First, there is a gap (in the literature) relating to what the key drivers of effective FTAs are.
- Second, there is a strong case for FTAs by a number of economists, and this has been supported by trade policies favouring FTAs (or a shift away from multilateralism) around the world, witnessed by their recent proliferation.
- Third, there is ample evidence to suggest that the gravity theory of international trade is the right one to use as the theoretical underpinning to a model that can help predict an effective FTA – the key is to choose the appropriate set of explanatory variables. Since the gravity theory has been used to assess trade flows, it seems logical to extent it into an analysis of trade performance pre- and post-FTA.

Having examined the theory in the literature, the model proposed for the author's study will necessarily draw on the gravity model as the underpinning theoretical foundation. A central element of the research in this paper is that the success of a trade agreement, measured through growth in imports and exports of a country post-FTA compared to that pre-FTA (and adjusted for world trade), depends on a number of causal factors. As noted, the gravity model provides some answers – economic size and distance – and as this research proposes to extend this theory, the two gravity causal variables will be included, although for distance, it is proposed to use shipping costs as a proxy, given the strong correlation between transport costs and distance. Other causal variables will be drawn from the literature reviewed, theory, commonsense and the experience of the author in the trade policy space.

This will be discussed in depth in the next section which documents the model employed, the data and methodology used as well as its justifications.

1.3 Model, Data and Methodology

1.3.1 Model

The author is interested in establishing what factors make for an effective free trade agreement and has therefore posed this question as the focus of this research. To help answer this, it is proposed that a conventional bilateral gravity trade model be used as the basis and a set of various causal variables be added to that. As outlined earlier, the basic bilateral gravity model comprises growth in trade being a function of income (GDP) and distance. Essentially, bilateral trade growth is positively correlated to income and negatively correlated to distance. The gravity model has a long history in international and regional trade and is well established (Rose 2005, Anderson and Wincoop 2004). It therefore makes sense to use the gravity model, as well as Rose's (2005) version, as both a theoretical foundation and to test the validity of the author's model.

The specification of the model is:

Bilateral TradeGrow(BTG) = FTA + FTA strength + Lang + Strength + Poten + Ship + GDP + GDPP + Free + FreeP + Tariff + TariffP + Non-tariff + Non-TariP + Reform + ReformP + Intra + IntraP + Trust + TrustP + Judic + JudicP + ComLaw + ComLawP.

Because the explanatory (or causal) variables have differing levels of impacts on the dependent variables, they are assigned different weights in the equation. The weights vary from 1 to 3, with 1 signifying a relatively low weight, 2 a moderate weight and 3 a relatively high weight. For example, membership of an FTA would be expected to have a strong impact on bilateral trade (and this is supported in the literature covered earlier), and so it is assigned a higher weight of 3; on the other hand, economic freedom in the initiating country (first) would not have the same impact on trade; hence, it gets a lower weight.

Because the above model is an extension of the gravity framework, much higher weights (50) are assigned to GDP of the partner country and shipping.

The dependent variable is growth in bilateral trade (BTG). It is a calculation of growth in bilateral trade post-FTA compared to pre-FTA. It looks at trade growth in a 5-year period post-FTA, which is compared to trade growth in a 5-year period pre-FTA. Five years is chosen because in the trade policy experience of the author, FTAs are commonly reviewed after 5 years, and Australia has been subject to trade policy reviews undertaken by the WTO every 5 years. Furthermore, 5 years should provide an adequate time period for which to assess the performance of trade, which in turn can be used as the basis for evaluation.

At the same time, growth in bilateral trade post-FTA needs to be adjusted; otherwise, it would pick up normal time trend growth in trade that would have occurred in the absence of an FTA or with GDP growth over that time period. Accordingly, bilateral trade growth of a country pair has been adjusted by taking into account world trade growth for the identical time period, that is, 5-year pre-FTA and 5-year post-FTA.

Therefore, the dependent variable (BTG) is in effect *growth in bilateral trade adjusted for world trade growth*. The value for the dependent variable for a given country pair is calculated as follows:

$$((\mathbf{1} + \mathbf{E10/100})/(\mathbf{1} + \mathbf{H10/100}))/((\mathbf{1} + \mathbf{D10/100})/(\mathbf{1} + \mathbf{G10/100})).$$

E = 5-year bilateral trade growth post-FTA, H = 5-year world trade growth post-FTA, D = 5-year bilateral trade growth pre-FTA, and G = 5-year world trade growth pre-FTA. It is considered that this calculation would yield a reliable measure of growth in bilateral trade following the entry into force of an FTA. In other words, and on the balance of probabilities, this is considered to be an accurate measure of the dependent variable.

BTG is a function of a number of causal variables which are:

- *FTA* – whether or not the country pair has a free trade agreement in force. A value of unity is assigned for an FTA in force; zero when the country pair is not in a free trade agreement. As the literature demonstrates, this variable is strongly proportional to trade. Accordingly, the weighting accorded to this variable is high – 3.
- *FTA strength* denotes the relative strength of that particular bilateral FTA – that is the degree to which it is trade liberalising or opens up the market. A value of unity is assigned when the FTA is judged to be a liberalising one; zero if not. This variable has a weight of 1.
- *Lang* denotes common language – this is a binary variable which is unity if both countries share a common language and zero otherwise. It is reasonable to assume that having a common language greatly facilitates communication which in turn stimulates trade which is why it has a weight of 3.
- *Strength* denotes strength of trade in the first period – if level of trade is relatively high (greater than $3 billion) in the second country, then the coding is unity; zero if less than $3 billion. It is reasonable to assume that a high level of trade in the partner or second country will more likely stimulate more trade and that such countries make for more effective FTA partners. This variable has a weight of 3, indicating its force in driving bilateral trade.
- *Poten* denotes potential for trade creation – essentially this is where the own-price elasticities of demand are judged to be high, and then the coding is unity; it is zero otherwise. It is reasonable to conclude that trade in goods where demand is elastic is a lot more sensitive to price changes (which occurs as tariffs fall when an FTA enters into force). In these situations, a lot more trade will likely occur than when trade comprises goods where demand is price inelastic. Consequently, this variable, proportional to trade, is assigned a relatively high weight of 3.
- *Ship* – this relates to the cost of shipping and is a good proxy for distance. This is a binary variable which is unity if costs are low – less than $1500 per full container load (FCL) – zero if higher. Other things being equal, trade is more likely to be generated when shipping costs are lower (as is typically the case when distances are shorter). So this variable, like distance, is inversely proportional to trade. Consistent with the gravity model discussed earlier in the paper, this variable is assigned a high weight of 3.
- *GDP* – this is the GDP of the first country of a pair. This is a binary variable which is unity if GDP is relatively high – greater than US$500 billion; it is zero if lower. Proportional to trade, GDP of the first (initiating) country of the pair is assigned a weight of 1.
- *GDPP* – this is the GDP of the second country of a pair. This is a binary variable which is unity if GDP is relatively high – again greater than US$500 billion; it is

zero if lower. GDP of a potential partner country would be expected to be highly proportional to bilateral trade, so this variable is assigned a weight of 3.

- *Free* denotes economic freedom – this relates to the degree to which a country is business friendly. It is a binary variable that is unity if a country is rated as moderately free; it is zero otherwise. As noted earlier in the literature review, economic freedom correlates positively with growth. A business friendly environment in the initiating (first) country would be expected to be proportional to trade, and it is assigned a weight of 1.
- *FreeP* denotes economic freedom in the second country in the pair. A value of unity is assigned if a country is free; zero otherwise. For the first country in the pair, seeking an FTA partner, economic freedom in that country, would be a highly positive factor, so this variable is assigned a weight of 2.
- *Tariff* stands for tariff barriers in the first country of a pair. A value of unity is assigned if the country's average tariff rate post-FTA is less than 5 %; it is zero if average tariffs are greater than 5 % post-FTA. Low tariff barriers in the initiating country would be proportional to trade though not to the same degree as low tariffs in the partner country (since the initiating country is seeking better access to the other country); hence, this variable has a weight of 1.
- *TariffP* stands for tariff barriers in the second country of a pair. A value of unity is assigned if the country's average tariff rate post-FTA is less than 5 %; it is zero if average tariffs are greater than 5 % post-FTA. As one would expect, low tariff barriers in the partner country would be proportional to trade by a greater degree; hence, the weight assigned for this variable is 3.
- *Non-tariff* stands for non-tariff barriers such as quotas or voluntary export restraints that form a feature of the first country's (in the pair) trade policies. A value of unity is assigned if the country is judged to have low non-tariff barriers; zero if they are high. Low non-tariff barriers are proportional to trade, and for the first country in a pair, this is assigned a moderate value of 2.
- *Non-tariP* denotes non-tariff barriers in the second country. Again, a value of unity is assigned if the country is judged to have low non-tariff barriers; zero if they are high. For the partner country to have low non-tariff measures, it is also a desirable outcome sought by an initiating country; this also is assigned a weight of 2.
- *Reform* denotes evidence of recent economic reform in the first country. A value of unity is assigned if the country is judged to have undertaken economic reform; zero if there was little evidence of reform. There was much in the literature reviewed earlier to suggest reform is an important component to driving trade. Evidence of recent economic reform in the first country of a pair is assigned a weight of 2.
- *ReformP* denotes evidence of recent economic reform in the second country (in the pair). A value of unity is assigned if the country is judged to have undertaken economic reform; zero if there was little reform. Evidence of economic reform in a partner country would be very proportional to trade; the assigned weight here is 3.

- *Intra* denotes intra-industry trade (trade in similar products belonging to the same industry) as a feature of the first country's bilateral trade. A value of unity is assigned when intra-industry is judged to be high from the data; zero when it is low. Intra-industry trade was supported in the literature. However, it is more prevalent for advanced, high-income countries and less so for developing countries. The weight assigned to this variable is 1.
- *IntraP* denotes intra-industry trade as a feature of the second country's bilateral trade. A value of unity is assigned when intra-industry is judged to be high from the data; zero when it is low. The weight assigned to this variable is also 1.
- *Trust* denotes trustworthy institutions (e.g. low corruption in the government) in the first country. A value of unity is assigned when the country is deemed to have trustworthy institutions; zero when it does not. As noted earlier in the literature review, trustworthy institutions have a positive correlation with economic growth and hence trade. A weight of 1 has been assigned to this variable.
- *TrustP* denotes trustworthy institutions (e.g. low corruption in the government) in the second country. Again, a value of unity is assigned when the country is deemed to have trustworthy institutions; zero when it does not. The weight assigned to this variable is also 1.
- *Judic* denotes an independent judicial system in the first country (of the pair). A value of unity is assigned when the country has an independent system; zero when it does not. An independent judicial system which better safeguards property rights is expected to have a positive impact on trade, and accordingly, this variable is assigned a weight of 1.
- *JudicP* denotes an independent judicial system in the second country. A value of unity is assigned when the country has an independent system; zero when it does not. The weight assigned to this variable is also 1.
- *ComLaw* denotes the effectiveness of commercial law in the first country (e.g. where property rights, including intellectual property rights, are strong). A value of unity is assigned when commercial law is assumed to be effective; zero when it is not.
- *ComLawP* denotes the effectiveness of commercial law in the second country. Again, a value of unity is assigned when commercial law is assumed to be effective; zero when it is not. The weight assigned to this variable is also 1.

The model specified above is comparable to the Rose (2005) model. The model Rose specifies is based on bilateral trade growth being a function of GDP, population, distance, common language, sharing of a land border, area, using the same currency, whether or not they shared the same colonial power, whether they were colonies, GSP (tariff preferences accorded to developing countries in the WTO), WTO membership, FTA membership, IMF membership and OECD membership. It makes sense to be able to test the validity of results obtained for the author's model with Rose's model.

1.3.2 Data

One hundred and ten country pairs were identified and used for this study. Of these, 62 country pairs have formal free trade agreements in place and 48 countries do not. Examples of FTAs used in the sample include well-known ones like the Australia–New Zealand Closer Economic Relations Trade Agreement, the Australia–US FTA and the China–New Zealand FTA as well as lesser well-known ones like the Armenia–Kazakhstan FTA, Ukraine–Belarus FTA and the Panama–Chile FTA. So the sample is not only a mix of FTA and non-FTA pairs but also a mix of FTAs where trade flows are small and relatively unknown and where they are large and have been in the public eye.

The mix of country pairs with FTAs and without is to provide comparison in examining the effects of FTAs in stimulating greater trade and also to provide a balanced picture since it is fair to assume that trade growth also occurs in the absence of FTAs. Providing a mix of country pairs also enables the researcher to better isolate the effects of growth in trade resulting from FTAs since it is possible to make this comparison. These country pairs are tabulated in the statistical annex appended to this paper that appears as an 'Excel' spreadsheet (refer Appendix 1 and 2).

Details of countries having entered into FTAs were obtained from the World Trade Organisation's (WTO) website – in particular the WTO's RTA database (http://rtais.wto.org/UI/PublicAllRTAList.aspx). Under WTO rules, member countries that enter into bilateral or regional free trade agreements must, under GATT Article XXVIII, formally notify the WTO since these agreements represent a departure from the most-favoured nation principle, a key pillar of WTO membership (where one country that makes say a tariff concession to another must accord the same level of access to all WTO members). An FTA or RTA accords preferential market access to its member partner(s) and not others, so all members of the WTO need to be advised so that they could make adjustments to their trade policies. The WTO site was therefore an appropriate source for bilateral FTAs to be used in the sample.

Data for the growth rates in bilateral trade for the country pairs were obtained from the large trade database of the United Nations Conference on Trade and Development (UNCTAD). These data can be obtained from the UNCTAD statistics portal which contains time series statistics on international trade, economic trends, foreign investment, commodities and maritime transport. In particular, the country pair bilateral trade growth rates were obtained from a section entitled 'Value growth rates of merchandise exports and imports, annual, 1950-2013' (http://unctadstat.unctad.org/wds/TableViewer/tableView.aspx?ReportId=102 refers). Only FTAs entered into before 2008 were included in this study since 5 years of post-FTA trade growth performance was required. This necessarily meant that many recent FTAs (where trade flows are large) could not be included in the study. The actual year when a particular FTA had entered into force has been documented in the spreadsheet (as a separate column), and average growth of 5 years prior to that year and 5 years after that year has been recorded in separate columns.

As earlier noted, growth in bilateral trade for the selected 112 country pairs has been adjusted for growth in world trade, and this has formed the dependent variable in the model (BTG). Values for the dependent variable in the model have been reported as a ratio. For example, the Ukraine–Kazakhstan FTA (observation number 97) shows a coefficient of 1.265, indicating that trade grew by over 26 % post-FTA, whilst for observation 10 – the Australia–New Zealand FTA (which is often seen as the 'gold standard' in FTAs because of the truly liberalising nature of the agreement) – the reported coefficient is 0.987 indicating a decline in bilateral trade of around 1.1 %. To a degree, the latter can be explained because of the different times when the FTAs were entered into and the size of bilateral trade. The Australia–NZ FTA came into force in 1983, so the 5 years post 1983 would have incorporated the severe global recession of 1982–1983 and anaemic growth during the 5-year period post-FTA, hence lower bilateral trade growth irrespective of an FTA. Whilst in the former case, the Ukraine–Kazakhstan FTA came into effect in 1998 at a time when most former Soviet Union countries were beginning to recover strongly as they made the transition from centrally planned to market economies. Not surprisingly, due to the sharp rebound in economic growth, trade growth was also strong at that time.

With respect to the 24 causal variables used in the model documented earlier, data for these were obtained from a number of sources. The first causal variable is whether or not a country pair has an FTA. A value of 1 is assigned in cases where there is an FTA in place, and 0 is assigned where there is no FTA. With regard to the strength of FTA, information on the type of FTA is documented on the WTO's RTA portal – elements such as the magnitude of tariff cuts, the sensitive sectors that are excluded from the open market disciplines of the FTA and its scope (whether it covers investment, services, government procurement and other sectors). A judgement is then made on each FTA, and a value of 1 is assigned when it is more liberalising and 0 if it is less liberalising. For non-FTA country pairs, a value of 0 is assigned.

With regard to common language, a value of 1 is assigned to a country pair where the language is common and 0 otherwise. For many cases (e.g. Canada–France, Australia–New Zealand and Panama–China), it is obvious. In some cases (e.g. Australia–India), though the main languages in India are not English and therefore different to Australia, the fact is that English is widely spoken in India and is the language used in commerce. It is reasonable in this case (and in many European countries) to assume common language where English is also the language of the trade partner. Where it was not known, information on languages used in country pairs was obtained from the Australian Department of Foreign Affairs and Trade's (DFAT) site under the section 'countries and regions'.

On the strength of trade in the first period (pre-FTA), the UNCTAD database was used to determine the value of bilateral trade. Bilateral trade (exports + imports) of $3 billion or more would be considered substantial, so trade in excess of this figure was assigned a value of 1, whilst less than that attracted a value of

0. With respect to trade creation, it is recognised that where goods have high price elasticities of demand, there is much more scope for trade creation as tariff levels fall (and hence market prices). The UNCTAD trade data for the country pairs was examined to determine the scope for trade creation; where the composition of trade was such where goods were more price elastic, bilateral trade was more amenable to trade creation and vice versa for goods where demand elasticities were considered to be low.

With regard to the cost of shipping, the following site – www.worldfreightrates.com/en/freight – provides a calculator that calculates shipping rates for a full container load of product. The rates vary proportionally with distance, so for longer voyages, the costs rise. This variable is very similar to the distance variable often used in gravity model studies (Rose 2005, 2007) and provides a good predictor for trade flows. As one would expect, shipping costs vary inversely with trade flows, so where shipping costs were less than $1500 per full container load, a value of 1 was assigned and 0 when costs were less than this figure.

For obtaining data on GDP of country pairs (first and second), the DFAT site was used. A moderately large country is considered to have a GDP of US$500 billion. According to both the World Bank and the International Monetary Fund in 2013, only 26 countries (of around 190) measured up to this level of GDP. Details on economic freedom (or its lack) were obtained from http://www.heritage.org/index/ which evaluates and ranks countries on the basis of several criteria including rule of law, degree of government intervention in an economy and regulatory efficiency.

Data on average tariff rates as well as non-tariff measures were obtained from the UNCTAD trade database – http://unctadstat.unctad.org/wds/TableViewer/tableView.aspx?ReportId=122 – which provides countries' average tariff rates over time. From these figures, it was possible to classify countries on the basis of low or high tariffs and assign values accordingly. Information relating to economic reforms in country pairs was obtained from the DFAT site – from uploaded individual country reports prepared by the Department's overseas missions.

Information on the extent (or lack) of intra-industry trade was obtained from the following location on the vast WTO site – http://www.wto.org/english/res_e/statis_e/its2011_e/its11_toc_e.htm – from gleaning country pairs' composition of trade, one can determine the extent of trade-in like goods (export and import of similar goods), and accordingly values can be assigned.

Information relating to the last three causal variables for the first and second countries, namely, trustworthy institutions, independent judicial systems and effectiveness (or lack) of commercial law, was obtained from the following site – www.internationalpropertyrightsindex.org/ranking – which ranks countries where property rights are most secure.

1.3.3 Methodology

To obtain whether there was a correlation between the dependent variable – growth in bilateral trade adjusted for world trade (BTG) – and the set of causal variables, the author created an index variable that summed all 24 of them. As noted earlier in the paper, the index numbers were based on the values (1 or 0) assigned to each causal variable and the weight assigned to each variable. This sum total was then listed in the column entitled 'Index Score' (TG index) where TG stands for trade growth. Generally speaking, the higher the TG index number for a given country pair (with or without an FTA), the stronger the likelihood that it would be correlated with the dependent variable.

Whilst previous gravity model studies used regression analysis, mainly ordinary least squares to correlate the dependent and causal variables (Rose 2005, 2007; Anderson and Wincoop 2003), for this research, the author considered the conditions were more suited to the index model given the large number of causal variables (24) and the moderate sample size (112). Compared to regression analysis which has a long history in economics, the index method for analysis and forecasting is relatively new. Nevertheless, in many respects, the index method is more effective than traditional regression methods such as ordinary least squares. This is especially so for forecasting purposes.

Essentially under the index method, numbers (typically 1 or 0) are assigned to each observation for the various causal variables, and each variable is provided a weight. The values for each observation are then summed to provide the index (in the case of this research, the index is the TG index). Graefe and Armstrong (2011) summarise the key conditions where the index method is useful for forecasting. Graefe and Armstrong claim 'the index method is an alternative to multiple regression models in situations with small samples and many variables'. They go on to note that the 'usefulness of multiple regression models for prediction depends on the availability of valid and reliable quantitative data relative to the number of causal variables'. As a guide, Graefe and Armstrong (2011) recommend that regression analysis for nonexperimental data (like the data used in this study) requires at least 100 observations (meaning a relatively large sample). And it is best that regression analysis be restricted to just a few causal variables (lest one runs into problems of say multicollinearity). Given that the identified causal variables for this study were 24, it made sense to choose the index method for analysis rather than regression.

Graefe and Armstrong (2011) also state that the index model is useful for cases where a large number of causal variables are important and for which one can assess the directional effect of each variable on the outcome. Again, for the FTA model of this paper, the index method is better, not just because of its lack of complexity but because it relies on the experience and prior knowledge of the researcher(s). In the context of this research, the author has over two decades' experience in trade policy with several Australian and State government agencies which can be brought to bear when making judgements about countries' trade performances. Importantly,

Graefe and Armstrong (2011) also lend much credibility to the notion that weights be applied to the various causal variables since, necessarily, some variables have a greater impact on the outcome than others; they can therefore be weighted accordingly.

In another paper, the same authors (Armstrong and Graefe 2011) used 59 biographical variables to create a 'bio-index' for forecasting US presidential elections. This index counted the number of variables for which each presidential candidate rated favourably with the forecast that the candidate with the highest 'score' would win the contest. Not surprisingly, the bio-index relied on information from a wide range of sources and included many more variables than that used by traditional econometric forecasting. To underscore the effectiveness of this research and forecasting method, the bio-index approach correctly predicted 27 of the 29 US presidential elections held from 1896 to 2008 (although one candidate, Al Gore in 2000,actually won the popular vote but not the presidency). Again, the authors state the 'index method is particularly valuable in situations with good prior domain knowledge'. Importantly, indexes are relatively easy to use, easy to understand and, if constructed properly, provide reasonably good forecasts.

In a more recent paper on this topic, Green and Armstrong (2014) also lend weight to the notion that complexity does not necessarily make for better forecasting. The authors found no evidence that 'complexification improved accuracy'. This further adds weight to the selection by the author of the index method as a rationale for the research methodology for this paper. Tellingly, Green and Armstrong (2014) state that 'a causal model with three variables selected and estimated by stepwise regression is more complex than a 50 variable index model that uses prior knowledge to select variables and specify weights and then sums across the variables'. This is exactly the approach used by the author in this paper.

Green and Armstrong (2014) also note that simple linear relationships (such as through the use of the index approach) can approximate more complex relationships (as the index incorporates a large number of diverse variables) and 'should be preferred' in cases where the true relationship(s) is unlikely to be correctly identified. In the case of this research, whilst 24 variables were selected as determinants of effective FTAs, in reality, a lot more could have been chosen – and indeed some of the chosen ones could well be subject to debate as to the validity of their inclusion.

To test the effectiveness and validity of the author's model, the Rose (2005) model variables described earlier were used, and values of 1 or 0 and weights for each variable were assigned so that an index was also created. The same dependent variable (BTG) was regressed alongside the Rose index which was based on his causal variables. Doing this would both test the validity of the Rose model and importantly would allow for a comparison to be made with the author's model.

Having outlined the model, data and methodology, the results of the research will be reported and discussed in the next section.

1.4 Model Results

The results of the FTA effectiveness model (i.e. growth in trade post-FTA compared to pre-FTA) are reported in Tables 1.1 and 1.4 in Appendices 1 and 2. A much more detailed outline of the research model which includes all 24 causal variables is included in a separate Excel document (submitted with this paper as an appendix). All 112 country pairs are listed in Tables 1.1 and 1.4. In Table 1.1, the dependent variable and the sole causal variable, which is the trade growth index, are listed, whilst in Table 1.4, details of growth in trade pre- and post-FTA together with growth in world trade pre- and post-FTA (and for non-FTA pairs, it is for 5 years before the relevant year listed in the column and 5 years after) are provided.

To summarise, the author developed an index model (full index model) based on trade theory and evidence to also predict change in a nation's 5-year growth of bilateral trade relative to the growth in world trade. The use of an index model allows the author to include those variables considered to have an important influence on the dependent variable BTG ratio without requiring significant amounts of quantitative data to estimate model coefficients. The 24 variables in the model are binary, and the variable weights (model coefficients) are determined judgmentally from trade theory. The heaviest weights are assigned to cost (cheapness) of shipping, which is a proxy for distance, GDP of trading partner and common language. The introduction of an FTA and an assessment of its strength are also overweighted. Other variables given higher weights (higher than 1) include whether the country pair is characterised by an FTA, the degree to which tariffs are low in the partner country and the strength of the FRA.

In order to test whether the variables with smaller weights in the full index model improve the predictive validity of the model, the author created a short index model that includes only the overweighted variables.

Using 50 of the total sample of 112 trade partner pairs, the author estimated single regression equations that relate the full index and short index scores to BTG ratio. The author then applied the regression equations to the index scores for the remaining 62 trade sample pairs in order to predict BTG ratio for each.

The summary page table (in the Excel spreadsheet at the appendix) shows that the mean absolute error (MAE) of out of sample forecasts of BTG ratio from the full index model is about 5 % (0.051) and is about 2 % smaller than the errors of the forecasts from the short index model. In other words, the lower-weighted variables in the full index model do contribute to predicting the dependent variable (BTG ratio).

The heaviest weighted variables in the index models either do not change or change slowly over time, which suggests that a naive no-change model would make sensible predictions of BTG ratio. This turned out to be the case: the MAE of the naive model forecasts was less than 5 % and somewhat less than the MAEs of both index models' forecasts. In other words, changes from one 5-year period to the next seem typically to have less effect on changes to BTG ratio than do the variables that stay more or less the same or expect most relative bilateral trade growth with partners that have a large GDP, low shipping costs and a common language.

The author also tested a simple implementation of a standard trade model, the Rose model which was also based on gravity theory. Forecasts from the Rose model were 22 % less accurate than forecasts from the naive model. This finding suggests that the Rose model may have excluded critical variables such as the strength of the FTA or shipping costs.

Finally, to test the hypothesis that periods of relatively strong bi-trade growth are followed by periods of relatively weak bi-trade growth, the author predicted that if the rate of bilateral trade growth was greater than the rate of world trade growth in the first 5-year period, it would be less by the same amount in the second 5-year period. In other words, relative growth spurts in bilateral trade would be followed by relatively modest growth and vice versa. The findings support this hypothesis that neither unusually strong nor unusually weak bilateral trade growth between particular country pairs persists beyond about 5 years: errors of the forecasts of BTG ratio from that 'reversal' model turned out to be 28 % smaller than those from the naive model.

The data analysis is provided at Table 1.2 at the base of Appendix 1 where the slope, intercept and correlation were calculated. The slope was calculated to be 0.001077, the intercept just under 1 at 0.95363 and the correlation 0.28154.

A key point note with respect to the correlation value of 0.28154 is that the coefficient was positive, indicating a positive relationship between the dependent variable (of trade growth post-FTA) and the TG index. In other words, the causal variables that form the index can be used to predict growth in bilateral trade. The positive sign was in the right direction.

It is fair to say that this study's determination of a positive relationship between the dependent and causal variables, based on the trade growth evidence for 112 country pairs, confirms the findings of the literature review. They also add weight to extending the gravity model. One could argue, at least tentatively, that the evidence lends support to the hypothesis that the 24 causal variables identified in this paper do, to a degree, explain what makes for an effective free trade agreement. That said, it is clear that more research in this area is needed to determine, with greater accuracy, what factors make for a successful FTA.

An out of sample test of forecast accuracy was conducted on country pairs 53–112, and the results are reported in Table 1.3. It can be seen that the CumRAE for the full index is 1.061. This is a result that adds further weight to the validity of the author's model using the index method and confirms the view (based on the literature) that growth in bilateral trade is driven by the 24 variables that make up the index. It means that the index model created provides forecasts that are 6 % more accurate than the naive model and are more accurate again than the forecasts from the other models (with CumRAEs greater than 1.061). The Rose model falls into this category as the CumRAE calculated was 1.217.

Also, the author used the judgemental weights that derived from the review of the literature, and the model with those weights provides forecasts that are more accurate than those from an equal-weights model. Furthermore, the short index

CumRAE (see Table 1.3) was 1.081. This indicates that the short index model also provides forecasts that are more accurate than the alternative models (other than the full index), but most importantly, having all the important variables (represented in the full index) provides the most accurate forecasts. As discussed in the methodology section earlier, this reinforces the value of the index model approach, which allows the inclusion of all important variables in a model.

As noted earlier, evidence from the forecasting literature – for example, Graefe and Armstrong (2011) – suggests the usefulness of the index model, particularly where a large number of causal variables are important in predicting the dependent variable and where it is possible to assess the directional effect of each variable on the outcome. The author tested this in the model he developed against Rose model and reasonable naive alternatives and found a strong relationship exists between the dependent and causal variables. This suggests that the use of the index method on the extended gravity model that included a large number of explanatory variables to predict growth in bilateral trade was sound.

There may be several ways to further improve the author's model. They include:

- The time period examined (5-year post-FTA compared to 5-year pre-FTA) could be extended. Though the author had earlier argued that 5 years made good sense given that this is the cycle for trade policy reviews to be conducted, it may be the case that comparing the evidence every 10 may yield a more positive correlation. This needs to be investigated.
- It may be the case that additional variables need to be included in the model. As noted earlier, in their paper, Armstrong and Graefe (2011) used no fewer than 59 causal variables to determine the index that was used to forecast the accuracy of US presidential elections. It could be that 24 variables were just not enough and that, quite possibly, some important causal variables were not included. Again, this requires further research.
- Given that increasingly investment is playing an important role in FTA negotiations, this could be included as a causal variable to an effective FTA.
- It may be that the weights assigned to the causal need to be revised which could make a difference to the correlation coefficient.
- It may also be the case that some causal variables included had a weak effect and may need to be removed.

Overall, the positive correlation obtained in this study by using the index method as well as the robust out of sample tests indicates that this research is on the right track. Importantly, it indicates that research of this nature – looking for reliable explanatory variables that help predict what makes for a good FTA – is worthy of further research.

1.5 Implications for Broader Trade Policy

As outlined earlier in this paper and also by the Australian Department of Foreign Affairs and Trade (www.dfat.gov.au), across the globe, there is an expanding network of FTAs. As shown in the literature review, FTAs can play an important role in supporting global trade liberalisation and, under Article XXIV of the GATT, are explicitly allowed for under WTO rules.

In recent times, in addition to goods trade, FTAs are also incorporating several other issues such as intellectual property rights, government procurement and competition policy. At the time of writing, Australia has seven FTAs currently in force with New Zealand, Singapore, Thailand, the USA, Chile, the Association of South East Asian Nations (ASEAN) (with New Zealand) and Malaysia, and the countries covered by these FTAs account for 26 % of Australia's total trade. Australia signed an FTA with Korea in April 2014 and an EPA with Japan in July 2014 and an FTA with China this month (November 2014). Korea and Japan account for 5 % and 11 % of Australia's total trade, respectively, whilst trade with China accounts for a significant 28 %. Taken together, Australia's trade with its FTA partners now accounts for a very significant 70 % of total trade.

Given the results of the research that show that FTAs have a positive impact on trade, Australia's trade policy switch (made prior to the Australia–Singapore FTA) to rely more heavily on FTAs as a route to enhanced market access was a sensible call.

With the analytical focus increasingly shifting to the choice of partner (rather than whether or not to enter into FTAs), it is clear that there is much at stake since it remains imperative that the choice of trade partner must be the right one. And at the same time, there remain budgetary pressures within government which mean that detailed cost/benefit and/or econometric FTA feasibility studies are time consuming and use much public resources. Therefore, policymakers need to have a 'checklist' of desirable characteristics for being able to predict the suitability of an FTA partner country as this would save resources that may otherwise have been spent on costly (and, in some cases, unnecessary) benefit/cost research. This would also lead to a better use of policymakers' time.

In effect, the research undertaken in this paper – and the development of a checklist of known drivers of effective FTAs – could be regarded as pre-benefit-cost research feasibility analysis. That is, it has the potential to lead to greater cost-effectiveness in FTA analysis typically undertaken by trade or commerce ministries in countries around the world.

1.6 Concluding Remarks

As indicated at the outset, the central purpose of this paper was to attempt to answer the question of what factors make for an effective free trade agreement. Whilst the results of the statistical analysis conducted cannot be too definitive, there is evidence to indicate that some of the main factors that make for an effective FTA include the strength (in terms of its liberalising impact) of the trade agreement, common language, shipping costs, degree of economic freedom in partner countries, degree of tariff and non-tariff measures in the country pair, GDP, degree of economic reforms undertaken in both countries, the potential for trade creation and degree of intra-industry trade. It also includes intangibles such as the degree of trustworthiness, whether or not there is an independent judiciary and the effectiveness of commercial law.

Many of these causal variables make common sense, and one can tentatively conclude that, based on the literature, theory and evidence, there is a case for these to be listed as determinants of a successful FTA.

There seems to be little doubt that by being able to isolate the drivers of a successful trade agreement, it should make it possible to undertake preliminary and relatively inexpensive 'desktop' research prior to expensive benefit/cost studies being commissioned as to whether another country is a suitable partner for a free trade agreement (FTA).

If this research has unearthed a set of causal variables that can be used for prediction purposes and in the process save public monies that would otherwise have been spent on more resource-intensive and by definition higher-cost research, then the resources devoted to this paper will not have been in vain.

Acknowledgement I would like to thank Dr Kesten Green for his considerable input, valuable guidance and time throughout the development of this thesis, without which the robustness of the results would not have been possible.

Appendix 1

Table 1.1 Results of FTA model

Bilateral FTA/Pair	BTG ratio	TG index
Armenia – Kazakhstan	**1.206976306**	117
Armenia – Moldova	**1.203022144**	67
Armenia – Russia	**1.123855835**	117
Armenia – Turkmenistan	**1.203154663**	66
Australia – Indonesia	**1.086762979**	121
Australia – Peru	**1.087816511**	67
Australia – Philippines	**1.07618929**	75
Australia – Mexico	**1.044003524**	125
Armenia – Ukraine	**1.175802443**	123
Australia – New Zealand	**0.986887552**	96
Australia – Singapore	**0.870530443**	90
Australia – Russia	**0.998257732**	67
Australia – Canada	**0.947408625**	78
Australia – Israel	**0.998185801**	28
Australia – Chinese Taipei	**0.970661558**	127
Australia – India	**1.009524351**	78
Australia – UK	**0.920940065**	77
Brunei – Japan	**1.075345909**	126
Canada – Chile	**1.133058293**	35
Canada – Japan	**1.084288979**	74
Canada – China	**1.138248157**	123
Canada – UK	**1.16535905**	134
Canada – Netherlands	**1.144468606**	129
Canada – Spain	**1.185373388**	129
Canada – France	**1.161128801**	84
Canada – South Africa	**1.180875375**	130
Canada – Chinese Taipei	**1.072368565**	78
Canada – Hong Kong	**1.092364603**	36
Canada – Germany	**1.154618031**	136
Canada – Italy	**1.097223303**	127
Canada – Poland	**1.144247816**	122
Canada – Costa Rica	**0.870935634**	71
Canada – Israel	**1.045626557**	83
Chile – China	**0.915558398**	80
Chile – Japan	**0.976324983**	78
Chile – Mexico	**1.037939975**	139

(continued)

Table 1.1 (continued)

China – Hong Kong	**0.820829866**	86
China – Macao	**0.74445941**	86
China – New Zealand	**1.011398138**	32
Egypt – Turkey	**0.951442475**	72
Georgia – Armenia	**1.245795864**	68
Georgia – Turkmenistan	**1.043387463**	71
Guatemala – Chinese Taipei	**0.957290996**	66
India – Singapore	**1.009813826**	86
India – Sri Lanka	**0.997664951**	83
Israel – Mexico	**0.881900764**	78
Japan – Indonesia	**1.094177651**	129
Japan – Malaysia	**0.978410491**	82
Japan – Philippines	**1.062830828**	74
Japan – Singapore	**0.975603458**	81
Japan – Russia	**1.00184834**	112
Japan – Turkey	**1.001122795**	62
Japan – Germany	**0.993724213**	71
Japan – France	**0.934200099**	67
Japan – Ukraine	**1.01952732**	60
Japan – UK	**0.982070847**	70
Japan – Turkmenistan	**0.989720985**	61
Japan – Azerbaijan	**0.963409332**	58
Japan – Kazakhstan	**1.011756457**	58
Japan – Uzbekistan	**1.006753501**	56
Japan – Kyrgyz Rep	**0.950752715**	57
Japan – Thailand	**1.019212772**	131
Jordan – Singapore	**0.987788616**	74
Korea – Chile	**0.860619128**	84
Korea – Singapore	**0.965822139**	35
Laos – Thailand	**1.137241858**	77
New Zealand – Singapore	**1.057430326**	91
New Zealand – France	**1.034913701**	124
New Zealand – Russia	**1.085270552**	64
New Zealand – USA	**0.990330027**	84
New Zealand – Germany	**0.997750608**	73
New Zealand – Indonesia	**1.025126299**	70
New Zealand – Netherlands	**0.990142718**	71
New Zealand – Spain	**1.010003556**	70
New Zealand – UK	**0.991016166**	82
New Zealand – Thailand	**1.038209945**	72

(continued)

Table 1.1 (continued)

New Zealand – Poland	**1.006581707**	71
New Zealand – Portugal	**1.082421641**	65
New Zealand – Malaysia	**1.020831904**	135
Nicaragua – Chinese Taipei	**1.112350559**	72
Pakistan – Sri Lanka	**1.020283945**	74
Pakistan – Malaysia	**1.032751719**	83
Panama – Chile	**0.933548392**	79
Panama – Chinese Taipei	**1.05437973**	124
Panama – Singapore	**0.881179462**	20
Russia – Serbia	**0.898022031**	19
Singapore – Australia	**0.975612226**	141
Thailand – Australia	**1.065177103**	139
Thailand – New Zealand	**1.028707807**	88
Turkey – Albania	**1.004079692**	66
Turkey – Georgia	**0.978565797**	65
Turkey – Israel	**1.139807862**	78
Turkey – Morocco	**0.947614024**	19
Turkey – Tunisia	**0.973138955**	61
Ukraine – Belarus	**0.912945555**	66
Ukraine – Macedonia	**1.087176624**	9
Ukraine – Kazakhstan	**1.265562554**	16
Ukraine – Moldova	**0.942541804**	66
Ukraine – Tajikistan	**1.024552307**	67
US – Kazakhstan	**0.964311141**	16
US – Japan	**1.008840777**	72
US – Germany	**1.059549249**	74
US – France	**1.054396424**	76
US – Australia	**1.078698401**	91
US – Bahrain	**1.003334962**	29
US – Chile	**1.052088723**	40
US – Israel	**1.099985564**	44
US – Jordan	**1.013906978**	23
US – Morocco	**1.021673783**	24
US – Singapore	**0.902442185**	46

Shaded pairs = no bilateral FTA

Table 1.2 Data analysis (112 observations)

0.000834	*Slope*
0.95363	*Intercept*
0.281535	*Correlation*

Table 1.3 Out of sample forecast accuracy (country pairs 53–112)

	Mean	90 percentile	Cumulative	Cumulative	% error
Model	*Absolute error*	*Absolute error*	*Absolute error*	*RAE*	*Reduction*
Naïve	0.048	0.103	2.878	1.000	
Reversal	0.035	0.065	2.079	0.722	28
Short index	0.052	0.124	3.112	1.081	−8
Full index	0.051	0.126	3.055	1.061	−6
Rose	0.058	0.136	3.502	1.217	−22

Appendix 2

Table 1.4 Trade growth pre- and post-FTA

Bilateral FTA/Country Pair	5 years trade growth - pre FTA	5 years trade growth - post FTA	5 years world trade growth - pre FTA	5 years world trade growth - post FTA
Armenia – Kazakhstan	3.06	31.55	4.6	10.62
Armenia – Moldova	–6.14	8.72	7.65	3.65
Armenia – Russia	0.34	12.56	8.59	8.39
Armenia – Turkmenistan	–0.66	15.3	8.44	4.61
Australia – Indonesia	6.45	11.6	8.44	4.61
Australia – Peru	3.45	8.56	8.44	4.61
Australia – Philippines	7.65	11.76	8.44	4.61
Australia – Mexico	7.99	8.76	8.44	4.61
Armenia – Ukraine	–0.8	12.52	8.44	4.61
Australia – New Zealand	0.71	12.85	–0.91	12.51
Australia – Singapore	11.82	10.04	3.19	16.65
Australia – Russia	0.88	13.84	3.19	16.65
Australia – Canada	3.68	11.04	3.19	16.65
Australia – Israel	3.67	16.98	3.19	16.65
Australia – Chinese Taipei	5.27	15.51	3.19	16.65
Australia – India	4.67	19.45	3.19	16.65
Australia – UK	2.76	6.98	3.19	16.65
Brunei – Japan	4.31	2.89	16.65	7
Canada – Chile	4.75	11.82	9.22	2.9
Canada – Japan	3.96	6.2	9.22	2.9
Canada – China	8.45	16.3	9.22	2.9
Canada – UK	3.65	13.8	9.22	2.9
Canada – Netherlands	3.65	11.76	9.22	2.9
Canada – Spain	2.67	14.66	9.22	2.9
Canada – France	6.77	16.8	9.22	2.9
Canada – South Africa	4.67	16.45	9.22	2.9
Canada – Chinese Taipei	5.66	6.75	9.22	2.9
Canada – Hong Kong	4.27	7.31	9.22	2.9
Canada – Germany	8.99	18.56	9.22	2.9
Canada – Italy	4.35	7.87	9.22	2.9
Canada – Poland	3.67	11.76	9.22	2.9
Canada – Costa Rica	5.49	2.25	2.9	14.52
Canada – Israel	8.21	6.6	9.22	2.9
Chile – China	22.25	10.47	10.62	9.18
Chile – Japan	12.16	5.23	14.51	10.04
Chile – Mexico	8.68	11.53	8.08	6.86
China – Hong Kong	17.75	9.26	3.19	16.65

(continued)

Table 1.4 (continued)

China – Macao	14.18	–3.91	3.19	16.65
China – New Zealand	18.72	10.14	16.65	7
Egypt – Turkey	22.29	11.81	14.51	10.04
Georgia – Armenia	5.79	25.47	8.39	3.19
Georgia – Turkmenistan	6	18.89	3.65	11.42
Guatemala – Chinese Taipei	12.56	6.35	10.62	9.18
India – Singapore	16.11	11.43	11.82	6.27
India – Sri Lanka	5.84	11.67	4.6	10.62
Israel – Mexico	12.14	6.31	3.65	11.42
Japan – Indonesia	6.54	6.93	16.65	7
Japan – Malaysia	7.79	4.09	10.62	9.18
Japan – Philippines	4.81	2.18	16.65	7
Japan – Singapore	1.08	9.75	2.9	14.52
Japan – Russia	1.32	12.97	2.9	14.52
Japan – Turkey	3	14.76	2.9	14.52
Japan – Germany	4.87	15.98	2.9	14.52
Japan – France	3.54	7.65	2.9	14.52
Japan – Ukraine	0.18	13.67	2.9	14.52
Japan – UK	7.56	17.56	2.9	14.52
Japan – Turkmenistan	0.31	10.49	2.9	14.52
Japan – Azerbaijan	9.83	17.76	2.9	14.52
Japan – Kazakhstan	4.04	17.15	2.9	14.52
Japan – Uzbekistan	–2.11	9.68	2.9	14.52
Japan – Kyrgyz Rep	1.52	7.42	2.9	14.52
Japan – Thailand	8.88	6.64	14.51	10.04
Jordan – Singapore	15.45	8.38	11.82	6.27
Korea – Chile	15.35	8.07	6.86	16.33
Korea – Singapore	12.94	7.66	10.62	9.18
Laos – Thailand	17.23	27.56	12.51	7.65
New Zealand – Singapore	0.01	11.84	4.6	10.62
New Zealand – France	6.8	16.89	4.6	10.62
New Zealand – Russia	0.25	15.06	4.6	10.62
New Zealand – USA	5.65	10.65	4.6	10.62
New Zealand – Germany	4.76	10.54	4.6	10.62
New Zealand – Indonesia	2.11	10.7	4.6	10.62
New Zealand – Netherlands	3.76	8.65	4.6	10.62
New Zealand – Spain	4.65	11.78	4.6	10.62
New Zealand – UK	6.76	11.89	4.6	10.62
New Zealand – Thailand	1.06	10.96	4.6	10.62
New Zealand – Poland	5.87	12.7	4.6	10.62
New Zealand – Portugal	3.65	18.65	4.6	10.62
New Zealand – Malaysia	1.78	9.88	4.6	10.62

(continued)

Table 1.4 (continued)

Nicaragua – Chinese Taipei	7.23	9.41	16.65	7
Pakistan – Sri Lanka	8.38	5.09	11.82	6.27
Pakistan – Malaysia	10.85	5.01	16.65	7
Panama – Chile	26.67	8.47	16.65	7
Panama – ChineseTaipei	5.94	21.6	6.86	16.33
Panama – Singapore	24.26	8.07	10.62	9.18
Russia – Serbia	22.11	8.23	10.62	9.18
Singapore – Australia	1.39	11.82	3.19	16.65
Thailand – Australia	10.49	11.85	11.82	6.27
Thailand – New Zealand	10.96	8.48	11.82	6.27
Turkey – Albania	22.43	12.76	16.65	7
Turkey – Georgia	23.16	10.55	16.65	7
Turkey – Israel	7.24	15.16	9.22	2.9
Turkey – Morocco	16.19	8.67	10.62	9.18
Turkey – Tunisia	17.88	9.02	11.82	6.27
Ukraine – Belarus	19.67	7.83	10.62	9.18
Ukraine – Macedonia	0.57	15.63	4.6	10.62
Ukraine – Kazakhstan	3.15	24.28	8.39	3.19
Ukraine – Moldova	19.82	7.33	11.82	6.27
Ukraine – Tajikistan	–0.82	13.09	2.9	14.52
US – Kazakhstan	15.46	9.89	10.62	9.18
US – Japan	4.85	4.4	10.62	9.18
US – Germany	6.87	11.76	10.62	9.18
US – France	3.76	7.98	10.62	9.18
US – Australia	6.92	9.61	11.82	6.27
US – Bahrain	6.93	5.89	10.62	9.18
US – Chile	6.89	11.9	6.86	6.33
US – Israel	0.39	14.25	–0.91	2.52
US – Jordan	3.1	10.55	4.6	10.62
US – Morocco	6.28	7.17	10.62	9.18
US – Singapore	8.06	6.16	6.86	16.33

Data source for country trade growth – http://unctadstat.unctad.org/wds/TableViewer/tableView.aspx?ReportId=102

Shaded areas denote non-FTA country pairs

References

Acemoglu D, Johnson S, Robinson J (2005) Income and democracy. Working paper 11205. National Bureau of Economic Research, Cambridge, MA

Anderson JE, Wincoop EV (2003) Gravity with gravitas: a solution to the border puzzle. Working paper 8079, National Bureau of Economic Research, 1050 Massachusetts Ave, Cambridge, MA 02138

Anderson JE, Wincoop EV (2004) Trade costs. Working paper 10480. National Bureau of Economic Research, Cambridge, MA

Antras P, Staiger RW (2012) Offshoring and the role of trade agreements. Am Econ Rev 102 (7):3140–3183

Armstrong JS, Graefe A (2011) Predicting elections from biographical information about candidates: a test of the index method. J Bus Res 64:699–706

Australian Department of Foreign Affairs and Trade website. www.dfat.gov.au

Australian Financial Review, 18 Nov 2014

Baier S, Bergstrand J (2008) Bonus vetus OLS: a simple method for approximating international trade-cost effects using the gravity equation. J Int Econ 77:77–85, Feb 2009

Baldwin RE (1995) What caused the resurgence of regionalism? Swiss J Econ Stat 131 (3):453–463

Bergstrand JH (1989) The generalised gravity equation, monopolistic competition and the factor-proportions theory in international trade. Rev Econ Stat 71(1):143–153

Bhagawati J (1993) The case for free trade. Sci Am 269(5):18–23

Department of Foreign Affairs and Trade, Media Releases, 8 July 2014 and 9 Apr 2014. www.dfat.gov.au

Eicher TS, Henn C (2011) In search of WTO trade effects: preferential trade agreements promote trade strongly but unevenly. J Int Econ 83:137–153

Eicher TS, Henn C, Papageorgiou C (2012) Trade creation and diversion revisited: accounting for model uncertainty and natural trading partner effects. J Appl Econ 27:296–321

Ethier WJ (1998) The new regionalism. Econ J 108(449):1149–1161

Foster N, Stehrer R (2011) Preferential trade agreements and the structure of international trade. Rev World Econ 147:385–409

Ghosh S, Yamark S (2004) Are regional trading arrangements trade creating? An application of extreme bounds analysis. J Int Econ 62(2):369–395

Graefe A, Armstrong JS (2011) Conditions under which index models are useful: reply to bio-index commentaries. J Bus Res 64:693–695

Green KC, Armstrong S (2014) Simple forecasting: avoid tears before bedtime. J Bus Res 11:271–279

Grossman G, Helpman E (1995) The politics of free trade agreements. Am Econ Rev 85 (4):667–690

Hoa TV (2008) Australia-China free trade agreement: causal empirics and political economy. Econ Pap 26(1):19–29

International Property Rights site: www.internationalpropertyrightsindex.org/ranking

Krugman P (1991) The move to free trade zones. Federal Reserve Bank of Kansas City – Economic review, Cambridge, MA, November/December

Lee H, Song B (2008) Quantitative estimates of the economic impacts of a Korea-United States free trade agreement. Asian Econ Pap 7(2):52–73

Rose AK (2005) Which international institutions promote international trade. Rev Int Econ 13 (4):682–698

Rose AK (2007) The foreign service and foreign trade: embassies as export promotion. World Econ 10(11):22–38

United Nations Conference for Trade and Development (UNCTAD). Statistics database. http://unctadstat.unctad.org/wds/TableViewer/tableView.aspx?ReportId=102

Wacziarg R, Welch KH (2008) Trade liberalization and growth: new evidence. World Bank Econ Rev 22:187–231
Whalley J (1998) Why do countries seek regional trade agreements. National Bureau of Economic Research, Cambridge, MA
World Freight Rates site: www.worldfreightrates.com/en/freight
World Heritage site: http://www.heritage.org/index/
World Trade Organisation: http://rtais.wto.org/UI/PublicAllRTAList.aspx
World Trade Organisation website: www.wto.org
Yaylaci O, Shikher S (2014) What would Korea-US free trade agreement bring? Int Econ J 28(1):161–182

Chapter 2
The Mode of Economic Cooperation in the "One Belt and One Road" Construction

Zongxian Feng and Hua Wang

Abstract In view of the regional economic cooperation and integration, this paper analyzes the strategic conception of "Silk Road Economic Belt" and "21st Century Maritime Silk Road"("One Belt and One Road" for short) raised by the Chinese people. It firstly discusses the major regional cooperation mechanism and the evolution of the type in this conception. Secondly, it discusses the competitive and cooperative relationship between the construction of "One Belt and One Road" and the current regional cooperation mechanism. Also, the possible effect which may exert on the construction of the "One Belt and One Road" from the emerging regional cooperation mechanism is also analyzed. Thirdly, it elaborates on the way China should adopt to guarantee the smooth implementation of "One Belt and One Road" by making use of the current regional cooperation mechanisms and cooperating with the ones that China has not yet participated. The result of this paper shows that China has been facing with two options currently in the construction of "One Belt and One Road." One is through the strategic means of free trade area, and the other one is through the cooperative means of regional and subregional combination. From the perspective of the feasibility and the profitability, the construction of the "One Belt and One Road" should implement an innovative cooperation model, which, at the current stage, is not a supranational mechanism, nor a model at the same level with the Customs Union or the Economic Union; it should be, on the contrary, a platform for friendly cooperation which can provide

This research was funded by the major projects of the National Social Science Foundation (No.12 & ZD070) the Chinese National Natural Science Foundation of China (No.71441039), major projects of the Key Research Base of Humanities and Social Sciences, the Chinese Ministry of Education (No.11JJD790013), and Silk Road thematic projects of 2013 Shaanxi Provincial Social Science Fund.

Z. Feng
School of Finance and Economics, Xi'an Jiaotong University, Xi'an, People's Republic of China

H. Wang (✉)
School of Finance and Economics, School of Foreign Studies, Xi'an Jiaotong University, Xi'an, People's Republic of China
e-mail: seablue@mail.xjtu.edu.cn

H.G. Djajadikerta, Z. Zhang (eds.), *A New Paradigm for International Business*, Springer Proceedings in Business and Economics, DOI 10.1007/978-981-287-499-3_2

the countries within the region with better economic exchanges and channel construction, a new idea and cooperative way to create better conditions and opportunities for collaboration among different countries, various mechanisms, and organizations. If conditions are right, it will form a higher and more extensive regional economic cooperation, including the institutional arrangements of the free trade area. Thus, this platform will promote the rejuvenation of the Silk Road and provide direct convenience to the integration of the region. This can also be called negative integration, a notion raised by Tinbergen, which is a development that seems to be doing nothing but can actually make contributions proactively.

2.1 Introduction

2.1.1 The Meaning and Spatial Range of "One Belt and One Road"

"One Belt and One Road" refers to the "Silk Road Economic Belt" and "21st Century Maritime Silk Road." It is a proposal made by President Xi Jinping in his visits to Kazakhstan and Indonesia in September and October 2013. "One Belt and One Road" is bordered by the Asia-Pacific economic circle in the east, enters the European economic circle in the west, and crosses the Eurasian continent. Historically, the "Land Silk Road" and the "Maritime Silk Road" were the great channels for trade, economic, and cultural communication between China and Central Asia, Southeast Asia, South Asia, West Asia, East Africa, and Europe. The "Silk Road Economic Belt" is from China to West Asia and leads to Europe. The "21st Century Maritime Silk Road" starts from China, crosses Southeast Asia, and extends to the Indian Ocean, Arabian Sea, and Gulf Area. In 2013, the trade volume between China and the countries along the route reached to one trillion US dollars, which account for a quarter of the Chinese total foreign volume. During the past 10 years, the trade volume between China and the countries along the route has grown at an average annual rate of 19 %, which increased by 4 % compared to the foreign trade at the same period. In the next 5 years, China will import commodities worth ten trillion US dollars, make foreign investment of more than 500 billion US dollars, increase the tourist quantity of approximately 500 million more passengers, and firstly benefit the surrounding countries and the countries along the route. To view from the space, "One Belt and One Road" covers an area of about more than ten countries and regions with disparity in economy and society. Thus, for discussion purposes, this paper will divide the countries and regions into two sections: domestic section and international section from the perspective of China. In the international section, regions like Asia, Europe, Africa, Pacific Ocean, Indian Ocean, and Atlantic Ocean are involved. To view from the time, the initial phase of the "One Belt and One Road" construction mainly concerns China and countries in Central Asia, South Asia, and Southeast Asia. In the future, the "One Belt and

One Road" will gradually extend to countries in West Asia and Central and Eastern Europe, with radiation effect even to North Africa and other European countries.

2.1.2 Literature Review

Tinburgen (1954) firstly raised the notion of regional economic integration and classified it into the negative one and the positive one. He believes that to introduce the liberalization of economic variables in the aim of eliminating discrimination and regulation institution is defined as the negative integration, while to reform the current condition with strong power and establish new liberalization policy and institution is defined as the positive integration. The American economist Balassa (1961, 1965) furthered the notion raised by Tinburgen by defining the integration as both a process and a state. He believes that the regional economic integration is the denial of any governmental discriminations and limitations during the move of the commodities and elements. In terms of the process, it includes various measures to eliminate the differences among the economic units in different countries. In terms of the state, it is shown by the elimination of all kinds of differential treatment in different countries. The American economist Jacob Viner (1950) firstly introduced his theory of customs union in the book *The Customs Union Issue*. He points out that the customs union will produce a dynamic effect of issues such as trade creation and trade diversion, economies of scale, competition, investment, and so on. And he employs the quantitative analysis to clarify that the trade creation could lead to the welfare increase of the member states, while the trade diversion could lead to the welfare decrease from the perspective of production. Another basic theory of the regional economic integration is the free trade area theory, on which the British scholar Peter Robson (2001) has launched comprehensive research. He believes that the elimination of the trade barriers within the region could realize the trade liberalization among the member states and the unified customs and trade policies should be adopted by them as the basic form of trade liberalization. In 1956, based on the economies of scale under a perfectly competitive market, Spark raised the theory of single market (Zhang Youwen 1999), and it was later developed from the dynamic perspective by the theory of big market raised by economists T Scitovsky and JF Deniau (Liang Shuanglu and Cheng Xiaojun 2007).

Economist Fritz Machlup (1979) argues that, in fact, the economic integration could either refer to several regions within the same country or among different countries. The latter one could be further classified into a regional and subregional one. Some other economists don't approve to explain economic integration as a process and state. As Peter Robinson stated, international economic integration is a mean, rather than a goal. He pointed out in 1961 that the integration should not be defined by means such as free trade, unified market, convertibility, liberalization, but as aim, equality, liberty, and prosperity.

As is shown in Graph 2.1, there are various kinds of regional cooperation mechanism in the "One Belt and One Road"; representative ones include the

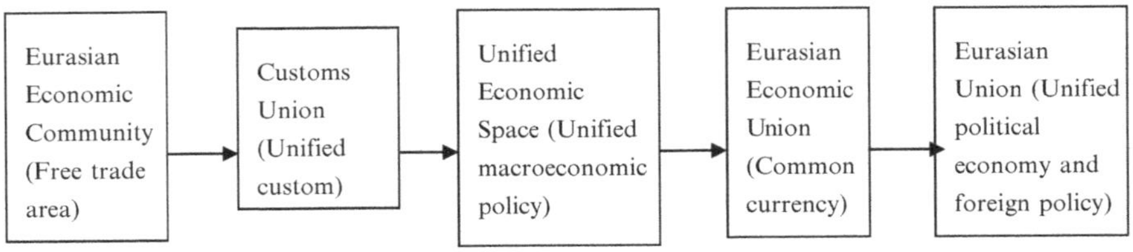

Graph 2.1 Road map of Eurasian Economic Community Integration (Source: Li Fuchuan (2011), *Market in Russian, Central Asia and Eastern Europe*)

Shanghai Cooperation Organization, Russia–Belarus–Kazakhstan Customs Union and China–ASEAN (10 + 1), APEC, European Union, and so on. In addition, there are also some others still under negotiations, such as the Trans-Pacific Partnership Agreement; Transatlantic Trade and Investment Partnership, which is called Europe–America free trade area by the international media; China–Japan–South Korea free trade area; Regional Comprehensive Economic Partnership; and the ongoing FTAAP feasibility research.

The effect on economic growth of the construction of infrastructure has always been the issue of common concern to many economists. From the classical theory to the newest theory of economic growth, the researches on the effect of infrastructure on economic growth have experienced the process from qualitative to quantitative and appeared three main stages of theory research and three main kinds of research methods. The first stage of theory research is named capital theory stage, the main idea of which is that the infrastructure is the capital of wealth assembling. Adam Smith noted in his *Wealth of Nations* in 1776 that the construction of traffic ways, bridges, ports, canals, and other transportation is the duty of the government and has important facilitations to the economic growth. The researches in this period were mainly qualitative, and the infrastructure was not separated from the factors which affect the economic growth. The successive stage of theory research is called the structural theory stage. There are mainly three views. The first one is that the economic growth could only be boosted if supply could be front-run in the infrastructures, with Paul Rosenstein-Rodan and Ragnar Nurkse as the typical representatives. They believe that only if infrastructure be developed at a heady speed could the economic growth be provided with a necessary prerequisite and could the speedy economic growth be sustained. The second one is that the economic growth could be boosted if the development of the infrastructure be laid out subsequently. This point of view is firstly stated by Albert Otto Hirschman in his famous *unbalanced growth*. The main content of it is that the investment capital should firstly be adopted in the direct productive activity and that to the infrastructures should be delayed temporarily, given the limited resources and abilities of investment, so that the revenue of investment could be obtained as soon as possible and output and income could be increased. After the direct productive sectors are developed and produce a large amount of income, part of which could be used to invest the infrastructure constructions. He believes that the way with more effect and less risk is that the direct productive activity should be carried out first. Thus, the pressure of shortage will subsequently emerge. Then the expenditures and allocations could be determined by this kind of pressure. The third one is that the basic condition of economic growth is the investment to the infrastructures. Representatives include Walt Whitman Rostow who believes that one prerequisite for economic takeoff is the construction of infrastructures, and he also emphasizes it with several theories and methods.

In terms of the strategic conception of the Chinese "One Belt and One Road" construction, this paper will analyze it from the perspective of the regional cooperation integration. The Chinese government also claims that it will make full use of the bilateral and multilateral mechanisms of China with the related countries and create the interest community of China and the countries along the route with the help of the existing and effective regional cooperation platform. The main issues that will be discussed in this paper are the competitive and cooperative relationship between the construction of "One Belt and One Road" and the current regional cooperation mechanism, the possible effect which may exert on the construction of the "One Belt and One Road" from the emerging regional cooperation mechanism, and the way China should adopt to guarantee the smooth implementation of "One Belt and One Road" by making use of the current regional cooperation mechanisms, combining the new supporting mechanism, and cooperating with the ones that China has not yet participated. The second part is about the Eurasian Economic Community and Eurasian Economic Union. The third part is about the China–Japan–South Korea free trade area, ASEAN 10 + 6, and Asia-Pacific free trade area. The fourth part is about the promotion of "One Belt and One Road" construction and option of regional economic integration mode.

2.2 From the Eurasian Economic Community to the Eurasian Economic Union

2.2.1 Eurasian Economic Community

In May 2001, the Eurasian Economic Community was established. The current member states are Russia, Belarus, Kazakhstan, Kyrgyzstan, and Tajikistan. Armenia, Moldova, and Ukraine are the observing countries.

2.2.1.1 From the Eurasian Economic Community to the Eurasian Customs Union

On January 1, 2010, Russia, Belarus, and Kazakhstan decided to set up the Customs Union under the framework of the Eurasian Economic Community. In July, the three countries have achieved the unification of their common external tariff. Since July 2011, they have abolished the mutual customs. On January 1, 2012, the

Eurasian Economic Commission, the superstate organization in charge of the initiation of the unified economic space and the process of the integration, has been put into operation.

The economic integration among Russia, Belarus, and Kazakhstan has created extremely strategic and fairly impressive short-term effect. For example, the mutual trade increase has become more than three times of the foreign trade increase, with the former one increased by 9 % and the latter one 3 %. Before the unified economic space was founded, the interior trade increase of the three countries was inferior to that of the foreign trade. In addition, according to statistics, the trade volume of machinery and technical products increases comparatively larger, including agricultural machinery, coaches, tractors, motorcycles, computers, televisions, and other high value-added products.

2.2.1.2 The Characteristic of the Eurasian Customs Union's Development

Firstly, Russia is the engine that can lead the Customs Union to a transformation of the unified economic space and realization of economic modernization and technological innovation economy. From the aspect of the economic strength, Russia has occupied a superstrong position where its market accounts for 90 % of the three countries' total. The GDP of Kazakhstan in 2009 was 10.6 billion US dollars, Belarus 5.19 billion US dollars, and Russia 1.3 trillion US dollars. Russia has a dominant role in this region.

Secondly, the customs rate has become Russianized. After the foundation of the Customs Union, Belarus and Kazakhstan have adjusted their standards of customs to fit that of Russia. 80 % of the products' customs were unchanged. Russia had a higher custom of those machinery and cars imported from Asian countries than Belarus and Kazak, so the two countries raised theirs while Russia left unchanged. The 350 items of customs were increased by 5 % on average. Some meat products like sausages and jars have increased greatly. Meanwhile, thousands of products like medical equipment, audio equipment, and home electrical appliances have been decreased by 5 %.

Thirdly, the Customs Union has exerted some positive demonstration effect on the promotion of the economic integration of other CIS countries. Different from the CIS countries founded in 1991, the Customs Union is a more real integration organization form with actual benefit. Currently, the main aim of Russia–Belarus–Kazakhstan Customs Union is to ensure the merchandise trade liberalization within the three countries. Looking ahead into the future, products with single market should match the services with the single market.

2.2.2 *Eurasian Economic Union*

The aim of Russia–Belarus–Kazakhstan integration is to establish the Eurasian Economic Union before 2015. What is the characteristic of it with Customs Union as its foundation? Andrei A. Slepnhev, the trade minister of the Customs Union, believes that this Union is more like the European Union than the Soviet Union. However, the early days of the Eurasian Union only witness a narrow range of coverage of the issues involved compared to the EU.

2.2.2.1 The "Road Map" of the Eurasian Union

The presidents of Russia, Belarus, and Kazakhstan have signed an agreement in Moscow on November 18, 2011. They decided to further promote the economic integration based on the Customs Union and build the Eurasian Economic Union in 2015.

According to the document signed by the presidents of the three countries, Russia, Belarus, and Kazakhstan started the building of the unified economic space since 2012, and their ultimate goal is to establish a Eurasian Economic Union with unified politics, economy, military, customs, and human space and to realize the free flow of labor, commodities, service, and capital. The leaders of the three countries also decided to establish a superstate organization, the Eurasian Economic Commission, which would take place of the Customs Union Commission and coordinate the economic integration of the three countries in an integrated manner. The new organization came into operation since 2012; the first leader of which is Viktor Khristenko, trade and industry minister of Russia. The agreement also formulated the "road map" of setting up the Eurasian Economic Union, which is the historical event in the regional integration process. Mikheyev, the Russian political analyst, thinks that this has meant that the founding of the European Economic Union has already turned from rhetoric to action, which signifies the actual movement plan and the leaders' political determination.

2.2.2.2 Symbolic Milestone

On May 29, 2014, the presidents of Russia, Belarus, and Kazakhstan officially signed the Eurasian Economic Union Treaty and established a limited economic union. The treaty includes 28 sections, 118 chapters, and 23 appendices, more than 700 pages in all. According to the treaty, Russia, Belarus, and Kazakhstan will achieve the free flow of commodities, service, capital, and labor before 2025. Their ultimate goal is to establish an economic union similar to the EU and form a unified market with a population of 170 million. The treaty covers a whole range of energy, transportation, industry, agriculture, customs, trade, revenue, government procurement, and so on. And it also develops a list of the free trade commodities, excluding sensitive products like cigarettes and wine. According to the treaty, the three countries promised to ensure the free flow of commodities, service, capital, and labor in the Union and strived to ensure the collaboration of policies in the major economic industry represented by energy, processing, agriculture, and transportation. The treaty formulates that the Eurasian Economic Union is an international organization where Russia, Belarus, and Kazakhstan enjoy equal authority and equal voting rights in the organizations of the Union. The Eurasian Commission's headquarters is based in Moscow. The court of the Eurasian Economic Union is based in Minsk, the capital city of Belarus. The financial regulator is based in Alma-Ata, a southern city of Kazakhstan. Different from the eurozone set by the EU, Russia, Belarus, and Kazakhstan have never discussed the possibility of providing a common currency.

It is important to note that Ukraine is the critical partner for Putin to establish the Eurasian Union, due to the fact that most of the countries in the Eurasian Union are located in Asia, while Ukraine is the largest economic entity in Europe. However, since the outbreak of the crisis, Ukraine has lost Crimea and faced with the intense demand for independence from the eastern part. Most importantly, Ukraine was absent from the meeting of the Eurasian Union (Feng Wei and Cheng Guoqiang 2014).

Russia has once suggested that Russia, Belarus, and Kazakhstan should carry out a unified trade policy within the Eurasian Economic Union framework. However, the final text of the treaty only regulates the three countries to coordinate the trade policy. In the meantime, Putin has indicated that the Economic Union would adopt the general international standards of trade, some even consistent with the WTO standards. Apart from that, Russia and Belarus once attempted to add issues concerning international cooperation, common nationality, immigration policy, visas, border security, etc., into the treaty, but turned down by Kazakhstan. According to Ordabayev, the vice foreign minister of Kazakhstan, the Union will be depoliticized and become a pure economic union. Putin said that the geographic position of the Union signifies the possibility that it might become the global transportation junction, which connected the trade flow between Asia and Europe.

2.2.3 The Prospect of Cooperation and Development Between China and the Eurasian Union

China adjoins two countries in the Eurasian Union, namely, Russia and Kazakhstan. Being the members of the Shanghai Cooperation Organization and each other's strategic cooperation partner, they have close relationships with each other. China also has close trade relationships with Russia, Belarus, and Kazakhstan. According to the statistics published by the Commerce Department, the bilateral trade volume between China and Russia has reached 7.509 billion US dollars in 2012. Among which, the main export products from Russia to China are minerals, chemical products, and wood works. The main import products from Russia to China are mechanical and electrical products, textile products, and raw materials. The bilateral trade volume between China and Kazakhstan has reached 2.568 billion US dollars in 2012, which mainly focused on the huge infrastructure construction projects like oil and gas pipelines, hydroelectric power stations, and so on. Comparatively speaking, the bilateral trade volume between China and Belarus was rather small, only 1.58 billion US dollars, which mainly focused on mechanical appliances, steel, and agricultural machinery. However, when we compared the data among Russia, Belarus, and Kazakhstan, to take 2012 as an example, we may find that minerals have the highest percentage of the trade volumes among the mutual trade of Russia, Belarus, and Kazakhstan, which account for 37 % of the total; followed by the machinery and transportation facilities, with a percentage of 21 %; the metal and metal works, with a percentage of 12.7 %; and the agricultural and chemical products, with a percentage of about 10 %. It is not hard to find that there are differences between China and each of the three countries in terms of trade volumes, but the trade structure and bilateral import and export products between China and each of them are very similar. Therefore, in the face of the emergence of the Eurasian Union, China has an urgent need to upgrade its structure. Not only that, when the time is right, China should also initiate negotiations with the Eurasian Union. In addition, the Eurasian Development Bank is also one financial institute that China needs to assess carefully and analyze the gains and losses if we are to participate in. The Eurasian Development Bank is an international economic institute, founded in January 2006. It specializes in the investment of infrastructure constructions, with a registered capital of 1.5 billion US dollars. Its member states include Russia, Kazakhstan, Tajikistan, Armenia, Belarus, and Kyrgyzstan. Among which, Russia, Kazakhstan, and Tajikistan are also member states of the Shanghai Cooperation Organization. Given that China has always been committed to the promotion of the founding of the SCO Bank, Siluanov, the treasury secretary of Russia, claimed that once China as one of the member states of SCO attends the Eurasian Development Bank, the Eurasian Development Bank might as well be turned into the SCO Bank.

There are some overlaps of the member states between the Silk Road Economic Belt raised by China and the Eurasian Union. The two have overlaps of regions and similarities of functions, but differences of geopolitics and trend of geoeconomics. If we set Central Asia as the center point, the gravitational pull of the Eurasian Union will drive Central Asia to become lopsided to Russia, while the Silk Road Economic Belt will connect Central Asia with China. Therefore, it is still unavailable for comment whether the establishment of the Eurasian Union will dilute the functions and prospects of the economic cooperation of the SCO. However, in terms of the national interests, the Silk Road Economic Belt will not do harm to the interests of the Eurasian Union. The basic function of the Silk Road Economic Belt is to promote the regional cooperation, which is beneficial to the stability and development of the regions. No matter in terms of politics, economy, or safety, the stability and development of Central Asia are in accordance with the interests of both China and Russia. Moreover, the Silk Road Economic Belt is not a threat to the Eurasian Union. However, some Russian scholars hold a skeptical attitude toward it. For example, Sergei Luzyanin, the deputy director of the Institute of Far Eastern Studies in the Russian Academy of Sciences, believes that with the promotion of the "One Belt and One Road" construction, China might influence the relationship of trade and economy and political ecology of the traditional sphere of influence in Central Asia. Moreover, Russian professor Yuri published an article on the Russian *Independence Newspaper* and pointed out that some sinologists in Russia believe that "One Belt and One Road" is the manifestation of Chinese hegemony and fight to the EU mechanism.

When it comes to the countries of Central Asia, this is not a problem of choosing one from the two alternatives. The Silk Road Economic Belt will not affect the prospects of the Eurasian Union. Fundamentally, the success of the Eurasian Union is determined by the relationship between China and Russia and by the interests it could bring to these nations but not much by the Silk Road Economic Belt. However, from the above analysis, although China and Russia are neighboring countries beside the countries in Central Asia and are the member states of SCO, it is rather difficult for them to reach consensus due to the disparity of economy, worries of manipulation by others, and some political reasons. Moreover, Russia always avoids the discussion of the Chinese conception to promote the FTA cooperation within the SCO framework, but firmly facilitates the Eurasian Economic Union based on the original Commonwealth of Independent States. And the countries of Central Asia which are located right between the two large states also decline to be deeply involved in order to maintain the balance.

2.3 China–Japan–South Korea Free Trade Area, ASEAN 10 + 6, and Asia-Pacific Free Trade Area

2.3.1 China–Japan–South Korea Free Trade Area

On the fifth China–Japan–South Korea trilateral meeting on May 15, 2012, the leaders of the three countries announced the launching of China–Japan–South Korea free trade area negotiation within the year. Specialists have shown that the launching of the FTA negotiation would open a new chapter of regional cooperation in Northeast Asia, which has a grand strategic significance. But it is by no means easy to accomplish the establishment of the free trade area and requires the firm confidence and common efforts to overcome. Before that, the joint study on China–ROK FTA was initiated in 2006 by the two countries' governments. Until now, there have already been five rounds and also made some achievements.

In the face of the global economic region integration, it is our combined interest and an irreversible trend to establish the China–Japan–South Korea free trade area. This has an important strategic significance to the three countries. To cooperate, they will reach a win–win situation. If not, they will all lose.

China, Japan, and South Korea are all located in the Northeast Asia, with a population of 1.5 billion people. In 2012, the GDP of the three countries added up to 14.3 trillion US dollars, which account for 90 % of that of the East Asia, 70 % of Asia, and nearly 20 % of the world's economy. The three countries are the large trading nations in the world. In 2012, the total volume of import and export in the three countries are mounted to 5.4 trillion US dollars, which account for 35 % of the global trade volume. The economic scales of the three countries are only after Europe and North America. Once the free trade area agreement was reached, China–Japan–South Korea free trade area will become the world's third largest free trade area only after the NAFTA and EU. It is predicted that China–Japan–South Korea FTA will become a single market with 1.5 billion population and 12 trillion US dollar GDP on its establishment and form the world's third economical plate. The profit of GDP will be increased in China, Japan, and South Korea by 1.1–2.9 %, 0.1–0.5 %, and 2.5–3.1 %, respectively.

However, China–Japan–South Korea FTA is not only faced with opportunities but also challenges. The GDP of the three countries all rank in the top ten in the world, but the level of trade and investment is far from satisfactory. Thus, the potential for cooperation and development is tremendous. Although to build the FTA is a general trend, the negotiations are by no means smooth. Since there are many obstacles like sensitive industries, political environment, and so on, the construction of the China–Japan–South Korea FTA is bound to be a long, slow, and difficult process. Future difficulties of the negotiation might include the impact that brings about to the Japanese and Korean markets from the Chinese agricultural export because of their high level of agricultural protections and the influence on Chinese automobile and steel industries from the import of those products from Japan and Korea. Besides, the shifts of American strategic centers to the East have intensified the complexity of the East Asian regional cooperation and the process of China–Japan–South Korea FTA. There are also many uncertainties in the FTA process.

Economically, there are diversities in the economic level of the three countries and imbalance of the industrial division. The disparity of economic development level will lead to the segmented demand of the entry standards and the differences of market capacity, market structure, and consumption structure, which increases the obstacles and conflicts in trade and investment. Besides, there are trade barriers and a prominent imbalance of revenue in China, Japan, and South Korea. The concern of the increase and decrease of the trade deficit by Japan and Korea affects the process of FTA to a large extent. Moreover, the differences of concerns toward the sensitive industries will also increase the difficulty of negotiations. For example, the sensitive industries of Japan include agriculture, steel, energy, service, textile, processing, and shipbuilding. The sensitive industries in Korea include the agricultural industry, energy industry, and processing industries like costume and textile. The sensitive industries in China include the chemical engineering industry, automobile industry, electric and information industry, mechanical equipment industry, financial industry, retail industry, medium- and high-end manufacturing industry, and transportation equipment industry Shi Jianhuai (2005). Among which, agriculture is recognized as the key problem in the free trade area negotiation.

Before the negotiation of China–Japan–South Korea FTA, there have been years of negotiations on the China–ROK FTA. Korea is fairly active in promoting China and Japan to build the FTA since it has already reached the agreements with Europe and the USA. The success of the China–ROK FTA will lay a solid foundation to the success of China–Japan–South Korea FTA. Since the establishment of the diplomatic relations between China and Korea, the bilateral economic and trade relationships have been developing rapidly over the past 22 years. In 2013, the volume of bilateral trade has added up to over 270 billion US dollars, and the mutual investment has mounted to 57 billion US dollars. China has become Korea's largest trading partner and import and export market. From January to March in 2014, the volume of bilateral trade has reached 67.63 billion US dollars, with a year-on-year increase of 6.8 %. Since its launching in May 2012, China–ROK FTA has had 11 rounds of negotiations in order to reach a comprehensive, balanced, and high-level free trade agreement. On May 30, 2014, the 11th round of China–ROK negotiation for five days was ended in Meishan, Sichuan Province. In this round, the two parties continued to have intensive and in-depth consultations in aspects of trade in goods and services and investment. In addition, they also held negotiations toward a wide range of issues including rule of origin, trade remedy, technical barriers to trade, sanitary and phytosanitary measures, intellectual property rights, e-commerce, environment, etc., and made positive progress. In November 2014, the two parties have announced the completion of China–ROK FTA substantial negotiations and the turning to technical consultation.

The first round of China–Japan–South Korea FTA was held from March 26 to 28, 2013, in Seoul, Korea, in which the three parties have discussed issues concerning the arrangements of the mechanism and the realm and means of negotiations of the FTA. The second round of the China–Japan–South Korea FTA was held from July 30 to August 2, 2013, in Shanghai, China, in which they intended to further the negotiation of means of consultations; discussed issues related to the commodities, service, and competitive fields; and planned to hold an expert meeting on issues like intellectual property rights and e-commerce. Currently, after the four rounds of negotiations, the three parties of China–Japan–South Korea FTA have already had in-depth consultations on trade in goods and services, investment, and so on and reached consensus on tax reduction mode of commodity trade including the basic structure of procedures of commodities, goods classifications, handling method, etc. Moreover, the three parties also agreed to bring several issues into the spectrum of the negotiations including trade in goods, trade in service, investment, rule of origin, customs procedures, trade remedy, sanitary and phytosanitary measures, technical barriers to trade, intellectual property rights, and competition policies and clauses and set up 11 working teams for negotiations. The next goal of the negotiation is to further clarify the means, areas, and levels of opening up in terms of the fields of cargos, service, and investment and make consultations of the texts already included in the scope of negotiations.

2.3.2 ASEAN 10 + 6

2.3.2.1 The Origin and Negotiation of ASEAN 10 + 6 (RCEP)

In 2003, China proposed to support East Asia in building the ASEAN and China–Japan–South Korea free trade area. In 2006, Japan suggested to bring India, Australia, and New Zealand (10 + 6) into the "10 + 3" system and establish the Comprehensive Economic Partnership in East Asia (CEPEA for short). According to the officials of the Japan External Trade Organization, Japan hopes to pull the three countries into the system because Australia and New Zealand have signed free trade agreements with high levels and have similar demands with Japan, while India has a close economic tie with Japan.

After that, ASEAN proposed the corresponding new framework, the RCEP conception on the East Asia Summit on November 19, 2011. This is the "10 + 6" of the ASEAN version, in which the set of working teams of trade in goods, trade in service, and investment are proposed. On the ASEAN Summit held in April 2012, the member states of ASEAN put out a statement to initiate RCEP at the end of that year. ASEAN also invited the six countries with which it signed the FTA to participate in the RCEP negotiation.

On the East Asia Summit held on November 18, 2012, the initiation of RCEP negotiation has become the focus of attention to all the factions. RCEP is the 10 + 6 system sponsored by the ASEAN countries and joined by the other six countries including China, Japan, South Korea, Australia, New Zealand, and India. Through means of tariff and nontariff reduction, it will form a free trade agreement of establishing the single market of the 16 countries.

According to the data released by the IMF, the overall economic scale of the 16 countries added up to 17.32 trillion US dollars, which account for 27 % of the global economy, smaller than the overall economic scale of 24.9082 trillion US dollars of TPP participating countries including Japan, Mexico, and Canada. But the big economic circle of the 16 countries includes the Asian countries right in the center of the global economic development. Once the RCEP is completed, it will become the world's largest free trade area with approximately 3.5 billion population and 23 trillion US dollar GDP, which account for one third of the world's total.

The ten ASEAN countries, along with six partners including Australia, China, India, Japan, Korea, and New Zealand, have held the first round of RCEP negotiation from May 9 to 13 in Brunei. The 16 member states have reached an agreement to advance the negotiation so that the goal of ending it by 2015 could be realized on schedule. This round of negotiation officially founded three working teams of trade in goods, trade in service, and investment and also made consultation on the issues of cargos, service, and investment. All the parties exchanged in-depth views on issues concerning the working plans, the range of responsibilities, and the possible future challenges of the three working teams and made preliminary discussions on the negotiation of other fields. The Joint Statement published by the RCEP negotiating committee explicitly points out that they will strive to finish the negotiation of RCEP by the end of 2015. The negotiation of RCEP admits the core position of ASEAN in the regional architecture and the profits the 6 FTA partners of ASEAN gain in promoting the integration of participating countries' economy, creating equal and fair economic development environment, and enhancing the economic cooperation among the member states.

The second round of RCEP negotiation was held from September 23 to 27 in Australia. The third round was held in Kuala Lumpur, Malaysia. China, Japan, Korea, Australia, New Zealand, India, and 10 ASEAN countries participated in the conference. The third round mainly focused on the market access mode, agreement on the framework of the chapters, text elements of the related fields, and so on. The fourth round of RCEP was started on March 31, 2014, in Nanning, Guangxi Province, and it lasted 5 days. Delegations of 500 representatives from ASEAN, China, Japan, Korea, India, Australia, and New Zealand participated in the negotiation.

2.3.2.2 The Obstacles of ASEAN 10 + 6 Integration

The obstacles of ASEAN 10+6 integration firstly lie in the disparity of the ten ASEAN countries. To reach a consensus between the world's poorest and wealthiest countries within this economic entity of great economic gap would be an unprecedented historical difficulty. ASEAN has shown its ambition to remove all the distractions and comprehensively promote the integration of East Asia and facilitate the regional development of a longer time, higher standards, and better qualities.

Secondly, the obstacle lies in how to integrate FTA, which has become the most concerned problem in the industry. Whether the open compliance in the previous bilateral FTA agreements signed by ASEAN and other parties, like the 10 + 1 which was implemented by ASEAN with China, Japan and Korea respectively and the bilateral free trade agreement between ASEAN and India, Australia, New Zealand, should be integrated and take effect to the other member states in the RCEP framework negotiations? In the joint conference, ASEAN proposed that all the bilateral FTA should also be opened to the third party, i.e., the most favored nation treatment. This has signified that China has to negotiate the issue of opening markets mutually with countries like India and Japan in 2 or 3 years' time according to RCEP's timetable. However, China hasn't signed any bilateral FTA agreement with India and Japan. In addition, some issues which are hard to reach consensus under the bilateral FTA will also be impossible to solve in the short term under the framework of RCEP Hu Weijia (2012). Moreover, there are also big diversities in the six member states in terms of economic development level and opening degree of trade. Australia and New Zealand have already achieved liberalization. China, Japan, and Korea are going on negotiations of FTA. India has even a lower level of opening degree.

The feasible method of negotiation is as follows: Firstly, unify the FTA of the six countries and ASEAN. Next, the 16 countries could negotiate and confirm the articles of agreement. Then the two parts could reach the two-way agreement and discuss the Sino-Japanese and Sino-Indian market openings.

This round of negotiation has formed the classical hub-and-spoke effect. Just like the wheels, the ASEAN becomes a core hub, and the other six countries become the spokes of the wheel. The two parts have together formed a complete circle and achieved the goal of regional economic integration. This means that the ASEAN plays a special leading role in the RCEP negotiation and there is a necessity to carry on the boosting of bilateral FTAs in inner Asia. Currently, the negotiations of China–Japan–South Korea FTA haven't been laid by under the influence of RCEP. On October 24, the Korean Foreign Affairs and Trade showed after the hearing: the Korean government will simultaneously promote the China–Japan–South Korea FTA and RCEP in pursuit of the maximization of the national interest. Actually, the bilateral FTA serves as the basis and crux of the success of RCEP Hu Weijia (2012).

In fact, except the problem of mutual opening ups within the six countries, to integrate the five FTA items signed by ASEAN with the other six countries, respectively, has already been very difficult. In the five FTAs, there are major differences not only in the rule of origins but also the liberalization levels. RCEP negotiation guidelines and goals point out that the level of trade liberalization of the RCEP trade agreement will be higher than those who have already been signed by ASEAN, which means that each country will be faced with the pressure of deepening their opening ups in different fields.

2.3.2.3 A Reversed Effect on Reform Boosting from the Opening Ups to the Outside World

To coordinate the different demands of different nations is the urgent problem for RCEP negotiation to be resolved. During the joint negotiation, each country should firstly clear up their mess. China will continue to deepen the China–ASEAN FTA Hu Weijia (2012). Since the supplemental agreements of FTA are expected to be signed in November, there might be a new progress in the China–ASEAN FTA. The contents of the supplemental agreements are mainly about the reduction of nontariff barriers between China and ASEAN, including technical barriers to trade (TBT) and SPS.

It is predicted that nontariff barrier, including service industries and investment liberalization, is the biggest challenge for China in the RCEP negotiation. Opening the service industries to the outside world is also the most sensitive and complicated part of the China–Japan–South Korea FTA negotiation soon to be initiated. In the RCEP negotiations, China will be faced with more pressures. To view from the number of the industries opened up, the level of opening up in the service industry of China is still lower than those developed countries like Japan, Korea, Australia, and New Zealand. If RCEP is to implement the strategy of keeping up with the highest standards, then the pressure of the Chinese service industries will become more apparent.

Here's a comparison of the opening-up levels of the Chinese service industries with the other five countries. In the service trade, the subsectors opened up to ASEAN in China are 33 ones, Korea 85 ones, Australia 85, and New Zealand 116 ones. The opening level of specific industries will also become the key of negotiations apart from the categories of opening ups. In its accession to the WTO, China has already made promises to open up industries including banking, insurance, bonds, distribution, telecommunication, etc. However, the overall opening level is not very satisfactory. According to the timetable published by ASEAN, RCEP high-level negotiation will be completed in 2015, which has seemingly set a deadline for the reform and opening ups to the Chinese monopolizing service industries including finance, telecommunication, and so on.

After the initiation of the RCEP negotiation, China will be faced with the new pressure of post-establishment national treatment, which only existed in the China–ASEAN FTA among the six countries. The post-establishment national treatment refers to the treatment to the foreign investment which is no less than the standards for the domestic investors in terms of access, founding, expansion, etc. This signifies that the foreign capital no longer needs examinations and approvals on entering China. China will be challenged even if it doesn't reform the policy of the foreign capital and system for examination and approval of foreign investment including the *Industrial Guide for Foreign Investment*.

2.3.3 TPP Challenges and the Asia-Pacific FTA

2.3.3.1 Analysis of China's Intention Toward TPP

The profound meaning of the American TPP strategies lies in its influence of the world's trade system. The United States has always been declaring that the TPP is a trade system that was established for the next generations and the twenty-first century with higher standards and wider range. TPP negotiations cover a great number of trade standards that are in favor of America, which will ensure the dominant place of which in the establishment of the new free trade area. The United States wishes to build a new regional trade agreement to enable the fast, convenient, and barrier-free entry to the Asia-Pacific region of the American enterprises, the expansion of export, the increase of the domestic employment, the promotion of economic persistent and stable growth, and, ultimately, the dominance of the international competition pattern. The new choice of strategic path by America is to make use of the TPP platform and crush one country after the other from regions to the whole world. Through the promotion of its trade rules, the United States wishes to obtain the inside dominance, i.e., the ability to decide the regional rules, acquire the exterior revenue of the regional cooperation, expand the bargain chips in the multilateral trade negotiations, and obtain the dominant power in the formulation of the international economic rules. Although there is a sign of rapid growth of the TPP under the proactive promotion of America, the key of TPP's success lies still in the increasing participation of the Asia-Pacific countries, to view from the strategy. Only by constant expansion of regional and economic scales can we achieve the promotion of export, creation of job, construction of the Asian-Pacific region's architectural momentum and finally stepping towards the realization of TPP (Liu Zhongwei, Shen Jiawen 2012), finally stepping toward the realization of the TPP, by constant expansion of regional and economic scales. Therefore, except China, the attitudes held or actions taken by the East Asian nations and regional integrated organizations like Japan, Korea, and ASEAN toward the TPP become rather important. Their judgments toward their interests have in some way decided the changes and adjustments toward the future geopolitical economic situation of East Asia, even the whole Asia-Pacific region. At present, the United States on the one hand makes great effort to persuade the ASEAN nations and its partner countries like Japan and Korea to join the TPP negotiations and on the other hand takes ambiguous actions toward China, the important partners of ASEAN, and member states of SCO, representing its complicated mentality.

For China, proactively developing the foreign trade and involving in the international market competition are the significant successful experiences it has obtained through the achievement of the economic construction. China has the resource endowment and industry base to participate in the international trade competitions and thus should go on its promotion of trade liberalization. America and Japan are the two biggest trade destinations of China. To realize the Sino-US and Sino-Japanese free trade is the biggest challenge for China to increase its openness of trade and competitiveness. Currently, whether China could join in the negotiation before the end of the first round is vital to its entry of the TPP. Since China still has many limitations toward the foreign-funded projects while the TPP is well known for its high standards of openness, China has to compromise to the high standards signed by the current 12 states in the second round and make opening ups on a large scale if it cannot join the negotiation in the first round to lower the standards. There is media commentary that this kind of huge openness in the short term for China may well be equal to the second entry of the WTO. Therefore, while China is proactively promoting the construction of "One Belt and One Road," the competition and cooperation relationship with the TPP has more to do with the Maritime Silk Road. On the basis of promoting the East Asian free trade area, China needs to speed up the research on TPP-related issues and advance the making of the TPP negotiation plan. According to the rules of the TPP, the member states without the free trade relationships have to make bilateral FTA negotiations. Therefore, the participation of China in the TPP negotiations has actually opened the gate of Sino-US FTA negotiations. And the ongoing negotiation of Sino-US investment agreement is a preview. After the TPP entry of Japan, the FTA negotiation gate between China and Japan will also be automatically opened, which serves great opportunities to break down the American- and Japanese-led policies to contain China, object their trade protectionism toward China, and demand their commitment to the position of China's market economy.

However, currently, it is still fairly difficult to promote the process of East Asian free trade area construction. China could consider the possibility to collaborate with America, not exclude its effects in the Asian economy, use its leverage to open the

Asia-Pacific market, integrate the original free trade agreement, reduce the transaction costs of regional trade, and thus create a more convenient international market environment for Chinese export industries. In the meantime, China, along with all the member states of APEC, should cooperate with each other to promote the construction of Asia-Pacific free trade area and make it a vital move to improve the Sino-US and Sino-Japanese relationships and promote the trade liberalization of Asia-Pacific and the whole world. Furthermore, China should speed up the promotion of the feasibility discussion of the free trade area within the SCO and accelerate the Sino-ROK and Sino-Australian free trade area negotiations and RCEP process. By which means, China could have more chips when negotiating in more than one system. In addition, China should make full use of its tremendous market superiority to increase its attractiveness to the foreign countries on one hand and speed up the transformation to domestic demand-oriented economy and reducing of economic external dependence.

2.3.3.2 Asia-Pacific Economic Cooperation

The Asia-Pacific Economic Cooperation (APEC for short), founded in 1989, is the most influential official forum for economic cooperation in the Asia-Pacific region. In its early days, it is merely a regional economic forum and consultation organization. For more than a decade, it has already developed into the most important economic cooperation forum and the highest level of intergovernmental economic cooperation mechanism in the Asia-Pacific region. The scale of trade within the region has increased from one trillion US dollars to three trillion US dollars, which accounts for 50 % of the total volume of the countries within the region, up from 50 %. However, there is still a big gap existing compared to EU. The regional economic integration is in accordance with the common interests of the countries within the region, and it requires the joint efforts of the member states to advance the trade liberalization and investment facilitation.

Currently, there are three main challenges for the development of APEC. The first one is the fast development of FTAs like bamboo shoots. The economic cooperation of APEC is in the crucial crossroad of whether to expand the fragmentation effect or choose the economic integration. The second one is that the mode of development for APEC has already become unsuitable for the new situations and the new infrastructure is rather weak. The development of this region has already confronted its bottlenecks given the weakness of infrastructure and defects of interconnections. The third one is the slow progress of the promotion of overall regional economic integration. Innovation and reform must be adopted to facilitate the economic growth and enhance the overall interconnections at all levels. The prospect of building the FTAAP has been laid out a decade ago and observed in the declaration of APEC leaders. They have reached the consensus and shown that the Asia-Pacific FTA will provide the opportunity for trade investment liberalization and facilitation raised by the *Bogor Goals*. In 2010, the APEC leaders expressed again their commitment to adopt the two free trade agreements, namely, the TPP and RCEP, as their method to the Asia-Pacific FTA.

2.3.3.3 Asia-Pacific FTA

In 2014, the APEC conference was held in Beijing, China. In order to promote the regional economic integration and adoption of concrete actions in the Asia-Pacific FTA, as well as to lay a solid foundation for the final completion of Asia-Pacific FTA, APEC agreed to establish the Friends of the Chair working team for regional economic integration enhancement and FTA promotion within the APEC Committee on Trade and Investment, initiate the Asia-Pacific FTA process, advance cooperation comprehensively and systematically, formulate the road map of the realization of the Asia-Pacific FTA, and promote support and guidance for the promotion of the FTA. China has put forward suggestions to implement the feasibility research of the Asia-Pacific FTA, not applying to any existing free trade agreements or negotiations of the region. As for the future constructions of the Asia-Pacific FTA, the first thing to do is to launch the feasibility research and to see if the current free trade agreements could also be employed by the other free trade agreements within APEC. However, the final establishment of the negotiation agenda for FTAAP would still require the consensus reached by both China and America. Currently, the United States still remained in the TPP negotiation and no consensus result has been reached. So it is not strange to see the negative attitudes of America toward the FTAAP. Moreover, there are still many questions except the specific and complicated details of negotiations. If the FTAAP was raised by China, should it be led by China or by America? Should we employ the prospect of facilitating the development of the developing countries or to adopt the original basis of TPP negotiation? Except Japan, most of the Asian countries which have joined the TPP hold positive attitudes toward the FTA. In the TPP negotiations, China had to propose new solutions under the pressure of the dominant party, America. This could also be a method to relieve the pressure.

2.4 Chinese "One Belt and One Road" and the Regional Cooperation Mode

The above analysis shows that in terms of the Silk Road Economic Belt construction, there can't be any progress of the FTA agreement negotiations when the great interests of the two countries haven't been overlapped in the regional economic integration. This will inevitably influence the countries of Central Asia which have close relationships with Russia. In terms of the Maritime Silk Road Construction, in its process of regional economic integration, China not only faces with the possible great opportunity brought about by the RCEP negotiation of ASEAN 10 + 6 negotiations but also confronts the challenges brought about by the American-led TPP negotiation and its exclusions toward China. Therefore, China needs to innovate the mode of regional cooperation given that there could be both advances and drawbacks in the Asia-Pacific FTA agreement negotiations.

To view the "One Belt and One Road" construction as a process of regional economic integration, the comparison of the regional economic cooperation mode of China with countries and regions in certain zones could be viewed in Table 2.1.

As the proverb goes, every journey begins with a single step which implies the significance of transport infrastructure. Interoperability is an important condition and base for the cooperation of "One Belt and One Road." Recently, "interoperability" means a global linkage with China's neighboring countries to China, which needs the hardware "infrastructure and transportation" and the software "institutions, rule-based interconnection" construction, and the "major thoroughfare" among China and relative countries which includes goods, capital, transportation, logistics, and information freedom. Stand in the perspective of economics, regional economic integration is relying on interoperability. If an area is not covered by the physical infrastructure, it is difficult to imagine how high the degree of integration is. Under the premise of no interconnection and cooperation, a city or a port could be useful for just one region. But with the existence of interconnection and cooperation, a city or a port could play a greater role. The interconnection network of "One Belt and One Road" will be effective to network economy. Its greatest feature is a network-based economic activity. And the network could be a medium to generate economic and trade activities. To make the "One Belt and One Road" function healthy, the transportation communication network must be open and efficient, which means the requirement of network capacity, speed requirements, and inter-network interconnection. Interoperability between national and regional networks is an inevitable requirement of regional economic integration. Without network interconnection, economic activity will be bound to be an isolated network island.

Developing countries are the majority of "One Belt and One Road." For the development of these countries, China plays an important role in foreign aid (foreign) output. And infrastructure interoperability is an important area of investment Xinhuanet (2014). American economists Hollis B. Chenery and Alan M. Strout discussed the relationship between foreign aid to developing countries (FDI) and economic development in the article "Foreign Aid and Economic Development." This paper established a two-gap model, which was widely cited later. The two-gap model is used to analyze the situation that investment is greater than the savings and imports are greater than an economic model for exports in developing countries. Furthermore, Hirschman created a "three-gap" and "four-gap" model by considering the revenue and expenditure restraint and the technology gap. The "four-gap" model includes makeup of the savings gap, the foreign exchange gap, the government revenue gap, and factors of the production gap. And this model discussed the special significance of foreign direct investment to the production factors (business management, entrepreneurship, technology, skills, information) gap. While some countries in "One Belt and One Road" region are

Table 2.1 The important regional economic cooperation in the construction of "One Belt and One Road"

Model	Characteristics				
	Reduce the products' custom within the region	Elimination of trade barriers within the region	Unified custom and trade policy	Free flow of staff, commodities, labor, and capital	Compromise of economic and monetary policy and development of superstate mechanism
PTA	√				
CEPA					
ECFA					
FTA	√	√			
South Asia					
China–ASEAN (10 + 1)					
ASEAN (10 + 6, RCEP*)					
Asia-Pacific: TPP*; Northeast Asia: China–South Korea*, China–Japan–South Korea*					
South Asia: China – Pakistan, China–Bangladesh*					
West Asia: China – GCC					
Europe: Iceland, Switzerland					
Oceania: New Zealand, Australia*					
Customs Union	√	√	√		
Russia–Belarus–Kazakhstan Customs Union					
Common market	√	√	√	√	
Economic Union	√	√	√	√	√
EU					
Eurasian Union					

Description: The items with asterisks in the table have not been implemented or are still under negotiations or the feasibility research on the savings gap and foreign exchange gap and they need construction funds, the introduction of capital will become the primary objective of these countries' foreign policy. At this moment, the focus of FDI policy objectives is to emphasize the size and number of foreign investment but not only the quality of foreign investment. On the contrary, in some countries without savings gap and foreign exchange gap, the building funds are sufficient. The FDI policy should take the advanced technology, management experience, highly qualified personnel, and other production factors into account first but not the size and number. In this regard, Chinese enterprises should also be fully prepared. In order to promote the construction of interconnection infrastructure, China and other 20 countries have initiated the Asian Infrastructure Investment Bank, the BRICS have initiated the BRICS Development Bank, and China has also established the Silk Road Construction Fund.

2.5 Conclusion

The analysis of this paper has shown that China has two options in the "One Belt and One Road" construction. One is the FTA strategic option, which is to sign the preferential trade arrangements with the countries along the route progressively to establish bilateral and multilateral FTAs, i.e., the positive integration option raised by Tinburgen. For more than a decade, the FTAs in China developed from none to presence, from less to more. China has signed 12 free trade agreements successively with free trade partners from more than 20 nations and regions including 15 countries like ASEAN, Pakistan, New Zealand, Chile, etc., and regions like Hong Kong, Macao, Taiwan, etc. The trade volume between China and these free trade partners has already covered 24 % of the total volume of Chinese foreign trade. Besides, China is now proactively promoting the final negotiations of FTA with Korea, Gulf Cooperation Council, Australia, Japan, and South Korea. It has already finished the joint feasibility research of China–India FTA and launched that of the China–Columbia FTA. Given that Asia, especially East Asia, has already become the center of the global economic growth, it is foreseeable that China, which is also one of it, will devote to the speed up of FTA constructions with neighboring countries in the near future. This trend has already begun to appear in the promotion of China–Japan–South Korea FTA and the initiation of ASEAN 10+6 FTA negotiations. However, it is necessary to find that the simple reliance on the promotion of FTA strategy will definitely affect the overall national strategies of the countries along the "One Belt and One Road" route and lead to possible stagnation and delay of position taking of the sovereign states along the route due to different reasons including the relationship with other major countries and national conditions. The progress and effects of the "One Belt and One Road" construction might also be affected by the state of haste making waste caused by long periods of negotiating cycles, huge block of the international community, and high cost of the policy adjustment.

The other kind is the regional and subregional cooperation method, which promotes gradually from point to surface with great varieties. Just like the report of the 18th CPC National Congress points out: make overall plans on multilateral, bilateral, regional, and subregional opening ups and cooperation, speed up the implementation of FTA strategy, and promote the interconnections with neighboring countries. Innovative mode of cooperation has thus been made. Multilateral, bilateral, and regional opening ups and cooperation are the three important pillars of the Chinese foreign economy, trade, and cooperation. For over 10 years since China's entering into the WTO, it has made many breakthroughs in the multilateral cooperation fields, but the regional cooperation development is still underdeveloped. The "One Belt and One Road" construction is a new mode of cooperation. In the current phase, it is neither a supranational mechanism nor a union at the same level with the customs union and the economic union. It is more likely to be a platform built for the friendly cooperation of economic exchanges and channel construction in the countries within the region. It can provide better conditions and opportunities for cooperation among each state, mechanism, and organization by adopting new ideas. Therefore, it is a platform, an important way to promote multilateral and bilateral cooperation, which is different from the traditional way of regional cooperation. It does not apply to the existing organizations and mechanisms in China, but starts all over again with a brand-new organization and mechanism aiming to compete with those existing and emerging ones. There can be better communications and cooperation among the multilateral economic organizations in this region, no matter the SCO, Eurasian Economic Union, or the other ones. Through this platform, the rejuvenation of the Silk Road and the direct convenience from regional integration like the breaking of the bottleneck of capital and communication and removal of infrastructure difficulties could all be achieved. China could launch joint consultations, constructions, and sharing with the countries or regions along the route. It will not intentionally seek the overall promotion in the short term, i.e., negative integration option raised by Tinbergen, which is also a development seems to be doing nothing but can actually make contributions proactively.

References

Balassa B (1961) The theory of economic integration. Irwin, Homewood

Balassa B (1965) Economic development and integration. CEMLA, Mexico

Feng Wei, Cheng Guoqiang (2014) Evaluation of the international community to the "One Belt and One Road" strategy "along the way" initiative. China Economic Times

Fritz M (1979) A history of thought on economic integration. Macmillan, London

Hu Weijia (2012) ASEAN edition of "10 + 6" ready. Caijing Magazine 2012(29)

Li Fuchuan (2011) Customs Union of Belarus, Kazakhstan and Russia and its influence on Shanghai Cooperation Organization. Russ Cent Asian East Eur Mark 2011(7):1–9

Liang Shuanglu, Cheng Xiaojun (2007) Summary of international regional economic integration theory. Inq Into Econ Issues 2007(1):40–46

Liu Zhongwei, Shen Jiawen (2012) The review of research frontier and frameworks of Trans-Pacific Partnership Agreement (TPP). J Contemp Asia Pac Stud 2012(1):36–59
Peter Robson (2001) The economics of international intergration (trans: Dai Bingran). Shanghai Translation Publishing House, Shanghai
Shi Jianhuai (2005) International symposium on "East Asian Economic Circle" reported briefing. http://www.ccer.edu.cn
Tinbergen J (1954) International economic integration. Elsevier, Amsterdam
Viner J (1950) The customs union issue. Carnegie Endowment, New York
Xinhuanet (2014) "One Belt and One Road" strategy will lead the new economic landscape China Open. http://news.xinhuanet.com/fortune/2014-12/16/c_1113666080.htm
Zhang Youwen (1999) The history of the world economic integration. Academia Press, Shanghai

Chapter 3
Simulation on Trade Effects of CJK FTA and the Prospects of Negotiation

Zongxian Feng, Hua Wang, and Liwei Zhao

Abstract The first part of the paper discusses and simulates the possible trade effect and boundary effect of the establishment of the China-Japan-South Korea free trade area. Firstly, it analyzes the trade creation effect, the trans effect, and the substitution effect of the realization degree of trade liberalization under different reduction proportions of the three countries in their free trade area negotiations, by means of GSIM model simulation. Secondly, the paper builds a boundary effect measurement model based on the gravity model and analyzes the changes of boundary effect to the principal trade partners caused by the tariff changes after the establishment of the free trade areas, by taking the China-Japan-South Korea free trade area as an example. The research shows that the reduction of tariff will lead to the reduction of the boundary effect not only to China, Japan, and South Korea but also to other trade partners to some extent. However, on the whole, the reduction of the tariff is not enough for the elimination of the boundary effect, due to the existence of many other trade barriers. What's more, this paper makes a review of the process of the China-Japan-South Korea free trade area negotiations, discusses the respective interest appeals, and negotiates strategies on the one hand and its future prospects on the other hand.

This research was funded by the Chinese National Natural Science Foundation of China (No. 71073123 and No. 71441039), the major projects of National Social Science Foundation (No. 12 & ZD070), Social Science Fund Project in Shaanxi Province (No. 13D193), and Shaanxi Science and Technology Research and Development Project (Soft Science Research) (No. 2014KRM94).

Z. Feng
School of Finance and Economics, Xi'an Jiaotong University, Xi'an, People's Republic of China

H. Wang (✉)
School of Finance and Economics, School of Foreign Studies, Xi'an Jiaotong University, Xi'an, People's Republic of China
e-mail: seablue@mail.xjtu.edu.cn

L. Zhao
Industrial and Commercial Bank of China Limited, Xi'an, People's Republic of China

H.G. Djajadikerta, Z. Zhang (eds.), *A New Paradigm for International Business*, Springer Proceedings in Business and Economics, DOI 10.1007/978-981-287-499-3_3

3.1 Introduction

3.1.1 Significance

After the entering of WTO, China has quickly adjusted its strategic emphasis of the foreign trade policies. While proactively taking part in the multilateral trading system, China is also vigorously promoting the regional economic integration and building free trade areas with other countries and regions. Since 2002, China has signed free trade agreement with 10 countries or regions and made some achievements. So far, China has signed free trade agreement with several countries and regions (see Table 3.1).

Table 3.1 Signed and in negotiation FTA agreements of China (Dec. 2014)

Status	FTA
Signed FTA	1. Closer Economic Partnership Arrangement between Mainland, Hong Kong, and Macao (January 1, 2004, and January 1, 2005) 2. APTA ("the Bangkok Agreement" (1975) was changed to "Asia-Pacific Trade Agreement" on November 2nd, 2005) 3. China-Chile FTA (signed on November 18, 2005, implemented since October 1, 2006) 4. FTA between China and Pakistan (in November 2003, the two sides signed preferential trade arrangements; in November 2006, they signed the "free trade agreement"; on February 21, 2009, they signed the "Agreement on Trade in Services") 5. China-ASEAN FTA (signed the "Framework Agreement" on November 4, 2002; "Early Harvest Program," "Trade in Goods Agreement," and "Agreement on Trade in Services" were, respectively, implemented on January 1, 2004, July 2005, and July 2007) 6. China and New Zealand FTA (signed the "Free Trade Agreement" on April 7th, 2008; implemented on Oct. 1st, 2008) 7. China and Singapore FTA (signed the "Free Trade Agreement" on October 23, 2008; implemented "Memorandum of Understanding on Bilateral Labor Cooperation" the next year) 8. China and Peru FTA (signed a "free trade agreement" on April 28, 2009, implementation since March 1, 2010) 9. China and Costa Rica FTA (signed the "Free Trade Agreement" on April 8, 2010, implementation on August 1, 2011) 10. China and Iceland FTA (signed on April 15, 2013) 11. China and Switzerland FTA (signed on July 6, 2013)
In negotiation	1. China and the GCC FTA (negotiations started in July 2004) 2. China and Australia FTA (negotiations started in April 2005) 3. China and Norway FTA (negotiations started in Sep. 2008) 4. China and Switzerland FTA (negotiations started in Jan. 2011) 5. China and South Korea FTA (negotiations started in May 2012) 6. China, Japan, and South Korea FTA (negotiations started in March 2013) 7. "Regional Comprehensive Economic Cooperation Partnership"(RCEP) 8. China-ASEAN FTA (upgraded version of "10 + 1") 9. China-Sri Lanka FTA
In feasibility study	1. China-India 2. China-Colombia

Source: China Free Trade Area Service Network (http://fta.mofcom.gov.cn)

However, it should be noted that except China and the Association of Southeast Asian Nations (ASEAN), the scale of other free trade areas is limited. Even the ASEAN is limited by the development disparity of its members, territory disputes, and other issues, which lead to the restriction of the breadth and depth of the China-ASEAN free trade area cooperation. Therefore, there is still a long way to go for the construction of Chinese free trade areas. China, Japan, and South Korea are three major world economies in the Northeast Asian region. The total GDP of the three countries is $15 trillion, accounting for 20 % of global GDP and 90 % of GDP in East Asia, which has exceeded the GDP of EU. However, the volume of trade among the three countries accounts for less than 20 % of the total foreign trade of them. Once completed, CJK FTA will form a market with over 1.5 billion people and will become an FTA with the world's largest population, the third total economy only after the FTA of EU and North America. It will undoubtedly have a significant role in the world economy.

But for a long time, they lack an overall arrangement for free trade, which stands in sharp contrasts with the North American free trade area (NAFTA) and European Union (EU). The reason may well contribute to the complicated geopolitical issue and historical problems in the Northeast Asian region. In the short run, if we are to build free trade areas of the same scale, depth, and high level as NAFAT or EU, the China-Japan-South Korea free trade area is undoubtedly our best choice. Moreover, it will also have an important influence on the US-led TPP negotiations and the ASEAN-led "Regional Comprehensive Economic Partnership" (RCEP).

However, the researches at present on China-Japan-South Korea free trade area are mainly concentrated on the qualitative analysis such as feasibility, and there are few researches made on the quantitative study of the economic effect after the establishment of the China-Japan-South Korea free trade area.

3.1.2 Literature Review

Based on the Armington model, Francois and Hall (1997) proposed the Commercial Policy Analysis System (COMPA) by combining the microeconomic price theory. COMPA has become the tool of many economists for assessing trade policies between two countries, and it has now been widely used by scholars and policy-making departments in many countries or regions, including the USA, Canada, and Taiwan. However, the COMPA only takes the market balance of one country into consideration, while the global simulation model (GSIM) may cater for needs of partial equilibrium in several countries, which may have a better effect.

GSIM, short for global simulation model, is firstly proposed by Francois and H. Keith Hall (2002) and mainly adopted in research of partial trade equilibrium model of the single industry and business analysis in multiple regions. This model is the improved version of the SMART Model developed by the World Bank. The most distinctive feature of GSIM is that it can be used to analyze the effect the economic and trade policies have on the target countries from the global viewpoint and industrial level in terms of state output, the volume of import and export, and social welfare. Compared with those which can only be used to measure ordinary equilibrium models, GSIM has more flexibility and operability. It can focus on several target branches or products without the consideration of other products and the equilibrium of production element markets.

The formation of a region-wide FTA in Asia is a key recommendation that has been made by recent studies on Asian economic integration (ADB 2008a, 2011). Such a region-wide FTA could also enable Asian countries to gradually speak up with unified positions on international trade and investment in global forums and institutions that are responsible for global economic governance (Madhur 2012a, b).

The literatures about preferential trade agreements (PTAs) are numerous. Recent empirical studies have allayed some of the worst fears of trade theorists about PTAs (Freund and Ornelas 2010; Anderson and Yotov 2011). Neighboring countries that already trade heavily among them tend to form PTAs as they have much to gain by their low natural trade (including transport) costs. Such PTAs by their very nature are likely to lead to trade creation rather than trade diversion (Wonnacott and Lutz 1989; Krugman 1991). More broadly, countries closer to each other in terms of distance and pairs of countries with huge complementarities and even similar economic sizes tend to form PTAs than countries that do not share these characteristics (Bergstrand et al. 2011; WTO 2011). Domino effects or the formation of a PTA inducing non-members to either join the PTA or to form another PTA have been a key driving force behind the rapid growth of PTAs (Baldwin 1995; Baldwin and Jaimovich 2010). It is possible to view PTAs as building blocks for eventual global multilateral free trade, although how far PTAs could act as such building blocks would very much depend upon the way PTAs are designed and implemented in practice (ADB 2008b; Menon 2009). Even though a CK FTA may be more feasible in the immediate future, it will still involve hard negotiations on a number of delicate issues (Kwon 2011). Based on model-simulation results, it is now generally accepted that the sum of the benefits from three separate bilateral FTAs among China, Japan, and Korea would be less than a single trilateral FTA (Lee 2006).

This paper measures the boundary effect with the gravity model. From the literature review of the boundary effect, we can see that the boundary effect is the key area where the gravity model is used. The finding and extension of boundary effect is also closely connected with the gravity model. McCallum (1995) is the first person to find the existence of boundary effect between the United States and Canada by employing the US-Canadian trade flow data. His findings are based on the gravity model, in which he added the dummy variables of interprovincial trade to measure the boundary effect. Wei (1996) has proposed a unique way to estimate the domestic trade flow in his measurement of the boundary effect. However, the basis of his research is still the gravity model, which remains unchanged. What he did is the proposal of a new estimation method to explain variables in his empirical researches, which, to some extent, has solved the problem of data missing in the method proposed by McCallum. There are some new methods to measure the boundary effect that emerged, but the abovementioned methods proposed by

McCallum and Wei remain to be the most classical ones, which served as the foundation of others. For example, Zhu Haixia and Gu Haiying (2008) launched a reconstruction of the traditional model to measure the boundary effect according to the particularity of trade of agricultural products by focusing on the changes of Sino-US trade of agricultural products after 2002 and introduced new variables of agricultural acreage and proportion of agricultural population. Then, based on the model, they launched empirical research by utilizing the flow data of Sino-US trade of agricultural products. They found that the boundary effect of the Sino-US trade of agricultural products is conspicuous, but the trend of which come down with each passing year. In the meantime, there are also differences among flows and regions that existed.

This paper intends to make quantitative analysis to the trade effect and welfare benefits under the different levels of tariff reductions in the China-Japan-South Korea free trade area based on the 2011 world trade, with the adoption of the global simulation model (GSIM).

3.2 GSIM Model Structure and Data Collection and Parameter Estimation

3.2.1 The Structure of GSIM

According to the research of Francois and Hall (2002), there are four assumptions of GSIM:

The underlying assumption of the model is Armington assumption, i.e., the imported commodities from different regions are not homogeneous but have incomplete substitutional relations. Additionally, according to Armington's research, the elasticity of substitution is a constant.

The elasticity of import demand and that of export supply of each country remain the same, and they are all the same constant.

More emphasis should be put on the change of partial factors. Compared to the CGE model, the limited factor input makes the analysis become more convenient and transparent and also of great flexibility.

The result of this model utilized the proportion change, rather than the volumes of import and export, which substitute the absolute amount change with the proportion change. In the structure of this model, the amount of equations is equal to that of the export markets. From the equation set, we can confirm the price balance of the global market and subsequently backward induct to the specific prices of each country's market.

According to the abovementioned assumption, the GSIM model of this paper can be described as follows:

Firstly, analyze the demand function of the product import.

Let volume of imported commodity i in country V be the function of imported commodity's domestic price $P_{(i,v),r}$, world price $P_{(i,v),s\neq r}$, and total expenditure $y_{(i,v)}$ of the imported product to the country V, i.e.,

$$\mathrm{M}_{(i,v),r} = f\left(P_{(i,v),r}, P_{(i,v),s\neq r}, y_{(i,v)}\right) \tag{3.1}$$

According to the formula (3.1), we could obtain the products' self-demand price elasticity $N_{(i,v),(r,r)}$ and cross-demand price elasticity $N_{(i,v),(r,s)}$:

$$\mathrm{N}_{(\mathrm{i},v),(r,s)} = \theta_{(i,v),s}(E_m + E_s) \tag{3.2}$$

$$\mathrm{N}_{(\mathrm{i},v),(r,r)} = \theta_{(i,v),r}E_m - \sum_{s\neq r}\theta_{(i,v),s}E_s = \theta_{(i,v),r}E_m - \left(1-\theta_{(i,v),r}\right)E_s \tag{3.3}$$

Among which $\theta_{(i,v),s}$ is the portion of the consumption product i of the country V in its total expenditure. E_m is the elasticity of demand of product i in country V; E_s is the elasticity of substitution.

Next, analyze the prices of the imported and exported products. Let $P_{i,r}{}^*$ be the export price of product i of the exporting country i, $P_{(i,v),r}$ be the domestic price of product i, and t be the import tax rate:

$$\mathrm{P}_{(i,v),r} = \left(1 + t_{(i,v),r}\right)P_{i,r}{}^* = T_{(i,v),r}P_{i,r}{}^* \tag{3.4}$$

Now, the function of export supply can be simplified so that it can be determined by the world price, i.e.,

$$\mathrm{X}_{i,r} = f\left(P_{i,r}{}^*\right) \tag{3.5}$$

From formula (3.1), (3.4), and (3.5), we could obtain the determining equation of price on one hand and import and export on the other hand expressed by the rate of change ($Ex_{(i,r)}$ is the elasticity of export supply):

$$\widehat{\mathrm{P}}_{(i,v),r} = \widehat{P}_{i,r}{}^* + \widehat{T}_{(i,v),r} \tag{3.6}$$

$$\widehat{X}_{i,r} = E_{X(i,r)}\widehat{P}_{i,\ r}{}^* \tag{3.7}$$

$$\widehat{\mathrm{M}}_{(\mathrm{i},v),r} = N_{(i,v),(r,r)}\widehat{P}_{(i,v),r} + \sum_{s\neq r}N_{(i,v),(r,s)}\widehat{P}_{(i,v),s} \tag{3.8}$$

Substituting formulas (3.6), (3.2), and (3.3) into (3.8), we can obtain the equation of the total global export:

$$\begin{aligned}\hat{\mathrm{M}}_{i,r} &= \sum_{v}\hat{M}_{(i,v),r} = \sum_{v}N_{(i,v),(r,r)}\hat{P}_{(i,v),r} + \sum_{v}\sum_{s\neq r}N_{(i,v),(r,s)}\hat{P}_{(i,v),s} \\ &= \sum_{\mathrm{v}}N_{(i,v),(r,r)}\left[P_r{}^* + \hat{T}_{(i,v),r}\right] + \sum_{\mathrm{v}}\sum_{s\neq r}N_{(i,v),(r,s)}\left[\hat{P}_s{}^* + \hat{T}_{(i,v),s}\right]\end{aligned} \tag{3.9}$$

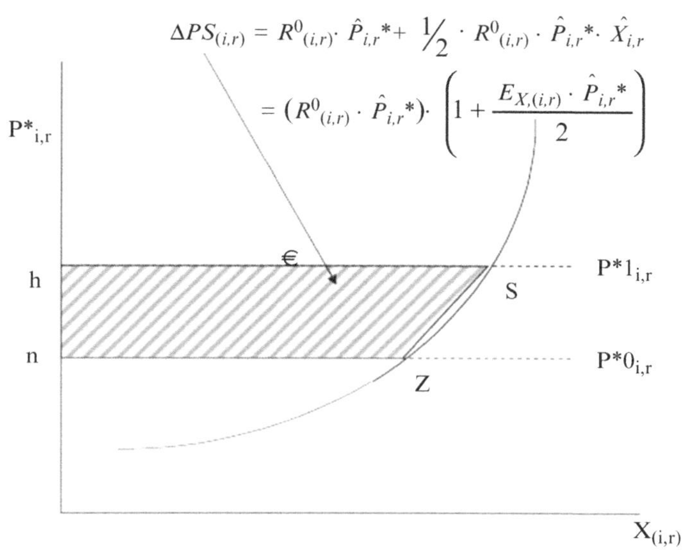

Chart 3.1 Producer surplus

On setting the total global export equal to total global import, we can obtain the following equation, which stands for the condition of the market clearing:

$$\begin{aligned} \hat{\mathrm{M}}_{\mathrm{i},r} &= \hat{X}_{i,r} \Rightarrow \\ E_{X(i,r)}\hat{P}_{i,r}^{*} &= \sum_{v} N_{(i,v),(r,r)}\hat{P}_{(i,v),r} + \sum_{v}\sum_{s\neq r} N_{(i,v),(r,s)}\hat{P}_{(i,v),s} \\ &= \sum_{v} N_{(i,v),(r,r)}\left[P_r^{*} + \hat{T}_{(i,v),r}\right] + \sum_{v}\sum_{s\neq r} N_{(i,v),(r,s)}\left[\hat{P}_s^{*} + \hat{T}_{(i,v),s}\right] \end{aligned} \tag{3.10}$$

The formula (3.10) is the core equation of global simulation model equation set. From formula (3.10), we can deduce that the set of world price met the demand of partial equilibrium condition, i.e., partial equilibrium data of the base period.

In order to analyze the welfare effect of the trade policy, here we introduce the consumer surplus and producer surplus and we use ΔPS to represent the producer surplus, which is shown in Chart 3.1:

$$\begin{aligned} \Delta PS_{(i,r)} &= R^{0}{}_{(i,r)}\hat{P}_{i,r}^{*} \\ &+ \tfrac{1}{2}R^{0}{}_{(i,r)}\hat{P}_{i,r}^{*}\widehat{X}_{i,r} = \left(R^{0}{}_{(i,r)}\widehat{P}_{i,r}^{*}\right)\left(1+\frac{E_{X,(i,r)}\widehat{P}_{i,r}^{*}}{2}\right) \end{aligned} \tag{3.11}$$

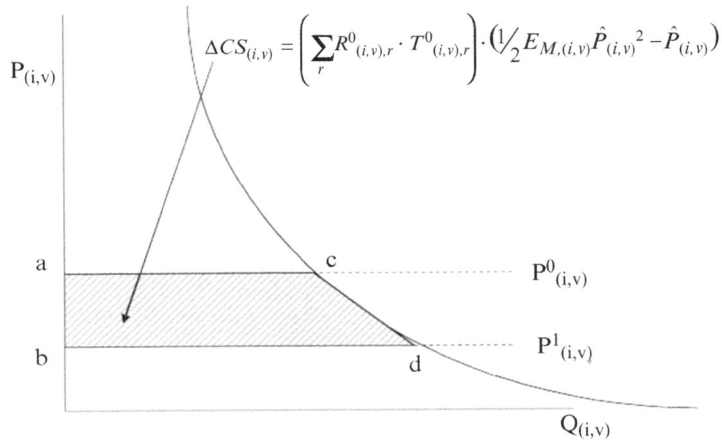

Chart 3.2 Consumer surplus

In formula (2.11), $R^0_{(i,r)}$ represents the balanced import revenue under the world price $P_{i,r}{}^*$ of the base period. Here, the utility function of the consumer is the CES of the joint goods:

$$Q_{iv} = A_v \left[\sum_{i=1}^{r} \gamma_{(i,v),r} M^{\rho}_{(i,v),r} \right]^{1/\rho} \tag{3.12}$$

$$\Delta CS_{(i,v)} = \left(\sum_r R^0{}_{(i,v),r} T^0{}_{(i,v),r} \right) \left(½\mathrm{E}_{\mathrm{M},\ (i,v)} \widehat{P}_{(i,v)}{}^2 sign\left(\widehat{P}_{(i,v)}\right) - \widehat{P}_{(i,v)} \right)$$

The consumer surplus can be represented as (clarified by the Chart 3.2)

$$\Delta CS_{(i,v)} = \left(\sum_r R^0{}_{(i,v),r} T^0{}_{(i,v),r} \right) \left(½\mathrm{E}_{\mathrm{M},\ (i,v)} \widehat{P}_{(i,v)}{}^2 sign\left(\widehat{P}_{(i,v)}\right) - \widehat{P}_{(i,v)} \right) \tag{3.13}$$

According to the structure of the model, we set the price of joint goods of partial balance in the base period to be 1. Additionally, the factor leading to the price changes caused by the model assumption is reduced to only one. Thus, the change rate of the price can be represented as

$$\widehat{P} = \frac{\mathrm{d}P}{P} = \sum_{i=1}^{r} \theta_{(i,v),r} \widehat{P}_{(i,v),r} = \sum_{i=1}^{r} \theta_{(i,v),r} \left[\left(1 + \widehat{P}^*{}_{i,r} \right) \frac{T_{1,(i,v),r}}{T_{0,(i,v),r}} \right] \tag{3.14}$$

This theoretical structure has constructed a closed economic system which meets the demand of partial equilibrium, which can be used to simulate economic effect issues of the tariff and export subsidy. Or we could transform the related trade policies into the equivalent tax rate or export subsidy rate for research. By setting the base period, we can calibrate the primary equilibrium of the model in the economic environment, in which the tariff wall and the export subsidy exist. In the meantime, there also exists a set of the balanced price. When the export subsidy does not exist, the tariff becomes the only reason that leads to the disparity of the domestic prices and world prices in terms of the imported commodity on the one hand and the loss of consumer surplus due to the rise in price and fall of consumption on the other. The manufacturing enterprises in importing countries may get some revenue from the rise of prices and sales volume. The government of the importing countries may also have more tariffs under the high tax rate. The tariff reduction of the related countries in the base period could lead to the reduction of the tariff barrier. In terms of the change of the tariff, we can get the new partial equilibrium from the model. On the basis of comparing the old and new sets of equilibrium solution, we can calculate the condition of economic effect and then confirm the specific effects to each side.

3.2.2 *Data Collection and Parameter Estimation*

3.2.2.1 Trade Flow and Tariff

One of the basic concepts of GSIM's simulation and analysis is, firstly, to set up a base period of the model, organize the data of the base period and substitute them into the model, change the variable stands for trade policy, and allow the others to remain unchanged. Then, according to the GSIM model, we can obtain the simulation value of the trade volume, output, social welfare, etc., of the related country's industry after the change of the variable. Finally, we compare the simulation value with the base value and obtain the range of the economic index caused by the change of the trade policy. Therefore, the main types of data needed in the GSIM are the data of the trade flow of the related nations and regions in the investigating base period; the elasticity data of supply, demand and substitution among products in the related countries and regions; and the variables of trade policies, for example, customs rate, export subsidy rate, etc.

This paper will make use of the GSIM to measure the boundary effect and welfare effect under different tax reductions of the China-Japan-South Korea free trade area on the basis of the world trade in 2011. The flow data of each side is the most important basic data in the model, from which we can calculate the market share of different sources of imports, which can serve as an important middle parameter. Table 3.2 shows the flow data of world goods trade obtained from the UN Comtrade. Table 3.3 shows the import tariff data of each country in the world in the year of 2011.

Table 3.2 Flow data of world goods trade (unit: 100 million US dollars)

Country	Australia	Brazil	Canada	China	EU	Hong Kong	India	Indonesia	Japan	South Korea	Malaysia	Russia	Singapore	Thailand	USA	others
Austria	0.00	16.52	15.69	751.28	170.54	27.53	140.02	51.38	519.52	240.99	41.18	9.74	49.25	72.35	96.98	397.24
Brazil	8.28	0.00	35.24	483.51	544.04	21.38	34.68	18.08	110.73	55.18	16.96	42.97	23.52	20.42	292.08	971.60
Canada	17.82	31.48	0.00	193.60	361.97	25.21	24.44	18.10	117.95	58.48	8.15	15.50	9.23	9.20	3,138.77	272.92
China	386.84	323.13	369.60	0.00	4,015.60	2,442.83	530.10	277.17	1,660.75	846.76	262.98	434.71	367.83	281.38	3,711.57	4,191.56
EU	421.71	477.78	467.26	2,004.18	0.00	412.02	554.87	112.58	741.18	462.15	181.06	1,368.03	418.61	167.07	3,711.56	9,796.84
Hong Kong	6.40	5.16	1.91	123.00	81.19	0.00	60.80	12.82	8.93	14.43	23.23	0.45	19.32	14.33	26.74	31.79
India	22.04	57.36	22.18	200.45	568.63	118.81	0.00	53.61	62.08	62.22	35.63	23.27	148.84	28.90	351.94	1,346.55
Indonesia	58.39	18.27	12.02	271.39	228.94	33.08	136.50	0.00	339.12	168.03	112.33	11.97	188.69	66.33	182.45	323.89
Japan	181.79	70.39	110.51	1,783.02	1,047.11	431.29	111.48	185.87	0.00	672.47	200.68	134.13	267.42	398.47	1,300.58	1,713.15
South Korea	77.68	109.59	58.01	1,484.51	558.65	257.89	125.08	132.82	397.45	0.00	69.03	109.40	212.89	88.29	575.01	1,406.57
Malaysia	84.86	17.00	15.35	459.79	268.38	108.35	91.58	86.05	282.99	94.53	0.00	11.99	339.69	120.00	226.68	423.83
Russia	5.49	25.23	9.18	375.27	2,424.78	7.41	43.58	11.30	166.24	120.91	3.91	0.00	27.77	33.08	255.69	1,960.96
Singapore	153.32	11.11	14.88	354.11	341.95	390.85	111.00	343.73	135.35	122.24	369.92	4.03	0.00	109.12	208.61	860.61
Thailand	83.55	23.33	22.06	332.21	259.41	136.77	51.19	102.42	242.99	49.95	118.38	15.44	114.03	0.00	238.19	579.38
USA	261.46	357.54	2,284.59	1,100.11	2,672.25	295.86	201.22	90.36	688.35	430.63	152.16	102.59	338.61	117.31	0.00	4,502.28
others	503.62	711.14	845.52	5,321.09	10,172.37	765.01	2,340.42	309.25	2,674.30	1,750.18	345.06	800.07	969.85	642.86	7,478.37	0.00

Table 3.3 Import tariff data of each country in the world in 2011 (unit: %)

Country	Australia	Brazil	Canada	China	EU	Hong Kong	India	Indonesia	Japan	South Korea	Malaysia	Russia	Singapore	Thailand	USA	Others
Australia	0	2.00	0.60	1.59	2.21	0	7.04	4.58	1.59	4.53	2.83	1.45	0	1.73	1.89	2.29
Brazil	1.89	0	0.71	2.33	11.18	0	11.32	2.75	1.67	54.23	1.15	3.48	0	5.03	2.46	7.01
Canada	2.23	5.44	0	2.87	4.09	0	15.25	4.27	1.32	4.28	1.50	5.44	0	4.22	1.77	3.76
China	3.39	13.47	4.13	0	6.81	0	7.03	5.71	2.83	7.16	3.85	6.44	0	5.80	2.76	4.96
EU	2.73	11.20	1.44	7.92	0	0	8.60	5.36	1.62	8.23	4.29	6.17	0	6.52	1.63	4.69
Hong Kong	3.38	13.46	2.74	3.99	7.31	0	8.26	5.09	1.62	2.77	2.25	3.87	0	2.91	2.85	4.32
India	3.18	6.19	4.57	2.60	8.01	0	0	5.57	1.82	9.91	3.58	6.75	0	5.00	3.39	4.33
Indonesia	1.77	11.83	4.50	3.27	7.42	0	7.7	0	0.81	2.90	4.29	3.23	0	6.25	5.27	4.23
Japan	3.36	13.05	2.58	6.07	7.74	0	8.77	6.95	0	4.55	7.62	2.61	0	7.28	1.18	5.13
South Korea	3.10	14.93	3.20	4.86	7.09	0	7.44	4.33	1.30	0	5.83	5.39	0	4.34	1.30	4.51
Malaysia	1.53	6.12	1.59	2.42	3.87	0	7.7	4.09	0.80	2.75	0	5.40	0	4.47	0.90	2.97
Russia	0.11	1.59	0.47	1.83	0.98	0	7.85	2.00	0.56	2.90	4.74	0	0	0.75	4.45	2.02
Singapore	0.73	5.76	0.37	3.69	2.83	0	5.19	2.64	1.90	1.60	2.48	4.58	0	4.61	1.03	2.67
Thailand	3.72	11.48	2.39	4.65	7.30	0	10.23	10.62	1.97	20.44	7.61	7.09	0	0	2.82	6.45
USA	2.46	7.56	2.21	5.45	4.54	0	6.94	4.01	1.72	28.77	2.18	4.73	0	4.56	0	5.37
Others	2.44	10.10	2.28	4.02	6.82	0.00	7.70	4.70	1.50	7.95	4.31	5.97	0.00	4.78	2.33	0.00

Table 3.4 GSIM elasticity parameters

Elasticity categories	Import demand elasticity	Export supply elasticity	Armington elasticity
Parameters	−1.68	4.46	5

3.2.2.2 Elastic Parameter

Elastic parameter directly affects the accuracy of the model estimates, so it is the most crucial parameter in GSIM. In GSIM, we need to obtain the three main elastic parameters first, which are export supply elasticity, import demand elasticity, and the substitution elasticity (Armington elasticity) among commodities of different countries. Currently, there are only a few studies of import demand elasticity and export supply elasticity, and they are limited to the research literature in the past. In the meantime, the elasticity data of the studies are rather scattered and differ greatly, which may easily result to large errors. Therefore, this paper mainly adopts the data of the commodities' elasticity from recent research published by the World Bank (http://wits.worldbank.org). According to the common practice of employing GSIM, we make the settings of the elastic coefficient to be symmetrical, i.e., we make the elasticity coefficient of each side to be equal. In terms of the substitution elasticity of Armington, we usually take 5. The specific elasticity data are as follows (see Table 3.4).

3.2.3 Parameters Calibration

According to the procedures of GSIM, on the basis of obtaining the original data of bilateral trade volume, bilateral level of tariff, import demand elasticity, export supply elasticity, and substitution elasticity, we need to firstly calibrate each parameter in order to simulate the economic effects under the different ranges of tariff reduction in the China-Japan-South Korea free trade area. The parameters that need to be calibrated are the expenditure portion $\theta_{(i,v),r}$ exported from the commodity's domestic price, the export portion $\phi_{(i,v),r}$ exported from the world price, self-price demand elasticity $N_{(i,v),(r,r)}$, cross-price elasticity $N_{(i,v),(r,s)}$, and tariff coefficient factor $T_{(i,v),r}$. Among them, tariff coefficient factor $T_{(i,v),r}$ is the most convenient one to be calibrated.

We calculate the expenditure portion by domestic price: $\theta_{(i,v),r} = \frac{M_{(i,v),r}T_{(i,v),r}}{\sum_s M_{(i,v),s}T_{(i,v),s}}$, as is shown in Table 3.5.

We calculate the export portion by world price: $\varphi_{(i,v),r} = \frac{M_{(i,v),r}}{\sum_w M_{(i,w),r}}$, as shown in Table 3.6.

According to formula (3.3) and formula (3.2), we can calibrate the commodities' self-price demand elasticity and cross-price elasticity. The calibration values are shown in Tables 3.7 and 3.8.

Table 3.5 Demand expenditure portion by the domestic price (unit: %)

Country	Australia	Brazil	Canada	China	EU	Hong Kong	India	Indonesia	Japan	South Korea	Malaysia	Russia	Singapore	Thailand	USA	Others
Australia	0.0	0.7	0.4	4.8	0.7	0.5	3.1	2.8	6.4	4.5	2.1	0.3	1.4	3.2	0.4	1.3
Brazil	0.4	0.0	0.8	3.1	2.4	0.4	0.8	1.0	1.4	1.5	0.8	1.4	0.7	0.9	1.3	3.5
Canada	0.8	1.3	0.0	1.2	1.5	0.5	0.6	1.0	1.4	1.1	0.4	0.5	0.3	0.4	14.3	0.9
China	17.1	14.7	8.8	0.0	17.1	44.6	11.6	15.5	20.6	16.2	13.5	14.2	10.5	13.0	17.1	14.6
EU	18.6	21.3	10.8	13.6	0.0	7.5	12.3	6.3	9.1	8.9	9.3	44.5	12.0	7.8	16.9	34.1
Hong Kong	0.3	0.2	0.0	0.8	0.3	0.0	1.3	0.7	0.1	0.3	1.2	0.0	0.6	0.6	0.1	0.1
India	1.0	2.4	0.5	1.3	2.4	2.2	0.0	3.0	0.8	1.2	1.8	0.8	4.3	1.3	1.6	4.7
Indonesia	2.5	0.8	0.3	1.8	1.0	0.6	3.0	0.0	4.1	3.1	5.8	0.4	5.4	3.1	0.9	1.1
Japan	8.1	3.2	2.6	11.9	4.5	7.9	2.5	10.5	0.0	12.5	10.7	4.2	7.7	18.7	5.9	6.0
South Korea	3.4	5.1	1.4	9.8	2.4	4.7	2.7	7.3	4.9	0.0	3.6	3.5	6.1	4.0	2.6	4.9
Malaysia	3.7	0.7	0.4	3.0	1.1	2.0	2.0	4.7	3.4	1.7	0.0	0.4	9.7	5.5	1.0	1.4
Russia	0.2	1.0	0.2	2.4	9.7	0.1	1.0	0.6	2.0	2.2	0.2	0.0	0.8	1.5	1.2	6.6
Singapore	6.6	0.5	0.3	2.3	1.4	7.1	2.4	18.6	1.7	2.2	18.7	0.1	0.0	5.0	0.9	2.9
Thailand	3.7	1.0	0.5	2.2	1.1	2.5	1.1	6.0	3.0	1.1	6.3	0.5	3.3	0.0	1.1	2.0
USA	11.5	15.4	53.3	7.3	11.1	5.4	4.4	5.0	8.4	9.9	7.7	3.3	9.7	5.4	0.0	15.8
Others	22.1	31.4	19.7	34.7	43.2	14.0	51.3	17.1	32.7	33.7	17.8	26.0	27.7	29.5	34.4	0.0

Table 3.6 Export volume portion by world price (Unit: %)

Country	Australia	Brazil	Canada	China	EU	Hong Kong	India	Indonesia	Japan	South Korea	Malaysia	Russia	Singapore	Thailand	USA	Others
Australia	0.0	0.6	0.6	28.9	6.6	1.1	5.4	2.0	20.0	9.3	1.6	0.4	1.9	2.8	3.7	15.3
Brazil	0.3	0.0	1.3	18.1	20.3	0.8	1.3	0.7	4.1	2.1	0.6	1.6	0.9	0.8	10.9	36.3
Canada	0.4	0.7	0.0	4.5	8.4	0.6	0.6	0.4	2.7	1.4	0.2	0.4	0.2	0.2	72.9	6.3
China	1.9	1.6	1.8	0.0	20.0	12.2	2.6	1.4	8.3	4.2	1.3	2.2	1.8	1.4	18.5	20.9
EU	2.0	2.2	2.2	9.4	0.0	1.9	2.6	0.5	3.5	2.2	0.9	6.4	2.0	0.8	17.4	46.0
Hong Kong	1.5	1.2	0.4	28.6	18.9	0.0	14.1	3.0	2.1	3.4	5.4	0.1	4.5	3.3	6.2	7.4
India	0.7	1.8	0.7	6.5	18.3	3.8	0.0	1.7	2.0	2.0	1.1	0.8	4.8	0.9	11.3	43.4
Indonesia	2.7	0.8	0.6	12.6	10.6	1.5	6.3	0.0	15.8	7.8	5.2	0.6	8.8	3.1	8.5	15.1
Japan	2.1	0.8	1.3	20.7	12.2	5.0	1.3	2.2	0.0	7.8	2.3	1.6	3.1	4.6	15.1	19.9
South Korea	1.4	1.9	1.0	26.2	9.9	4.6	2.2	2.3	7.0	0.0	1.2	1.9	3.8	1.6	10.2	24.8
Malaysia	3.2	0.6	0.6	17.5	10.2	4.1	3.5	3.3	10.8	3.6	0.0	0.5	12.9	4.6	8.6	16.1
Russia	0.1	0.5	0.2	6.9	44.3	0.1	0.8	0.2	3.0	2.2	0.1	0.0	0.5	0.6	4.7	35.8
Singapore	4.3	0.3	0.4	10.0	9.7	11.1	3.1	9.7	3.8	3.5	10.5	0.1	0.0	3.1	5.9	24.4
Thailand	3.5	1.0	0.9	14.0	10.9	5.8	2.2	4.3	10.3	2.1	5.0	0.7	4.8	0.0	10.1	24.5
USA	1.9	2.6	16.8	8.1	19.7	2.2	1.5	0.7	5.1	3.2	1.1	0.8	2.5	0.9	0.0	33.1
Others	1.4	2.0	2.4	14.9	28.6	2.1	6.6	0.9	7.5	4.9	1.0	2.2	2.7	1.8	21.0	0.0

Table 3.7 Self-price demand elasticity $N_{(i,v),(r,r)}$

Country	Australia	Brazil	Canada	China	EU	Hong Kong	India	Indonesia	Japan	South Korea	Malaysia	Russia	Singapore	Thailand	USA	Others
Australia	−5.00	−4.98	−4.99	−4.84	−4.98	−4.98	−4.90	−4.91	−4.79	−4.85	−4.93	−4.99	−4.95	−4.89	−4.99	−4.96
Brazil	−4.99	−5.00	−4.97	−4.90	−4.92	−4.99	−4.97	−4.97	−4.95	−4.95	−4.97	−4.95	−4.98	−4.97	−4.96	−4.89
Canada	−4.97	−4.96	−5.00	−4.96	−4.95	−4.98	−4.98	−4.97	−4.95	−4.96	−4.99	−4.98	−4.99	−4.99	−4.52	−4.97
China	−4.43	−4.51	−4.71	−5.00	−4.43	−3.52	−4.62	−4.49	−4.32	−4.46	−4.55	−4.53	−4.65	−4.57	−4.43	−4.52
EU	−4.38	−4.29	−4.64	−4.55	−5.00	−4.75	−4.59	−4.79	−4.70	−4.70	−4.69	−3.53	−4.60	−4.74	−4.44	−3.87
Hong Kong	−4.99	−4.99	−5.00	−4.97	−4.99	−5.00	−4.96	−4.98	−5.00	−4.99	−4.96	−5.00	−4.98	−4.98	−5.00	−5.00
India	−4.97	−4.92	−4.98	−4.96	−4.92	−4.93	−5.00	−4.90	−4.97	−4.96	−4.94	−4.97	−4.86	−4.96	−4.95	−4.85
Indonesia	−4.92	−4.97	−4.99	−4.94	−4.97	−4.98	−4.90	−5.00	−4.86	−4.90	−4.81	−4.99	−4.82	−4.90	−4.97	−4.96
Japan	−4.73	−4.89	−4.91	−4.61	−4.85	−4.74	−4.92	−4.65	−5.00	−4.58	−4.65	−4.86	−4.75	−4.38	−4.80	−4.80
South Korea	−4.89	−4.83	−4.95	−4.68	−4.92	−4.84	−4.91	−4.76	−4.84	−5.00	−4.88	−4.88	−4.80	−4.87	−4.91	−4.84
Malaysia	−4.88	−4.98	−4.99	−4.90	−4.96	−4.93	−4.93	−4.84	−4.89	−4.94	−5.00	−4.99	−4.68	−4.82	−4.97	−4.95
Russia	−4.99	−4.97	−4.99	−4.92	−4.68	−5.00	−4.97	−4.98	−4.93	−4.93	−4.99	−5.00	−4.97	−4.95	−4.96	−4.78
Singapore	−4.78	−4.98	−4.99	−4.92	−4.95	−4.76	−4.92	−4.38	−4.94	−4.93	−4.38	−5.00	−5.00	−4.83	−4.97	−4.90
Thailand	−4.88	−4.97	−4.98	−4.93	−4.96	−4.92	−4.96	−4.80	−4.90	−4.96	−4.79	−4.98	−4.89	−5.00	−4.96	−4.93
USA	−4.62	−4.49	−3.23	−4.76	−4.63	−4.82	−4.85	−4.84	−4.72	−4.67	−4.75	−4.89	−4.68	−4.82	−5.00	−4.48
Others	−4.27	−3.96	−4.35	−3.85	−3.57	−4.54	−3.30	−4.43	−3.91	−3.88	−4.41	−4.14	−4.08	−4.02	−3.86	−5.00

Table 3.8 Commodities cross-price elasticity $N_{(i,v),(r,s)}$

Country	Australia	Brazil	Canada	China	EU	Hong Kong	India	Indonesia	Japan	South Korea	Malaysia	Russia	Singapore	Thailand	USA	Others
Australia	0.00	0.02	0.01	0.16	0.02	0.02	0.10	0.09	0.21	0.15	0.07	0.01	0.05	0.11	0.01	0.04
Brazil	0.01	0.00	0.03	0.10	0.08	0.01	0.03	0.03	0.05	0.05	0.03	0.05	0.02	0.03	0.04	0.11
Canada	0.03	0.04	0.00	0.04	0.05	0.02	0.02	0.03	0.05	0.04	0.01	0.02	0.01	0.01	0.48	0.03
China	0.57	0.49	0.29	0.00	0.57	1.48	0.38	0.51	0.68	0.54	0.45	0.47	0.35	0.43	0.57	0.48
EU	0.62	0.71	0.36	0.45	0.00	0.25	0.41	0.21	0.30	0.30	0.31	1.47	0.40	0.26	0.56	1.13
Hong Kong	0.01	0.01	0.00	0.03	0.01	0.00	0.04	0.02	0.00	0.01	0.04	0.00	0.02	0.02	0.00	0.00
India	0.03	0.08	0.02	0.04	0.08	0.07	0.00	0.10	0.03	0.04	0.06	0.03	0.14	0.04	0.05	0.15
Indonesia	0.08	0.03	0.01	0.06	0.03	0.02	0.10	0.00	0.14	0.10	0.19	0.01	0.18	0.10	0.03	0.04
Japan	0.27	0.11	0.09	0.39	0.15	0.26	0.08	0.35	0.00	0.42	0.35	0.14	0.25	0.62	0.20	0.20
South Korea	0.11	0.17	0.05	0.32	0.08	0.16	0.09	0.24	0.16	0.00	0.12	0.12	0.20	0.13	0.09	0.16
Malaysia	0.12	0.02	0.01	0.10	0.04	0.07	0.07	0.16	0.11	0.06	0.00	0.01	0.32	0.18	0.03	0.05
Russia	0.01	0.03	0.01	0.08	0.32	0.00	0.03	0.02	0.07	0.07	0.01	0.00	0.03	0.05	0.04	0.22
Singapore	0.22	0.02	0.01	0.08	0.05	0.24	0.08	0.62	0.06	0.07	0.62	0.00	0.00	0.17	0.03	0.10
Thailand	0.12	0.03	0.02	0.07	0.04	0.08	0.04	0.20	0.10	0.04	0.21	0.02	0.11	0.00	0.04	0.07
USA	0.38	0.51	1.77	0.24	0.37	0.18	0.15	0.16	0.28	0.33	0.25	0.11	0.32	0.18	0.00	0.52
Others	0.73	1.04	0.65	1.15	1.43	0.46	1.70	0.57	1.09	1.12	0.59	0.86	0.92	0.98	1.14	0.00

3.3 Economic Effect Simulation in China-Japan-South Korea Free Trade Area

3.3.1 Trade Effect

According to the theory of Customs Union raised by American economists Wiener and Lipsey, the economic effect of customs union should be divided into the static effect and the dynamic effect. The dynamic one includes economies of scale and stimulation of investment. In terms of economies of scale, the arrangements of regional economy and trade could enlarge the scale and volume of the members' markets through rules of free trade. Thus, the industries which are more competitive within the region could make full use of their advantages to enlarge the scale of production, reduce the product costs, enhance the economic efficiency, and ultimately occupy the market of the whole region and produce internal and external economies of scale (internal economies of scale are economies of scale with low cost, while external economies of scale derive from the total national economy and economic development within the integration organization). In terms of the stimulation of investment, generally speaking, the increasement of the regional investment always comes from two aspects: one is that the original producers would increase their investment for the improvement and updating of the products in order to enhance their competitive capacity; the other one is that the producers beyond the region would try any way they can to invest, produce, and sell within the region in order to bypass the tariff wall due to the fact that the nonmembers may suffer from discrimination from the free trade areas which keep tariff and other barriers to them while removing those things from their members. The static effects include the trade creation and trade diversion effects. The trade creation mainly refers to the phenomenon that, caused by international market separation and the removal of trade and non-trade barriers, the member's domestic high cost products being replaced by the imported low cost products from other members and the export enlargement of domestic low cost products which were once affected greatly by the transaction expenses together bring comparative economic benefits to all parts in the region. Trade diversion means that the original trade contacts beyond the region are transferred into the trade contacts within the region where the transaction expenses have been reduced. From realistic feasibility, there is still a long way to go for the China-Japan-South Korea free trade area to reach the level of customs union, but there are similarities in their economic effects. Restricted by the range of research, this paper will mainly focus on the static effect of the China-Japan-South Korea free trade area.

In the process of China-Japan-South Korea free trade area negotiations, the three parties have reached consensuses on some basic framework issues including steps of negotiations, classifications of commodities, ways of handling problems, etc. The next goal of negotiation is to further clarify the way, region, and level of opening in terms of commodities, services, and investments as well as to exchange views on the texts with the range of negotiations among the three parties. The first and foremost measure to be taken is to reduce the mutual import duties. This paper sets a basis of customs duty rate of each country in 2011 and simulates the trade effects and welfare effects under the condition that each party reduce the tariff by 20 %, 50 %, and 80 %, respectively. Table 3.9 shows how the export volume of different countries changes when the members reduce their tariff by 50 % simultaneously. Table 3.10 is the comparison and contrast of the changes of trade when the ranges of tariff reduction are varied.

We can make several conclusions from Table 3.9:

- There exists prominent trade creation effect. After the mutual lowering of import tariff among the three members, there is a sharp increase in the mutual exports. The volumes of export from China to Japan and South Korea increase by 8.76 billion US dollars and 11.4 billion US dollars, respectively. The volumes of export from Japan to China and South Korea increase by 19.83 billion US dollars and 4.6 US dollars, respectively. The volumes of export from South Korea to China and Japan increase by 12.82 billion and 380 million, respectively. On the whole, the volumes of exports in China, Japan, and South Korea increase by 17.5 billion, 18.3 billion, and 9.9 billion US dollars, respectively. It is true that the trades in China, Japan, and South Korea all benefit a lot from the tariff reductions.
- There exists transparent trade diversion effect. Except that the volumes of export to other countries and regions in China and Japan increase by 3.88 billion and 380 million US dollars, respectively, the competitive capacity of the commodities in these two countries is also improved due to the lower cost of export caused by internal tariff alleviation and reduction of tariff wall. China, Japan, and South Korea all have more commodities exported to the members while their volumes of export in the USA and other EU members have negative changes.
- There exists clear substitution effect. Parts of the exported commodities in third-party countries or regions are substituted by those more competitive ones of other member states. Those countries that failed the competition had to increase export to the countries beyond the free trade areas in order to consume the existing capacity and increase the volume of trade to different levels.

Table 3.10 shows that the export volume of the three countries increases with the increase of the rate of tariff reduction. Every time when the tariff reduces 1 %, the export volume of China, Japan, and South Korea would approximately increase 351, 368, and 200 million US dollars, respectively. Every time the tariff reduces 80 %, the export volume of China, Japan, and South Korea would increase 28.08, 29.46, and 15.97 billion, respectively. The revenues of China and Japan are higher than that of the South Korea. Certainly, this is due to the reason that the economic scale and export scale in China and Japan are much higher than those in South Korea. In terms of the percentage of increasement, Japan is the first one, then South Korea, while China is the last one with 50 % less than Japan.

Table 3.9 The change of world trade under 50 % reduction of tariff of the members

Country	Australia	Brazil	Canada	China	EU	Hong Kong	India	Indonesia	Japan	South Korea	Malaysia	Russia	Singapore	Thailand	USA	Others
Australia	0.00	0.08	0.06	−10.05	0.81	0.20	0.56	0.31	−3.11	−5.20	0.23	0.05	0.25	0.48	0.49	0.99
Brazil	0.03	0.00	0.06	−7.51	1.41	0.11	0.06	0.07	−0.90	−1.31	0.06	0.11	0.07	0.09	0.86	0.35
Canada	0.03	0.03	0.00	−3.31	0.38	0.09	0.01	0.04	−1.14	−1.48	0.01	0.02	0.01	0.03	4.38	−0.32
China	−1.89	−1.79	−2.36	0.00	−22.32	−7.30	−3.33	−1.17	87.57	114.87	−1.25	−2.43	−1.90	−1.04	−19.30	38.84
EU	1.12	0.96	0.54	−32.34	0.00	1.87	0.70	0.37	−6.47	−11.24	0.50	2.68	0.99	0.64	8.67	−2.40
Hong Kong	0.02	0.02	0.00	−1.84	0.26	0.00	0.15	0.06	−0.07	−0.33	0.09	0.00	0.07	0.07	0.09	0.03
India	0.05	0.09	0.02	−3.31	0.91	0.50	0.00	0.16	−0.57	−1.54	0.09	0.04	0.30	0.10	0.69	−0.83
Indonesia	0.22	0.06	0.03	−4.07	0.71	0.19	0.32	0.00	−2.58	−3.90	0.44	0.04	0.66	0.33	0.63	0.28
Japan	−2.57	−1.04	−1.73	198.26	−15.49	−5.27	−1.73	−2.50	0.00	46.02	−2.81	−1.99	−3.85	−5.16	−18.77	1.97
South Korea	−0.88	−1.32	−0.75	128.24	−6.73	−2.44	−1.60	−1.42	3.77	0.00	−0.78	−1.32	−2.48	−0.90	−6.72	−5.19
Malaysia	0.29	0.05	0.03	−7.07	0.73	0.57	0.18	0.35	−2.26	−2.23	0.00	0.03	1.06	0.55	0.70	0.21
Russia	0.01	0.04	0.01	−6.16	4.15	0.03	0.04	0.03	−1.50	−2.97	0.01	0.00	0.06	0.12	0.53	−1.00
Singapore	0.38	0.02	0.01	−5.78	0.61	1.70	0.12	1.07	−1.21	−3.00	0.95	0.01	0.00	0.40	0.45	−0.37
Thailand	0.25	0.06	0.03	−5.24	0.61	0.67	0.08	0.38	−2.03	−1.20	0.37	0.04	0.31	0.00	0.65	0.08
USA	0.70	0.73	2.70	−17.72	5.36	1.35	0.26	0.30	−5.99	−10.46	0.43	0.20	0.81	0.45	0.00	−0.98
Others	1.57	1.76	1.38	−83.34	24.93	3.84	4.04	1.17	−22.09	−41.74	1.12	1.94	2.75	2.76	21.01	0.00

Table 3.10 The change of export volume under different tax rate

The rate of tariff reduction (%)	China			Japan			South Korea		
	Original volume of export	Change	Rate of change (%)	Original volume of export	Change	Rate of change (%)	Original volume of export	Change	Rate of change (%)
20	20,102.8	70.0	0.35	8,608.4	73.0	0.85	5,662.9	39.6	0.70
50	20,102.8	175.2	0.87	8,608.4	183.3	2.13	5,662.9	99.5	1.76
80	20,102.8	280.8	1.40	8,608.4	294.6	3.42	5,662.9	159.7	2.82

Table 3.11 The change of welfare under 50 % tax reductions in GSIM

Country	The rate of tariff reduction (%)	Producer surplus A	Consumer Surplus B	Tariff revenue C	Net social benefits D = A + B + C
China	20	12.82	33.25	−33.58	12.49
	50	32.16	83.52	−89.39	26.28
	80	51.61	134.27	−151.80	34.07
Japan	20	13.40	9.89	−9.92	13.37
	50	33.76	24.78	−25.56	32.98
	80	54.43	39.76	−42.11	52.08
Korea	20	7.27	17.28	−18.54	6.02
	50	18.30	43.43	−49.43	12.29
	80	29.46	69.85	−84.05	15.26

3.3.2 *Welfare Effect*

Theoretically, if we successfully build the China-Japan-South Korea free trade area, the mutual reduction of import tariff among members will not only affect themselves but will also bring effect to the welfare of producers and consumers as well as the tax revenues in the related countries and regions. The mere problem is how much or in which direction these effects are. Table 3.11 shows the change of welfare in China, Japan, and South Korea under different ranges of tax reductions.

Table 3.11 shows that:

- When the member states reduce their taxes, producers could easily sell the products to other markets, enlarge the market area and obtain benefits from scale of economies, and in the meantime increase the competitive capacity of the industries in the member states against their counterparts in the nonmember states so that they could obtain more benefits in the competition of the world market. Therefore, the producer surplus increases with the increase of the tax reductions in the three countries. To put it more specifically, every time the tariff reduces by 1 %, the producer surplus will increase by 0.65, 0.68, and 0.37 US dollars in China, Japan, and South Korea, respectively.
- After the tariff reduction, the consumer could turn to buy the exported commodities of good quality and low prices from member states rather than buy consumer goods of high prices in their own countries. The reduction of prices also accompanies with the rise of the demand, which may definitely lead to the constant increase of consumer surplus. When the tax is reduced by 80 %, the consumer surplus in China, Japan, and South Korea will increase by 13.43, 3.98, and 7 billion, respectively.
- Since the overall level of tariff is not high, usually under the most related tax rate, the tariff revenue of each country will undoubtedly be negatively affected with the reduction of the tariff in the member states. Among them, the tariff revenue of China reduces at the fastest speed. Every time when the tariff reduces 10 %, the tariff revenue will reduce nearly 190 million US dollars.

- During the process of tariff reduction, the government could gain more producer surplus and consumer surplus while at the same time lose part of the tariff revenues. Comprehensively, the reduction of tariff undoubtedly boosts the effective allocation of production factors in the free trade area and gain member states with genuine net welfare. Among the three countries, Japan will become the biggest beneficiary, with 5.208 billion US dollars net welfare revenue when the tariff reduces 80 %, while the numbers for China and South Korea are 3.407 and 1.526 billion US dollars, respectively.

3.3.3 The Boundary Effect of China-Japan-South Korea Free Trade Area

This chapter will reexamine the boundary effect of each country under different levels of tariff reduction by employing the country boundary effect examination model on the basis of the new trade flow simulated from the construction revenue of China-Japan-South Korea free trade area. The results are shown in Table 3.12.

We can make several conclusions from Table 3.12.

- With the reduction of tariff, the boundary effect of the world's main countries has been in decline. The boundary effect of Malaysia has dropped by 80 % from 1.19 to 0.85, which signifies that under the same circumstances, the condition of the volume of selling domestically surpassing that of exporting to foreign countries has reversed.
- In terms of the three countries of the China-Japan-South Korea free trade area, China dropped from 4.87 to 4.47, Japan from 1.2 to 1.13, and South Korea from 0.79 to 0.72, which are quite conspicuous. However, with the reduction of the tariff, the level of reduction is also lowered.
- On the whole, even if the tariff reduces by 80 % in the three countries, the level of boundary effect reduction is still not satisfactory compared to the whole. This is mainly due to two reasons. The first reason is that the boundary effect within the three countries does connect not only to their own levels of tariff but also to those of the other countries. The other reason is that it is really more than tariff that constitutes the boundary barriers. Except the related variables in the model, there are also other factors including non-tariff barriers, languages, and other cultural barriers.

3.4 The Progression and Prospects

3.4.1 The Negotiations of China-Japan-South Korea Agreement of Investment

On May 13, 2012, the representatives from China, Japan and South Korea officially signed the Agreement on the Promotion, Facilitation and Protection of Investment

Table 3.12 Boundary effect coefficient under different levels of tariff reduction in China-Japan-South Korea free trade area

	Country	Australia	Brazil	Canada	China	EU	H.K.	India	Indonesia	Japan	Korea	Malaysia	Russia	Singapore	Thailand	USA
Original	Coefficient	1.68	1.52	2.10	1.58	1.29	1.41	1.63	1.03	0.22	−0.23	0.17	2.17	−3.64	0.73	1.85
	Boundary effect	5.38	4.57	8.17	4.84	3.63	4.09	5.11	2.81	1.24	0.79	1.19	8.74	0.03	2.07	6.34
20 %	Coefficient	1.61	1.49	2.05	1.52	1.26	1.42	1.61	1.01	0.16	−0.29	−0.14	2.12	−2.71	0.62	1.80
	Boundary effect	4.98	4.45	7.78	4.55	3.52	4.12	5.00	2.74	1.17	0.75	0.87	8.30	0.07	1.86	6.07
50 %	Coefficient	1.59	1.48	2.04	1.51	1.25	1.40	1.60	0.99	0.14	−0.31	−0.15	2.12	−2.73	0.61	1.79
	Boundary effect	4.93	4.38	7.73	4.51	3.49	4.04	4.97	2.70	1.15	0.74	0.86	8.30	0.07	1.85	6.01
80 %	Coefficient	1.58	1.46	2.04	1.50	1.24	1.38	1.60	0.98	0.12	−0.32	−0.16	2.12	−2.75	0.60	1.78
	Boundary effect	4.87	4.32	7.68	4.47	3.46	3.97	4.94	2.67	1.13	0.72	0.85	8.30	0.06	1.83	5.95

among the Government of People's Republic of China, Japan and Republic of South Korea. Since 2007 when China, Japan, and South Korea started the investment agreement, it took 5 years, 13 times of formal negotiations and several times of informal consultations, for the three countries to finally put a successful end to the signing of the agreement in the end of March 2012. This agreement includes all the important issues for the general international investment treaties, including 27 items and an additional memorandum of agreement. The signing of the agreement serves as an important milestone for the development of the economic and trade relations among China, Japan, and South Korea. It does not only provide the construction of China-Japan-South Korea free trade area with a solid foundation but also ensure a safer and more stable investment environment for the investors of the three countries.

3.4.2 China-South Korea Free Trade Area Negotiations

During the past 30 years, the economic exchanges in China and South Korea have experienced rapid development. In terms of trade, the bilateral trade has been greatly improved since the establishment of diplomatic ties between China and South Korea in 1992. In 2013, the bilateral trade in goods has surpassed 270 billion US dollars. As the biggest trade partners of South Korea, China is responsible for a quarter of the total volume of South Korea's foreign trade, which is more than those to the USA, Japan, and Russia put together. South Korea stands as China's third largest trade partner, with market share of 9.24 %, and first largest source of imports, which has surpassed Japan. Currently, China and South Korea are in different places of the global value chain as they vary in terms of economic development, industrial structures, and natural economic endowment. So China and South Korea have strong economic complementary. China could provide more labor-intensive products and intermediate products to South Korea, while South Korea could provide more productive goods and high-end consumer goods to China.

The negotiations on the establishment of China-South Korea free trade area have experienced a marathon. Leaders of the two countries have already reached their consensus as early as 2004 at the APEC meeting and have had feasibility research by the experts from both countries. After that, the China-ROK has launched joint studies as a continuity of the private researches. The joint studies covered issues of macroeconomic effect, domain area of the free trade area agreement, the effect to industries from trade and investment liberalization, and ways to tackle the problem of sensitive products or area. When the feasibility research was finished, each side will submit a research report to their own government.

In terms of direct investment, the direct investment between the two countries serves as the pillar and supplementary of mutual trade, which also carries great importance. The negotiation was officially started on May 2012, but it did not until September of next year that some breakthrough was made in the seventh round of the negotiation. China and South Korea have concluded the first-stage negotiations by reaching primary consensus on the percentage of products to be abolished tariffs

(90 %) and the percentage of export volume (85 %). A year later, China and South Korea have had six more rounds of negotiations, but they have made slow progresses so that the negotiation cannot be concluded.

The negotiations on China-South Korea free trade area was started on March 2012, and it took 2 years and 6 months, 14 rounds of negotiation, to finally reach the conclusion. According to the agreement, the percentage of trade liberalization of goods from both China and South Korea should surpass 90 % in tax items and 85 % in trade volume. After the reduction or removal of the tariff, the export competitive capacity of both countries will be greatly enhanced. Estimated by South Korea, the volume export of South Korea's commodities to the Chinese market has reached to 29 % of its total. The foreign economic policy institute of ROK predicted that the GDP of South Korea is expected to have a 1.25 % increase since the agreement of free trade area took effect. China's GDP has become six times more than that of South Korea, so the Chinese market can undertake the massive entering of commodities from South Korea, which could not only benefit the Chinese consumers but also exploit new markets for Chinese competitive products. On the whole, the negotiation on China-South Korea free trade area has reached the goal of relative balance of interests, comprehensiveness, and high level.

3.4.3 *China-Japan-South Korea Free Trade Area Negotiations*

In the view of East Asia or the whole world, China, Japan, and South Korea are extremely important economic entities. Japan, as the old capitalization nation, enjoys advanced science and technology and is well capitalized. South Korea, as one of the Four Asian Tigers, has achieved Han River Miracle only within decades and became the medium-developed country. China has achieved rapid development of industrial economy after the reform and opening up and become a significant production center of the whole world. In 2012, the total economic volume of China, Japan, and South Korea is mounted to 14 trillion US dollars, with an estimated percentage of 20 % of the world's total and 90 % of East Asia. In the perspective of trade, the three countries are all worthy of the name of the world's big trading nations. China and Japan are the biggest trade surplus countries. In 2012, the three parties' total volume of export and import are mounted to five trillion US dollars, which are one third of the world's total volume of trade. In the meantime, the outflow and inflow of the direct investment in this region account for 12.8 % and 9.2 % of the world's total, respectively.

In 2011, China has run a trade surplus with Japan and South Korea, while Japan has run a trade surplus with South Korea (see Chart 3.3).

On November 20, 2012, the trade ministers of the three countries have held a conference during the series of East Asia Summit meetings and declared the official launching of the China-Japan-South Korea free trade area. However, the negotiation of China-Japan-South Korea free trade area did not go smoothly.

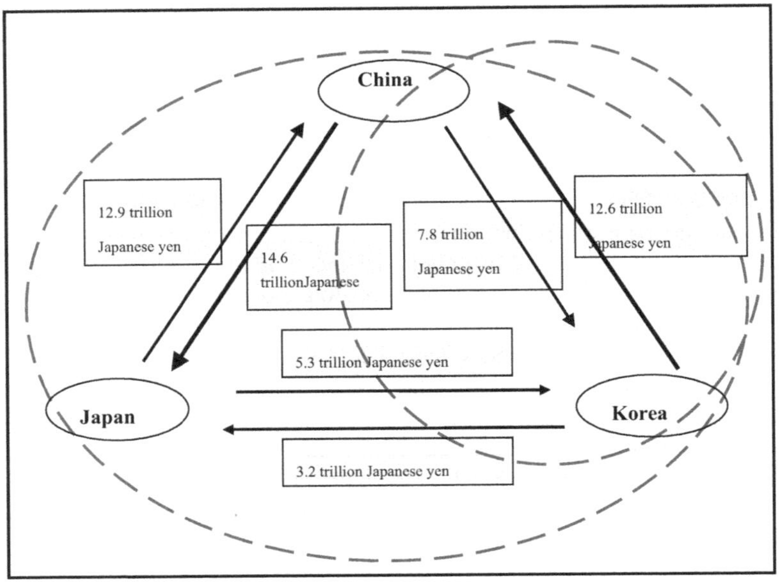

Chart 3.3 Trade between China, Japan, and South Korea (Reproduced from Nikkei Chinese network)

On March 2013, the first round of China-Japan-South Korea free trade area negotiation was held in Seoul, capital of South Korea. Representatives from the three countries made consultations on important issues of the negotiation, including the coordinating mechanism, covered areas or ways, etc., and they decided to put the next two rounds of negotiations of this year to the other two countries, respectively. China, Japan, and South Korea all indicated that they will make joint efforts to construct the free trade area, create better political and economic environment for further negotiations, and facilitate the negotiations to reach important phased objectives.

From the first round of negotiations on March 2013, there have been four rounds among China, Japan, and South Korea successively, but they are still hovering around the insubstantial issues like the structure of negotiations and the work to be focused. To view from the perspective of the process, the speed of the negotiation was far less than that of the North America FTA horizontally and also less than that of the China-ROK FTA vertically which has opened nearly at the same time. There have already been four rounds among the three countries. They have made in-depth consultations about goods trade, service trade, investment, and other contents or methods and reached consensus on the basic framework of tax reduction mode such as procedures of negotiations, classifications of products, mode of processing, and so on.

Moreover, the three sides also agreed to bring several issues into the negotiations, including goods trade, service trade, investment, rules of origin, customs cooperation, trade remedy, sanitation and phytosanitation, technical barriers, intellectual property rights, legal provisions, competition policy, etc., and they have also set up 11 consultative groups.

The next phase of the negotiation objectives on China-Japan-South Korea free trade area will continue to focus on the goods, service, and investment: issues about further confirming the domains, method, and scale of the opening are included, and there are also consultations on the texts about the items of negotiation.

However, as matters stand, it is difficult for China, Japan, and South Korea to reach consensus on the negotiations because there is still a disparity that existed among the three countries in terms of economic development level, industrial competitive ability, degree of opening up, and tariff level, let alone the complex and difficult situation in Northeast Asia and the fierce multilateral game process among China, America, Japan, and South Korea. Moreover, given that the China-ROK FTA negotiation is earlier than that of the China-Japan-South Korea FTA, the result of the China-ROK FTA negotiation will significantly influence the result of the China-Japan-South Korea FTA negotiation.

3.4.4 The Negotiating Stance and Offense-Defense State of the China-Japan-South Korea Cross-Setting Issue

3.4.4.1 The Issue of Farming Products Is One of the Important Key Issues in the China-Japan-South Korea FTA Negotiation

Both Japan and South Korea are the biggest farming product-importing countries in the world. The high tariff of the farming products, the strict protectionism, and the large government grants have limited the market access of the foreign farming products. The two countries also employ various non-tariff barriers, for example, access system including strict technical standards and inspection and quarantine standards and so on. The market access has become a bottleneck of the China-Japan-South Korea FTA negotiation. And the result of the negotiations on farming products will directly influence the success of the China-Japan-South Korea FTA negotiation.

Chart 3.4 shows the distribution of benefits among China, Japan, and South Korea. Take China as one side (here we will call 1) and Japan and South Korea as the other side (here we call 2) to have negotiation on agricultural issues. U1 and U2 are the utilities of the two sides, respectively.

For discussion purpose, let's assume that each side will choose the most favorable point on the utility curve to reach their agreement. Assume that D is the initial point, the negotiation will drive each side to the frontier, and the several points on the border are the feasible solutions to the forming of the agreement. S is the point where two sides have equal utility. Q is the point which is more favorable to 1 while R is the point which is more favorable to 2. To get more specific to the three modes of negotiation, we can think that the first mode of negotiation is more favorable to

Chart 3.4 Analysis of the bilateral feasible set of the farming products' access mode in the China, Japan, and South Korea negotiation

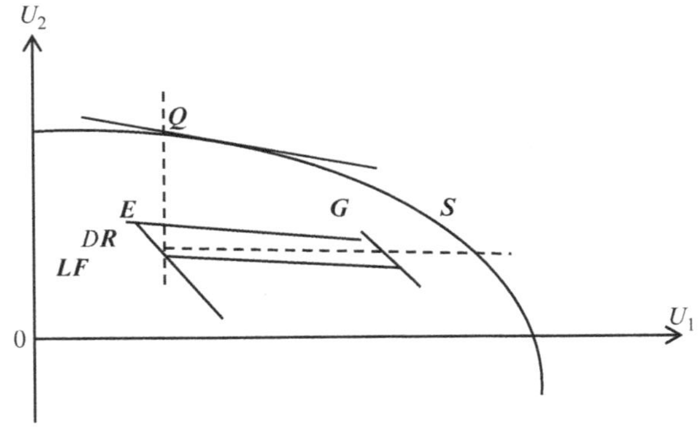

2, the second mode has equal utility to both sides, and the third mode is more favorable to 1. Then, $U_2 = \text{f}(U_{11} + U_{12})$; $U_2 < \text{f}(U_{11} + U_{12})$; $U_2 > \text{f}(U_{11} + U_{12})$.

The tax rate of farming products in China is lower than that of Japan and South Korea, so obviously China has a relatively favorable offense position in the negotiation of the farming products. But the process of negotiation will be affected if the offense is too aggressive and the opposite side refuses to bid.

3.4.4.2 Negotiation of the Cross-Setting Issue and the Stances of the Three Sides

In Chart 3.5, take China as one side (here we will call 1) and Japan and South Korea as the other side (here we call 2) to have negotiation on cross-agricultural and nonagricultural product issues. Assume D as the initial point of the farming product issue; the negotiation will drive the two sides to the efficient frontier, i.e., point S on Q-S-R. Assume S to be the point which is more favorable to 1 and the point where the nonagricultural products' access is to be negotiated.

In order to incorporate and balance the issues to be negotiated of each side, and benefit the new negotiation of equal utility, which is to integrate the negotiation of agricultural and nonagricultural blanket agreements, we could not start only from the new bifurcation point *D'* but from the point S where the agricultural issues reached to the agreement. In the nonagricultural issues, if one side, take 2 as the example, feels that its utility is lower than the other side, it will strive to drive the current condition of the two sides from S to the efficient frontier, any point on *a-r-SNN*, so that both sides could reach to the relative utility balance in the cross-agricultural and nonagricultural issues. To get more specific to the cross-setting issues, there are further negotiations concerning cost, revenue, and risk for each side to reach their own interactive decisions. Thus, it is fairly difficult for the agreement reached in the single issue to realize the equal utility for both sides. However, since the China-Japan-South Korea FTA negotiation is cross-set and the market access negotiation also includes agricultural and nonagricultural issues, the

Chart 3.5 Analysis of the feasible set of the cross-agricultural and nonagricultural market access mode negotiation among China, Japan, and South Korea

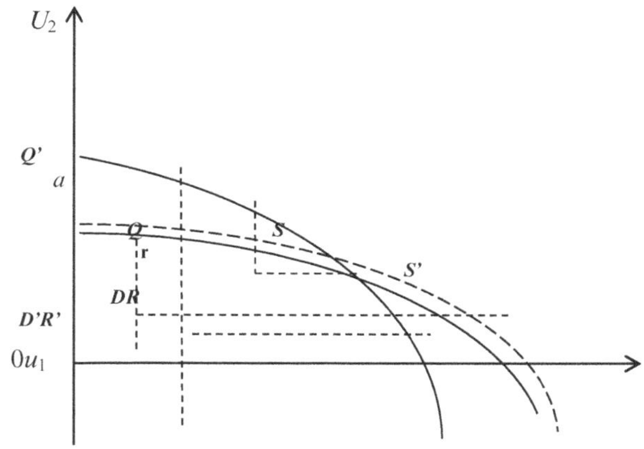

negotiating groups could reach a new balance through cross-setting issues. But it also requires mutual trust to come to a compromise, which is also very difficult.

3.4.4.3 The Effect to the China-Japan-South Korea Cross-Setting Issue from the End of the China-Japan-South Korea FTA Negotiation

The substantive negotiation of the China-ROK FTA agreement has already concluded. Most of the commodities have tax cuts in the two countries; some are protected as sensitive products. To view from the newly published negotiation results, both China and South Korea have found a balanced point in market opening and protection of the sensitive industry.

Due to the conclusion of China-ROK FTA negotiation, the floor of China-Japan-South Korea FTA negotiation was also fundamentally predetermined. At least at current levels, due to the fact that the common interests of China and South Korea have been largely achieved, the three sides of the negotiating groups have turned to two sides: Japan as one side while China and South Korea as the other.

As mentioned in this article, on the first day in the sixth round of talks of CJK FTA negotiations, China and South Korea proposed to Japan the liberalization rate target (the proportion of zero-tariff varieties) based on the content of their bilateral consensus. China-ROK FTA commits to cancel more than 90 % of the tariff types in 20 years, but so far, very little mention has been made of specific types. Japan rejected the proposal with the excuse that liberalize rate is too low, and the setting of the target liberalization rate was postponed. In the next phase of the negotiations, in order to achieve results acceptable to the three sides, Japan has to either accept the agreement reached by China-ROK FTA negotiation or put forward higher demand to China and South Korea from the possible agreement of the ongoing TPP negotiation with America and other countries so that its influence in the China-Japan-South Korea FTA negotiation could be realized.

Chart 3.6 Analysis of the feasible set of the cross-agricultural and nonagricultural market access mode negotiation among China, Japan, and South Korea under the new circumstances

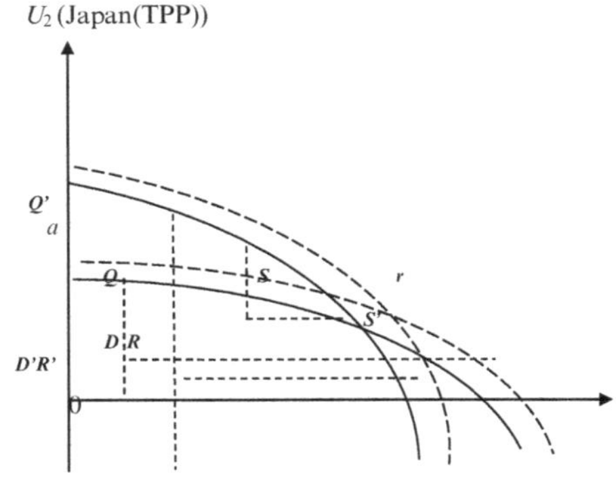

In Chart 3.6, take China and South Korea as one side (here we will call 1) and Japan as the other side (here we call 2) to have negotiation on cross-agricultural and nonagricultural product issues.

It can be assumed that the new program that China and South Korea will propose will be, on the basis of their substantive negotiated solutions, an expansion to a new boundary of agricultural and nonagricultural issues (see the dotted line in Chart 3.6). But Japan will ask China and South Korea to clarify the substantive content in their bilateral negotiation or will make defensive or offensive negotiations on the two issues by taking advantage of TPP.

TPP member economies account together for 40 % of the global economy. After three years of negotiations, these countries have growing pressures to achieve some results from the negotiations. In principle, TPP negotiations require members to remove all tariffs on imports of goods, including agricultural products. Now, the Japanese agriculture groups hope that five agricultural products, rice, wheat, beef and pork, dairy products, and sugar, will not be included in the zero-tariff list. Differences on the issue of agricultural tariffs lead TPP negotiations to an impasse that failed to achieve a major breakthrough. On October 28, 2014, Wall Street Journal reported that Japan does not want to open their agricultural and automotive markets, which hinders the TPP negotiations. On December 11, 2014, on the "President's Export Council" meeting held in the White House, US President Barack Obama said that although the TPP negotiations have not yet been completed, he believes the probability of TPP members to reach a final agreement has been significantly higher than 50 %, and the prospect of negotiations is much better than the last year. However, these are not easy.

RCEP was the arrangements to promote regional trade agreement negotiations proposed and led by ASEAN in 2011. It includes the 10 ASEAN member countries and the other countries that signed FTAs with ASEAN: China, Japan, Korea, Australia, New Zealand, and India. Because China, Japan, and South Korea are negotiating parties in RCEP, CJK FTA negotiations are critical to reach RCEP. If the progress of CJK FTA is slow, RCEP negotiations are bound to be affected. Positive and closer cooperation between China and South Korea, as well as the push of RCEP by other countries in ASEAN and Asia-Pacific region, is giving pressures on Japan. Because Japan emphasizes domestic market protection and is good at calculating, it will make use of the parallel process of TPP negotiations with CJK FTA negotiations in order to obtain maximum benefits. As the third largest power in East Asia, South Korea may use its third-party status to deal between China and Japan and to play a positive role in the integration process in East Asia.

3.5 Conclusion

This paper firstly constructs a global model that includes China, Japan, and South Korea and the associated 13 countries and regions and makes trade flow analysis.

Secondly, it makes simulated analysis of the economic and trade effects of the CJK FTA and gets the different results of trade effects and welfare effects of all the parties in different proportions of tariff reduction. The results show that there is significant trade creation effect, trade diversion effect, and trade substitution effect among China, Japan, and South Korea.

Thirdly, from the perspective of feasible set of negotiations, it discusses the single issue negotiation and across issues negotiation among China, Japan, and South Korea in agricultural and nonagricultural negotiations, which shows that the three parties may get consensus in their major interested industries in the agricultural and nonagricultural negotiations. And it further explores the prospect of CJK FTA in the situation that the substantive bilateral FTA negotiations between China and South Korea have ended: the results will not be less than the lower limit of the bilateral FTA between China and South Korea, and the upper limit may keep abreast of TPP negotiation. It also pointed out the feasibility and difficulties to achieve this goal and that, to some extent, the CJK FTA negotiation will affect the specific end time of RCEP negotiations in 2015.

References

ADB (2008a) Emerging Asian regionalism: a partnership for shared prosperity. ADB, Manila

ADB (2008b) How to design, negotiate, and implement a free trade agreements in Asia. ADB, Manila

ADB (2011) Institutions for regional integration: toward an Asian economic community. ADB, Manila

Anderson JE, Yotov YV (2011) Terms of trade and global efficiency effects of free trade agreements: 1990–2002. NBER working paper no 17003, National Bureau of Economic Research, Cambridge, MA

Baldwin RE (1995) A domino theory of regionalism. In: Baldwin RE, Haaparnta P, Kiander J (eds) Expanding membership of the European Union. Cambridge University Press, New York, pp 25–53

Baldwin R, Jaimovich D (2010) Are free trade agreements contagious? NBER working paper No 16084. National Bureau of Economic Research, Cambridge, MA

Bergstrand JH, Egger P, Larch M (2011) Economic determinants of the timing of preferential trade agreement formations and enlargements. Working papers, University of Notre Dame, Notre Dame

Francois J, Hall HK (1997) Applied methods for trade policy analysis. Cambridge University Press, Cambridge

Francois J, Hall HK (2002) Global simulation analysis of industry-level trade policy. Word Bank. http://wits.worldbank.org/WITS/docs/GSIMMethodology.pdf

Freund C, Ornelas E (2010) Regional trade agreements. Policy research working paper no. 5314, World Bank, Washington, DC

Krugman P (1991) Is bilateralism bad? In: Helpman E, Razin A (eds) International trade and trade policy. MIT Press, Cambridge, pp 9–23

Kwon, Hyuk-jae (2011) Free trade agreement between Korea and China. KBS World

Lee S (2006) The political economy of FTAs in Northeast Asia: a South Korean perspective. Paper presented at the conference on Northeast Asia's economic and security regionalism: old constraints and new prospects, Center for International Studies, University of Southern California

Madhur S (2012a) 21st century global economic governance: evolving architecture, emerging issues, and Asia's role, 2011 visiting scholars' paper series. Korea Institute for International Economic Policy, Seoul, pp 153–191

Madhur S (2012b) Asia's role in twenty first century global economic governance. Int Aff 88 (4):817–833

McCallum J (1995) National borders matter: Canada—US regional trade patterns. Am Econ Rev 85(3):615–623

Menon J (2009) Dealing with the proliferation of bilateral free trade agreements. World Econ 32(10):1381–1407

Shang-Jin Wei (1996) Intra-national versus international trade: how Stubborn is nations in global integration? NBER working paper No 5531. National Bureau of Economic Research, Cambridge, MA

Wonnacott P, Lutz M (1989) Is there a case for free trade areas? In: Schott JJ (ed) Free trade areas and U.S. trade policy. Institute for International Economics, Washington, DC, pp 59–84

WTO (2011) World trade report 2011 – the WTO and preferential trade agreements: from co-existence to coherence. Geneva

Zhu H, Gu H (2008) The border effect of Sino – US agricultural trade based on gravity model. Financ Trade Res 03:58–65

Chapter 4
Foreign Trade and Economic Growth in Recent China: A Granger Causality Analysis

Kin-Yip Ho, Kun Wang, and Wanbin (Walter) Wang

Abstract Many studies have investigated the relations between China's foreign trade and economic growth. Most of these studies found bidirectional causality between trade and economic growth. In this study, we analyze the causal relationship between foreign trade and economic growth in China using quarterly data from 2005 to 2013. The empirical results show evidence of unidirectional causality between China's GDP and China's export. Our results are different with most existing literature and show the new economic growth pattern in China.

4.1 Introduction

Since the open-door policy in 1978, China, the largest developing country in the world, has undergone far-ranging reforms of trade system that have steadily reduced the role of planning and increased the importance of market forces. In 1978, China's total imports and exports of $20.6 billion ranked 32nd among all nations and accounted for less than 1 % of global trade. In 2013, China's total merchandise trade exceeded $4.16 trillion, 202 times the level of 1978. China now accounts for 11.8 % and 10.3 % of global exports and imports, making it the world's largest commodity exporter and second largest commodity importer.

Many studies have investigated the relations between China's foreign trade and economic growth. They focus on the causal relationship between trade and growth, i.e., whether China's trade expansion is caused by its rapid economic growth and/or whether the higher level of openness leads to higher economic growth. For example, Liu et al. (1997) examine the direction of causality between external trade (exports and imports) and GNP. Shan and Sun (1998) test for causality between exports and real industrial output. Liu et al. (2002) investigate the causal links between trade, economic growth, and inward foreign direct investment in China at the aggregate level. They all find bidirectional causality between trade and

K.-Y. Ho • K. Wang • W. Wang (✉)
College of Business and Economics, The Australian National University, Canberra, ACT, Australia
e-mail: Walter.Wang@anu.edu.au

H.G. Djajadikerta, Z. Zhang (eds.), *A New Paradigm for International Business*, Springer Proceedings in Business and Economics, DOI 10.1007/978-981-287-499-3_4

economic growth, implying that China's economic growth and trade reinforce each other.

Understanding the economic growth pattern has important policy implications (Ho and Tsui 2004). China's growth trajectory poses a number of serious problems such as pollution and rising inequality. Zhu and Kotz (2011) analyze the growing role played by domestic market, exports, and investment in China's rapid economic growth since 1978. They question the sustainability of the recent dependence on exports and investment.

While many earlier studies find bidirectional causality between foreign trade and economic growth in China, it is plausible that the relations may have evolved over time because of the transitional nature of China's economy and the Chinese government's gradual structural adjustment to its economic growth model in recent years. Therefore, using recent quarterly data, we analyze the causal relationship between foreign trade and economic growth in China using quarterly data from 2005 to 2013. The remainder of this paper is organized as follows. Section 4.2 describes the data and research methodology employed. Section 4.3 discusses the findings and the concluding remarks are summarized in Sect. 4.4.

4.2 Research Methodology and Data

4.2.1 Methodology

Unit Root Test When dealing with time-series data, we have to be certain that the data are stationary prior to the causality test. A time series is said to be stationary if its statistical properties such as mean, variance, autocorrelation, etc. are all constant over time. That is, the value of the covariance between the two time periods depends only on the distance or gap or lag between the two time periods and not the actual time at which the covariance is computed. If the time-series variables are found to be nonstationary and integrated of the same order, tests can be performed to see if the variables are cointegrated. The unit root test, such as augmented Dickey–Fuller (ADF) test, Phillips–Perron (PP) test, and KPSS test, is a widely popular used methodology to examine the presence of stationary and the order of integration in the time series.

ADF test consists the following OLS estimation (Dickey and Fuller 1981):

$$\Delta Y_t = \beta_0 + \delta Y_{t-1} + \sum_{i=1}^{m} \alpha_i \Delta Y_{t-i} + u_t$$

where u_t is the pure white-noise error term and where $\Delta Y_{t-1} = (Y_{t-1} - Y_{t-2})$, $\Delta Y_{t-2} = (Y_{t-2} - Y_{t-3})$, etc. Akaike's information criteria (1971) are used to determine the optimal choice of lag length. The null and alternative hypothesis for the existence of unit root is $H_0 : \delta = 1$, which indicates that the time series is nonstationary, versus $H_0 : \delta < 1$, which denotes stationarity in the series.

Granger Causality Granger causality test is a technique for determining whether one time series is significant in forecasting another. Granger (1969) defines the causality for two scalar-valued, stationary, and ergodic time series $\{X_t\}$ and $\{Y_t\}$ using a simple model:

$$X_t = \sum_{j=1}^{m} a_j X_{t-j} + \sum_{j=1}^{m} b_j Y_{y-j} + \varepsilon_t$$

$$Y_t = \sum_{j=1}^{m} c_j X_{t-j} + \sum_{j=1}^{m} d_j Y_{y-j} + \eta_t$$

where ε_t, η_t are two uncorrelated white-noise series. If some b_j is not zero, the knowledge of past values of Y helps to predict current and future values of X values, and Y is said to Granger cause X. Similarly, X causes Y if some c_j is not zero. That is, one variable (X) is said to Granger cause another variable (Y) if the lagged values of X can predict Y. Linear least squares predictors are used in implementing this test. The null hypothesis is that X (Y) does not Granger cause variable Y (X).

4.2.2 Data

The data set we used in this study is from January 2005 to December 2013. Figure 4.1 shows the year-over-year growth rate of China's quarterly import and export. Import, export, and GDP growth rates show similar trends. They experienced a dramatic drop in the first quarter of 2009 due to the spread of the 2008 international financial crisis but recovered quickly in 2010, following which the growth rates have slowed down.

Spring Festival is the most important holiday in China. Spring Festival is subject to lunation and it can be in January or February. Thus it affects the import (export) of January and February heavily. Therefore we utilize quarterly data instead of monthly data since both January and February fall in the first quarter. We transform the monthly import and export time series into quarterly data. We calculate quarterly import and export year-over-year growth rate using the following formulas:

$$\mathrm{IMR}_{q,year} = \frac{IM_{m1,year} + IM_{m2,year} + IM_{m3,year} - \left(IM_{m1,year-1} + IM_{m2,year-1} + IM_{m3,year-1}\right)}{IM_{m1,year-1} + IM_{m2,year-1} + IM_{m3,year-1}} * 100 \quad (4.1)$$

$$\mathrm{EXR}_{q,year} = \frac{EX_{m1,year} + EX_{m2,year} + EX_{m3,year} - \left(EX_{m1,year-1} + EX_{m2,year-1} + EX_{m3,year-1}\right)}{EX_{m1,year-1} + EX_{m2,year-1} + EX_{m3,year-1}} * 100 \quad (4.2)$$

where $IM_{m1,year}$, $IM_{m2,year}$, and $IM_{m3,year}$ are the total volume of imports in the first, second, and third months in quarter q; $IM_{m1,year-1}$, $IM_{m2,year-1}$, and $IM_{m3,year}$ are the

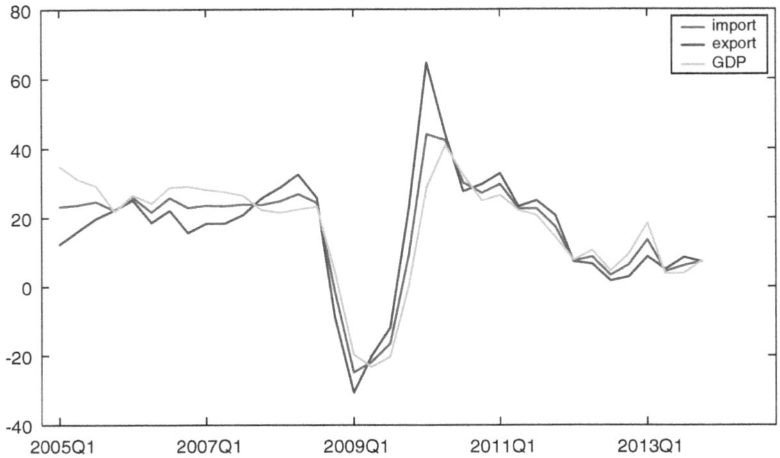

Fig. 4.1 China's quarterly import and export year-over-year growth rate (2005Q1-2013Q4)

total volume of imports in the first, second, and third months in the same quarter of last year. $EX_{m1,year}$, $EX_{m2,year}$, and $EX_{m3,year}$ are the total volume of exports in the first, second, and third months in quarter q; $EX_{m1,year-1}$, $EX_{m2,year-1}$, and $EX_{m3,year}$ are the total volume of exports in the first, second, and third months in the same quarter of last year.

The quarterly GDP year-over-year growth rate is calculated as:

$$\mathrm{GDPR}_{q,year} = \frac{GDP_{q,year} - GDP_{q,year-1}}{GDP_{q,year-1}} * 100 \tag{4.3}$$

where $GDP_{q,year}$ is the gross domestic product in quarter q; $GDP_{q,year-1}$ is the gross domestic product in the same quarter of the last year.

4.3 Empirical Results

Order of Integration

Table 4.1 reports the results of unit root tests for the quarterly time series of the import and export variables using the modified Dickey–Fuller t test (known as the DF-GLS test). DF-GLS test (Elliott et al. 1992) is an augmented Dickey–Fuller test, and it has significantly greater power than the previous versions of the augmented Dickey–Fuller test.

Causality Test

The results of pairwise Granger causality between import, export, and GDP growth rates are reported in Table 4.2. Our results show that we only reject the hypothesis

Table 4.1 Test for unit roots in the index of macroeconomic variables

Variable	Level (trend)	Critical value (5 %)	Level (no trend)	Critical value (5 %)
China IMR	−3.562*	−3.190	−3.519*	−1.950
China EXR	−3.371*	−3.190	−2.821*	−1.950
China GDPR	−3.064	−3.190	−2.517*	−1.950

Note: *indicate significance at the 5% level

Table 4.2 Pairwise Granger causality test

Hypothesis	*p*-value	Conclusion
China's IMR does not Granger cause China's EXR	0.004	Reject
China's EXR does not Granger cause China's IMR	0.910	Accept
China's IMR does not Granger cause China's GDPR	0.395	Accept
China's GDPR does not Granger cause China's IMR	0.158	Accept
China's EXR does not Granger cause China's GDPR	0.956	Accept
China's GDPR does not Granger cause China's EXR	0.002	Reject

that China's IMR does not Granger cause China's EXR and the hypothesis that China's GDPR does not Granger cause China's EXR. In other words, China's import is the Granger cause of China's export; China's GDP is the Granger cause of China's export. Our results show that China's foreign trade is not the Granger cause of China's GDP. This is different with the literature examining the relations using earlier data. For example, the dataset used by Liu et al. (2002) is from 1981 to 1997. The dataset used by Yao (2006) is over the period 1978–2000. Our results suggest that China's economic growth model has changed in recent years.

4.4 Conclusion

Foreign trade has played a major role in China's economic growth. Questions have been raised about the sustainability of China's growth trajectory. Our results about the relations between China's foreign trade and economic growth are different with the existing research examining the relations for earlier periods. Our results show that foreign trade expansion is not the Granger cause of economic development in China, while China's GDP is the Granger cause of China's export, suggesting that China's economic model has changed over time.

References

Akaike H (1971) Autoregressive model fitting for control. Ann Inst Stat Math 23:163–180

Dickey DA, Fuller WA (1981) Likelihood ratio statistics for autoregressive time series with a unit root. Econometrica 49:1057–1072

Elliott G, Rothenberg TJ, Stock JH (1992) Efficient tests for an autoregressive unit root. National Bureau of Economic Research, Cambridge, MA
Granger CW (1969) Investigating causal relations by econometric models and cross-spectral methods. Econometrica 37:424–438
Ho KY, Tsui AK (2004) Analysis of real GDP growth rates of greater China: an asymmetric conditional volatility approach. China Econ Rev 15:424–442
Liu X, Song H, Romilly P (1997) An empirical investigation of the causal relationship between openness and economic growth in China. Appl Econ 29:1679–1686
Liu X, Burridge P, Sinclair PJ (2002) Relationships between economic growth, foreign direct investment and trade: evidence from China. Appl Econ 34:1433–1440
Shan J, Sun F (1998) On the export-led growth hypothesis: the econometric evidence from China. Appl Econ 30:1055–1065
YAO, S (2006) On economic growth, FDI and exports in China. Appl Econ 38:339–351
Zhu A, Kotz DM (2011) The dependence of China's economic growth on exports and investment. Rev Radic Polit Econ 43:9–32

Chapter 5
Price Discovery and Dynamic Correlations: The Case of the Chinese Renminbi Markets

Kin-Yip Ho, Yanlin Shi, and Zhaoyong Zhang

Abstract The Chinese renminbi (RMB) currency system has undergone several major developments in the past two decades, including the adoption of a managed-floating system since July 2005, the expansion of an offshore RMB non-deliverable forward (NDF) market, and the relaxation of certain regulatory controls to promote the increased use of the RMB in the region. These developments have sparked intense debate on the potential of RMB internationalization and its pros and cons. In view of these developments, this paper provides a comprehensive analysis of the dynamics of the RMB in both the spot and NDF markets since 2005 by examining the role and significance of the RMB NDF by quantifying the contributions of the RMB spot and NDF rates in the price discovery process and the volatility dynamics of the RMB markets by adopting two different frameworks with multivariate Student's t-distribution and time-varying conditional correlations. The results indicate that asymmetric volatility effects are significant for several NDF contract maturities and the spot-NDF correlations are significantly time-varying. Moreover, shocks to the volatility levels are highly persistent. Causality tests on the spot and NDF volatilities further suggest that the NDF markets impact the future fluctuations of the spot market, but the spot market does not have predictive power for the volatility of the NDF markets.

5.1 Introduction

China has become the second largest economy worldwide in 2010. This has been expected to happen for some time, but the fact that it is happening currently has far-reaching implications for the dynamics of the global economy and international

K.-Y. Ho (✉)
College of Business and Economics, The Australian National University,
Canberra, ACT, Australia
e-mail: kin-yip.ho@anu.edu.au

Y. Shi
The Australian National University, Canberra, ACT, Australia

Z. Zhang
Edith Cowan University, Perth, WA, Australia

H.G. Djajadikerta, Z. Zhang (eds.), *A New Paradigm for International Business*,
Springer Proceedings in Business and Economics, DOI 10.1007/978-981-287-499-3_5

financial architecture. Having pursued an export-led growth strategy since the early 1980s, China has run up a large current account surplus and accumulated foreign exchange reserves exceeding two trillion US dollars as of 2008 (Park 2010). Despite its increasingly prominent role in international trade, China's financial system is still considered relatively backward compared with other developed countries. Furthermore, the Chinese renminbi (RMB) regime is subject to many regulatory controls and not fully convertible.

Since the mid-1990s, the Chinese government has stepped up its efforts to introduce reforms to its currency regime. In 1994, the dual-track regime involving a swap rate system was replaced by a unified fixed rate of 8.26 RMB per US dollar (USD), which implied a one-off depreciation of the official exchange rate (Zhang and Sato 2012). At about the same period, the RMB non-deliverable forward (NDF) market began to expand, with rapid increases in trading volume since 2002 (Zhang 2004; Peng et al. 2007; Zhang and Chan 2010). Subsequently, on July 21, 2005, the rigid fixed-rate system was superseded by the current managed-floating regime, which maintained the RMB against a basket of currencies (Liu and Pauwels 2008). Concurrently, the average daily trading volume in the RMB NDF market was around US$ 1 billion, and this increased to around US$ 2.5–3 billion per day in 2007 (Peng et al. 2007).

The pressure to de-peg the RMB from the USD and adopt a managed-floating system came from two sources (Nair and Sinnakkannu 2010): foreign countries (especially the United States) were of the view that China was enjoying unfair international trade competitiveness, and the local export businessmen were thinking that their exports were undervalued in terms of foreign currency earnings. There is a widespread view that the RMB is significantly undervalued in real terms against the USD, with some arguing that this is contributing to the rising trade imbalances between China and the rest of the world, especially the United States (Goldstein 2003; Tung and Baker 2004; Sun and Ma 2005). Complaints from US manufacturers over the competitive challenges posed by cheap Chinese imports and concerns that US jobs are lost due to unfair Chinese trade practices have induced the US government to accuse China of currency manipulation and to apply political pressure on its Chinese counterpart to revalue the RMB. Despite switching to a managed-floating regime with gradual appreciation against the USD, China's foreign reserves continue to accumulate, and the trade surplus still persists.

China's surging trade flows with the rest of the world have also raised a related issue: the potential of internationalizing the RMB. As noted by several researchers (Li 2004; Dobson and Masson 2009; Chen and Peng 2010; Park 2010; Wu et al. 2010), there are early signs of regional use of the RMB. For example, the RMB has been used in the settlement of cross-border trade between China and some neighboring countries. More significantly, in 2004, banks in Hong Kong started to offer RMB retail banking services. The scope of the renminbi business in Hong Kong has been expanded twice, in 2005 and in 2007, with Hong Kong now possessing a renminbi bond market outside Mainland China. The rising significance of the RMB mainly has to do with the strengthening of China's trade ties with the rest of the world. China is well integrated in manufacturing production with its Asian neighbors, and the size of its regional trade is far in excess of its trade with

Europe or North America, or even both combined. In fact, even though China is a net exporter to Europe and the USA, she runs a trade deficit with Asia's larger economies, such as Japan, Taiwan, and South Korea.

With increased trade, the demand for hedging against foreign exchange risk has risen. Indeed, the RMB NDF market was launched in the early 1990s in Singapore and Hong Kong to meet the demand of multinational corporations who want to preserve the value of their RMB holdings. This is truly an offshore unregulated market populated by both onshore and offshore participants, including importers, exporters, banks, and investors. However, participation of mainland entities in the NDF market is restricted by guidelines issued by the State Administration of Foreign Exchange (SAFE). Nonetheless, compared with other offshore RMB markets (such as the offshore deliverable RMB market recently launched in Hong Kong), the RMB NDF market is still considered relatively more popular, as it provides liquidity for large positions. Furthermore, as noted by Zhang and Chan (2010), with Chinese enterprises increasingly involved in the global economy, coupled with the fact that foreign direct investments are expanding, the RMB NDF market looks set to become more important to both international and domestic investors. A vibrant NDF market not only provides key instruments with which international traders hedge their risk but also lays the foundation for China's broader strategic plan to internationalize the RMB in the long run.

The purpose of this paper is to provide a comprehensive analysis of the dynamics of the RMB in both the spot and NDF markets since 2005 by examining the role and significance of the RMB NDF by quantifying the contributions of the RMB spot and NDF rates in the price discovery process and the volatility dynamics of the RMB markets by adopting two different frameworks with multivariate Student's t-distribution and time-varying conditional correlations. The results indicate that asymmetric volatility effects are significant for several NDF contract maturities and the spot-NDF correlations are significantly time-varying. Moreover, shocks to the volatility levels are highly persistent. Causality tests on the spot and NDF volatilities further suggest that the NDF markets impact the future fluctuations of the spot market, but the spot market does not have predictive power for the volatility of the NDF markets.

5.2 Methodology and Model

According to Tse (1999), the log spot price multiplied by 100, S_t, and the log of corresponding future price (NDF rates) multiplied by 100, $F_{x,t}$ (x is the various mature dates), are cointegrated (i.e., move together in the long run) with a common stochastic trend. Thus, the Vector Error Correction (VEC) model proposed by Engle and Granger (1987), which employs the Vector Autoregressive (VAR) structure to model the cointegrated variables, can be used to fit our data as follows:

$$\begin{aligned}\Delta S_t &= c_1 + \alpha_1 z_{t-1} + \sum_{i=1}^{2} A_{1i}\Delta F_{x,t-i} + \sum_{i=1}^{2} A_{2i}\Delta S_{t-i} + \varepsilon_{1t} \\ \Delta F_{x,t} &= c_2 + \alpha_2 z_{t-1} + \sum_{i=1}^{2} A_{3i}\Delta F_{x,t-i} + \sum_{i=1}^{2} A_{4i}\Delta S_{t-i} + \varepsilon_{2t}\end{aligned} \tag{5.1}$$

where $z_{t-1} = S_{t-1} + \beta_2 F_{x,t-1}$ is the error correction (cointegration) term and k is the number of lags included in the estimation. The value of k is selected according to Akaike Information Criterion (AIC) and Bayesian Information Criterion (BIC) of the original VEC models.

The idea of price discovery, defined by Lehmann (2002), is the efficient and timely incorporation of the information implicit in investor trading into market prices. There are two popular common factor models due to Hasbrouck (1995) and Gonzalo and Granger (1995). Based on these models, Lien and Shrestha (2009) propose an improved measure, while the three existing models all rely on VEC models of the market prices.

If we use the vector $P_t = (S_t, F_t)^T$ to represent the bivariate cointegrated series, Equation (5.1) can be compacted into the following equation:

$$\Delta P_t = \Pi P_{t-1} + \sum_{i=1}^{k} A_i \Delta P_{t-i} + \varepsilon_t,\ \Pi = \alpha\beta^T \tag{5.2}$$

where A_i is the coefficient matrix and α and β are 2×1 vectors. ε_t is the random disturbance vector with the dimension 2×1. The columns of β consist of the cointegrating vector and each column of α consists of adjustment coefficients. The matrix Π is decomposed in a way that $\beta^T P_t$ consists of one stationary series vector. The covariance matrix of the error term is then given by $E(\varepsilon_t \varepsilon_t^{\,T}) = \Omega$.

Following Stock and Watson (1988) and Hasbrouck (1995), Equation (5.2) can be transformed into the following vector moving average (VMA) representation:

$$\Delta P_t = \Psi(L)\varepsilon_t \tag{5.3}$$

or, alternatively,

$$P_t = P_0 + \Psi(1)\sum_{i=1}^{t} \varepsilon_i + \Psi^*(L)\varepsilon_t \tag{5.4}$$

Because the series are cointegrated, De Jong (2002) shows the following facts are true:

$$\beta^T \Psi(1) = 0 \text{ and } \Psi(1)\alpha = 0 \tag{5.5}$$

Therefore, Equation (5.4) can be written as (De Jong 2002)

$$P_t = P_0 + \beta_\perp \alpha_\perp^T \sum_{i=1}^{t} \varepsilon_i + \Psi^*(L)\varepsilon_t \tag{5.6}$$

where $\alpha_\perp$ and $\beta_\perp$ are orthogonal vectors to α and β, respectively. According to Lien and Shrestha (2009), $\alpha_\perp^T \sum_{i=1}^{t} \varepsilon_i$ represents the common stochastic trend component, which follows a random walk process. Furthermore, $\Psi(1)\varepsilon_t$ represents the long-run impact of innovations on prices, which is the main focus of all the three price discovery measures.

We then turn to the conditional correlation series of spot and NDF rates by using the multivariate generalized autoregressive conditional heteroskedasticity (MGARCH) family models for this matter, including both the BEKK specification defined in Engle and Kroner (1995) and the VECH specification proposed by Bollerslev et al. (1988).

5.3 Data Description

Table 5.1 displays the summary statistics of the natural logarithms of the RMB spot (S_t) and NDF ($F_{x,t}$) series from July 21, 2005, to December 31, 2010, and their first-differenced series. The datasets are daily observations obtained from Thomson Reuter's DataStream International. As shown in Panel B, all the mean values of the first-differenced series are negative and fairly close to one another. In contrast, the standard deviation increases with the maturity period of the NDF contract. All the NDF series have higher standard deviations compared with the spot series. Additionally, all the first-differenced series are highly leptokurtic, with the 12-month NDF contract ($\Delta F_{12m,t}$) exhibiting the highest excess kurtosis. This is a preliminary indication that it is more appropriate to model all the first-differenced series with a fat-tailed distribution. Another noteworthy feature of all the first-differenced series is the presence of nonlinear dependencies, as shown by the statistically significant BDS test statistics (Brock et al. 1996). The BDS test is a nonparametric portmanteau test for time-based dependence in a series. As suggested by Brock et al. (1996), the test can be used for testing against a variety of possible deviations from independence, including conditional heteroskedasticity. The highly significant test statistics indicate the possible presence of time-varying volatility.

Figure 5.1 shows the logarithmic spot and NDF rates and their first-differenced series. In Panel A, the NDF rates apparently exhibit more variability compared with the spot rates. Both the NDF and spot rates have declined in the past 3 years, and this reflects the gradual appreciation of the RMB since the start of the managed-floating regime. Panel B of Fig. 5.1 displays the first-differenced series, which exhibit the phenomenon of volatility clustering, whereby large (small) changes in

Table 5.1 Summary statistics of log NDF and spot rates

Panel A: Natural logarithm of spot and NDF rates					
	S_t	$F_{3m,t}$	$F_{6m,t}$	$F_{9m,t}$	$F_{12m,t}$
Mean	198.4912	197.7733	196.9554	196.1425	195.3187
Median	194.6410	193.6660	193.8274	193.6199	193.5362
Max.	209.4084	208.8116	207.9279	207.0489	206.2384
Min.	188.5644	188.5735	187.4261	185.4077	183.4659
Std. Dev.	7.1206	6.7129	6.5022	6.3905	6.3492
Skew.	0.3171	0.3955	0.4166	0.3963	0.3266
Kurt.	1.3815	1.4637	1.5410	1.6332	1.7490
Obs.	1,422	1,422	1,422	1,422	1,422
Panel B: First difference in the natural logarithm of spot and NDF rates					
	ΔS_t	$\Delta F_{3m,t}$	$\Delta F_{6m,t}$	$\Delta F_{9m,t}$	$\Delta F_{12m,t}$
Mean	−0.0147	−0.0130	−0.0122	−0.0115	−0.0110
Median	−0.0029	−0.0050	0.0000	0.0000	0.0000
Max.	0.8848	1.5272	2.3245	2.8249	3.3083
Min.	−0.6878	−1.6416	−2.4249	−2.6423	−2.8430
Std. Dev.	0.1014	0.1689	0.2350	0.2808	0.3131
Skew.	0.3194	0.0694	0.0822	0.4095	0.6894
Kurt.	14.5005	19.4259	24.2169	22.4510	25.6500
Obs.	1,421	1,421	1,421	1,421	1,421
BDS. (10)	38.6152***	37.8895***	34.0875***	36.3294***	35.4274***

Note: This table reports the descriptive statistics of the log NDF and spot rates
Max. is the maximum of the data, *Min.* is the minimum of the data, *Std. Dev.* stands for the standard deviation of the data, *Skew.* is the skewness of data, *Kurt.* is the kurtosis of data, and *Obs.* is the number of observations
BDS. (10) is the BDS independence test on dimension 10

the return are followed by large (small) changes subsequently. Apparently, the NDF series are more volatile compared with the spot series.

Table 5.2 reports the unconditional correlation matrix for the first-differenced logarithmic spot and NDF series. One noteworthy feature is the set of fairly low correlations between the spot and all the NDF series. Among all the pairs, the correlation between the spot and the 12-month NDF contract (0.3953) is the lowest. In comparison with the findings reported in the literature on the correlations between foreign exchange spot and forward contracts, the correlations between the spot and the NDF rates appear weak. For example, in Kroner and Sultan (1993), the correlation coefficients are mostly above 0.95. In contrast, the NDF rates with various maturities appear to exhibit strong co-movements with one another, since the correlation coefficients are above 0.9. This may indicate that if information were impounded in one of the NDF rates, other NDF rates will also move swiftly together.

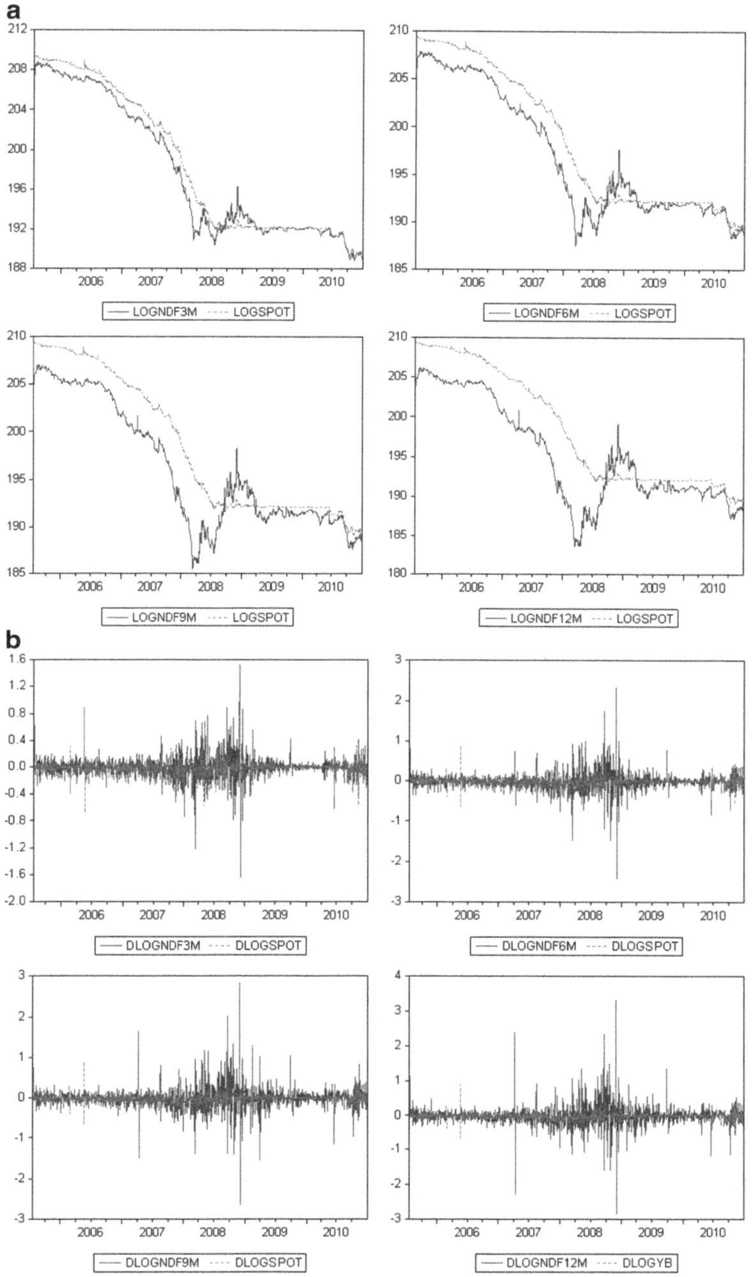

Fig. 5.1 *RMB spot and NDF rates*. **Panel A**: Natural logarithm of the RMB spot (*logspot*) and NDF (*logndf*) rates (Note (*clockwise* from *top left*): natural logarithm of 3-month NDF contract (*LOGNDF3M*); natural logarithm of 6-month NDF contract (*LOGNDF6M*); natural logarithm of 12-month NDF contract (*LOGNDF12M*); natural logarithm of 9-month NDF contract (*LOGNDF9M*)). **Panel B**: Natural logarithm of the RMB spot (*dlogspot*) and NDF (*dlogndf*) rates (Note (*clockwise* from *top left*): first difference of natural logarithm of 3-month NDF contract (*DLOGNDF3M*); first difference of natural logarithm of 6-month NDF contract (*DLOGNDF6M*); first difference of natural logarithm of 12-month NDF contract (*DLOGNDF12M*); first difference of natural logarithm of 9-month NDF contract (*DLOGNDF9M*))

Table 5.2 Correlation matrix of differenced log of spot and NDF rates

	ΔS_t	$\Delta F_{3m,t}$	$\Delta F_{6m,t}$	$\Delta F_{9m,t}$	$\Delta F_{12m,t}$
ΔS_t	1.0000	0.5139	0.4480	0.4146	0.3953
$\Delta F_{3m,t}$	0.5139	1.0000	0.9358	0.8613	0.8416
$\Delta F_{6m,t}$	0.4480	0.9358	1.0000	0.9331	0.9333
$\Delta F_{9m,t}$	0.4146	0.8612	0.9331	1.0000	0.9439
$\Delta F_{12m,t}$	0.3953	0.8416	0.9333	0.9430	1.0000

5.4 Empirical Findings

To test for cointegration and estimate the VEC model, the first step is to check the order of integration of the series. We have conducted both the Augmented Dickey-Fuller (ADF) and Phillips-Perron (PP) tests and reported the results in Table 5.3. As it can be seen in Table 5.3, for all the logarithmic spot and NDF series, the null hypothesis of a unit root cannot be rejected, as the test statistics are insignificant. Once the logarithmic series are differenced, the null hypothesis can be rejected. This suggests that the spot and the NDF series are nonstationary in their levels, but attain stationarity after first differencing.

Given that the spot and forward prices are integrated of order one (I(1)), cointegration tests are conducted, the results of which are reported in Table 5.4. The Johansen cointegration test results indicate that the spot and NDF rates, at each term to maturity, share a long-run equilibrium relationship with each other. Both the trace and maximum eigenvalue test statistics are significant at the 1 % level. The finding of cointegration across all the maturity periods appears consistent with the concept of market efficiency, since it suggests that the markets where the underlying securities and their derivatives are traded are observed to be structurally and strategically related with each other. More specifically, the spot price reflects the information that is impounded in the forward price; likewise, the value of the forward contract reflects the information contained in the spot price.

The significance of cointegration allows for the development of a VEC model that describes the systematic disequilibrium adjustment process and the nature of the short-run causal relationship between spot and forward prices. Notably, this model has been enhanced to account for the presence of conditional heteroskedasticity. Table 5.5 presents the detailed results of the bivariate VEC for the spot and NDF rates for each maturity period. Based on the Schwarz Bayesian Criterion (SBC), two lags are found to be adequate for all the estimated models. To make inferences into the systematic adjustment process of the spot and NDF variables to disequilibrium shocks, we examine the error correction term (z_{t-1}). For all the maturity periods, the error correction term is significant at the 1 % level in the RMB spot rate equation; this indicates that past equilibrium errors have an impact on the current change in the RMB spot rate. In contrast, for all the NDF rate equations, the error correction term is insignificant. Furthermore, the parameter estimates for the lagged ΔS_t and $\Delta F_{x,t}$ are mostly significant in the spot rate equation, whereas they are usually not so in the NDF rate equation. These results indicate that when the

Table 5.3 Unit root tests on log NDF and spot rates

Variables	Adj. t-Stat. (ADF)	Adj. t-Stat. (PP)
S_t	−0.5098	−0.6381
ΔS_t	−14.1308***	−41.6203***
$F_{3m,t}$	−1.3734	−1.3613
$\Delta F_{3m,t}$	−36.3065***	−36.2899***
$F_{6m,t}$	−1.6516	−1.5762
$\Delta F_{6m,t}$	−37.4617***	−37.5215***
$F_{9m,t}$	−1.7251	−1.5779
$\Delta F_{9m,t}$	−38.5040***	−38.6984***
$F_{12m,t}$	−1.6824	−1.5857
$\Delta F_{12m,t}$	−37.3857***	−37.4933***

Note: This table reports the Augmented Dickey-Fuller (*ADF*) and Phillips-Perron (*PP*) unit root tests on the log NDF and spot rates
Adj. t-Stat. is the adjusted t-statistic
***, **, and * indicate significance at 1 %, 5 %, and 10 % level, respectively
The critical values are calculated based on MacKinnon (1996)

Table 5.4 Johansen cointegration tests

Variables	Hypothesized number of cointegration(s)	Eigenvalue	Trace Stat.	Max. Eigen. Stat.
S_t and $F_{3m,t}$	None	0.0227	33.3307***	32.6152***
	At most 1	0.0005	0.7155	0.7155
S_t and $F_{6m,t}$	None	0.0228	33.5376***	32.7130***
	At most 1	0.0006	0.8246	0.8246
S_t and $F_{9m,t}$	None	0.0228	33.6402***	32.6699***
	At most 1	0.0007	0.9703	0.9703
S_t and $F_{12m,t}$	None	0.0225	33.3953***	32.3131***
	At most 1	0.0008	1.0822	1.0822

Note: This table reports the Johansen cointegration tests on the log spot rates and different NDF rates. All tests are under the assumption there are linear deterministic trends in the variables, and conintegrations only contain the intercepts. Lags from order 1–5 are included in the tests
Trace Stat. is the trace statistic, and *Max. Eigen.* Stat. is the maximum eigenvalue statistic
***, **, and * indicate significance at 1 %, 5 %, and 10 % level, respectively
P-values are calculated according to MacKinnon et al. (1999)

cost-of-carry relationship is perturbed, it is the cash price that makes the greater adjustment in order to reestablish the equilibrium. Put differently, the NDF rate leads the spot rate in price discovery. These error correction results are further expanded upon by applying the Gonzalo-Granger (1995) permanent-transitory components model. It is found that the short-term NDF contracts (such as 3 months) have higher contributions to the price formation process in comparison with the long-term contracts. This could be because of the higher liquidity associated with short-term contracts (Zhang and Chan 2010).

Table 5.5 VEC estimations of log spot rates against log NDF rates

	S_t and $F_{3m,t}$	S_t and $F_{6m,t}$	S_t and $F_{9m,t}$	S_t and $F_{12m,t}$
β_2	−1.0627***	−1.1150***	−1.1638***	−1.2180***
	(0.0214)	(0.0413)	(0.0603)	(0.0819)
c_1	−0.0183***	−0.0185***	−0.0185***	−0.0184***
	(0.0027)	(0.0027)	(0.0027)	(0.0027)
c_2	−0.0139***	−0.0128**	−0.0112	−0.0104
	(0.0046)	(0.0064)	(0.0076)	(0.0085)
α_1	−0.0150***	−0.0081***	−0.0057***	−0.0043***
	(0.0030)	(0.0016)	(0.0011)	(0.0008)
α_2	0.0016	0.0028	0.0026	0.0021
	(0.0051)	(0.0037)	(0.0031)	(0.0026)
A_{11}	−0.2156***	−0.1879***	−0.1807***	−0.1749***
	(0.0309)	(0.0297)	(0.0292)	(0.0290)
A_{12}	−0.1248***	−0.1129***	−0.1048***	−0.0989***
	(0.0309)	(0.0298)	(0.0293)	(0.0290)
A_{21}	0.0745***	0.0349***	0.0254**	0.0196**
	(0.0185)	(0.0127)	(0.0104)	(0.0093)
A_{22}	−0.0207	0.0081	0.0021	−0.0039
	(0.0183)	(0.0126)	(0.0104)	(0.0092)
A_{31}	0.0033	0.0570	0.0573	0.0971
	(0.0523)	(0.0700)	(0.0823)	(0.0909)
A_{32}	−0.0353	−0.0497	0.0601	0.0255
	(0.0523)	(0.0702)	(0.0825)	(0.0911)
A_{41}	0.0283	−0.0073	−0.0317	−0.0019
	(0.0312)	(0.0299)	(0.0293)	(0.0291)
A_{42}	0.0049	0.0198	−0.0163	−0.0363
	(0.0310)	(0.0297)	(0.0292)	(0.0289)

Note: This table displays the estimated results of the VEC models of log spot rates against various log NDF rates with the following specifications:

$$\Delta S_t = c_1 + \alpha_1 z_{t-1} + \sum_{i=1}^{2} A_{1i}\Delta F_{x,t-i} + \sum_{i=1}^{2} A_{2i}\Delta S_{t-i} + \varepsilon_{1t}$$

$$\Delta F_{x,t} = c_2 + \alpha_2 z_{t-1} + \sum_{i=1}^{2} A_{3i}\Delta F_{x,t-i} + \sum_{i=1}^{2} A_{4i}\Delta S_{t-i} + \varepsilon_{2t}$$

$$z_{t-1} = S_{t-1} + \beta_2 F_{x,t-1}$$

where z_{t-1} is the cointegration term, ε_{1t} is the residual of log spot rates, and ε_{2t} is the residual of log NDF rates

***, **, and * indicate significance at 1 %, 5 %, and 10 % level, respectively

The values in the brackets are corresponding standard errors

Furthermore, we have conducted the Granger causality tests to assess the causal relationships between the Chinese RMB spot rates and future rates. The test results are reported in Table 5.6. As it can be seen in Table 5.6, the results provide more corroborating evidence that the NDF markets are significant in the price formation process. As illustrated by the Granger causality tests based on the VEC model, the

Table 5.6 Granger causality tests (VEC model)

Null hypothesis	D.F.	Chi-sq Stat.
$\Delta F_{3m,t}$ *does not granger cause* ΔS_t	2	17.2816***
ΔS_t *does not granger cause* $\Delta F_{3m,t}$	2	0.4941
$\Delta F_{6m,t}$ *does not granger cause* ΔS_t	2	7.8426**
ΔS_t *does not granger cause* $\Delta F_{6m,t}$	2	1.4162
$\Delta F_{9m,t}$ *does not granger cause* ΔS_t	2	5.9911**
ΔS_t *does not granger cause* $\Delta F_{9m,t}$	2	0.8679
$\Delta F_{12m,t}$ *does not granger cause* ΔS_t	2	4.7152*
ΔS_t *does not granger cause* $\Delta F_{12m,t}$	2	1.1516

Note: This reports the results of Granger causality tests on the VEC models of log spot and NDF rates

D.F. is the degree of freedom of the chi-square distribution; *Chi-sq Stat.* is the chi-square statistic of the test

***, **, and * indicate significance at 1 %, 5 %, and 10 % level, respectively

lagged values of the RMB NDF series have predictive power for the current values of the spot series, with the future rates of the 3-month future contract being the strongest, but not vice versa. The number of lags in the tests is chosen based on the SBC, and our findings are robust to changes in the number of lags.

Finally, to analyze the conditional volatility dynamics of the RMB spot and NDF markets, we estimate the MGARCH models of log spot rates and various log NDF rates with both the BEKK and VECH specification, respectively. The estimation results of both models are reported in Tables 5.7 and 5.8. As it can be seen in Table 5.7, there is evidence that some of the NDF series exhibit significant asymmetry. Hogan and Melvin (1994) and Tse and Tsui (1997) attribute this to the existence of heterogeneous expectations in the foreign exchange market. Furthermore, shocks to the volatility seem persistent as evidenced from the sum of the parameters A_i and B_i, which is very close to one. Most of the parameters in the conditional covariance equation are also statistically significant. This finding suggests that the covariance between the spot rates and the future rates is most likely time-varying. The results in Table 5.8 based on the VECH model further confirm the finding that the spot and the NDF series exhibit time-varying conditional variances and covariances.

5.5 Conclusion

In this paper we have examined the dynamics of the RMB in both the spot and NDF markets since 2005 by assessing the role and significance of the RMB NDF and quantifying the contributions of the RMB spot and NDF rates in the price discovery process. We have also studied the volatility dynamics of the RMB markets by adopting two different frameworks with multivariate Student's t-distribution and time-varying conditional correlations. Our empirical analysis shows that the RMB

Table 5.7 MGARCH by diagonal BEKK estimations

	S_t and $F_{3m,t}$	S_t and $F_{6m,t}$	S_t and $F_{9m,t}$	S_t and $F_{12m,t}$
M_1	6.05e-6*	9.57e-6**	1.10e-5**	1.26e-5**
	(3.63e-6)	(4.51e-6)	(5.14e-6)	(5.51e-6)
M_2	6.95e-6	3.31e-5**	4.25e-5*	5.60e-5**
	(5.66e-6)	(1.51e-6)	(2.30e-5)	(2.57e-5)
M_3	1.48e-5	0.0002**	0.0005***	0.0006***
	(1.08e-5)	(7.18e-5)	(0.0002)	(0.0002)
A_1	0.2959***	0.3307***	0.3638***	0.3631***
	(0.0243)	(0.0246)	(0.0288)	(0.0307)
A_2	0.2619***	0.2977***	0.2966***	0.3131***
	(0.0271)	(0.0301)	(0.0305)	(0.0285)
D_1	−0.1375***	−0.0109	0.0032	−0.0803
	(0.0508)	(0.0848)	(0.0779)	(0.0868)
D_2	−0.2016***	0.1314*	0.1782***	0.1203
	(0.0446)	(0.0743)	(0.0619)	(0.0736)
B_1	0.9629***	0.9577***	0.9517***	0.9505***
	(0.0035)	(0.0044)	(0.0052)	(0.0053)
B_2	0.9644***	0.9578***	0.9515***	0.9512***
	(0.0036)	(0.0049)	(0.0055)	(0.0053)
v	3.3443***	3.3472***	3.2338***	3.2505***
	(0.2303)	(0.2210)	(0.2080)	(0.2041)
Q-stat.(10)	35.2146	36.6029	39.1914	39.7178
BIC.	−4.5066	−3.7248	−3.2359	−3.0465

Note: This table displays the regression results of the conditional variance equations from the MGARCH models of log spot rates and various log NDF rates with diagonal BEKK specifications:

$$\varepsilon_t = \begin{pmatrix} \varepsilon_{1t} \\ \varepsilon_{2t} \end{pmatrix} | Q_{t-1} \sim Student - t(0, H_t, v),\ H_t \equiv \begin{pmatrix} h_{1t} & h_{12t} \\ h_{12t} & h_{2t} \end{pmatrix}$$

$$h_{1t} = M_1 + A_1^2 \varepsilon_{1,t-1}^2 + D_1^2 \varepsilon_{1,t-1}^2 I(\varepsilon_{1,t-1} < 0) + B_1^2 h_{1,t-1}$$

$$h_{2t} = M_2 + A_2^2 \varepsilon_{2,t-1}^2 + D_2^2 \varepsilon_{2,t-1}^2 I(\varepsilon_{2,t-1} < 0) + B_2^2 h_{2,t-1}$$

$$h_{12t} = M_3 + A_1 A_2 \varepsilon_{1,t-1} \varepsilon_{2,t-1} + D_1 D_2 \varepsilon_{1,t-1} \varepsilon_{2,t-1} I(\varepsilon_{1,t-1} < 0) I(\varepsilon_{2,t-1} < 0) + B_1 B_2 h_{12,t-1}$$

where ε_t is the residual matrix, H_t is the conditional variance-covariance matrix, $\varepsilon_{s,t}$ is the residual of log spot rates, $\varepsilon_{ndf,t}$ is the residual of log NDF rates, $h_{s,t}$ is the conditional variance of log spot rates, $h_{ndf,t}$ is the conditional variance of log NDF rates, $h_{s,ndf,t}$ is the conditional covariance of log spot and log NDF rates, Q_{t-1} is the information set at time $t - 1$, and v is the degree of freedom of the multivariate Student's t-distribution (Bollerslev 1987). *I()* is the function that when the condition inside the brackets is true returns 1, otherwise returns 0. *Q-stat.(10)* is the adjusted chi-square statistic of the system residual portmanteau tests for autocorrelations up to order 10, where Lutkepohl (1991) type of standardized residuals is tested. *BIC* is the Bayesian information criteria. All the estimates are maximum likelihood (*ML*) using BHHH algorithm (Berndt et al. 1974)

***, **, and * indicate significance at 1 %, 5 %, and 10 % level, respectively

The values in the brackets are corresponding standard errors

NDF market has a significant role in the price discovery process, despite the fact that some researchers (such as Peng et al. 2007) have noted that the pricing in the NDF market is not tied to financial fundamentals. Furthermore, the Granger causality tests in volatility suggest that past values of the NDF volatility have

Table 5.8 MGARCH by diagonal VECH estimations

	S_t and $F_{3m,t}$	S_t and $F_{6m,t}$	S_t and $F_{9m,t}$	S_t and $F_{12m,t}$
M_1	6.90e-6*	1.07e-5**	1.38e-5**	1.26e-5**
	(3.60e-6)	(5.12e-6)	(6.53e-6)	(5.92e-6)
M_2	8.10e-6	3.54e-5**	4.65e-5*	4.71e-5*
	(6.10e-6)	(1.56e-5)	(2.60e-5)	(2.44e-5)
M_3	2.99e-5**	0.0003***	0.0009***	0.0009***
	(1.49e-5)	(9.41e-5)	(0.0002)	(0.0002)
A_1	0.0675***	0.1303***	0.1931***	0.1509***
	(0.0153)	(0.0241)	(0.0362)	(0.0299)
A_2	0.0735***	0.0972***	0.1040***	0.0891***
	(0.0145)	(0.0194)	(0.0232)	(0.0198)
A_3	0.0954***	0.1367***	0.1407***	0.1300***
	(0.0183)	(0.0255)	(0.0276)	(0.0249)
D_1	0.0364*	−0.0133	−0.0354	−0.0007
	(0.0205)	(0.0281)	(0.0391)	(0.0348)
D_2	0.0324*	−0.0007	0.0157	0.0147
	(0.0182)	(0.0218)	(0.0280)	(0.0238)
D_3	0.0315	−0.0036	0.0196	0.0141
	(0.0216)	(0.0272)	(0.0310)	(0.0283)
B_1	0.9329***	0.9076***	0.8809***	0.8949***
	(0.0067)	(0.0094)	(0.0125)	(0.0112)
B_2	0.9278***	0.9149***	0.8984***	0.9119***
	(0.0059)	(0.0086)	(0.0105)	(0.0092)
B_3	0.9133***	0.8871***	0.8648***	0.8776***
	(0.0072)	(0.0110)	(0.0139)	(0.0123)
v	3.3558***	3.3695***	3.2355***	3.2372***
	(0.2323)	(0.2231)	(0.2095)	(0.2051)
Q-stat. (10)	36.9023	34.1211	36.7732	36.6454
BIC	−4.5004	−3.7203	−3.2316	−3.0405

Note: This table displays the regression results of the conditional variance equations from the MGARCH models of log spot rates and various log NDF rates with diagonal VECH specifications:

$$\varepsilon_t = \begin{pmatrix} \varepsilon_{1t} \\ \varepsilon_{2t} \end{pmatrix} \Big| Q_{t-1} \sim Student - t(0, H_t, v),\ H_t \equiv \begin{pmatrix} h_{1t} & h_{12t} \\ h_{12t} & h_{2t} \end{pmatrix}$$

$$h_{1t} = M_1 + A_1\varepsilon^2_{1,t-1} + D_1\varepsilon^2_{1,t-1}I(\varepsilon_{1,t-1} < 0) + B_1h_{1,t-1}$$

$$h_{2t} = M_2 + A_2\varepsilon^2_{2,t-1} + D_2\varepsilon^2_{2,t-1}I(\varepsilon_{2,t-1} < 0) + B_2h_{2,t-1}$$

$$h_{12t} = M_3 + A_3\varepsilon_{1,t-1}\varepsilon_{2,t-1} + D_3\varepsilon_{1,t-1}\varepsilon_{2,t-1}I(\varepsilon_{1,t-1} < 0)I(\varepsilon_{2,t-1} < 0) + B_3h_{12,t-1}$$

where ε_t is the residual matrix, H_t is the conditional variance-covariance matrix, ε_{1t} is the residual of log spot rates, ε_{2t} is the residual of log NDF rates, h_{1t} is the conditional variance of log spot rates, h_{2t} is the conditional variance of log NDF rates, h_{12t} is the conditional covariance of log spot and log NDF rates, Q_{t-1} is the information set at time $t-1$, and v is the degree of freedom of the multivariate Student's t-distribution. *I()* is the function that when the condition inside the brackets is true returns 1, otherwise returns 0. *Q-stat.(10)* is the adjusted chi-square statistic of the system residual portmanteau tests for autocorrelations up to order 10, where Lutkepohl (1991) type of standardized residuals is tested. *BIC* is the Bayesian information criteria. All the estimates are maximum likelihood (*ML*) using BHHH algorithm (Berndt et al. 1974)

***, **, and * indicate significance at 1 %, 5 %, and 10 % level, respectively

The standard errors are in the brackets

predictive ability for the current values of the spot volatility. Moreover, the conditional volatilities of several NDF series are substantially time-varying and asymmetric, which could indicate the presence of heterogeneous expectations in the NDF markets. The results are consistent with the findings in Hogan and Melvin (1994) and Tse and Tsui (1997). In addition, shocks to the volatility are found to be quite persistent.

These findings have some important implications. The results confirm that strong linkages between the RMB spot and NDF markets, which implies that NDFs are not only an important hedging tool for offshore investors and companies with exposure to the RMB but also instruments for investors to bet on the future movements of the RMB. The interaction between the two markets would facilitate the development of the onshore market, with domestic market participants benefiting particularly from the transferable skills and experience of international market players. The existence of time-varying correlations suggests that the optimal (minimum-variance) hedge ratio is dynamic and has to be regularly adjusted by hedgers.

References

Berndt E, Hall B, Hall R, Hausman J (1974) Estimation and inference in nonlinear structural models. Ann Econ Soc Meas 3:653–665

Bollerslev T (1987) A conditionally heteroskedastic time series model for speculative prices and rates of return. Rev Econ Stat 69:542–547

Bollerslev T, Engle RF, Wooldridge JM (1988) A capital asset pricing model with time-varying covariances. J Polit Econ 96:116–131

Brock W, Dechert D, Sheinkman J, LeBaron B (1996) A test for independence based on the correlation dimension. Econ Rev 15:197–235

Chen P, Peng W (2010) The potential of the renminbi as an international currency. In: Peng W, Shu C (eds) Currency internationalization: global experiences and implications for the renminbi. Palgrave-Macmillan, London

De Jong F (2002) Measures of contributions to price discovery: a comparison. J Financ Mark 5:323–327

Dobson W, Masson P (2009) Will the renminbi become a world currency? China Econ Rev 20:124–135

Engle RF, Granger CWJ (1987) Co-integration and error correction: representation, estimation, and testing. Econometrica 55:251–276

Engle RF, Kroner KF (1995) Multivariate simultaneous generalized ARCH. Econ Theor 11:122–150

Goldstein M (2003) China's exchange rate regime. Testimony at the US House of Representatives, Washington, DC, 1 Oct 2003

Gonzalo J, Granger C (1995) Estimation of common long-memory components in cointegrated systems. J Bus Econ Stat 13:27–35

Hasbrouck J (1995) One security, many markets: determining the contributions to price discovery. J Financ 50:1175–1199

Hogan KC Jr, Melvin MT (1994) Sources of meteor showers and heat waves in the foreign exchange market. J Int Econ 37:239–247

Kroner K, Sultan J (1993) Time-varying distributions and dynamic hedging with foreign currency futures. J Financ Quant Anal 28:535–551
Lehmann BN (2002) Some desiderata for the measurement of price discovery across markets. J Financ Mark 5:259–276
Li J (2004) Regionalization of the RMB and China's capital account liberalization. China World Econ 12:86–100
Lien D, Shrestha K (2009) A new information share measure. J Futur Mark 29:377–395
Liu L, Pauwels L (2008) Do external political pressures affect the renminbi exchange rate? Hong Kong Monetary Authority working paper, 0805. Hong Kong Monetary Authority, Hong Kong
Lütkepohl H (1991) Introduction to multiple time series analysis. Springer, Berlin
MacKinnon JG (1996) Numerical distribution functions for unit root and cointegration tests. J Appl Econ 11:601–618
Mackinnon JG, Haug AA, Michelis L (1999) Numerical distribution functions of likelihood ratio tests for cointegration. J Appl Econ 14:563–577
Nair M, Sinnakkannu J (2010) De-pegging of the Chinese renminbi against the US dollar: analysis of its effects on China's international trade competitiveness. J Asia Pac Econ 15:470–489
Park Y (2010) RMB internationalization and its implications for financial and monetary cooperation in East Asia. China World Econ 18:1–21
Peng W, Shu C, Yip R (2007) Renminbi derivatives: recent development and issues. China World Econ 15:1–17
Stock JH, Watson MW (1988) Testing for common trends. J Am Stat Assoc 83:1097–1107
Sun H, Ma Y (2005) Policy strategies to deal with revaluation pressures on the renminbi. China Econ Rev 16:103–117
Tse Y (1999) Price discovery and volatility spillovers in the DJIA index and futures markets. J Futur Mark 19:911–930
Tse Y, Tsui A (1997) Conditional volatility in foreign exchange rates: evidence from the Malaysian ringgit and Singapore dollar. Pac-Basin Financ J 5:345–356
Tung C, Baker S (2004) RMB revaluation will serve China's self-interest. China Econ Rev 15:331–335
Wu F, Pan R, Wang D (2010) Renminbi's potential to become a global currency. China World Econ 18:63–81
Zhang P (2004) Chinese Yuan (renminbi) derivative products. World Scientific, Singapore
Zhang P, Chan T (2010) The Chinese Yuan: internationalization and financial products in China. Wiley, New York
Zhang ZY, Sato K (2012) Should Chinese renminbi be blamed for its trade surplus: a structural VAR approach. World Econ 35:632–650

Chapter 6
Public News Flows and Chinese Renminbi: A Volatility Regime-Switching Analysis

Kin-Yip Ho, Yanlin Shi, and Zhaoyong Zhang

Abstract In recent years the Chinese foreign exchange rate policy and the internationalization of Chinese renminbi (RMB) have been hotly debated both in the academic world and in practice as the growing weight of China's foreign trade and investment flows in the world economy. Most of the existing studies tend to review the process and impact of the RMB internationalization issues. The great interest of RMB internationalization is probably with financial institutions doing international business in the currency and also the Chinese firms conducting international business. This paper examines the impact of public information flows on the volatility of the Chinese RMB spot and non-deliverable forward (NDF) exchange rates using a regime-switching framework. Two major types of news items – articles that report on the RMB and those that report on the US dollar (USD) – are used to measure information flows. The results indicate that the impact of news flows is more significant in the calm (low volatility) regime rather than in the turbulent (high volatility) regime. These findings have important implications for policy-makers in both the public and private sectors and for business firms who wish to hedge their exposures.

6.1 Introduction

Since the mid-1990s, the Chinese government has stepped up its efforts to introduce reforms to its currency regime. In 1994, the dual-track regime involving a swap rate system was replaced by a unified fixed rate of 8.26 RMB per US dollar (USD), which implied a one-off depreciation of the official exchange rate. At about the

K.-Y. Ho (✉)
College of Business and Economics, The Australian National University, Canberra, ACT, Australia
e-mail: kin-yip.ho@anu.edu.au

Y. Shi
The Australian National University, Canberra, ACT, Australia

Z. Zhang
Edith Cowan University, Perth, WA, Australia

H.G. Djajadikerta, Z. Zhang (eds.), *A New Paradigm for International Business*, Springer Proceedings in Business and Economics, DOI 10.1007/978-981-287-499-3_6

same period, the RMB non-deliverable forward (NDF) market began to expand, with rapid increases in trading volume since 2002 (Zhang 2004; Peng et al. 2007; Zhang and Chan 2010). Subsequently, on July 21, 2005, the rigid fixed-rate system was superseded by the current managed-floating regime, which maintained the RMB against a basket of currencies (Liu and Pauwels 2012). Concurrently, the average daily trading volume in the RMB NDF market was around US$1 billion, and this increased to around US$2.5–3 billion per day in 2007 (Peng et al. 2007). Until the end of 2011, further changes to the RMB exchange rate policy were announced by the People's Bank of China (PBC). Since January 4, 2006, a "more market-driven" price mechanism was introduced to set the central parity rate, a new reference trading spot rate of RMB. Initially, the intraday fluctuation of the RMB/USD was within a tightly controlled range of ±0.3 %. The band was subsequently widened to ±0:5 % on May 18, 2007. As a result of the 2008 global financial crisis, the appreciation of RMB/USD rate was temporarily halted toward the end of July 2008. On June 19, 2010, China ended its 23-month-long peg to the USD (Liu and Pauwels 2012).

This paper examines the impact of public information flows on the volatility of the RMB spot, NDF, and future exchange rates after the RMB reform. While the currency is still greatly influenced by the central government policy and the political environment, we hypothesize that RMB/USD becomes more sensitive to the arrival of public news as it moves toward a market-driven regime. The theoretical underpinning of our empirical analysis is the "mixture of distribution hypothesis" (MDH) which studies the relationship between financial volatility and public information arrival. We apply MDH (Melvin and Yin 2000; Bauwens et al. 2006) and the idea of Veronesi (1999) to the exchange rate market and test how the volatility of RMB/USD spot, NDF (1, 3, 6, 9, and 12 months' maturity), and future exchange rate returns behave with the quantity and quality of public information arrival. To model the volatility process of daily return on RMB/USD rate, we use the Markov regime-switching generalized autoregressive conditional heteroskedasticity (RS-GARCH) framework, the idea of which has been widely used in the study of exchange rate (Engel and Hamilton 1990; Bekaert and Hodrick 1993; Engel 1994; Bollen et al. 2000; Dewachter 2001; Ichiue and Koyama 2011). From economic theory point of view, Beine et al. (2003) state that coordinated central bank interventions can lead to either a stabilizing or a destabilizing effect. Since central bank intervention is a key factor to volatility of exchange rate return, employing the regime-switching approach is a more efficient way to study the effects of news on return volatility. Besides, as pointed out by Liu and Pauwels (2012), the RMB/USD spot rate was temporarily halted from the end of July 2008 until June 2010 since the "managed-float" system had been announced. Therefore, there are two main regimes implemented for RMB/USD spot rate during the entire period, the pegging system and "managed float." Given two different systems existing, Wilfling (2009) argues that two-state regime-switching approach should be used to study the effects of official announcement on exchange rate return volatility. For the study of foreign exchange rate policy of China, Funke and Gronwald (2008) suggest that the approach to allow volatility transition is needed.

From modeling point of view, GARCH family model is not appropriate when structure changes are present. Lamoureux and Lastrapes (1990), Hamilton and Susmel (1994), and Klaassen (2002) argue that GARCH family model always implies a high volatility persistence, which may originate from structural changes in the variance. Furthermore, to examine the effects of conditional volatility on the contemporaneous returns, we construct and fit our data with the two-state regime-switching EGARCH-in-mean (RS-EGARCH-M) model, where "calm" and "turbulent" states are the low and high volatility states, respectively. Finally, in comparison, the ordinary GARCH framework is also employed, as is widely employed in the field of finance (Bollerslev et al. 1992; Melvin and Yin 2000; Kalev et al. 2004; Bauwens et al. 2006; Park 2010).

To control for information arrival rate, we use the newswire messages obtained from the RavenPack News Analytics—Dow Jones Edition, which is a comprehensive database covering more than 1,700 types of firm-specific and macroeconomic news events. RavenPack automatically tracks and monitors relevant information on tens of thousands of companies, government organizations, influential people, key geographical locations, and all major currencies and traded commodities. The service includes analytics on more than 170,000 entities in over 100 countries and covers over 98 % of the investable global market. Among the many benefits, RavenPack delivers sentiment analysis and event data most likely to impact financial markets and trading around the world – all in a matter of milliseconds. It continuously analyzes relevant information from all major real-time newswires and trustworthy sources, such as *Dow Jones Newswires*, regional editions of the *Wall Street Journal* and *Barron's*, Internet sources including financial sites and blogs, and local and regional newspapers, to produce real-time news sentiment scores. All relevant news items about entities are classified and quantified according to their sentiment, relevance, topic, novelty, and market impact. In terms of the sentiment, RavenPack uses a proprietary computational linguistic analysis algorithm to quantify positive and negative perceptions on facts and opinions reported in the news textual content. The core of the algorithm can be divided into two steps. Firstly, RavenPack builds up a historical database of the words which have affected the corresponding financial price. Then, the text in the specific news story is compared with the historical database, and the sentiments score is generated accordingly. Among the various (sub)categories provided, we construct our news variables from RMB-related and USD-related subcategories.

Consistent with the MDH, our empirical findings show that the volatility persistence of all the spot, NDF, and future RMB/USD exchange rate returns is reduced by including either RMB or USD news (reduction caused by including RMB news is generally greater) in certain state. More specifically, the reductions in calm state are greater for all the NDF and future rates. For spot rate, the reduction in turbulent state is greater. Secondly, marginal effects of news are different across different exchange rates, origin of news variables (related to RMB or USD), and states. Nevertheless, in general, effects of negative news are greater than positive news, effects of RMB news are greater than USD news, and effects on spot, short-term maturity NDF (1 and 3 months), and future rate are greater than effects on long-term maturity NDF (6, 9, and 12 months) rate. Thirdly, the estimated smooth probability of spot rate demonstrates that our model can produce consistent identification of states as the real economic case affected by macro foreign exchange rate policy. Also, the state structure of spot, short-term maturity NDF, and future rate is similar, while the state structure of long-term maturity NDF rates is all close to each other. Finally, in most of cases, the effects of conditional volatility on contemporaneous returns are insignificant.

6.2 The Theoretical Framework and Method

The theoretical underpinning of our empirical analysis is the "mixture of distribution hypothesis" (MDH) which studies the relationship between financial volatility and public information arrival. The idea of MDH is firstly proposed by Clark (1973) and extended by Tauchen and Pitts (1983) and Harris (1986, 1987). Building on the MDH, Lamoureux and Lastrapes (1990) argue that persistence in the conditional volatility of return reflects the time-series properties in the information arrival process. Andersen (1996) concludes that the idea of MDH as the variance of returns at a given interval is proportional to the rate of information arrival on the market. Kalev et al. (2004) use the number of firm-specific announcements as proxy for the rate of information arrival. Based on the argument of MDH, they propose that the conditional volatility of the stock return at a given interval could be proportional to the number of news received. Bauwens et al. (2006) further show that the idea of MDH can be extended to the foreign exchange rate market. Moreover, Veronesi (1999) suggests that because of asymmetric information about the state of the economy, investors overreact to bad news in good times and underreact to good news in bad times. In other words, the quality of news articles or news sentiment can also affect the volatility of financial return. This argument is supported by many recent research such as Laakkonen and Lanne (2008), Mitra et al. (2011), and Chen and Ghysels (2011).

Based on the theory of MDH and conclusion of Veronesi (1999), we argue the following relationship:

$$\log(h_t) \propto f(n_t, Q_\tau) \tag{6.1}$$

where h_t is the conditional volatility of exchange rate return at time t, n_t is number of relevant news arrival at the interval $[t-1, t]$, and Q_τ is the sentiment of news story τ ($\tau \in [t-1, t]$), which is a nonnegative value. Furthermore, in our research, $f(n_t, Q_\tau)$ will be determined by the variables $WNN_{c,t}$, $WNP_{c,t}$, $WNN_{u,t}$, and $WNP_{u,t}$, where $WNN_{c,t}$, $WNP_{c,t}$, $WNN_{u,t}$, and $WNP_{u,t}$ are, respectively, defined as the logarithm of weighted numbers of negative and positive global macro news stories about the Chinese RMB and the USD.

In order to test the effect of conditional volatility on return, we modify the EGARCH-M(1,1) model by including the news variables in the mean and conditional variance equations:

$$r_t = b_0 + b_\lambda h_t + b_1 WESS_t + \varepsilon_t$$
$$\varepsilon_t = \eta_t \sqrt{h_t} \text{ where } \eta_t \overset{iid}{\sim} t(0, 1, v)$$
$$\log(h_t) = c + \alpha \frac{\varepsilon_{t-1}}{\sqrt{h_{t-1}}} + \beta \log(h_{t-1}) + \gamma \left\{ \left| \frac{\varepsilon_{t-1}}{\sqrt{h_{t-1}}} \right| - E\left(\left| \frac{\varepsilon_{t-1}}{\sqrt{h_{t-1}}} \right| \right) \right\} + \lambda_1 WNN_t + \lambda_2 WNP_t \tag{6.2}$$

where ε_t is the error at time t. h_t is the conditional volatility of ε_t at time t. η_t is the standardized residual at time t and is independently and identically distributed following Student-t distribution, with 0 mean and unit standard deviation. v is the degree of freedom of the η_t.[1] α is the asymmetry term. *WESS* is the weighted scores of both the event sentiment score (ESS) and event novelty score (ENS), with the latter specifying whether the news story conveys positive or negative sentiment about the global macro environment. The reason for including $WESS_t$ (about RMB or USD) in the mean equation is that we want to control for the potential impact of news sentiment on the exchange rate return (Veronesi 1999; Hafez 2009; Leinweber and Sisk 2011; Moniz et al. 2011).

The coefficient β captures the level of volatility persistence, which measures how fast the current shock dissipates. Large volatility persistence means the current shock will affect the volatility in the long run. As argued by Nelson (1991), when $\beta < 1$, the EGARCH-M(1,1) process is covariance stationary. Based on Lamoureux and Lastrapes (1990) and Bauwens et al.'s (2006) results, the persistence of conditional volatility of exchange rate return may be generated by serial correlation in the information arrival process. This implies that the volatility persistence β will be significantly reduced after the inclusion of WNN_t and WNP_t (about RMB or USD) in the conditional variance equation.

6.3 Data and Empirical Results

Our foreign exchange rate samples comprise of daily data of RMB/USD spot rate, 1 month, 3 months, 6 months, 9 months, and 12 months' maturity NDF rates, and future rate, all from July 22, 2005, to December 31, 2011 (future rate only available from August 29, 2006). Our spot rate data are sourced from Thomson Reuters and NDF and future rate data are sourced from WM/Reuters. Define $\{S_0, S_1, \ldots, S_{T-1}, S_T\}$ as

[1] The reason for using the Student-t distribution assumption of the residuals rather than the Normal distribution is that the former can accommodate the excess kurtosis of the innovations (Bollerslev 1987). Besides, Susmel and Engle (1994) point out the importance of using t-distribution for more efficient estimation than Normal distribution.

the sequence of daily closing exchange spot (NDF or future) rate at times $\{0, 1, \ldots, T-1, T\}$. The corresponding daily return at time t is calculated as:

$$r_t = 100 \times \log(S_t/S_{t-1})$$

To proxy for public information arrivals, we use the RavenPack News Analytics database, which captures more than 1700 types of intraday global macro[2] news events starting from January 2000 onward. In order to account for the qualitative impact of these news releases, RavenPack offers an analytical output for global macro news release on a global basis. These news releases are obtained from *Dow Jones Newswires* and the *Wall Street Journal* and the *Barron's*. Among dozens of the analytical outputs in the database, we use the event sentiment score (ESS) and event novelty score (ENS).

The descriptive statistics of all the returns of RMB/USD rates and their absolute values are summarized in Panel A Table 6.1 (all in percentage). All the means of ordinary returns are less than 0. The standard deviations of spot and 1-month NDF returns are very close to each other at around 0.11. For other NDF returns, longer-term maturity rates tend to have greater standard deviations, indicating they are more volatile. The future return has a similar standard deviation to the 6 months NDF rate at around 0.20. The skewness of all the returns is positive, except for future rate. Kurtosis of spot and 1-month NDF return are still very close. Longer-term maturity NDF returns also have greater kurtosis. As to the absolute returns, the story is almost the same. The statistics of spot and 1-month NDF returns are quite similar. Longer-term maturity NDF returns tend to be more volatile, right skewed, and leptokurtic. Future return has roughly similar statistics as 6-month NDF return.

All the exchange rates and returns over the entire period are plotted in Fig. 6.1. Generally, all the return series have the similar shape, and they are more volatile between 2008 and 2009, the financial crisis period, and after the second half of 2010. It is clear that between late 2008 and the first half of 2010, when the RMB/USD spot rate was temporarily halted (Liu and Pauwels 2012), the spot rate is kept in the flat line, and all the returns tend to be comparatively less volatile. The plots of spot, short-term maturity NDF, and future exchange rate are very similar, while the plots of long-term maturity NDF exchange rate are close to each other. It is also true for the return series.

The descriptive statistics of the four sentiment scores $ESS_{c,\tau}$, $ENS_{c,\tau}$, $ESS_{u,\tau}$, and $ENS_{u,\tau}$ used to construct our news variables are summarized in Panel B Table 6.1. The mean $ESS_{c,\tau}$ is a bit greater than 50, indicating that on average, the news stories about RMB are slightly positive. The mean $ESS_{u,\tau}$ is 48.3602, less than 50,

[2] Altogether RavenPack provides five general news categories (Business, Economy, Environment, Politics and Society) and many subcategories. In our research, news variables are constructed from the subcategories "Chinese Renminbi" and "U.S. Dollar" of Economy category. Although pointed out by Liu and Pauwel (2012), political news can also affect conditional volatility of exchange rate return, the corresponding number of news stories in RavenPack is very small. Therefore, we exclude the Politics category.

Table 6.1 Descriptive statistics of the daily data

Var.	Mean	Std. dev.	Median	Min.	Max.	Skew.	Kurto.	Obs.
Panel A: returns of CNY/USD rates								
$r_{s,t}$	−0.0151	0.1064	−0.0037	−0.6878	0.8848	0.2123	12.5178	1,681
$r_{1n,t}$	−0.0145	0.1178	−0.0038	−0.7616	0.8698	0.1430	10.3959	1,681
$r_{3n,t}$	−0.0136	0.1627	−0.0044	−1.6416	1.5272	0.0321	19.3821	1,681
$r_{6n,t}$	−0.0128	0.2222	0.0000	−2.4249	2.3246	0.0650	25.7215	1,681
$r_{9n,t}$	−0.0120	0.2645	0.0000	−2.6423	2.8250	0.4003	24.2045	1,681
$r_{12n,t}$	−0.0112	0.2942	0.0000	−2.8430	3.3083	0.6937	27.8916	1,681
$r_{f,t}$	−0.0166	0.1960	0.0000	−1.9273	1.6461	−0.2119	24.8474	1,394
$\|r_{s,t}\|$	0.0683	0.0830	0.0409	0.0000	0.8848	3.0741	19.1663	1,681
$\|r_{1n,t}\|$	0.0764	0.0909	0.0479	0.0000	0.8698	2.7858	15.3184	1,681
$\|r_{3n,t}\|$	0.0993	0.1295	0.0605	0.0000	1.6416	4.0323	32.0491	1,681
$\|r_{6n,t}\|$	0.1298	0.1808	0.0763	0.0000	2.4249	4.7257	41.7970	1,681
$\|r_{9n,t}\|$	0.1529	0.2161	0.0886	0.0000	2.8250	4.5787	37.9330	1,681
$\|r_{12n,t}\|$	0.1681	0.2416	0.1038	0.0000	3.3083	4.9981	44.0069	1,681
$\|r_{f,t}\|$	0.1091	0.1636	0.0598	0.0000	1.9273	4.6916	35.9889	1,394
Panel B: news database								
$ESS_{c,\tau}$	53.8656	32.7752	83.0000	17.0000	83.0000	−0.2359	1.0557	6,855
$ENS_{c,\tau}$	62.2814	27.4856	56.0000	1.0000	100.0000	−0.0475	1.8810	6,855
$ESS_{u,\tau}$	48.3602	32.9594	17.0000	17.0000	83.0000	0.0995	1.0099	97,463
$ENS_{u,\tau}$	61.8725	29.3045	56.0000	0.0000	100.0000	−0.1609	1.8642	97,463

(continued)

Table 6.1 (continued)

Var.	Mean	Std. dev.	Median	Min.	Max.	Skew.	Kurto.	Obs.
Panel C: news variables								
$WESS_{c,t}$	2.0941	18.8161	0.0000	−33.0000	33.0000	−0.1389	1.7678	1,681
$WNN_{c,t}$	1.9951	2.1581	0.0000	0.0000	5.1940	0.1954	1.1094	1,681
$WNP_{c,t}$	2.4606	2.1570	3.9283	0.0000	5.4816	−0.2127	1.1413	1,681
$WESS_{u,t}$	−0.8033	9.0738	−1.1984	−28.8750	28.8750	0.1119	2.3059	1,681
$WNN_{u,t}$	6.2467	0.6966	6.3627	0.0000	7.5471	−2.5219	18.9562	1,681
$WNP_{u,t}$	6.1276	0.8091	6.2399	0.0000	7.4550	−3.1937	23.1718	1,681

Var. variable, *Std. dev.* standard deviation, *Min.* minimum, *Max.* maximum; *Skew.* skewness, *Kurto.* kurtosis, *Obs.* the number of observations

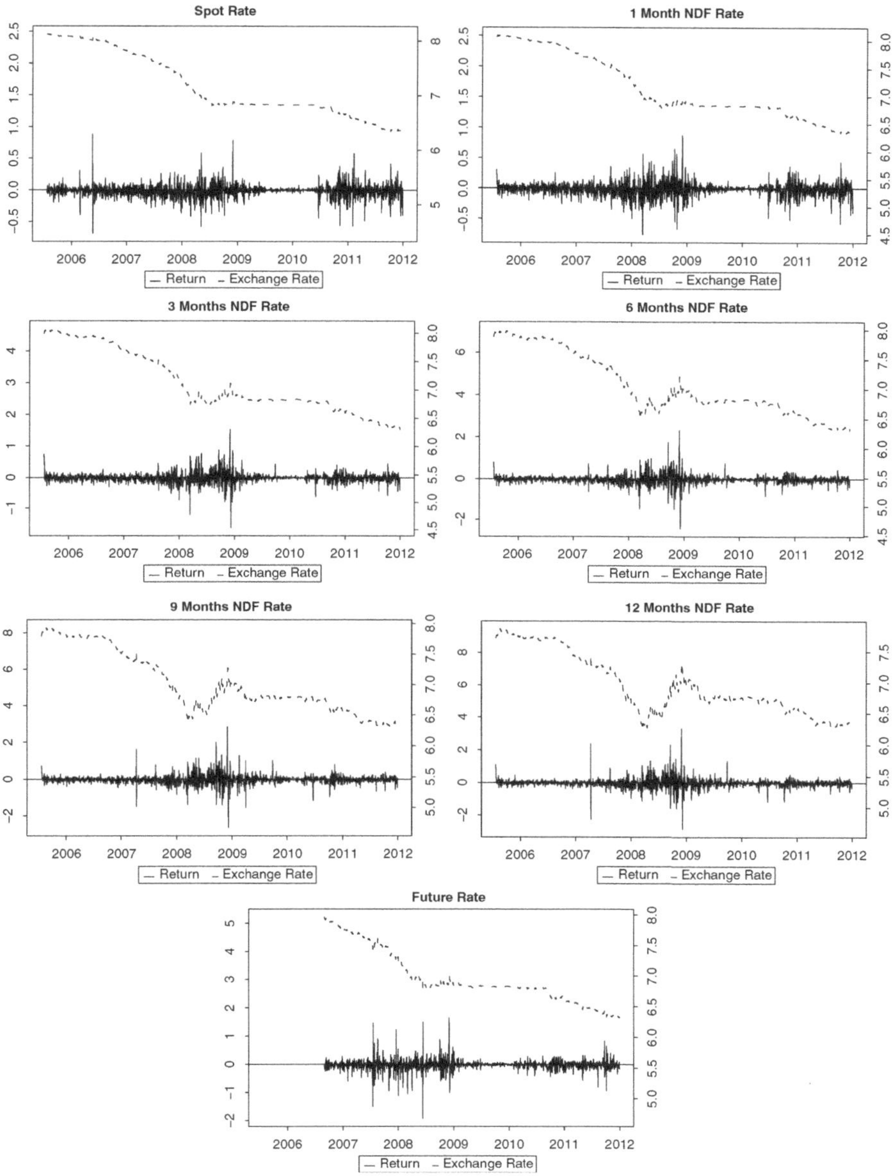

Fig. 6.1 Daily CNY/USD exchange rates and returns

suggesting that the macro news about USD during the entire period are overall slightly negative. It is interesting that number of news about USD is much greater than the number of news about RMB.

The descriptive statistics of news variables are summarized in Panel C Table 6.1. Generally, the weighted number of news about USD is much more negatively skewed and leptokurtic. $WESS_{c,t}$ has a positive mean of 2.0941 with standard deviation 18.8161. $WESS_{u,t}$ has a negative mean of −0.8033 with less variation (standard deviation is 9.0738). Most of the statistics of $WNN_{c,t}$ and $WNP_{c,t}$ are quite similar, while $WNP_{c,t}$ has slightly larger mean and median and is negative skewed. $WNP_{u,t}$ has about the same mean and standard deviation as $WNN_{u,t}$ but is more negative skewed and leptokurtic.

We then estimate the EGARCH-M model. All the returns of RMB/USD spot, NDF, and future rate are firstly fitted into the models without news variables (reduced models) and then the models with news variables (full models). The estimates are reported in Table 6.2.

For the reduced models, it seems that in all the reduced models, volatility persistence is considerably large, ranging from 0.9894 to 0.9967. The effects of conditional volatility on contemporaneous return are estimated to be significantly negative for spot, 1-month NDF, 3-month NDF, and future rates and insignificant for the others. It is indicated that conditional volatility can negatively affect the contemporaneous returns of spot, future, and short-term NDF rates, with spot rate affected most and future rate affected least (−0.9262 and −0.1774, respectively). On the other hand, long-term NDF returns will not be significantly affected. Finally, the estimates of asymmetry term α are insignificant for all rates.

For the full models, news variables of RMB and USD have different effects on conditional volatility. First, USD news can reduce volatility persistence in all rates. RMB news can only lead to reduction for spot, future, and short-term NDF rates, where the reductions are greater than USD news. However, generally speaking, all the reductions are considerably small. As we discussed earlier, due to structural changes in the volatility, GARCH family model always implies high volatility persistence. Our early findings show that the volatility of all the RMB/USD exchange rates is apparently not constant over the entire period, which could be the reason for the small reductions we have. Second, the estimated marginal effects of news are mostly insignificant. Compared with the reduced models, the log-likelihood values are remarkably improved in all cases (RMB news has greater log likelihood only for spot and 1-month NDF rates), and the Akaike information criterion (AIC) also prefers the models with either RMB or USD news. Therefore, the insignificance can be explained as that negative (positive) news variable cannot bring in extra explanation give the other news variable included. In the return equations, the estimates of $WESS_t$ are significant in all cases. However, the estimates of RMB news are all negative, while for USD news they are all positive. The implication is worth noticing, that is, positive USD news can significantly increase contemporaneous returns, while positive RMB news will reduce them. Finally, the absolute value of estimated $WESS_t$ suggests that both RMB and USD news can

Table 6.2 Regression outputs of the EGARCH-M models

	Spot rate			1-month NDF rate			3-month NDF rate		
	Wo. news	Wt. CNY	Wt. USD	Wo. news	Wt. CNY	Wt. USD	Wo. news	Wt. CNY	Wt. USD
b_λ	−0.9262	−0.9244	−1.0123	−0.8355	−0.9101	−0.9712	−0.3984	−0.4010	−0.4448
	(0.0000)	(0.0000)	(0.0000)	(0.0000)	(0.0001)	(0.0000)	(0.0005)	(0.0000)	(0.0067)
b_1		−0.0006	0.0008		−0.0009	0.0019		−0.0012	0.0027
		(0.0000)	(0.0000)		(0.0000)	(0.0000)		(0.0000)	(0.0000)
α	−0.0185	−0.0264	−0.0207	0.0072	0.0137	0.0083	−0.0301	−0.0162	−0.0144
	(0.2123)	(0.1310)	(0.1724)	(0.6591)	(0.5083)	(0.6550)	(0.0358)	(0.2652)	(0.3384)
β	0.9967	0.9890	0.9957	0.9947	0.9866	0.9914	0.9967	0.9926	0.9938
	(0.0000)	(0.0000)	(0.0000)	(0.0000)	(0.0000)	(0.0000)	(0.0000)	(0.0000)	(0.0000)
γ	0.1795	0.2106	0.1880	0.2230	0.2083	0.2200	0.1671	0.1555	0.1709
	(0.0000)	(0.0000)	(0.0000)	(0.0000)	(0.0000)	(0.0000)	(0.0000)	(0.0000)	(0.0000)
λ_1		−0.0007	−0.0008		0.0031	−0.0162		−0.0005	−0.0082
		(0.9349)	(0.9540)		(0.6942)	(0.2826)		(0.9456)	(0.5223)
λ_2		0.0151	0.0001		0.0188	−0.0037		0.0089	−0.0017
		(0.0768)	(0.9931)		(0.0172)	(0.8207)		(0.0667)	(0.9048)
ν	3.3766	3.2397	3.4095	4.0386	3.7266	4.1266	3.7068	3.6820	3.8923
	(0.0000)	(0.0000)	(0.0000)	(0.0000)	(0.0000)	(0.0000)	(0.0000)	(0.0000)	(0.0000)
log lik.	1983.714	2064.278	2021.040	1773.236	1868.282	1862.581	1316.000	1392.081	1416.966
AIC	−3951.428	−4108.556	−4022.08	−3530.472	−3716.564	−3705.162	−2616.000	−2764.162	−2813.932

(continued)

Table 6.2 (continued)

	6-month NDF rate			9-month NDF rate			12-month NDF rate			Future rate		
	Wo. news	Wt. CNY	Wt. USD	Wo. news	Wt. CNY	Wt. USD	Wo. news	Wt. CNY	Wt. USD	Wo. news	Wt. CNY	Wt. USD
b_λ	−0.1368	−0.0930	−0.1053	−0.0258	−0.0217	−0.0174	0.0071	0.0111	0.0075	−0.1774	−0.1569	−0.2071
	(0.1138)	(0.3871)	(0.3756)	(0.7059)	(0.8041)	(0.8628)	(0.9135)	(0.8922)	(0.9327)	(0.0007)	(0.0613)	(0.0314)
b_1		−0.0019	0.0041		−0.0022	0.0048		−0.0024	0.0053		−0.0007	0.0020
		(0.0000)	(0.0000)		(0.0000)	(0.0000)		(0.0000)	(0.0000)		(0.0000)	(0.0000)
α	−0.0119	−0.0143	−0.0083	−0.0177	−0.0182	−0.0165	−0.0185	−0.0233	−0.0210	0.0082	0.0260	0.0099
	(0.4205)	(0.3627)	(0.5981)	(0.2225)	(0.2155)	(0.2732)	(0.1341)	(0.0550)	(0.0964)	(0.7720)	(0.4866)	(0.7529)
β	0.9927	0.9935	0.9921	0.9927	0.9935	0.9897	0.9943	0.9960	0.9928	0.9894	0.9806	0.9850
	(0.0000)	(0.0000)	(0.0000)	(0.0000)	(0.0000)	(0.0000)	(0.0000)	(0.0000)	(0.0000)	(0.0000)	(0.0000)	(0.0000)
γ	0.1731	0.1558	0.1643	0.1549	0.1443	0.1473	0.1329	0.1182	0.1273	0.2709	0.2911	0.2671
	(0.0000)	(0.0000)	(0.0000)	(0.0000)	(0.0000)	(0.0000)	(0.0000)	(0.0000)	(0.0000)	(0.0000)	(0.0001)	(0.0000)
λ_1		−0.0032	−0.0033		−0.0006	0.0034		0.0022	−0.0041		0.0055	−0.0398
		(0.6282)	(0.7872)		(0.9216)	(0.7733)		(0.6920)	(0.6905)		(0.6224)	(0.0826)
λ_2		0.0067	0.0031		0.0049	0.0138		0.0063	0.0145		0.0174	−0.0198
		(0.1323)	(0.8292)		(0.2318)	(0.3419)		(0.0772)	(0.2674)		(0.0522)	(0.3094)
v	3.6659	3.2945	3.6440	3.2385	3.0126	3.3667	3.4138	3.1105	3.3117	2.4169	2.3370	2.4555
	(0.0000)	(0.0000)	(0.0000)	(0.0000)	(0.0000)	(0.0000)	(0.0000)	(0.0000)	(0.0000)	(0.0000)	(0.0000)	(0.0000)
log lik.	852.543	948.804	982.451	552.068	646.2268	676.947	408.200	503.529	540.257	941.878	978.877	994.232
AIC	−1,689.086	−1,877.608	−1,944.902	−1,088.136	−1,272.454	−1,333.894	−800.400	−987.058	−1,060.514	−1,867.756	−1,937.754	−1,968.464

log lik. log likelihood, *AIC* Akaike information criterion, *Wo.* without, *Wt.* with, *CNY* Chinese renminbi, *USD* US dollar; numbers inside the parentheses are the p-values affect NDF rates more than spot and future rates, with longer-term NDF rates affected greater.

In all cases, including either RMB or USD, news variables can greatly improve log-likelihood values and are preferred by AIC (RMB news has greater log likelihood and AIC only for spot and 1-month NDF rate compared with USD news). However, the stories of the estimates are quite different regarding the various exchange rates, related origin of news variables, and states. For spot rate, both RMB and USD news can reduce the volatility persistence in both states. The reduction is greater in turbulent state, and reductions introduced by RMB news are greater than USD news in both states. For short-term maturity NDF rates, both RMB and USD news can only reduce volatility persistence in calm states, with reduction from RMB news much greater. For long-term maturity NDF rates, volatility persistence is reduced in both states from both RMB and USD news, though the reductions in turbulent state are much smaller, except for the 9-month NDF rate with USD news. In calm state, reductions from RMB and USD news are closer than in the case of short-term maturity NDF rates. For future rate, the story is very similar to short-term NDF rates, except that here volatility persistence is also reduced in turbulent state, with much smaller reduction. Particularly, for spot, future, and short-term maturity NDF rates, some significant positive effects of conditional volatility on contemporaneous returns are observed in calm state. However, in turbulent state, the significant estimates still indicate negative effects.

6.4 Conclusion

This study empirically examines the role of public news arrivals on RMB/USD spot, NDF, and future exchange rate return volatility using a novel news database that utilizes a text analytic algorithm to quantify the sentiment of each news story based on its textual content. The news database is provided by RavenPack News Analytics—Dow Jones Edition. It tracks and continuously monitors relevant news on tens of thousands of companies, government organizations, influential people, key geographical locations, and all major currencies and traded commodities. To form the basis of the theory behind our empirics, we merge two streams of the literature; the mixture of distribution hypothesis (MDH) literature, proposed by Clark (1973), Tauchen and Pitts (1983), Harris (1986, 1987), and Andersen (1996), argues that the variance of returns at a given interval is proportional to the rate of information arrival on the market. The literature on the asymmetric effect of different news on financial return volatility, led by Veronesi (1999), argues that in the presence of asymmetric information, investors overreact to bad news in good times and underreact to good news in bad times. This literature suggests that news sentiment plays an important role in explaining the financial return volatility, and its effect depends on the state of volatility.

To test Veronesi's (1999) argument, we classify news into negative and positive type using the sentiment score based on RavenPack's proprietary algorithm. Unlike extant studies that use the price impact of news to classify the news type, this classification overcomes the problem of endogeneity. Using the RS-EGARCH-M models with two states on daily returns of RMB/USD spot, NDF, and future exchange rate return from July 22, 2005, to December 31, 2011, we find support of the MDH. Our empirical findings show that, firstly, the volatility persistence of all the exchange rate returns is reduced by including either RMB or USD news. More specifically, reductions caused by including RMB news are generally greater. Reductions in calm state are greater for all the NDF and future rates. For spot rate, the reduction in turbulent state is greater. Secondly, marginal effects of news are different across different exchange rates, origin of news variables (related to RMB or USD), and states. Nevertheless, in general, effects of negative news are greater than positive news, effects of RMB news are greater than USD news, and effects on spot, short-term maturity NDF, and future rate are greater than effects on long-term maturity rate. Thirdly, the estimated smooth probability of spot rate demonstrates that our model can produce consistent identification of states as the real economic case affected by macro foreign exchange rate policy. Also, the state structure of spot, short-term maturity NDF, and future rate is similar, while the state structure of long-term maturity NDF rates is all close to each other. Finally, in most of cases, the effects of conditional volatility on contemporaneous returns are insignificant. These findings have important implications for policy-makers in both the public and private sectors and for business firms who wish to hedge their exposures.

References

Andersen TG (1996) Return volatility and trading volume: an information flow interpretation of stochastic volatility. J Financ 51:169–204

Bauwens L, Rime D, Sucarrat G (2006) Exchange rate volatility and the mixture of distribution hypothesis. Empir Econ 30:889–911

Beine M, Laurent S, Lecourt C (2003) Official central bank interventions and exchange rate volatility: evidence from a regime-switching analysis. Eur Econ Rev 47:891–911

Bekaert G, Hodrick B (1993) On biases in the measurement of foreign exchange risk premiums. J Int Money Financ 12:115–138

Bollen NPB, Gray SF, Whaley RE (2000) Regime switching in foreign exchange rates: evidence from currency option prices. J Econ 94:29–276

Bollerslev T (1987) A conditional heteroskedastic time series model for speculative prices and rates of return. Rev Econ Stat 69:542–547

Bollerslev T, Chou RY, Kroner KF (1992) ARCH modelling in finance: a review of the theory and empirical evidence. J Econ 52:5–59

Chen X, Ghysel E (2011) News good or bad and its impact on volatility predictions over multiple horizons. Rev Financ Stud 24:46–81

Clark P (1973) A subordinated stochastic process model with finite variance for speculative Prices. Econometrica 41:135–155

Dewachter H (2001) Can Markov switching models replicate chartist profits in the foreign exchange market? J Int Money Financ 20:25–41

Engel C (1994) Can the Markov switching model forecast rates? J Int Econ 36:151–165

Engel C, Hamilton JD (1990) Long swings in the dollar: are they in the data and do markets know it? Am Econ Rev 80:689–713

Funke M, Gronwald M (2008) The undisclosed renminbi basket: are the markets telling us something about where the renminbi-US dollar exchange rate is going? World Econ 31:1581–1598

Hafez PA (2009) Impact of news sentiment on abnormal stock returns. White paper, RavenPack

Hamilton JD, Susmel R (1994) Autoregressive conditional heteroskedasticity and changes in regime. J Econ 64:307–333

Harris L (1986) A transactions data study of weekly and intraday patterns in stock returns. J Financ Econ 16:99–117

Harris L (1987) Transactions data tests of the mixture of distributions hypothesis. J Financ Quant Anal 22:127–141

Ichiue H, Koyama K (2011) Regime switches in exchange rate volatility and uncovered interest parity. J Int Money Financ 30:1436–1450

Kalev PS, Liu WM, Pham PK, Jarnecic E (2004) Public information arrival and volatility of intraday stock returns. J Bank Financ 28:1441–1467

Klaassen F (2002) Improving GARCH volatility forecasts with regime-switching GARCH. Empir Econ 27:363–394

Laakkonen H, Lanne M (2008) Asymmetric news effects on volatility: good vs. bad news in good vs. bad times. MPRA paper 8296

Lamoureux CG, Lastrapes WD (1990) Heteroskedasticity in stock return data: volume versus GARCH effects. J Financ 45:221–229

Leinweber D, Sisk J (2011) Relating news analytics to stock returns. In: Mitra G, Mitra L (eds) The handbook of news analytics in finance. Willey, Chichester, pp 149–171

Liu L, Pauwels L (2012) Do external political pressures affect the renminbi exchange rate? J Int Money Financ 31:1800–1818

Melvin M, Yin X (2000) Public information arrival, exchange rate volatility, and quote frequency. Econ J 465:644–661

Mitra L, Mitra G, Bartolomeo D (2011) Equity portfolio risk estimation using market information and sentiment. In: Mitra G, Mitra L (eds) The handbook of news analytics in finance. Willey, Chichester, pp 289–303

Moniz A, Brar G, Davies C, Strudwick A (2011) The impact of news flow on asset returns: an empirical study. In: Mitra G, Mitra L (eds) The handbook of news analytics in finance. Willey, Chichester, pp 211–228

Nelson DB (1991) Conditional heteroscedasticity in asset returns: a new approach. Econometrica 51:485–505

Park Y (2010) RMB internationalization and its implications for financial and monetary cooperation in East Asia. China World Econ 18:1–21

Peng W, Shu C, Yip R (2007) Renminbi derivatives: recent development and issues. China World Econ 15:1–17

Susmel R, Engel R (1994) Hourly volatility spillovers between international equity markets. J Int Money Financ 13:3–25

Tauchen G, Pitts M (1983) The price variability–volume relationship on speculative markets. Econometrica 51:485–505

Veronesi P (1999) Stock market overreaction to bad news in good time: a rational expectations equilibrium model. Rev Financ Stud 12:975–1007

Wilfling B (2009) Volatility regime-switching in European exchange rates prior to monetary unification. J Int Money Financ 28:240–270

Zhang P (2004) Chinese yuan (renminbi) derivative products. World Scientific, Singapore

Zhang P, Chan T (2010) The Chinese yuan: internationalization and financial products in China. Wiley, New York

Chapter 7
The Perceptions and Challenges of Corporate Sustainability Reporting in China

Junru Zhang, Hadrian Geri Djajadikerta, and Zhaoyong Zhang

Abstract The connection between the respect of sustainable development and joint rules of conduct in international trade has increased dramatically in recent years. Many countries have promoted sustainability development and requirement with their trading partners both in the West and the East-Asian Region. This has led corporate sustainability disclosures to become a vital role that facilitates international trade. Although recently there have been numerous studies that investigate corporate sustainability disclosures in China, understanding the perceived importance of this form of disclosure cannot be ignored for analyses. Consequently, the purpose of this study is to provide exploratory evidence, showing the users' perceived importance in corporate sustainability in China and addressing to what extent it is different from what was intended in the GRI guidelines. This study examines three sustainable aspects, which are corporate environmental, economic and social disclosures. The findings in this study provide an indication that what was intended in GRI may not be so important in China. Although there are indicators shown to be different from what was intended in the GRI guidelines, 50 % of the items remain to be significant when analysing CSD in China.

7.1 Introduction

The connection between the respect of sustainable development and joint rules of conduct in international trade has increased dramatically in recent years. Many countries have promoted sustainability development and requirement with their trading partners both in the West and East-Asian Region. This has led corporate sustainability disclosures to become a vital role that facilitates international trade. Corporate sustainability disclosure (CSD) is considered the most effective and efficient way to facilitate the empowerment and satisfaction of stakeholders in their quest for and understanding of sustainability. According to the triple-bottom reporting, corporate sustainability (CS) includes environmental, social and economic sustainability. The concept of corporate sustainability was introduced in the

J. Zhang (✉) • H.G. Djajadikerta • Z. Zhang
Edith Cowan University, Perth, WA, Australia
e-mail: j.zhang@ecu.edu.au

H.G. Djajadikerta, Z. Zhang (eds.), *A New Paradigm for International Business*, Springer Proceedings in Business and Economics, DOI 10.1007/978-981-287-499-3_7

1990s by multinational companies; however, this attracted little attention. In 2001, China entered the World Trade Organisation, and a significant number of Chinese companies became members of the global supply chain (Zhang 2013). Due to the high level of competition in the global market as well as the national demand, the Chinese President Hu Jin Tao proposed the concept of a 'Harmonic Society' in 2005, which placed corporate sustainability problems, together with companies' social responsibility on top of the government agenda (Zhou et al. 2012). However, the legal concept of CS has never been included in the Company Law in China. Accountability for CS requires a more thorough understanding of the quality of CSD in the context of China. In addition, although a significant number of sustainability disclosing guidelines have been recommended by CS literature, they cannot be strictly applied to all countries, particularly to China (Li et al. 2013; Ling 2009). The degree of influence of corporate policies about being sustainably orientated can be significantly different in Western and Asian contexts. Hence, it is of importance and interest for researchers to investigate the Chinese perceptions and understanding of corporate sustainability. This study will provide evidence to build the most up-to-date and accurate instrument suitable for empirical studies of CSD in China.

The GRI has been widely adopted both internationally and nationally in China. While this set of initiatives remains one of the most authoritative existing guidelines, the standard and framework are based on the fundamentals and the perceptions of the Western countries. Therefore, this study seeks to fill a gap in the literature by providing up-to-date evidence on the quality of CSD in Chinese-listed companies and the perceptions of the Chinese CSD users. Corporate sustainability disclosure is comprised of three different disclosures, which are corporate environmental, social and economic disclosures. Subsequently, this study strives to achieve the following objectives:

1. To understand the CSD users' (financial analysts) perceived importance of corporate sustainability reporting in China
2. To understand to what extent the users perceive the sustainability indicators in GRI differently from what was intended

This study provides a deeper insight into the practices focus of Chinese companies when disclosing sustainability. The results provide an indication of future research by identifying the Chinese report users' (financial analysts) perceptions of CSD. The existing research in China focuses on the report preparers' perceptions rather than the users'; thus, little attention has been given to this aspect in the literature. In this study, the research considers whether companies wanting to achieve improved CSD should rely on the GRI, which has not been extensively investigated according to the literature. Therefore, this study fills a research gap in the Chinese CSD studies by providing the most up-to-date evidence of users' perceptions of CSD from the listed companies in China.

7.1.1 Corporate Sustainability Reporting in China

The notion of corporate sustainability in China has attracted much attention over the past 20 years due to the advent of globalisation and international trade. While the government in China has traditionally assumed sole responsibility for ensuring quality of the living conditions of the population, there is an expectation that organisations will take a greater responsibility in this area (Gao 2009). Corporate sustainability, which is incorporated with triple-bottom line reporting, rather than solely related to economic responsibility, includes the interrelationship between environmental and social perspectives (GRI 2013).

China is the world's largest developing country and is experiencing dramatic economic development. It managed to survive the 1997 Asian financial crisis (AFC) and to quickly recover from the 2008 global financial crisis (GFC) (Guo et al. 2013). However, in tandem with the significant boost in its economy in the past 15 years, China has experienced severe environmental deterioration, and this has raised significant environmental and social issues which have been criticised nationally and internationally. For example, in 2008 serious milk powder corporate scandals in mainland China have raised extreme concern for companies' corporate sustainability. The scandals destroyed people's confidence in the Chinese milk powder supply industry. The 300,000 victims triggered considerable social pressure, which consequently caused thousands of workers to lose their job and become redistributed in the labour market (Noronha et al. 2013). The community, as a result, had to bear this significant social cost. In terms of the environmental aspect, it has been identified that more than 90 % of rivers close to cities are heavily polluted, and the air pollution in many cities is so serious that it is likely to cause health consequences (Nie 2009). The International Energy Agency (IEA), which gives advice to developing countries to ensure reliable, affordable and clean energy, suggests that in 2013, China's emissions of greenhouse gases exceeded those of the USA. In the next 25 years, if this trend is not checked, the amount of carbon dioxide from China alone will be twice as much or more than that coming from the entire OECD countries (Bezlova 2007). China had become the number one country in terms of total annual carbon emissions by 2013 and a crucial player in negotiations under the United Nations Framework Convention on Climate Change (Jost 2013).

Due to this situation, Chinese enterprises have been increasingly pressured by numerous stakeholders to engage in social and environmental sustainability. Despite increased attention to corporate sustainability performances in China in recent years, enterprises' awareness is still at the infancy level, and there is very limited research evidence of completeness and comparability of sustainability reports in China. Diao (2013) revealed that there was significant variation among large companies in sustainability information disclosures. In addition, China had a completely different culture and political system than the West (Li-Hua and Lu 2013). In this context, Chinese stakeholders' perceptions of corporate sustainability have been progressively more focused and driven by strong public sentiment due to the increased focus corporate sustainability. Studies have investigated Chinese enterprises using initiatives based on Western theoretical foundations, which indicate that environmental reporting in listed companies is growing with most companies reporting 'material', 'energy', 'emission, effluents and waste' types of information (Yuan 2007; Peng 2009; Niu 2009; Zhang 2013). This result may provide some indication of which aspects are more likely to be focused on when preparing an environmental disclosure; however, it is of interest to the regulators, practitioners and the users of sustainability report to understand whether the report users find this information useful and it meets their perceptions of sustainability reporting.

7.1.2 Global Reporting Initiative

The Global Reporting Initiative (GRI) was formed in 1997 by the Coalition for Environmentally Responsible Economies in collaboration with the Tellus Institute. This initiative attempts to provide a sound conceptual basis for sustainability reporting framework, which is designed to improve the quality, accuracy and usefulness of corporate, environmental and social reporting (Frost 2007). Nowadays the emerging trend for companies is to disclose social, economic and environmental information concurrently in a format similar to the triple-bottom line. Therefore, it is significant to develop information transparency and discussion surrounding companies' viability, strategy and operations. Not being socially responsible leads to companies being vulnerable to lawsuits, boycotts and loss of reputation and brand value, which in turn causes negative impacts on market acceptance, positioning and demands (Burritt and Schaltegger 2012). Various guidelines have been developed by several organisations. These include the Dow Jones Sustainability Index (DJSI), ISO 14000 Series by the ISO, SA 8000 by Social Accountability International, AA1000 AccountabilityAbility Principles Standard 2008 by the Account Ability (AA), FTSE4 Good Index Series by the Financial Times and London Stock Exchange Group (FTSE) and Global Reporting initiative Sustainability Reporting Guidelines/the third generation (G3) by the Global Reporting Initiative (GRI).

After the conception of sustainability, the GRI rapidly became the leader among voluntary worldwide sustainability reporting systems based on three institutional innovations: initiating a multi-stakeholder process for developing reporting guidelines, institutionalising the process for producing successive generations of the guidelines and creating an organisation to serve as the steward of the guidelines and of the process (Brown et al. 2009). The formation and amendments of the GRI are largely dependent on its annual meeting in Amsterdam, where 'over a thousand representatives of global business, investment capital, civil society organisational, professionals, and idea entrepreneurs, politicians, corporate CEOs and high-level members of multilateral institutions' attend (Brown et al. 2009, p. 2). However, although the editing process involves many multinational influences and consideration of the needs of different countries, the GRI is based on the needs and circumstances of Western countries. The framing of the GRI has been considered by many studies as 'an efficiency gain for all actors' because the foundation of the initiatives is stakeholder theory, which allows for balancing sets of competing objectives. According to Brown et al. (2009), those objectives include individual and collective interests, broad consultation and efficient pursuit of technical objectives and a vision of social change and attainable instrumental goals, as well as building a new institution and not challenging the existing institutions and power relations. Consequently, the creation of the GRI has been based on a number of corporate behaviour theories, including legitimacy theory, institutional theory and stakeholder theory.

Although compliance with the guidelines is entirely voluntary, in its 2008 survey of the Global Fortune 250 (G250) and the 100 largest companies measured by revenue in 22 countries (N100), KPMG found that there were 75 % of G250 and 70 % of N100 companies using these initiatives. In China, the GRI has gained high praise from both industries and academics as the most comprehensive guidelines for social reporting (Zhang 2013). The Shenzhen Stock Exchanges published the social disclosure instructions in 2006 based on the frame of the GRI. However, many Chinese scholars employed it to measure the extent and the degree of the CSD (Chu 2007; Yuan 2007; Nie 2009; Peng 2009; Xue 2011).

7.1.3 The Influence of Chinese Culture on Corporate Sustainability Disclosure

Corporate sustainability disclosure is heavily influenced by both the external and internal environmental factors of a nation. Hofstede (1980) defines culture as collective mental programming, which has been indicated as a variable that significantly affects the corporate disclosure environment in a country. Diao (2013) suggests that companies that are both profitable and sustainable are directly influenced by an old Chinese paradox of being rich and generous. He explains that the social structure of China was strongly associated with the male-controlled clan system and family blood relationship of all types of business, in which an intense degree of ethical quality issues would exist (Diao 2013). The moral standard is heavily influenced by Confucius, who lived in the sixth and fifth century BC and took the view that harmonising was in the best interests of each member in a society. This idea proposes that wealth may not be well appreciated and meaningful if people do not live harmoniously and questions the essential component of the paradox and the belief of the Chinese, because 'moral problems and social philosophy override questions of logic, epistemology and metaphysics, and these are featured by a strong conservativeness and closed character' (Qu and Leung 2006, p. 245). Therefore, the transparency of corporate disclosure by Chinese publicly listed companies has always been an issue that influences significantly both the corporate sustainability reporting systems and stakeholders' perceptions of them.

Table 7.1 Confucius' three different layers

Category	Value	Focus
Bottom standard	Not tempted by profit	Business operating, managing, ethical activities. No profit, no action
Medium standard	Profit over righteousness[a]	Social development through accumulated social capital while maintaining a certain amount of economic benefit
Top standard	Everything over righteousness	Benefit transferred from corporate stakeholders

[a]Righteousness prescribes the world where peace prevails, order abounds and the social and natural harmony results in material well-being for everyone (Liu 2008)

Empirical studies into Chinese culture and corporate sustainability have explored the 'profits' from 'righteousness' (Yi) from Confucius. Xia et al. (2009) supported the idea of righteousness before profits, when they stated that business values should be reflected by the fundamental value of being ethical. Concerns should all be closely related to customers' value, employees' value and shareholders' value. Liu (2008) considered the Confucianism from three different layers (Table 7.1).

In the commodity economic market, culture differences between the West and the East also affect their perceptions. Most Western firms value profits over righteousness, whereas Chinese firms, the government-owned ones in particular, consider both social welfare and financial profit. Profit over righteousness implies that people are kind and generous to others to improve profits, which is why profits exist before righteousness. Wang and Juslin (2009) found that the Western corporate social responsibility and corporate sustainability concepts did not adapt well to the Chinese market, because they had rarely defined the primary reason for corporate sustainability. The ethical approach to the corporate sustainability concept does not take the Chinese reality and culture into consideration. The Wang and Juslin research was conducted purely based on reviewing literature and defining terms within the West and the East contexts. Under this perception, Wang and Juslin (2009) pointed out that corporate sustainability is a term that can be legitimately interpreted within the Chinese culture; however, Confucianism and Taoism, which emphasise the 'cultivation of virtue and morality, as well as the core of its harmony notion, is the harmonious society' (Wang and Juslin, 2009, p. 446), which offers a better understanding of corporate sustainability in the Chinese context.

Overall, studies of Chinese culture linked with corporate sustainability have provided insight into self-cultivation of virtues that may guide companies to a new way of improving their corporate sustainability performance. The studies also pointed out the differences in understanding of sustainability between the West and the East. Although the previous studies may seem to have been significant for explaining the economics, they are not practical for setting standards for corporate disclosure activities nor for cultural influence towards companies' reporting system.

7.2 Theoretical Background and Research Hypotheses

7.2.1 *Signalling Effect Theory*

Signalling theory considers that information asymmetry may often exist in a capital market. Under this assumption, information obtained from the management level is exceedingly more accurate and reliable than from the market. Investors, therefore, cannot respond quickly enough to make rational decisions about the most effective investment. As a result, market resources are not allocated efficiently. Signalling theory delivers the most reliable and valuable information to investors, because it suggests companies to disclose information that is unknown by the market (Yang 2011). Companies with sound performance will deliver their positive image to the public and be distinguished examples among the peers. However, if investors do not receive this information because a company chooses to not disclose negative images, the market value of a company may decrease in the long run.

Signalling theory has been getting attention in corporate disclosure studies in recent years, because it assumes that people send and explain signals to reduce information asymmetry (Lin 2010). Companies that disclose nonfinancial information signal their willingness to communicate with their stakeholders about sustainability issues; and companies produce stand-alone reports when the profit of providing such disclosure outweighs the related costs. Lin (2010) suggests that sustainability disclosure may be considered with signals of companies' sustainable performance as well as profitability to stakeholders of a company. This theory is important to test the perception of CSD in China because the ordinary companies in China are not willing to disclose voluntary information; therefore, every single indicator is considered important to disclose. However, companies who choose not to disclose may exert significant pressure on the public, the government and industrial association. Consequently, based on the theoretical assumption from this theory, all the indicators from GRI will be perceived to be important by the users.

7.2.2 *Research Hypotheses*

The research assumes that understanding users' perceived importance of corporate sustainability disclosure is important. If users perceive a strong and significant relation between sustainability reports and long-term corporate performance, they will use data in these reports to predict the long-term survival of companies. Consequently it improves the transparency and accuracy of the reports. Since corporate sustainability incorporates environmental, social and economic perspectives according to triple-bottom line reporting, the research questions and hypotheses are stated as follows:

Question 1 What is the users' perceived importance of environmental disclosure and to what extent do users perceive the environmental indicators in GRI differently from what GRI intended?

This question leads to hypothesis one:

Ho1 (Null) There is no statistically significant difference between the users' perceived importance of environmental disclosure and what was intended by GRI.

Ha1 (Alternative) There is statistically significant difference between the users' perceived importance of environmental disclosure and what was intended by GRI.

Question 2 What is the users' perceived importance of economic disclosure and to what extent do users perceive the social indicators in GRI differently from what GRI intended?

This question leads to hypothesis two:

Ho2 (Null) There is no statistically significant difference between the users' perceived importance of economic disclosure and what was intended by GRI.

Ha2 (Alternative) There is statistically significant difference between the users' perceived importance of economic disclosure and what was intended by GRI.

Question 3 What is the users' perceived importance of social disclosure and to what extent do users perceive the sustainable economic indicators by GRI differently from what was intended?

This question leads to hypothesis three:

Ho3 (Null) There is no statistically significant difference between the users' perceived importance of social disclosure and what was intended by GRI.

Ha3 (Alternative) There is statistically significant difference between the users' perceived importance of social disclosure and what was intended by GRI.

7.3 Research Methods

7.3.1 Research Design

Data collection for this study involved collecting data from survey questionnaire sent out to financial analysts. As for recruiting report users who are financial analysts, the sample will be solicited from the listed security organisations provided by the China Securities and Regulatory Commission (CSRC) (http://www.csrc.gov.cn). There are 111 companies registered on CSRC, and the designed questionnaire survey was sent out to 11 companies, where financial analysts work in these registered security companies, by email. They were asked to provide responses for the questionnaires, and they sent their response back.

According to the central limit theorem, a sample of 30 is sufficient to draw numeric conclusions. The central limit theorem considers only the mean of a sufficiently large number of independent random variables, and each with finite mean and variance will be approximately normally distributed (Chakrapani 2011). The theorem provides a sample number of 30 which can converge to normality, and this statement has been empirically tested and a profound implication for business and social research. As the central limited theorem is based on pure random samples, they are not subject to coverage, nonresponse and non-sampling errors (Chakrapani 2011). Hence, a sample of 30 in a study will be statistically significant, because the *t*-test values begin to get close to the z-scores based on the normal curve. To ensure there would be enough responses, 40 questionnaires were sent out. Fortunately 34 responses came back, and they were used in this study.

The rationale of choosing financial analysts was that corporate sustainability information has always been a useful input for financial analysts to evaluate and predict firm value, on the basis of financial factors influencing companies' performances, such as sales, costs, operational efficiency, financing and litigation risk (Dhaliwal et al. 2012). It was assumed that a better corporate sustainability reputation captured by financial analysts would improve companies' brand value and reputation, which in turn would significantly enhance the evaluation of firm products by consumers (Brown and Dacin 1997), and it translates the reputation into increased sales (Dhaliwal et al. 2012). According to a survey conducted by Deloitte in 2003 among 400 mainstream fund managers and financial analysts in Europe, approximately 80 % of the respondents indicated that corporate sustainability disclosures and management were focused section, and they had positive impacts on companies' market value. Hence, it was clear that financial analysts used CSD, and it was a vital resource to use when analysts evaluated firm value that significantly influenced investors' decision-making process. In addition, Lin (2010) suggested that financial analysts were experts who assessed corporate policies and performance on various issues of sustainability in China, and they were considered to be the prime CSD users who influenced other investors extensively. Therefore, because this study solely considered the users' perception, financial analysts were included as the primary respondents of the survey questionnaire.

7.3.2 Survey Design

Billing and Halstead (2005) suggested that one of the best ways to obtain information about beliefs, behaviours views and perceptions of individuals in the business world was to ask questions with closed ends. They found that this survey method was cost-effective, valid, easy and time efficient. The survey method also added benefit to reliability by providing higher consistency than the interview method because data to be collected were more measureable (Lin 2010). Therefore, the survey was selected for this study to formulate the instrument.

The survey had 23 questions in total, with 13 for environmental perspective and 5 questions for each social and economic perspective, respectively. The survey measurement included questions based on Likert scale, which is one of the three most adopted scales that address responses to a series of attitudinal dimensions (Brace 2004). A five-point scale was adopted because it provides sufficient discrimination for most purposes and can be easily understood by the respondents (Brace 2004). Subsequently, this study used this scale to indicate the degree to which respondents agreed or disagreed that it was important or not important. In order to measure the GRI, respondents were asked to write from 1 to 5 (1 for least important/completely disagree, 5 for most important/completely agree). The second part of the survey involved an open-ended question, where the respondents were encouraged to write anything that they thought should be added about sustainability guidelines or standards. See Appendix A, B and C for the survey design.

The results from the survey were then imported into SPSS (statistical package for the social sciences). Descriptive statistics and one-sample *t*-test were used to examine the research questions and hypotheses.

7.4 Result and Discussion

7.4.1 Descriptive Statistics

Environmental Indicators Table 7.2 shows descriptive statistics of environmental indicators. The respondents were asked to rate the importance of the information items in terms of their desirability to be included in companies' environmental disclosures. There are five different levels from the least important to the most important. All items are major environmental performance indicators suggested by GRI guidelines.

The results reveal that all of the indicators were considered to be either 'important' or 'most important'. Q3 and Q6 regarding 'water' and 'effluents and waste' were the most concerned items, where 50 % and 44.1 % of the responses were 'most important'. There were no respondents who rated 'least important' and 'not important' in Q6, Q7 and Q8. Q7 was about 'products and services', where 52.9 % of respondents chose important and 14.7 % selected most important. Q8 was about 'compliance': 52.9 % and 35.3 % rated it 'important' and 'most important', respectively. The only indicators that received 'least important' were Q4, Q9 and Q12, which were concerned about 'biodiversity', 'transportation' and 'environmental grievance mechanisms'. Nevertheless, the most selected options for these two questions were 'important'. It is notable that 'most important' was chosen in all responses, and the majority of the respondents considered that these items were 'important'.

Table 7.2 Frequency table of environmental indicators (sample size $N = 34$)

	Least important	Not important	Neutral	Important	Most important	Mode
Material usage	0	1 (2.9 %)	6 (17.6 %)	23 (67.6 %)	4 (11.8 %)	Important
Energy	0	1 (2.9 %)	5 (14.7 %)	22 (64.7 %)	6 (7.6 %)	Important
Water	0	1 (2.9 %)	2 (5.9 %)	14 (41.2 %)	17 (50 %)	Most important
Biodiversity	1 (2.9 %)	1 (2.9 %)	6 (17.6 %)	22 (64.7 %)	4 (11.8 %)	Important
Emission	0	1 (2.9 %)	2 (5.9 %)	18 (52.9 %)	13 (38.2 %)	Important
Effluents and waste	0	0	5 (14.7 %)	14 (41.2 %)	15 (44.1 %)	Most important
Products and services	0	0	11 (32.4 %)	18 (52.9 %)	5 (14.7 %)	Important
Compliance	0	0	4 (11.8 %)	18 (52.9 %)	12 (35.3 %)	Important
Transportation	1 (2.9 %)	3 (8.8 %)	10 (29.4 %)	18 (52.9 %)	2 (5.9 %)	Important
Environmental overall sustainability	0	1 (2.9 %)	7 (20.6 %)	23 (67.6 %)	3 (8.8 %)	Important
Supplier environmental assessment	0	2 (5.9 %)	6 (17.6 %)	21 (61.8 %)	5 (14.7 %)	Important
Environmental grievance	1 (2.9 %)	2 (5.9 %)	11 (32.4 %)	19 (55.9 %)	1 (2.9 %)	Important
Q13	No response					

Q13 is an open-ended question, asking 'What other aspects do you think are important for a company to disclose economic information?' No response was obtained for this question.

In summary, the results in descriptive statistics show that these 12 environmental indicators should be included in a sustainability report or an environmental reporting. 'Water' and 'effluents and waste' should take more weight when examining environmental disclosures, because overall they were considered to be more important than the other indicators.

Economic Indicators Table 7.3 presents the descriptive statistics of the economic indicators.

The results show that only slightly over 60 % rated either 'important' or 'most important' in Q1 and Q2, which questions were concerning 'economic performance' and 'market presence'. However, there were over 30 % who rated either 'not important' or 'neutral'. Q3 and Q4 were rated much less important than Q1 and Q2. Although the mode for Q3 (indirect economic impacts) was 'important', 50 %

Table 7.3 Frequency table of economic indicators (sample size $N = 34$)

	Least important	Not important	Neutral	Important	Most important	Mode
Q1	1 (2.9 %)	1 (2.9 %)	11 (32.4 %)	19 (55.9 %)	2 (5.9 %)	Important
Q2	0	2 (5.9 %)	10 (29.4 %)	20 (58.8 %)	2 (5.9 %)	Important
Q3	0	4 (11.8 %)	13 (38.2 %)	17 (50 %)	0	Important
Q4	0	6 (17.6 %)	14 (41.2 %)	14 (41.2 %)	0	Important *and* neutral
Q5	CPI of employees within a company; accumulated unemployment					

of the respondents rated it 'not important' and 'neutral'. This question indicated that information about indirect economic impact was not considered important in sustainability reporting. This is because users can find out indirect economic impact information through other types of measures or reports rather than using CSD. Q4 is regarding procurement practices, and the most common answers were 'neutral' and 'important'. There were also 17.6 % who rated 'not important'.

There were only two responses for Q5, which is an open-ended question in sustainable economic aspect. The report users responded that they would like to see the consumer price index of the employees within a company and the accumulated unemployment in companies' sustainability report. It is important to see that financial analysts were linking the financial perspective with corporate sustainability when examining CSD.

Overall, the result suggests that Q3 may be included in a sustainability report, but the weight of this indicator must be reconsidered. Q4 may not need to be included since the majority considered it less than important. Companies may also need to consider including the CPI of their employees as well as the unemployment in their sustainability reports.

Social Indicators Corporate social disclosure is a major focus in sustainability reporting outlined in GRI. There are four main categories in this form of report – labour practice and decent work, human right, society and product responsibility. There are subcategories within each of the main categories. However, this study considered only the main categories because they were the most representative.

Table 7.4 shows the results of the responses from the users' most desired social items in corporate sustainability reports. The items are the major social categories in the GRI guidelines. In this section, although all indicators were considered as important, the level of importance falls into different degrees. There were 64.7 % who rated labour practice and decent work 'important' and 8.8 % rated them 'most important', but 26 % rated either 'not important' or 'neutral'. Just over 60 % rated human right and society to be either 'important' or 'most important'. Notably, over 80 % of the users believe that product responsibility is significant in sustainability reporting.

Table 7.4 Frequency table of the level of importance among the social sustainability aspects

	Least important	Not important	Neutral	Important	Most important	Mode
Labour practice and decent work	0	2 (5.9 %)	7 (20.6 %)	22 (64.7 %)	3 (8.8 %)	Important
Human right	1 (2.9 %)	1 (2.9 %)	10 (29.4 %)	14 (41.2 %)	8 (23.5 %)	Important
Society	0	3 (8.8 %)	9 (26.5 %)	20 (58.8 %)	2 (5.9 %)	Important
Product responsibility	0	2 (5.9 %)	3 (8.8 %)	22 (64.7 %)	7 (20.6 %)	Important
Q5	Sexism					

Sexism was written in the open-ended question. Although the GRI guidelines have included an item about sexism (such as equal remuneration for women and men), this suggests that companies may consider putting more activities and protections for equal gender in their sustainability reports.

In summary, all four questions were regarded as important in sustainability reports, and companies should consider including activities about gender equality reports as well.

7.4.2 Hypotheses Test

Environmental Disclosures The three hypotheses given in the previous section tested using one-sample *t*-test. The results are shown in Tables 7.5, 7.6 and 7.7 regarding environmental, economic and social indicators, respectively. All items included in the GRI guidelines were intended to be important for companies' reporting. Therefore, the test values in *t*-test were set to 4, which represents important.

Hypothesis one states that there is no statistically significant difference between the users' perceived importance of environmental disclosure and what was intended in GRI. Table 7.5 presents the result from *t*-test for environmental indicators, and it answers partially research question two. Evidently, there are six questions that are statistically significant: Q3, Q5, Q6, Q8, Q9 and Q12. It means that the users' perceived importance of these questions was significantly different from what GRI was intended. Therefore, the null hypotheses for these questions are rejected. It suggests that when measuring and analysing sustainability reports in China, the weight and importance of these items included in these questions must be reconsidered.

Q3 indicates that the environmental performance indicator 'water' is significantly important, and it needs to be included in a sustainability report. The t-statistic is 3.016 and $p = 0.005$, claiming that the results are significant at 0.01 level, higher

Table 7.5 *t*-test table for environmental indicators (sample size $N = 34$)

	Mean	Std. deviation	*t*-test 95 % confidence interval	
			t	Sig. (two tailed)
Q1	3.88	0.640	−1.071	0.292
Q2	3.97	0.674	−0.255	0.801
Q3	4.38	0.739	3.016	0.005***
Q4	3.79	0.808	−1.485	0.147
Q5	4.26	0.710	2.175	0.037**
Q6	4.29	0.719	2.385	0.023**
Q7	3.82	0.673	−1.529	0.136
Q8	4.24	0.654	2.098	0.044**
Q9	3.50	0.862	−3.384	0.002***
Q10	3.82	0.626	−1.643	0.110
Q11	3.85	0.744	−1.153	0.257
Q12	3.50	0.788	−3.699	0.001***

**Significant at 0.05 level; ***Significant at 0.01 level

Table 7.6 *t*-test table for economic indicators (sample size $N = 34$)

	Mean	Std. deviation	*t*-test 95 % confidence interval	
			t	Sig. (two tailed)
Q1	3.59	0.783	−3.066	0.004***
Q2	3.65	0.691	−2.978	0.005***
Q3	3.38	0.697	−5.167	0.000***
Q4	3.24	0.741	−6.018	0.000***

***Significant at 0.01 level

Table 7.7 *t*-test table for the level of importance among the social sustainability aspects

	Mean	Std. deviation	*t*-test 95 % confidence interval	
			t	Sig. (two tailed)
Labour practice and decent work	3.76	0.699	−1.963	0.058*
Human right	3.79	0.946	−1.268	0.214
Society	3.62	0.739	−3.016	0.005***
Product responsibility	4	0.739	0.000	1.000

*Significant at 0.1 level; ***Significant at 0.01 level

than the test value. The mean of 4.38 also indicates that 'water' is extremely important when reporting environmental responsibility.

Q9 is also significant at the 0.01 level, with a slightly lower mean of 3.50. This indicates that environmental impact created by transportation must be considered in sustainability reporting. The t-statistic is −3.384, and the p-value is 0.002, meaning that the result is statistically significant. Therefore, the null hypothesis is rejected for Q9, suggesting that the perceived important for 'transportation' is different from what was intended in GRI.

The question regarding 'environmental grievance mechanisms' has the indicial mean as Q9. Although the p-value is slightly better, it is significant at the 0.01 level. Hence, the null hypothesis is also rejected for Q12.

For Q5, Q6 and Q8, users had an average of 4.26, 4.29 and 4.24, respectively, at the 0.05 significance level, revealing that users cared enormously about 'emissions', 'effluents and waste' and 'compliance'. This was consistent with the recent trend that carbon offsets and the serious carbon emissions in many major cities in China, which have gradually gained significant international attention. Carbon offset refers to a monetary investment that abates greenhouse gas emission or sequesters carbon from the atmosphere that is used to compensate for greenhouse gas emission from companies' own activities. For resecuring the severe air pollution, recently Beijing had 'APEC blue' sky because the government shut down temporarily the industrial area in Hebei. In order to achieve long-term performance, companies disclosing emission may have become a determinant that reflects their value. Therefore, according to the *t*-test results, the null hypotheses are rejected for these three questions.

In summary, hypothesis one is rejected for Q3 and Q9 at 0.01 significance level and Q5, Q6 and Q8 at 0.05 significance level. This hypothesis is accepted for Q1, Q2, Q4, Q7, Q10 and Q11.

Economic Disclosures Hypothesis two states that there is no statistically significant difference between the users' perceived importance of economic disclosure and what was intended in GRI. All the economic indicators are shown to be significant at 0.01 level. Interestingly, their average values are below the test value 4, suggesting that economic indicators from the users' perceptions were not as important as they were intended in the GRI guidelines.

Q2, which is regarding 'market presence', has the highest mean of 3.65 among the four indicators with a t-value of −2.978. It means that users care less about market presence in sustainability reporting. The t-value and p-value show that it is statistically significant. Q1 and Q3 had similar means, which are 3.59 and 3.39, respectively. These again show that users care less about 'economic performance' and 'indirect economic impacts'. The t-statistic is −3.066 for Q1 and −5.167 for Q3, showing that they are significant statistically. Q4 is similar to the previous indicator as well, where the mean is 3.24. Q4 is also statistically significant.

In summary, users considered the economic indicators less important. Since the results are statistically significant, therefore, hypothesis two is entirely rejected.

Social Disclosures Hypothesis three states that there is no statistically significant difference between the users' perceived importance of social disclosure and what was intended in GRI. The results in Table 7.7 reveal that the social sustainability indicators about product responsibility were much concerned by the report users. Human right had an average of 3.79, indicating that the report users were less than importantly concerned. The t-value and p-value are −1.268 and 0.214, showing that this question is not statistically significant; therefore, the null hypothesis is not rejected. For product responsibility, although the t-value and the p-value are insignificant, the mean for this question presents that the users cared about product responsibility in sustainability report. The other questions, which were society, human right and labour practice and decent work, were shown to be less than the test value. The question about society has an average of 3.62, showing that this area was less concerned by report users. The t-value and p-value were −3.016 and 0.005, showing that the responses for society were statistically significant. Similarly, labour practice and decent work had a mean of 3.76 slightly higher than society. The t-statistic was −1.963 and $p = 0.058$, indicating that the result is significantly different from what GRI was intended.

In summary, research hypothesis three is accepted for human right and product responsibility, and it is rejected for labour practice and decent work at the 0.1 significance level and for society at the 0.01 significance level.

7.5 Conclusion

The purpose of this study was to provide exploratory evidence of the users' perceived importance in corporate sustainability in China and to address to what extent perceptions were different from what was intended in the GRI guidelines. This study research examines three sustainable aspects, which were corporate environmental, economic and social reporting. The results in this study were based on 34 responses of the questionnaires designed using the GRI guidelines from financial analysts. For the environmental indicators, 'water', 'emission', 'effluents and waste', 'compliance', 'transportation' and 'environmental grievance mechanisms', responses were different and regarded as more important than was intended in the GRI guidelines. In the economic aspect, all four indicators, 'economic performance', 'indirect economic impact', 'procurement practices' and 'market presence', are different, and they were less important than what was intended in GRI. For social indicators, 'labour practice' and 'society' are less important, whereas 'product responsibility' is the most important in this aspect.

Regarding the question of the users' perceived importance in environmental reporting in China, Table 7.2 shows that all 12 environmental indicators need to be included in sustainability reports. The environmental indicators were 'material', 'energy', 'water', 'biodiversity', 'emissions', 'effluents and waste', 'products and services', 'compliance', 'transportation', 'environmental overall sustainability', 'supplier environmental assessment' and 'environmental grievance mechanisms'. In particular, 'biodiversity' and 'water' were shown to be the most important among the 12 indicators. This suggests that these two indicators were regarded as more important than what GRI was intended; therefore, companies need to include more information about these areas in their environmental disclosures. Results from *t*-test in Table 7.5 indicate that 'water', 'emission', 'effluents and waste', 'compliance', 'transportation' and 'environmental grievance mechanisms' are statistically significant; hence, the null hypotheses for these items were rejected. In the Chinese context, these three indicators are much more important than what was intended by GRI.

In relation to the users' perceived importance in economic reporting, Table 7.3 shows that 50 % of the respondents rated 'economic performance', 'indirect economic impact' and 'market presence' as important. This suggests that it may not be as important to include these indicators in sustainability disclosures. Nevertheless, 50 % of the respondents wanted to see this information. 'Procurement practices' was deemed either important or not important, indicating that it is not necessary to include this item in CSD. Besides, the CPI of employees from a disclosing company and unemployment were also regarded as two important indicators in CSD. The *t*-test later showed that all indicators were not significant, and their importance was below the test value by GRI; therefore, the economic indicators are different from the GRI guidelines, and they are much less important in CSD in the Chinese context.

For social indicators, descriptive statistics indicate that in sustainability disclosures, 'labour practice and decent work', 'human rights' and 'society' are equally important, whereas 'product responsibility' is the most important. Sexism was also another concern by two of the users, which suggests that companies may need to include more information about gender equality in sustainability, as well as for product responsibility. The *t*-test indicates that 'labour practice' and 'society' are less important in China than what GRI was intended. 'Product responsibility' should be focused when disclosing sustainability. However, due to only a small sample was focused in this study, it provides an indication for future research: what are perceived to be important by GRI may not be considered as so important by Chinese report users; and what are perceived to be important by Chinese report users may not be as important by users from other countries with different culture backgrounds.

In summary, this study provides insight into users' perceived importance of corporate sustainability disclosures in China. Although there are indicators shown to be different from what was intended in the GRI guidelines, more than half of the items remain significant when analysing CSD in China.

Appendix A

Sustainable Environmental Information

How do you perceive the importance of the following aspects in environmental disclosure?

1. Material usage (materials used from recycled materials).

Least important	*Not important*	*Neutral*	*Important*	*Most important*

2. Energy (energy consumption, energy intensity, reduction of energy consumption or reduction in energy requirements of products and services).

Least important	*Not important*	*Neutral*	*Important*	*Most important*

3. Water (the amount of water withdrawal by source, influence from such withdrawal and percentage and total volume of water recycled and reused).

Least important	*Not important*	*Neutral*	*Important*	*Most important*

4. Biodiversity (operational sites owned, leased, managed in or adjacent to, protected areas and areas of high biodiversity value outside protected areas. It may also include description of significant impacts of activities, products and services on biodiversity in protected areas and areas of high biodiversity value outside protected areas or habitats protected or restored, as well as the total number of IUCN Red List species and national conservation list species with habitats in areas affected by operations and by level of extinction risk).

Least important	*Not important*	*Neutral*	*Important*	*Most important*

5. Emissions (direct or indirect greenhouse gas emissions, greenhouse gas emission intensity, reduction of greenhouse gas emissions, emissions of ozone-depleting substances and NOx, SOx and other significant air emissions).

Least important	*Not important*	*Neutral*	*Important*	*Most important*

6. Effluents and waste (total water discharge by quality and destination; total weight of waste by type and disposal method; total number and volume of significant spills; weight of transported, imported, exported or treated waste deemed hazardous under the terms of the Basel Convention annexes i, ii, iii and viii; percentage of transported waste shipped internationally; identity, size, protected status and biodiversity value of water bodies and related habitats significantly affected by the organisation's discharges of water and run-off).

Least important	*Not important*	*Neutral*	*Important*	*Most important*

7. Products and services (the extent of impact mitigation of environmental impacts of products and services, percentage of products sold and their packaging materials that are reclaimed by category).

Least important	*Not important*	*Neutral*	*Important*	*Most important*

8. Compliance (monetary value of significant fines and total number of nonmonetary sanctions for non-compliance with environmental laws and regulations).

Least important	*Not important*	*Neutral*	*Important*	*Most important*

9. Transportation (environmental impacts of transporting products and other goods and materials for the organisation's operations and transporting members of the workforce).

Least important	*Not important*	*Neutral*	*Important*	*Most important*

10. Environmental overall sustainability (total environmental protection expenditures and investments by type)

Least important	*Not important*	*Neutral*	*Important*	*Most important*

11. Supplier environment assessment (percentage of new suppliers that were screened using environmental criteria, significant potential negative environmental impacts in the supply chain and actions taken).

Least important	*Not important*	*Neutral*	*Important*	*Most important*

12. Environmental grievance mechanisms (the number of grievances about environmental impacts filed, addressed and resolved through formal grievance mechanism).

Least important	*Not important*	*Neutral*	*Important*	*Most important*

13. What other aspects do you think are important for a company to disclose environmental information? Please specify here and rate it.

Least important	*Not important*	*Neutral*	*Important*	*Most important*

Appendix B

Sustainable Economic Information

How do you perceive the importance of the following aspects in economic disclosure?

1. Economic performance (direct economic value generated and distributed, financial implications and other risks and opportunities for the organisation's activities due to climate change, coverage of the organisation's defined benefit plan obligation and financial assistance received from the government).

Least important	*Not important*	*Neutral*	*Important*	*Most important*

2. Market presence (ratios of standard entry level wage by gender compared to local minimum wage at significant locations of operation and proportion of senior management hired from the local community at significant locations of operation).

Least important	Not important	Neutral	Important	Most important

3. Indirect economic impacts (development and impact of infrastructure investments and services supported and significant indirect economic impacts, including the extent of impacts).

Least important	Not important	Neutral	Important	Most important

4. Procurement practices (proportion of spending on local suppliers at significant location of operation).

Least important	Not important	Neutral	Important	Most important

5. What other aspects do you think are important for a company to disclose economic information? Please specify here and rate it.

Least important	Not important	Neutral	Important	Most important

Appendix C

Sustainable Social Information

How do you perceive the importance of the following aspects in social disclosure?

1. Labour practice and decent work.

Least important	Not important	Neutral	Important	Most important

2. Human right.

Least important	Not important	Neutral	Important	Most important

3. Social.

Least important	Not important	Neutral	Important	Most important

4. Product responsibility.

Least important	Not important	Neutral	Important	Most important

5. What other aspects do you think are important for a company to disclose economic information? Please specify here and rate it.

Least important	*Not important*	*Neutral*	*Important*	*Most important*

References

Bezlova A (2007) China racing to be world's worst polluter. The Click 14:2
Billings DM, Halstead JA (2005) Corporate social reporting and reputation risk management. Account Audit Account 21(3):337–361
Brace I (2004) Questionnaire design: how to plan, structure and write survey material for effective market research. Kogan Page, London/Sterling
Brown TJ, Dacin PA (1997) The company and the product: corporate associations and consumer product responses. J Mark 61:68–84
Brown HS, Jong M, Lessidrenska T et al (2009) The rise of the global reporting initiative: a case of institutional entrepreneurship. Environ Polit 18(2):182–200
Burritt R, Schaltegger S (2012) Measuring the sustainability of industrial biomass production and use. Manag Policy J 3(2):109–133
Chakrapani C (2011) Statistical reasoning vs. magical thinking. Available via VUE. http://ww.chuckchakrapani.com/articles/pdf/0411chakrapani.pdf. Accessed 12 Mar 2014
Chu X (2007) Empirical study on the relation between taking society responsibility and market performance of listed company – take the Shanghai industrial enterprise as the example. Dissertation, Xinjiang University of Finance
Dhaliwal DS, Radhakrishnan S, Tsang A, Yang YG et al (2012) Nonfinancial disclosure and analyst forecast accuracy: international evidence on corporate social responsibility disclosure. Account Rev 87(3):723–759
Diao Y (2013) Min ying qi ye yuan gong she hui ze ren de zhan lue ding wei ji shi shi xiao ji (Strategy and performance of corporate sustainability in Chinese private sectors). Dissertation, Zhe Jiang Industry and Commerce University
Frost G (2007) The introduction of mandatory environmental reporting guidelines: Australian evidence. Abacus 43(2):190–216
Gao Y (2009) Corporate social performance in China: evidence from large companies. J Bus Ethics 89(1):23–35
Global Reporting Initiative GRI (2013) G4 guidelines. http://www.globalreporting.org/ReportingFramework. Accessed 2 Oct 2013
Guo XD, Marinova D, Hong J (2013) China's shifting policies towards sustainability: a low-carbon economy and environmental protection. J Contemp China 22(81):428–445
Hofstede GH (1980) Culture's consequences: international difference in work related values. Sage, Beverley Hills
Jost W (2013) China's climate change expert community – principles, mechanisms and influence. J Contemp China 22(82):7–12
Li HR, Lu L (2013) Technology strategy and sustainability of business. J Technol Manag China 8 (2):62–82
Li Q, Luo W, Wang Y, Wu L et al (2013) Firm performance, corporate ownership and corporate social responsibility disclosure in China. Bus Ethics A Eur Rev 22(2):159–173
Lin I (2010) Users' and preparers' perception of sustainability reporting and corporate sustainability. Dissertation, ProQuest Dissertation and Theses database. (UMI 3427306)

Ling L (2009) Shang shi gong si she hui ze ren bao gao pi lu wen ti yan jiu (Research on the disclosure of listed companies' social responsibility reporting). Dissertation, Industrial University of He Fei

Liu G (2008) Xian qin ru jia li yi guan yu she hui ze ren jian she biao zhun (The influence from Confucianism to the corporate sustainability system). Acad J Renmin Univ China 2:79–85

Nie J (2009) Research on information disclosure of corporate social responsibility. Dissertation, The University of Finance and Economics of Tianjin

Niu HQ (2009) Empirical study about motivation to disclose the social responsibility report of the listed companies. Dissertation, Zhejiang Gongshang University

Nornha C, Tou S, Guan J et al (2013) Corporate social responsibility reporting in China: an overview and comparison with major trends. Corp Soc Responsib Environ Manag 20:29–42

Peng HG (2009) Research on corporate social disclosure in China. Dissertation, The University of Jilin

Qu W, Leng P (2006) Cultural impact on Chinese corporate disclosure – a corporate governance perspective. Manag Audit J 21(3):241–264

Wang L, Juslin H (2009) The impact of Chinese culture on corporate social responsibility: the harmony approach. J Bus Ethics 88:431–451

Xia J, Li S, Long C et al (2009) The transformation of collectively owned enterprises and its outcomes in China 2001–05. World Dev 37(10):1651–1662

Xue HY (2011) Research on factors on corporate social responsibility information disclosures. Dissertation, Tianjin University of Business

Yang J (2011) Shang shi gong si she hui ze ren bao gao pi lu yin su yan jiu (Factors influencing listed companies' corporate social responsibility report disclosure). Dissertation, Southwestern University of Finance and Economics

Yuan Y (2007) Information disclosure of corporate social responsibility. Dissertation, Southwestern University of Economics and Finance

Zhang J (2013) Determinants of corporate environmental and social disclosure in Chinese listed mining, electricity supply and chemical companies annual reports. Dissertation, Edith-Cowan University

Zhou S, Quan X, Jiang W (2012) Corporate social responsibility and sustainable development in China: literature review and case analysis. J Supply Chain Oper Manag 10(1):54–65

Chapter 8
Shadow Economy and Corruption in the ASEAN: Complement or Substitute?

Duc Hong Vo, Dao Thi-Thieu Ha, and Thinh Hung Ly

Abstract Very few empirical studies have been attempted to investigate the possible link between shadow economy and corruption for developing and transition economies, in particular, for the Association of Southeast Asian Nations (ASEAN). The lack of the studies can be explained by the fact that both "shadow economy" and "corruption" are ultimately unobservable. Using the MIMIC approach, this empirical study fills the gap. Data from the ASEAN (excluding the two high-income countries – Singapore and Brunei) for the period from 1995 to 2014 are utilised in this study. The findings from this study indicate that (i) there is a positive causal relationship between shadow economy and corruption in the ASEAN and that (ii) the effect from corruption on shadow economy is more profound than the effect from shadow economy on corruption. Shadow economy and corruption are complement, not substitute, for the ASEAN. The implication for macroeconomic policies in these countries is that controlling corruption is a good starting policy to minimise the growth of the shadow economy.

8.1 Introduction

Shadow economy and corruption are generally known as unobservable factors. Nonetheless, there exists evidence of a relationship between these two factors reported by the World Bank and few empirical studies. A very few empirical studies have been attempted to examine a possible link between shadow economy and corruption for a group of countries. Some empirical studies concluded that shadow economy and corruption are complement. This means that an increase of shadow economy will result in an increase of corruption and vice versa. Other

D.H. Vo (✉)
Open University of Ho Chi Minh City, Ho Chi Minh City, Vietnam

Economic Regulation Authority, Perth, WA, Australia
e-mail: Duc.Vo@erawa.com.au

D.T.-T. Ha
Banking University of Ho Chi Minh City, Ho Chi Minh City, Vietnam

T.H. Ly
Open University of Ho Chi Minh City, Ho Chi Minh City, Vietnam

H.G. Djajadikerta, Z. Zhang (eds.), *A New Paradigm for International Business*, Springer Proceedings in Business and Economics, DOI 10.1007/978-981-287-499-3_8

empirical studies provided the opposite findings in which shadow economy and corruption are negatively correlated.

In their study, Johnson et al. (1997) argued that the existence of a shadow economy will result in a reduction of an official economy. As such, businesses and individuals have motivations to work in the shadow economy, and they are prepared to pay for corruption to avoid getting caught by the government. As a result, shadow economy and corruption are complement. In other studies, Hindriks et al. (1997) and Hibbs and Piculescu (2005) provided the same conclusions on the link between shadow economy and corruption. In contrast, Choi and Thum (2005) and Dreher et al. (2009) argued that as long as businesses and individuals are joining in the shadow economy, there are no more opportunities for corrupt government officials to exploit. As a result, it is expected that an existence of a shadow economy will reduce a level of corruption in the official economy.

This study is conducted in response to a lack of empirical evidence designed for the ASEAN in particular. Following this Introduction, Sect. 8.2 provides brief definitions of shadow economy and corruption and the possible links between them. In applying the MIMIC approach, both cause variables and indicator (consequence) variables for both shadow economy and corruption are identified. These variables are presented in Sects. 8.3 and 8.4 of the paper. Section 8.5 provides a brief framework of the MIMIC approach together with the data used in this study. Research findings are presented in Sect. 8.6, followed by concluding remarks and policy implications in Sect. 8.7.

8.2 Shadow Economy and Corruption

8.2.1 Shadow Economy

Shadow economy is defined in theoretical and empirical studies to include economic activities which are measured but not reported into the gross national products (GNP) of a particular nation (Feige 1986, 1989). Smith (1994) defined shadow economy to include all economic activities taking place in the markets for goods and services which may be legal or illegal and are not officially measured and included in the national gross domestic products (GDP). In plain language, shadow economy includes all economic activities and incomes which avoid the interference of the government through the tax system (Feige (1989), Dell' Anno and Schneider (2004, 2006)). There is also an alternative view on a shadow economy which is developed through time and arguably followed the *water flow principle*: shadow economy adjusts automatically to be suitable with the tax system, the mechanism of punishment of the taxation office and the altitude of the society to activities taking place in the shadow sector (Mogensen et al. 1995). Table 8.1 classifies activities in the shadow economy.

Table 8.1 A classification of activities in the shadow economy

<table>
<tr><td rowspan="3">Illegal activities</td><td colspan="2">Monetary transactions</td><td colspan="2">Nonmonetary transactions</td></tr>
<tr><td colspan="2" rowspan="2">Trade in stolen goods, drug dealing and manufacturing, prostitution, gambling, smuggling, fraud</td><td colspan="2">Barter of drugs, stolen, or smuggled goods</td></tr>
<tr><td colspan="2">Producing or growing drugs for own use. Theft for own use</td></tr>
<tr><td rowspan="3">Legal activities</td><td>Tax evasion</td><td>Tax avoidance</td><td>Tax evasion</td><td>Tax evasion</td></tr>
<tr><td>Unreported income from self-employment</td><td rowspan="2">Employee discounts, fringe benefits</td><td rowspan="2">Barter of legal services and goods</td><td>All do-it-yourself</td></tr>
<tr><td>Wages, salaries and assets from unreported work related to legal services and goods</td><td>Work and neighbour help</td></tr>
</table>

Source: Rolf Mirus and Roger S. Smith (1997, p. 5)

8.2.2 *Corruption*

A very typical definition of corruption is that corruption represents the abuse of public power for private benefits (Tanzi 1998, p. 8). In this definition, the abuse of public power in a private sector is not considered. Corruption can also be defined as an intentional ignorance of regulations for the use of relationship for private benefits. Corruption has caused significant losses to the society. *First*, corruption is a barrier to a democracy in which public power cannot be used for private benefits. *Second*, corrupt government officials have delivered lower-than-expected quality of public infrastructure such as hospitals and schools which is not in accordance with the costs involved. *Third*, corruption contributes to a distortion of equality in the economy and a reduction of competition in goods production and services provision. Fourth, corruption damages trust from the public to the government and its political regime (Transparency International 2009).

8.2.3 *A Relationship Between Shadow Economy and Corruption*

Evidence from studies on a relationship between shadow economy and corruption provides mixed findings. Conclusions from some studies indicated that shadow economy and corruption are complement. This means that an increase in corruption will be associated with an increase in shadow economy (Johnson et al. 1998a, b; Friedman et al. 1999). In contrast, some argued that it is not feasible for businesses and individuals to give bribes to corrupt government officials when their activities in the shadow economy are noticed. As such, it is argued that the presence of corruption is independent with shadow economy. However, Choi and Thum (2005) and Dreher et al. (2007) provided evidence to argue that the presence of shadow economy can reduce a distortion of resources allocation because corrupt government's officials have no chance to corrupt. As a result, they argued that corruption and shadow economy are substitute.

For low-income nations, businesses starting their business provide bribes to corrupt government officials with an expectation that their economic activities in the shadow sector will not get caught by the government (Hindriks et al. 1999). Corrupt government officials receiving bribes will allow businesses to maximise their profits in the shadow sector (Hibbs and Piculescu 2005). As a result, corruption and shadow economy are positively correlated. In conclusion, a relationship between corruption and shadow economy appears to rely on the national income level and the effectiveness of the legal system. Johnson et al. (1997) concluded that corruption and shadow economy are complement. Using a full employment model, workers can choose to work in either the shadow economy or an official economy. It is argued that an increase in the shadow economy will result in the reduction of an official economy. In addition, corruption will provide an incentive for businesses and individuals to join a shadow economy. As a result, an increase in corruption will lead to an increase in shadow economy.

In relation to the effect of shadow economy to corruption, Dreher et al. (2008) concluded corruption leads to a reduction of a shadow economy. Shadow economy and corruption are substitute. The presence of economic activities in the shadow sector will reduce the official economy. Payments will take place in a hidden environment. Corrupt government officials are not provided any chance to be corrupt because all transactions are now hidden. As a result, they argued that shadow economy is negatively related to corruption.

It is noted that empirical studies on corruption have utilised a perception index of corruption representing for a level of corruption in the economy. However, it is argued that the perception-based indices reflect the quality of a country's institutions rather than its actual degree of corruption. Mocan (2004) argued that a perception of corruption is not related to the actual level of corruption in the economy because perception of corruption from businesses and individuals is distorted. Weber Abramo (2005) provided a similar conclusion that perceived corruption is not related to bribery.[1]

In response to this criticism of a perception-based index, this study utilises the MIMIC approach to estimate corruption (a latent variable) based on a set of cause variables and a set of indicator variables. This approach is similar to the approach adopted to estimate the shadow economy. In conclusion, both corruption and shadow economy are estimated using the MIMIC approach in this study. The MIMIC approach requires a set of cause variables and a set of indicator variables for any latent (unobservable) variable to be estimated. As a result, it is fundamental

[1] See Bjorvatn and Soreide (2005) for a detailed criticism of a perception index.

for the study to determine the sets of cause and consequence variables for each latent variable, being the shadow economy and corruption.

8.3 Causes and Consequences of the Shadow Economy

8.3.1 Causes Affecting the Shadow Economy

Literature presents the following causes which affect significantly the size of the shadow economy.

8.3.1.1 Tax and Social Security Contribution Burdens

In previous empirical studies, one of the most important and significant causes for an existence and growth of a shadow economy is an increase in tax and social security contribution burdens (Tanzi 1999; Schneider and Enste 2000). The higher the tax rate, the lower the *morality of taxation*, encouraging people working in a shadow economy to evade taxes (Torgler and Schneider 2009; Alm and Torgler 2006; Alm et al. 2006). Various studies concluded that the higher the net income in the (official) economy, the lower the level of labour joining a shadow economy. In addition, a gap between gross income and net income increases; more and more people will join to work in a shadow economy. As such, it is argued that a difference between gross income and net income depending heavily on tax and social security contribution burdens. In this study, a tax burden and a social security contribution burden are used as proxies for causes of a shadow economy for the ASEAN:

- *A tax rate*: a tax rate is used to determine a tax liability to be paid to the government.
- *A fiscal freedom index*: this index measures directly an extent to which regulations from the government affect individuals and businesses in the economy. This index is one of many indices calculated and made available to the public by the Heritage Foundation. The index varies within the range of 0 and 100 in which 0 represents the lowest level of a fiscal freedom and 100 represents the highest level of the freedom (Heritage Foundation 2014).

8.3.1.2 Intensity of Regulation

Schneider and Enste (2000) argued that an increase in intensity of regulation will reduce choices for individuals in the official economy (Note 1). An intensity of regulations generally measures a number of regulations and required certificates to work or operate regulations for a labour market. In Germany, the Deregulation Commission (1991) and Monopol-kommission (1998) concluded that various regulations from the government contribute to the cost for labour in the official economy. In response to these increases in labour costs, businesses will reduce a number of jobs required for their businesses. As a result, workers join a shadow economy where these costs can be avoided. A model developed by Johnson et al. (1997) predicts that, inter alia, countries with more general regulation applied to economic activities in their economies tend to have a higher share of the unofficial economy in the total GDP. A study by Friedman et al. (1999) provides the same conclusion. On the ground of previous studies, two variables representing as causes of a shadow economy are adopted in this study to represent an intensity of regulations across countries in the ASEAN:

- *A business freedom index*: this index measures an extent to which individuals can establish and run a business without being heavily reported to the government. Unnecessary and unreasonable regulations will no doubt increase costs for businesses. These regulations will play as a barrier for business activities to enter into the official economy. These regulations will increase costs, and as a result, products and services provided by businesses in the official economy become less competitive in the marketplace. This index also varies within the range of 0, being the lowest level, and 100, being the highest level of a freedom (Heritage Foundation 2014).
- *A labour freedom*: this index measures an extent to which individuals can work anywhere without any regulations from the government. This index is considered one of the most important indices developed by the Heritage Foundation. It is argued that when a labour freedom increases, businesses will have more capacity to offer jobs to workers. As a result, an unemployment rate is expected to be lower. This is an important mechanism to improve productivity and to ensure economic growth for a nation because labour market is as important as a good and service market (Heritage Foundation 2014).

8.3.1.3 Public Sector Services

A study by Johnson et al. (1998) indicates that an increase in the size of a shadow economy will be associated with a loss of government revenue. In return, quantity and quality of public goods and services provided are lower. To ensure quality and quantity of public goods and services being provided to the economy, an increase in tax on the official sector is expected. This increase in tax burdens will result in an increase of economic activities taking place in the shadow economy, and individuals and businesses have now more incentive to join the unofficial economy. This study also presents evidence to support the view that a smaller size of the shadow economy is in relation with a country with a large revenue collection, lower intensity of regulations and lower level of bribe and corruption.

As such, on a ground of this study, *government spending* is used as an indicator to represent a capacity of a government in providing public goods and services. *Government spending* measures a total spending of a government in comparison with total expenditure of the national economy which generally includes public and private spending. Government spending can be classified into different categories: government investment (infrastructure, research funds or human capital investment) and provision of public goods and services. The Heritage Foundation also produces the index representing a level of government spending across nations. As usual, this index varies within the range of 0 and 100 (Heritage Foundation 2014).

8.3.1.4 The Official Economy

It is argued that a prevailing condition of the official economy will determine the choice of individuals and businesses to join a shadow economy or an official economy (Bajada and Schneider 2005; Feld and Schneider 2010). In an economic expansion period where individuals can find jobs easily within the official economy, they have no incentive to join a shadow economy. However, this choice may not be available when the economy faces its downturn. Individuals may decide to join a shadow economy to find work. On the ground of this consideration, *an unemployment rate* will be used in this study.

8.3.2 Consequences of the Shadow Economy

A size of a shadow economy cannot be directly measured. As such, the approach adopted in this study is to link some observable variables with the size of a shadow economy. Based on previous empirical studies, some indicators below are used in this study.

8.3.2.1 Money Market

A money market is considered through some indicators such as total money supply into the economy. A money supply M_0 represents a level of the monetary base (cash which can be spent instantly) and M_1 represents a total of a money supply M_0 and deposits. Individuals and businesses joining a shadow economy generally avoid using transactions through banks because their activities may be noticed by the government. As a result, cash is the preferred means of settlement for transactions in the shadow economy.

8.3.2.2 Labour Market

A labour market index is used to measure a ratio of people joining a labour force. This is an index to represent a proportion of total population joining in economic activities to produce and provide goods and services in a specified period of time (World Bank 2014).

8.3.2.3 Tax Revenue

A tax revenue for any government is a total of compulsory collections from individuals and businesses in the form of tax. For any government, tax revenue is one of the most important factors for the government to determine the level of goods and services provided to the economy. Empirical studies indicate that a presence of a shadow economy will negatively affect tax collection for the government. As such, tax revenue is used as a proxy for a consequence of a shadow economy in this study.

8.3.2.4 An Increase of GDP Per Capita

It is argued that economic activities taking in a shadow economy will contribute to the official economy. Money earned from activities taking place in a shadow sector is argued to be spent in the official sector. As such, an increase of GDP per capita will be used as an index to measure an effect from the shadow economy to the official economy.

8.4 Causes and Consequences of Corruption

8.4.1 Causes

8.4.1.1 Political Regime and Judicial System

A political regime and a judicial system are factors to indicate the level of a country's democratic and institutional quality. Shleifer and Vishny (1993) were of the view that corruption is associated with weaknesses of political system, corporate governance and regulations in place to prevent corruption. In addition, they argued that an improvement in a political environment and transparency will also lead to a reduction of corruption in the economy. Other characteristics of a country's political system such as electoral rules and the degree of decentralisation also affect corruption.

All these political and judicial factors are very typical in research on the importance of the government to economic growth and development. In particular, North (1990) and Easterly and Levine (1997) argued that an effectively and enforced fully legal system will provide a strong framework for economic activities and for a protection of asset ownership of businesses and individuals. They also argued that a weak legal system will lead to economic transactions taking place in the shadow sector, reducing incentive for businesses and individuals in production and encouraging them to join the shadow economy. Based on the findings of previous empirical studies, three proxies used as *causes* representing *a political regime and a judicial system* are as follows:

- *Bureaucracy cost*: this cost measures an effectiveness of standards adopted in relation to goods production and services provision and other legal requirements in the nation (World Bank 2014).
- *Government's effectiveness*: this efficiency level measures the independence of publicly provided services, the quality of public institutions and the reliability on agencies which carry on the tasks of implementing legal requirements stipulated and adopted by the government such as the police (World Bank 2014).
- *Rule of law*: the rule of law measures the reliability and the quality of contract enforcement enforced by decisions from the court and implemented by the police towards businesses and individuals (World Bank 2014).

8.4.1.2 Fiscal Freedom

The government can interfere with economic activities in the economy through the use of regulations, policy and financial burden such as taxation and social security contribution to the private sector. Such an interference will contribute to a reduction of economic freedom. It is argued that an increase in economic freedom will be associated with a reduction of corruption because businesses and individuals have now more choices in relation to the industry they wish to join for goods production and services provision. Economic freedom also requires for a reduction of regulations stipulated and adopted which is associated with a reduction of bureaucracy of the government's official. A heavy interference from the government into the economy will create an environment in which givers and receivers of corruption will increase to avoid regulations. An increase in corruption will lessen the impact of policies and regulations on economic activities (Schneider 2012).

Tanzi (1998) and Dreher et al. (2007) emphasised that with a larger size of the public sector, government officials are assigned greater responsibility in terms of goods production and services provision. As a result, the extent of corruption may also be greater. Van Rijckeghem and Weder (2001) concluded that the above relationship between the size of a public sector and the shadow economy is more profound if government officials are paid low salaries to carry out their duties. Based on the considerations of the previous empirical studies, a variable representing for *fiscal freedom* is included in the model to compare the extent of this freedom across countries in the sample:

- *Fiscal freedom*: this index measures a freedom of individuals and businesses to manage their assets. These assets are used for the benefits of businesses and individuals (Heritage 2014).

8.4.2 Consequences

In order to identify and measure corruption, many studies have considered factors that can be used to measure a level of corruption in the economy. By the natural choice, these studies adopted an index representing a corruption in the society. This index was measured using the responses to the question: "In your industry, how commonly would you estimate that firms make undocumented extra payments or bribes?" (Gwartney et al. 2008, p. 194). As a result, this study utilises the *bribe payers index* as an index representing the *consequences* of corruption in the model:

- *Bribe payers index:* this index is developed based on perception of individuals to the extent in which bribes and corrupt activities are conducted without reporting and recording (World Bank 2014).

Buehn and Schneider (2009, 2012) and Schneider (2006) considered that, together with a bribe payers index, a variable representing a judicial independence is also required because this index indicates a level of equality of a judicial system in the influence of government officials, lobbyists and special interest groups, as well as private citizens and/or businesses. As such, this study utilises an index measuring *an independence of a judicial system* as an indicator representing *consequences* of corruption in the research model:

- *Judicial independence*: this index measures judicial independence of the judiciary in a country which is independent from political influences of members of the government, citizen and firms (World Bank 2014).

An extensive literature review also indicates that the *GDP per capita* is also widely used in empirical studies on corruption. As a result, this study uses *GDP per capita* as a variable representing *consequence* of corruption in the model.

8.5 Data and Research Method

8.5.1 A MIMIC Approach

Among various approaches which can be used to estimate the size of the shadow economy, a MIMIC approach is classified as a model approach which can be used to estimate the size and the trend of the shadow economy. While some methods such as a *monetary demand approach* or an *electricity consumption approach* only focus on one indicator to estimate the size of the shadow economy, an extensive economic literature review indicates that the shadow economy is influenced by various factors such as production, labour and monetary market. This approach focuses on causes and consequences of the shadow economy simultaneously. This approach is based on the DYMIMIC (dynamic multiple-indicators multiple causes) model which includes two different models: (i) a *measurement model* which is used to link observable indicators to the size of the shadow economy and (ii) *a structural equation model* which is used to present the link between causes and consequences among various indicators. This model approach is argued to be a more comprehensive approach than other previous models. However, a limitation of this approach is that it requires a large amount of data which may not be available in the developing countries.

In this study, a MIMIC model is adopted – a type of the structural equation model (SEM) to estimate the size of the shadow economy for ASEAN nations, including Vietnam. A key contribution of the SEM is to link and investigate the relationship between latent variables and observable variables by using the covariance matrix. In the MIMIC model, a shadow economy is an unobservable variable which can be analysed based on observable variables. For this purpose, first of all, a variable representing a shadow economy is linked to observable variables in the factor analytical model or to be named *a measurement model*. After that, a relationship between a variable proxied for a shadow economy and explanatory variables is determined using *the structural equation model*. As such, a MIMIC model is to use both models including factor model and a structural equation model.

A structural equation model can be expressed as below:

$$\eta = \gamma' X + \zeta \tag{8.1}$$

where $X = (x_1, x_2, \ldots, x_q)$ is a $(q * 1)$ vector and each x_i, $i = 1, \ldots, q$ is a potential cause of the latent variable η and $\gamma' = (\gamma_1, \gamma_2, \ldots, \gamma_q)$ is a $(1 * q)$ vector of coefficients describing the relationships between the latent variable and its causes. As such, the latent variable η is determined by a set of exogenous causes.

A measurement model can be expressed as below:

$$y = \lambda\eta + \varepsilon \tag{8.2}$$

where $y = (y_1, y_2, \ldots, y_p)$ is a $(p * 1)$ vector of several indicator variables. λ is the vector of regression coefficients, and ε' is a $(p * 1)$ vector of white noise disturbances.

When equations (8.2) and (8.3) are combined, a multivariate regression model is formed in which endogenous variables y_j, $j = 1, \ldots, p$ are *indicator variables* of a shadow economy variable η and exogenous variables x_i, $i = 1, \ldots, q$ are *cause variables* of a shadow economy variable η. A general equation can be expressed as below:

From (8.3), $\Leftrightarrow \eta = \lambda^{-1}(y - \varepsilon)$.

From (8.2) and (8.3):

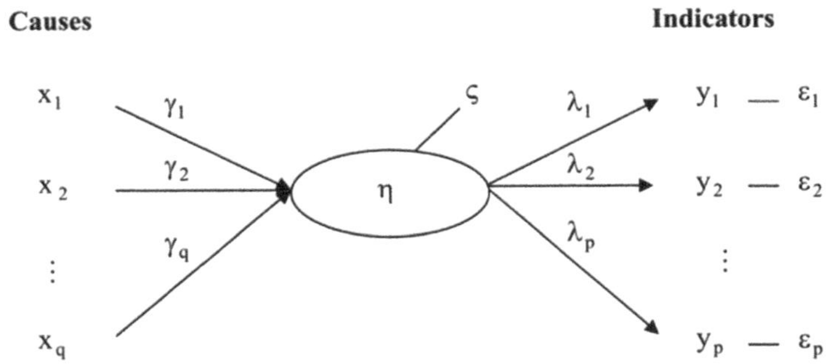

Fig. 8.1 General structure of a MIMIC model

$$\begin{aligned} \gamma' \mathrm{X} + \zeta &= \lambda^{-1}(y - \varepsilon) \\ \Leftrightarrow y &= \lambda\gamma' \mathrm{X} + \lambda\zeta + \varepsilon \\ \Leftrightarrow \mathrm{y} &= \Pi \mathrm{X} + \mathrm{z} \end{aligned} \tag{8.3}$$

For simplicity, Fig. 8.1 presents a general structure of the MIMIC model.

In summary, a MIMIC approach to estimating the shadow economy is to determine a hypothesis on a relationship between shadow economy (latent variable) and observable variables including causes and indicators. However, this approach is only to produce *a relative estimate* of the size of the shadow economy in comparison with a shadow economy at base value in a particular *base year*.

This study uses data for countries with low and average GDP per capita in the ASEAN nations including Vietnam, Laos, Cambodia, Indonesia, Malaysia, Thailand, Myanmar and the Philippines for the period from 1995 to 2014. Singapore and Brunei are not included in the sample because these two countries are at a high income level. East Timor is not included in the sample because of missing data for the research period. A MIMIC model is adopted in this study which can be illustrated as in Fig. 8.2.

Table 8.2 and Table 8.3 present descriptive statistics of cause and indicator variables for both shadow economy and corruption.

8.6 Findings

The MIMIC approach is adopted to identify and quantify the relationship between shadow economy and corruption for the ASEAN for the period from 1975 to 2014. The estimated coefficients for cause variables and indicator variables are presented in Table 8.4.

The chi-square value indicates the level of suitability of the research model to the data, and its p-value measures the probability of achieving this chi-square value. The results from the research model indicate that the reliability of the model is approximately at 90 %. In addition, the chi-square/Df which is smaller than

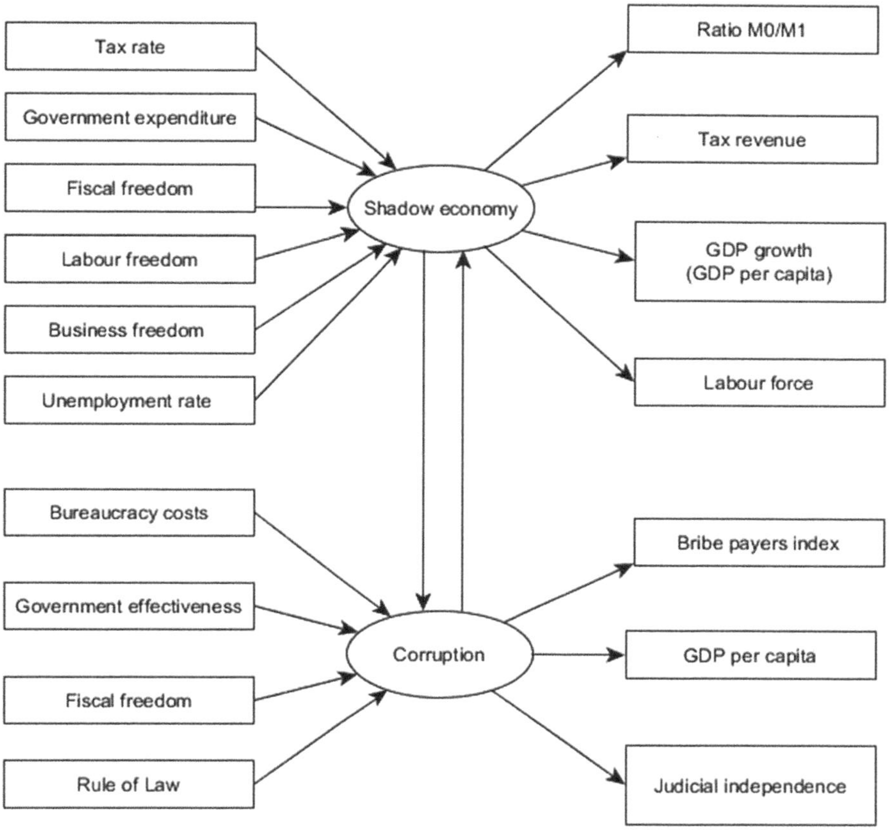

Fig. 8.2 A link between a shadow economy and a corruption: a MIMIC approach

2 indicates that the estimates are appropriate and reliable in consistence with the conclusions from Carmines and Mciver (1981). Browne and Cudeck (1993) concluded that the value of RMSEA of smaller than 0.05 indicates that the model is correctly specified, and as such, estimates are reliable and valid.

An important conclusion from the research findings is that there is a causal positive relationship between the shadow economy and corruption. This finding is consistent with the findings from other studies which concluded that the shadow economy and corruption are complements in developed countries. The findings from this study indicate that the effect from corruption on the shadow economy is greater than the effect of shadow economy on corruption.

Table 8.2 Descriptive statistics of *cause* variables and *indicator* variables for *shadow economy*

	Mean	Median	Max	Min	Std. dev.	Skewness	Kurtosis	Jarque-Bera	Obs.
Tax rate (% profits)	37.59	37.5	52.7	21.4	8.79	−0.09	2.68	0.94	160
Government expenditure	87.65	89.3	98.7	66.5	6.35	−0.77	3.379	17.04	160
Fiscal freedom	76.64	77.65	91.7	32.2	11.81	−2.02	8.21	290.69	160
Labour freedom	55.3	53.8	79.3	20	16.88	−0.72	2.87	14.15	160
Business freedom	54.14	55	85.6	20	15.07	−0.12	2.77	0.73	160
Unemployment rate (% population)	4.28	3.84	11.82	0.1	2.85	0.84	3.01	18.97	160
Ratio M_0/M_1 (%)	12.24	0.544	96.96	0.19	31.12	2.27	6.15	204	160
Tax revenue (%GDP)	10.21	11.77	19.75	0	5.64	−0.59	2.15	14.16	160
GDP growth (%)	8.27	9.36	45.18	−56.4	12.67	−1.23	8.27	226.17	160
Labour force (% population)	73.67	76.2	85.8	59.1	7.88	−0.22	1.76	11.53	160

Source: Authors' calculations

Note: Business freedom, fiscal freedom, government expenditure and *labour freedom* vary within the range of 0–100

Table 8.3 Descriptive statistics of *cause* variables and *indicator* variables for *corruption*

	Mean	Median	Max	Min	Std. dev.	Skewness	Kurtosis	Jarque-Bera	Obs.
Bureaucracy costs	4.58	4.15	8.4	1.5	1.28	0.99	3.69	29.74	160
Government effectiveness	−0.33	−0.31	1.25	−1.65	0.72	0.34	2.53	4.58	160
Fiscal freedom	76.64	77.65	91.7	32.2	11.8	−2.02	8.21	290.69	160
Rule of law	−0.55	−0.57	0.61	−1.68	0.62	0.33	2.19	7.2	160
Bribe payers index	4.13	3.8	7.4	2.3	1.05	1.34	3.96	54.28	160
GDP per capita (USD)	1971.66	1126	10422	125	2236.98	1.99	6.91	207.18	160
Judicial independence	4.32	4.3	7.3	2.3	1.02	0.71	3.07	13.48	160

Source: Authors' calculations

Note: Rule of law and *fiscal freedom* vary within the range of 0–100. *Bureaucracy costs*, *judicial independence* and *bribe payers index* vary within the range of 1–10. *Government effectiveness* varies within the range of −2.5 and 2.5

Table 8.4 Regression results

	Shadow economy	Corruption
Cause variables		
Tax rate[a]	1	
Fiscal freedom	1.952 (6.205)***	
Government expenditure	−0.167 (3.001)***	
Labour freedom	0.259 (10.916)***	
Business freedom	0.15 (6.177)***	
Unemployment rate	−0.316 (2.561)***	
Bureaucracy costs		−0.006
Government effectiveness		0.039 (4.213)***
Fiscal freedom		−0.033 (6.271)***
Rule of law		−0.03 (3.002)***
Indicator variables		
Ratio M_0/M_1[b]	1	
Tax revenue	−0.032 (2.235)***	
GDP growth	0.045	
Labour force	0.117 (6.285)***	
Bribe payers index		−0.972 (6.879)***
Judicial independence[c]		−1
GDP per capita		−2.278
A relationship between shadow economy and corruption		
Shadow economy → corruption		0.021 (9.225)***
Corruption → shadow economy		62.942 (9.495)***
Goodness-of-fit statistics		
RMSEA[d]	0.037	
Chi-square (p-value)	25.665 (0.08)	
Observations	160	
Df	87	

Source: Author calculations

Note: *** $p < 0.01$; ** $p < 0.05$; * $p < 0.10$

[a]Previous studies assume that *tax rate* is positively correlated with shadow economy. As such, its estimated coefficient is fixed

[b]The MIMIC approach requires that the estimated coefficient of one of the indicator variables is fixed. A ratio of M_0/M_1 is selected for consistency with other studies

[c]As above, *judicial independence* is selected

[d]Root mean square error of approximation

8.7 Concluding Remarks and Policy Implications

This study has been attempted to examine and quantify the link between shadow economy and corruption for the ASEAN for the period from 1995 to 2014. The MIMIC approach is used in this study. It is noted that the MIMIC approach requires a set of *cause* variables, which cause the presence of the shadow economy, and a set of *indicator* variables which are considered as the consequences of the presence of the shadow economy. On the ground of theories on the shadow economy and previous empirical studies, the *cause* variables and the *consequence* (indicator) variables have been identified and utilised in this study.

In relation to the causes of the shadow economy, *the fiscal freedom, government's expenditure, labour freedom, business freedom* and *unemployment* are all statistically correlated with the shadow economy. *Government's expenditure* and *unemployment* are negatively correlated with the shadow economy, whereas all the others have a statistically positive relationship with the shadow economy. While it may be clear from the negative relationship between government's expenditure and shadow economy, it may not be that clear for the unemployment. It can be argued that, at least for developing countries in the ASEAN, a reduction of unemployment does not guarantee for a reduction of the shadow economy. The research finding from this study indicates that a shadow economy is expected to be greater when unemployment is lower. It means, people have the jobs in an official economy who also want to join the shadow economy if their income aren't enough for living. This finding may provide evidence to support the view that reforms aiming to reduce unemployment are not necessarily associated with a reduction in the shadow economy.

In relation to corruption, *the effectiveness of the government, fiscal freedom* and *rule of law* are statistically correlated with a level of corruption. This study fails to find evidence to support the view that there is a link between *government's bureaucracy cost* and *corruption* for the ASEAN in the period from 1995 to 2014.

In particular, this study finds empirical evidence to support the view that there is a causal relationship between the shadow economy and corruption for the ASEAN for the period from 1995 to 2014. On one side, the shadow economy is positively correlated with corruption, and, on the other end, the corruption is also positively correlated with the shadow economy. These two relationships are statistically significant. In addition, it is noted that the effect of corruption into the shadow economy is more significant than the effect of shadow economy on corruption.

The findings from this study indicate that controlling shadow economy (and/or corruption) may be a better way to reduce the level of corruption (and/or shadow economy). However, for developing countries in the ASEAN, it may be more appropriate to start with the policies to reduce the corruption level than the other way round. Controlling corruption in those developing countries in the ASEAN will also mean that shadow economy is now controlled.

References

Alm J, Torgler B (2006) Culture differences and tax morale in the United States and Europe. J Econ Psychol 27:224–246

Alm J, Martinez-Vazquez J, Torgler B (2006) Russian attitudes toward paying taxes – before, during, and after the transition. Int J Soc Econ 33:832–857

Bajda C, Schneider F (2005) The shadow economies of the Asia-Pacific. Pac Econ Rev 10(3):379–401

Bjorvatn K, Soreide T (2005) Corruption and privatization. Eur J Polit Econ 21(4):903–914, Elsevier
Browne MW, Cudeck R (1993) Alternative ways of assessing model fit. In: Bollen KA, Long JS (eds) Testing structural equation models. Sage, Newbury Park, pp 445–455
Buehn A, Schneider F (2009) Institute for the Study of Labor (IZA), IZA discussion papers 4182. http://ideas.repec.org/p/iza/izadps/dp4182.html
Buehn A, Schneider F (2012) Corruption and the shadow economy: like oil and vinegar, like water and fire? Int Tax Public Financ 19:172–194
Carmines EG, McIver JP (1981) Analyzing models with unobserved variables. Sage, Beverly Hills
Choi JP, Thum M (2005) Corruption and the shadow economy. Int Econ Rev 46(3):817–836
Dell'Anno R, Schneider F (2004) The shadow economy of Italy and other OECD countries: what do we know? Department of Economics, University of Linz, Linz, Discussion paper. J Public Financ Public Choice 2005
Dell'Anno R, Schneider F (2006) Estimating the underground economy by using MIMIC models: a response to T. Breusch's critique. Working paper No 0607. University of Linz, Department of Economics, Linz
Deregulation Commission (1991) Opening of markets and competition. Report presented to German Fed. Government, Bonn
Dreher A, Kosogiannis C, McCorriston S (2007) Corruption around the world: evidence from a structural model. J Comp Econ 35(3):443–446
Dreher A, Kosogiannis C, McCorriston S (2008) Corruption around the world: evidence from a structural model. J Comp Econ 35(3):443–446
Dreher A, Kotsogiannis C, McCorriston S (2009) How do institutions affect corruption and the shadow economy? Int Tax Public Financ 16:773–796
Easterly W, Levine R (1997) Africa's growth tragedy: policies and ethnic divisions. Quart J Econ 112(4):1203–1250
Feige EL (1986) A re-examination of the 'underground economy' in the United States. IMF Staff Pap 33(4). Suppl Public Financ/Financ Publiques 49:119–136
Feige EL (ed) (1989) The underground economies: tax evasion and information distortion. Cambridge University, Cambridge
Feld L, Schneider F (2010) Survey on the shadow economy and undeclared earnings in OECD countries. Invited paper written for publication in the German Economic Review, Department of Economics, University of Linz, Linz
Friedman E et al (1999) Dodging the grabbing hand: the determinants of unofficial activity in 69 countries. World Bank discussion paper, published by J Public Econ (2000). 76(3):459–493
Gwartney J, Lawson R, Norton S (2008) Economic freedom of the world: 2008 annual report. The Fraser Institute, Data retrieved from www.freetheworld.com
Heritage Foundation (2014) Index of economic freedom, Chapter 5: Defining economic freedom. Heritage Foundation, Washington, DC
Hibbs DA Jr, Piculescu V (2005) Institutions, corruption and tax evasion in the unofficial economy. Discussion paper, Göteburg University
Hindriks J, Muthoo A, Keen M (1997) Corruption, extortion and evasion. J Public Econ 74 (3):395–430
Johnson S, Kaufmann D, Shleifer A (1997) The unofficial economy in transition. Brook Pap Econ Act 2:159–221
Johnson S, Kaufmann D, Zoido-Lobatón P (1998) Regulatory discretion and the unofficial economy. Am Econ Rev 88(2):387–392
Johnson S, Kaufmann D, Zoido-Lobatón P (1998a) Regulatory discretion and the unofficial economy. Am Econ Rev 88(2):387–392
Johnson S, Kaufmann D, Zoido-Lobatón P (1998b) Corruption, public finances and the unofficial economy. Discussion paper. The World Bank, Washington, DC
Johnson S, Kaufmann D, McMillan J, Woodruff C (1999) Why do firms hide? Bribes and unofficial activity after communism. J Public Econ 76:495–520

Mirus R, Smith RS (1997) Canada's underground economy: measurement and implications. In: Lippert O, Walker M (eds) The underground economy: global evidence of its size and impact. Fraser Institute, Vancouver

Mocan N (2004) What determines corruption? International evidence from micro data. NBER working paper 10460. National Bureau of Economic Research, Cambridge, MA

Mogensen GV, Kvist HK, Kormendi E, Pedersen S (1995) The shadow economy in Denmark 1994: measurement and results, Study No 3. Rockwool Foundation Research Unit, Copenhagen

Monopol-kommission (1998) Marktöffnung umfassend verwirklichen: Hauptgutachten 1996/97

North D (1990) Institutions, institutional changes and economic performance. Cambridge University Press, Cambridge

OECD (2002) Measuring the non-observed economy. OECD Publication, Paris

Schneider F (2006) Shadow economies and corruption all over the world: what do we really know? Economics discussion papers, No 2007–9, Kiel Institute for the World Economy. http://www.economics-ejournal.org/economics/discussionpapers/2007-9

Schneider F, Enste DH (2000) Shadow economies – size, causes, and consequences. J Econ Liter 38(1):77–114

Shleifer A, Vishny RW (1993) Corruption. Quart J Econ 108(3):599–618

Smith P (1994) Assessing the size of the underground economy: the Canadian statistical perspectives. Canadian Econ Observer, Cat. No 11–010, 3.16–33, at 3.18

Tanzi V (1998) Corruption around the world: causes, consequences, scope and cures. IMF Staff Pap 45(4):559–594

Tanzi V (1999) Uses and abuses of estimates of the underground economy. Econ J 109 (456):338–340

Torgler B, Schneider F (2009) The impact of tax morale and institutional quality on the shadow economy. J Econ Psychol 30(2):228–245

Van Rijckeghem C, Weder B (2001) Bureaucratic corruption and the rate of temptation: do wages in the civil service affect corruption and by how much? J Dev Econ 65(2):307–331

Weber Abramo C (2005) How far perceptions go. Transparency Brazil working paper. The World Bank, Washington, DC

World Bank (2014) World Bank: world development indicators definition. World Bank Data, data.worldbank.org

Chapter 9
Singapore as a 'Global City': Governance in a Challenging International Environment

Ian Patrick Austin

Abstract Singapore's success as a 'global city' focused on the free trade of goods, services and human capital into, and out of, the island nation is barely questioned by international policy and business practitioners today. The reason for this is clear; Singapore continued to attract high-quality global enterprises based on the provision of high-quality governance, human capital, communication and technology, transportation, logistical and other key infrastructure. None of this came about by accident, being the result of decade-long planning centred on turning Singapore into a truly 'global city' attracting the best 'talent' (corporate and individual) from within strategic sectors (wealth management, biotechnology, advanced manufactures, research-focused tertiary education). However, recent economic events, most notably the global financial crisis (GFC), have revealed structural cracks in this 'global city' planning that has seen the long-ruling (1959–current) People's Action Party (PAP) suffer two of its worst election results (2011 general election and 2013 by-election). Various political and policy opponents to the ruling elite have successfully highlighted that the 'global city' model has come at the cost of growing inequality and a real sense of displacement amongst citizens. In examining Singapore, nominally one of the truly great benefactors of globalisation, the author highlights that key factors in this processes, including free trade and human mobility, must always be constantly secured through the ascent of the polity if it is to be sustainable.

9.1 Introduction

For the second time since 2000, Singapore quickly dropped into recession in 2008 following a sharp decline in American consumer, business and travel demand, as a direct consequence of the global financial crisis (GFC 2007–2009). This was despite concerted policy effort since the 1997 Asian financial crisis and the 2001 global electronics slump by the state's leadership which has worked hard to

I.P. Austin (✉)
Edith Cowan University, Perth, WA, Australia
e-mail: i.austin@ecu.edu.au

H.G. Djajadikerta, Z. Zhang (eds.), *A New Paradigm for International Business*,
Springer Proceedings in Business and Economics, DOI 10.1007/978-981-287-499-3_9

re-create Singapore as a global city[1], at the forefront of global best practice across various services and research-oriented sectors (with reforms across the financial, multinational enterprise (MNE) engagement, education, research and others). Following the 2001 electronic sector-derived national recession, Singapore's elite, most notably the current prime minister (PM) Lee Hsien Loong, led a series of in-depth macroeconomic reviews concerning the country's future economic direction. Following a detailed consultation process with leading global corporate and academic figures, this policy introspection concluded that Singaporean economic development would be best served through achieving a 'global city' status, including an expanded policy of financial sector internationalisation, higher levels of MNE engagement to achieve overall sectorial diversification and the redevelopment of Singapore's urban space to incorporate these activities (Marina Bay Financial District) and new social, cultural (New National Reference Library, Esplanade Theatre on the Bay) and sporting infrastructure (Formula 1 Racing and the new National Stadium). Through the state directive of transforming Singapore into a 'global city', a form of *uber*-globalisation was embraced at all policy levels to ensure Singapore would serve as an ideal economic and social platform for MNEs and local innovative enterprises including multiple state-owned enterprises (for studies on Singapore as a global city, see Sanyal 2007; Tan 2009a; da Cunda 2010, 2012b; Lim 2012; Saitharan 2012; Seng 2012). The policy, however, in no way signalled a weakening of the state's hold over the domestic business community. The former prime minister Lee Kuan Yew built into the political DNA of the People's Action Party (PAP) the essential need to control domestic commercial life as a means to cut off the alternative political oppositions' human and financial capital resources. This PAP political-commercial nexus continues unabated under Lee's son who is the current PM, Lee Hsien Loong (since 2004). At the peak of this state-control-over-domestic-business regime are the state-owned enterprises, the Government Investment Corporation (GIC) and Temasek Holdings (TH), the two large investment vehicles whose boards include Singapore's political, policy and select business elite, with PM Lee holding the position of chair of the GIC (Neo and Chen 2007; da Cunda 2010).

The rapid free fall in Singapore's economic growth in 2008 exposed the limitations of this policy approach (having already been subject to criticism to no effect by the highly respected Ngiam Tong Dow in 2006) and in turn has opened up unprecedented political opposition to the PAP's domestic and international

[1] The concept of the global city in economic terms incorporates the free flow of commercial activity, trade and professional skills into, and out of, the city in a highly efficient manner. Quality airports, ports and internal transport facilitate the presence of corporate headquarters and manufacturing/innovation centres and are supported by high-quality education, medical, sporting and cultural infrastructure. 'Its simple definition is that it is a city that is an important nodal point in the global economic system...A global city has to be global in all its dimensions, not just in its economic and infrastructure characteristics. And it cannot be a derivative of other cities. It has to be unique in a number of ways, so as to give a competitive edge internationally' (da Cunda 2012a, pp. 17 & 20).

economic strategy (Giam 2010; Lim 2012). Despite a decade of significant government expenditure amounting to tens of billions of dollars aimed at national economic diversification through the establishment of new sectors in biotechnology, medicine, industrial design, advanced manufactures, the arts and others, the Singapore economy proved no more capable of handling external economic shock than its pre-2001 model. Unlike in 2001, however, the rapid rebound of the national economy post-2009 has not provided cover for the PAP from mounting criticism that their macro-strategic policy settings were misplaced. The principal task of this paper will be to examine the Singapore leaderships' open embrace of globalisation through a 'global city' policy dynamic and ask how it can continue to legitimise this position, to secure a sustainable mandate with Singaporeans, when that same policy is seen by a significant number of citizens (40 % based on the 2011 general election results) to have failed to provide a stable and equitable economic environment for the broader polity for over a decade. The two severe economic downturns (2001, 2008) are utilised here not to detract from the fact that the global economic forces impacting upon Singapore are constant, for Singaporean citizens have long recognised this fact, but to highlight a period in time in which the Singapore government's embrace of *uber*-globalisation and their desire to forge ahead as a global city has been openly exposed as being a process beyond their 'control'. Singapore's very existence of course derives from long-term global economic forces as Turnbull (1989) make clear, and this will continue to be the case as Saitharan (2012) makes clear. So in choosing to examine the changing nature of Singapore's governance through the impact of two economic downturns on the self-proclaimed 'global city', this author acknowledges the limitations arising.

9.2 A Global City: Which Type? And Impact on Domestic Politics

> For Singapore, becoming a global city is not merely an aspiration. It is a pre-requisite for our survival... Being open allows us to connect and trade with the rest of the world, and, in doing so, attract the best investments and talents to Singapore.... This is how, for example, despite having zero oil production, we became a global leader in oil trading, oil refining, oil-rig building, and so on. (Deputy Prime Minister Wong Kan. Seng 2012, p. 6)

Since the 1990s, Singapore's policymakers have openly and consistently identified the island state as a global city and as such sought to attract innovation-oriented MNEs by touting Singapore's advantageous location as a regional and global centre (Sanyal 2007; Bhaskaran 2009a, b; Ghesquiere 2007; Neo and Chen 2007; Ngiam 2006; Ong 2009; Tan 2009a, b; Saitharan 2012). Policymakers identified a strategic over-reliance on a particular economic sector – electronics – which had led to overexposure to global fluctuations in this and related sectors (such as air freight logistics) as amply highlighted by the 2001 downturn. To offset this exposure, Singapore's policymaking elite, in an act of macro-risk management, have undertaken extensive 'global city' planning processes aimed at enhancing the capabilities of existing sectors such as finance, tourism and medicine, whilst nurturing new ones, such as biotechnology, specialised design, innovative engineering and most controversially gambling (Sanyal 2007; da Cunda 2010). MNEs seen as being at the leading edge of their respective industries have consequently been courted and offered favourable policy environments to encourage them to either upgrade existing operations to even higher-value-adding activities or to headquarter themselves in Singapore through tax, infrastructure and state incentives (advanced manufactures, finance, logistics, medical services, gambling and technology).

The PAP elite have taken a leading role in selecting those key sectors sought for their innovative processes through direct state investment via bodies such as the GIC and TH. Bhaskaran (2009a, p. 83) places Singapore's movements towards a global city status within the broader global trends:

> The global economy is increasingly a network economy that links different global cities all over the world. Each of these global cities is like a node that switches all kinds of flows, be it flows of people, capital, ideas, telecommunications or tourists. These are nodal points, and what is important is that they create a lot of value. People in such cities can generate a lot of income, and, therefore welfare, if a city succeeds in becoming and maintaining itself as a regional hub. That is what is in it for us.

With the achievement of a global city status, so the policy prescription of the PAP cabinet throughout the first decade of the 2000s goes, comes a matrix of self-reinforcing economies of scale as professionals across a spectrum of industries are attracted to the city because for the very presence of the 'other/s'. That, in turn, MNEs from multifaceted sectors are attracted to such environments because of this self-reinforcing dynamic and diverse professional ecosystem generates both the talent and markets needed for their products and services (Lim and Lee 2010).

Ngiam (2006, p. 196) asserts that global 'cities compete on ideas, and ideas spring from the mind of the individual. Unlike oil from the ground, ideas derive from knowledge. And knowledge is acquired from learning' and 'they thrive because size alone is not the key determinant of success, but competiveness through knowledge acquisition via education, training of labour and stable good governance'. The global city theory advocates that the presence of a wide range of academic/research theorists and professional practitioners should create critical knowledge which provides for sustainable economic and social progress. These cities with extensive human capital in banking, other financial institutions, universities, legal circles, think-tanks and media enterprises would avoid the pitfalls of an over-reliance on a singular or a few sectors. This has been Singapore's explicit elite policy objective over the past decade and a half (Bhaskaran 2009a, b; Ghesquiere 2007).

Just how wrong this theory proved was apparent to all as New York, and more specifically Wall Street, the archetype of the global city with multitude of banks, financial institutions, universities, think-tanks and intellectual capital, far from negating risk, was instead the epicentre of the GFC. Equally so, Singapore's effort to develop into a global city proved no safeguard as its financial sector, despite applying and maintaining arguably the highest financial and corporate governance standards, suffered significantly in 2008 in the wake of financial collapses elsewhere. Other economic growth pillars, from finance services, wealth management, biotechnology, medical research and services, transport (air, freight, port) to tourism and leisure, built up over the previous decade through PAP elite support and billions of dollars in public investment and were consequently expected to buoy the national economy in the event of one sector alone staggering, all slide into economic downturn (Basu 2010; YoSS 2013). Serious questions that were in fact being asked prior to the GFC by long-time policymakers such as Ngiam (2006) now took full voice as policy thinkers and activists (found almost exclusively online due to their exclusion from the mainstream PAP-dominated media) questioned the validity of continuing the global city strategy, including the proactive policy to attract international MNEs (Lim 2009; Giam 2010).

Singapore's global city policy prescriptions are part of an extensive international consultation, including highly paid academic advice through Harvard University and Stanford University; it has taken little time for considerable domestic questioning to emerge regarding the validity of global city policy and the appropriateness of expertise garnered in Boston and San Francisco to the current lives and future well-being of a Singaporean (Australian Broadcasting Corporation, 28th March, 2009). The PAP has countered this critique by pointing to the fact that whilst they garner international advice from elite Western sources, it is a process of garnering policy advice only and in no way signifies an abrogation of policy sovereignty and that the continued prominence of state-owned enterprise throughout the national economy shows the PAP cabinet are no blind adherents to any doctrine other than the 'national interests' (da Cunda 2012b).

Despite the forceful nature of the PAP's response, including the prime minister's 2011 principal election speech which largely centred on responding to his government critics, the vocal and forceful nature of the criticism directed at the Singapore government post-GFC, and PAP's subsequent underwhelming 2011 general electoral results (the PAP's popular vote decline to 60.14 % compared to 66.6 % in the 2006 general election) shows that increasing numbers of Singaporean citizens expect to have meaningful input into the government's long-term economic strategy (da Cunda 2012b). The third generation cabinet of PM Lee simply does not have the same founding legitimacy of the Lee Kuan Yew cabinets or the solid backing of the second-generation Goh Chok Tong cabinets which themselves consisted of Lee Sr. and long-serving policy heavyweights such as Tony Tan (one-time deputy prime minister and holder of several crucial cabinet portfolios).

Whilst the PAP retained office in 2011, it has become clear that the 2009 GFC downturn and the 2011 general election marked a significant change to the intellectual environment in which Singapore's future governance will be structured. Post-GFC has seen an increasing number of Singaporeans challenging and questioning the PAP over its core governance foundation: economic management through transformation into an *uber*-global city.

Sylvia Lim, prior to the 2011 national election and as a Worker's Party member of the Parliament for Aljunied GRC, has been one of the most consistent, forceful and articulate of these critics. She has asked: why is it that whilst the Economic

Strategies Committee (ESC) Report of 2010 identified one of the 'key goals' of government as being the advancement of Singapore as a Global City in the same year (2010) the Economist Intelligence Unit ranked Singapore 53rd out of 140 cities in liveability, with the cultural and artistic environment in particular detrimentally affecting the ranking outcome? How can Singapore be a global city if creativity remains politically stifled, particularly given that creativity is crucial to attracting the entrepreneurship needed to fulfil such lofty ambitions? She has particularly attacked PAP-developed educational and cultural systems, 'Some of the contributing factors, in my view, are an education system and culture that reward conformity and obedience, the fear of failure and the drastic consequences of failure' (p. 25), whilst asking which type of global city the PAP has in mind when it has failed to (in her view and at least 40 % of the electorate according to 2011 GE results) sufficiently address the continued exodus of Singaporean talent to other shores, concerns over high levels of foreign immigration, well-documented strains on public infrastructure and housing, growing wealth inequality and perceived failures in looking after the aged (Lim 2012, pp. 25–290) (Table 9.1).

Sylvia Lim is but one member of a Singaporean polity that has effectively questioned and challenged the PAP's economic legitimacy foundations, and her effectiveness in doing so must be viewed within the broader context of post-GFC Asian political and intellectual shifts. Singapore's long-term political paradigm is hardly alone in Asia in being challenged with 2014 witnessing extensive protests on the streets of Hong Kong and rejections of traditional political powers through the ballot boxes of Taipei and Indonesia (Murray 2014). How can anyone today seriously argue that scholars of Harvard, Yale, Chicago, Oxford and Western others (commonly referred to in policy circles as Washington consensus) know any more about the 'right' path of economic development than Asian and international analysts found in Singapore, Beijing, Shanghai, Taipei, Seoul and others (Mahbubani 2008)? Clearly, the long-term political implications of the GFC-derived intellectual power shift will be profound as Singapore's elite have historically consistently leant on US academic and policy elite thinking, to justify the PAP policymaking model. The PAP has utilised the free market ideology of Harvard and Chicago as the legitimacy language for the creation of a global city-state entirely focused on *uber*-globalisation, with competition and free trade openly advocated for international externalities and consumption. As a trade-dependent port city, the Singapore elite frequently proclaim that free trade has raised not only Singapore to new heights, but is doing the same across Asia (Mahbubani 2008). However, their domestic critics are now asking: if this is the case, why aren't residents of the global city given greater free internal domestic competition in business which remains restricted through state-owned enterprise dominance? And how can it be that if the free trade of goods and services is universally beneficial for a global city, but the same does not equally apply to open political/policy competition which remains under continuing state restriction (Saitharan 2012; da Cunda 2012b; Lim 2012)?

Table 9.1 Singapore population, equity, workforce, education and immigration shifts in the 2000s

The Singapore Yearbook of Statistics 2013 reveals the PAP's political opposition has chosen fertile ground upon which to sustain a political campaign	
Demographics	1.8 Population Growth 2007–2013 and 3.1 Population and Growth Rate: reveals the substantive increase in foreign migration to Singapore over the 5-year period
Work force changes	1.11 Employment, 1.12 Income from Work
	4.5 Average Monthly Income from Work, 5.1 Labour Force, 5.2 Age-Specific Resident Labour Force Participation Rates and 5.5 5.6 Employment Residents Aged 15 Years and Over by Occupation: collectively reveal stagnation in the income of the lower 50 percentile of the working age population. Changing labour force structures (5.1) has impacted negatively on Singapore's working class 'heartland'
Decline in 'blue-collar' manufacturing	The picture is in fact one familiar to Australia, one of disappearing mass production manufacturing jobs (5.5), replaced by imports and advanced manufactures produced by a significantly lower number of high-skilled employees and the ascendancy of low-skilled service employment for those without a tertiary education
Growing inequality	4.7 GINI Coefficient Among Resident Employed Households: highlights the growing gap in income between the top 10 percentile and the remaining 90 percentile. Collective analysis of these figures highlights structural inequity (4.5)
Tertiary education	Tertiary education has become the default education level attainment for middle-class Singaporeans 20.1: readers should note that these figures exclude significant numbers of Singaporeans in international university programmes inside and outside of Singapore
Affordable housing for citizens and immigration	Access to affordable housing for citizens (section 12) has created increasing anxiety over Singapore's high foreign immigration levels. Given that the immigrant population has doubled from 754,000 in 2000 to 1,494,000 in 2012 whilst over the same period the Singapore citizen/PR population only grew from 3.73 million to 3.8 million at the same time (3.1), this anxiety hardly surprising

Source: Department of Statistics Singapore. Yearbook of Statistics 2013. www.singstat.gov

In sum, the body of critical policy analysis that has emerged in opposition to the PAP's economic strategy since the GFC, and formally expressed during the 2011 general election, is for the first time putting forward a *sustained* challenge to the PAP's own specific strategic positioning of Singapore being a singular type of *uber*-global city.

9.3 The Global City as a New National Economic Strategy: The 2001 Electronics Recession and Rapid Economic Growth (2002–2007)

Whilst the severity of the Asian financial crisis (1997–1998) moved the Singaporean government to initiate the global city concept as a national economic strategy, it was the 2001 global electronics recession that caught the nation's policymakers by complete surprise and led to even further analysis and reshaping of the national economic policy settings. Coming just 5 years after Singapore's first economic downturn under PAP rule (established 1959), which itself had broken decades of uninterrupted high levels of economic growth, meant that the political legitimacy impact was far more profound than that had resulted from the Asian financial crisis. The severity of the economic decline and the negative politics of mass retrenchments in 'heartland' electorates in which most of the factories were located resulted in the PAP government committing to even greater concerted efforts to see economic diversification into higher-value-added sectors, a key platform within the global city strategy, come to fruition.

The extent to which the electronics downturn wrong-footed Singapore's elite was fully reflected in the fact that the annual budget of that year (February 2001) made no provisions for a downturn and as a result had to be adjusted (Koh and Mariano 2006, p. 5). In particular, government leadership was surprised by the extent of the job losses. Foreign electronics MNEs that senior government policymakers had actively courted and extended much policy, goodwill and resources towards had quickly abandoned production in the city-state. The PAP's self-stated ability to engage with the world's MNE leadership counted for naught as the global electronics leadership fought for their sheer survival in 2001–2003. Most moved without hesitation to China to take advantage of cheaper labour and infrastructure options (Crispin 2009). It was a brutal lesson for the Singapore elite on the speed and mobility of a sector totally dependent on global supply chains attuned keenly to any fluctuation in market conditions.

As a direct result, the Singaporean government moved to select specific MNE manufactures, industry and service sectors identified as being at the forefront of future global innovation and therefore deemed acceptable within a global city landscape, targeting them through the Economic Development Board (EDB), the GIC and other state agencies. It moved policy setting to enable it to pick sectorial winners rather than specific MNEs. For example, the government established a biotechnology hub at One North (located geographically in proximity to the National University of Singapore) by providing the infrastructure and actively recruiting international research stars and their teams to the campus and at the same time promoting new arms of financial services by attracted wealth management services through legislation and taxation arrangements and advanced education-training via establishing Singapore Management University (SMU). The government made it clear that only those MNEs willing to bring internationally benchmarked innovative practice, such as Boeing, General Electric, Siemens

Nixdorf and others, would obtain substantive Singapore state support. Advanced manufactures, financial services, logistics and international service sectors would all be heavily invested in and compelled to be at the upper echelon of the international innovation chain or be cast adrift (Neo and Chen 2007, p. 253; da Cunda 2010).

From 2001 onwards, the PAP government utilised vast sums of the national savings and government-managed investment resources (over $S150 billion in the GIC alone) in an attempt to end the national economy's over-reliance on mass manufactures and to reinvigorate global-oriented services (most notably financial services, medical care and international tourism) whilst introducing new high-end services across medical, scientific, niche engineering, financial and creative industries (Chua 2007, p. 13). Then, deputy Prime Minister (1990–2004) Lee Hsien Loong, the cabinet and the government's agencies all actively engaged the leadership of Singapore-headquartered MNEs and those MNEs residing outside but identified as key players within innovative sectors through a series of cabinet member-chief executive officer level consultative committees. As stated previously, this engagement of MNE had not only economic but political reasoning. A strong MNE sector means that the PAP has no reliance on the local private business community for any political or financial support. These consultative committees gave company executives not only direct input into Singapore's policy prescription aimed at enhancing current MNE operations as well as attracting new ventures, but also into key national development goals across urban planning and tertiary education and training. All with the view to ensuring Singapore obtained the expressed branding of their city as a global one at the forefront of international operations by the world's top corporate leaders and enterprises. Indeed, it is doubtful that MNE executives enjoy as much input into any other nation's policy framework as they have under Lee's stewardship in Singapore (Lim and Lee 2010). For example, the use of consultative committees ensured that the Swiss-giant bank, UBS, located important wealth management operations on the island as the Singapore government deemed it a clear global innovative leader in wealth management services and as part of the far larger objective of diversifying the Singapore financial sector and positioning the nation as a viable alternative to Switzerland and other havens for the rich. As part of the consultative process, the Singapore government introduced legislation to ensure that UBS's wealthy clients are ensured absolute confidentiality (Lim 2009; Ngiam 2006).

Another policy emphasis of the Lee-driven policy review was to shift the nation towards an 'aggressive pro-growth attitude', and between 2004 and 2007, corporate tax slashed (from 26 % to 20 %), net investment in advance manufactures rose (from S$7.5 billion in 2003 to $8.3 billion in 2004 and $8.5 billion in 2005) and massive state and private international investments in two integrated resort casinos (Marina Bay Sands IR owned by the Sands group based in Las Vegas and Sentosa Island IR owned by the Genting Group based in Malaysia) were approved despite public resistance (and opened their doors in mid-2010). The result was GDP growth averaging 7.6 % between 2004 and 2007 and significant reduction in unemployment (4.8 % in September 2003 to 2.7 % in 2006) (Chua 2007, pp. 7–16; MITI

Singapore; MAS Singapore). Lee assured doubters that these significant policy shifts and the subsequent public investments undertaken represented Singapore's best bet at avoiding future economic recessions generated by external economic shocks (Bhaskaran 2009a; Tan 2009a, b). Collectively, these moves began to be shaped into the 'global city' policy framework: a space for international-oriented individuals and enterprise backed by a supportive government delivering a high-quality lifestyle, education and urban environment.

The impact of the 2001 electronic MNE exodus and the subsequent PAP-concerted redirection of the national economic strategy, however, must be viewed beyond the economic parameters and placed in the sphere of political legitimacy. The ruling PAP places sound long-term economic strategy and management alongside national security as the key legitimacy basis on which its monopoly on political power rests. The resulting mass unemployment in the manufacturing and logistics 'heartlands' of Jurong, Woodlands and Tampines during the 2001 electronics slump caused a significant political loss of face for the ruling elite. And whilst the Singapore economy emerged from the 2001 recession to enjoy a 5-year period (2001–2007) of robust national economic growth, a new caution had entered the political landscape. In a 2007 speech, the now PM Lee Hsien Loong stated that Singapore's success was attributed to 'a willingness to work hard, make changes and adapt to the world as it is and not as we wish it to be' (Neo and Chen 2007, p. 15). Whilst for outsiders this statement might seem innocuous, it is in fact a significant change in the political economy rhetoric for the PAP leadership. The founding patriarch of the party, Lee Kuan Yew, never hesitated to state that he and his cabinet colleagues had *forged* the Singapore national economy through sheer political will: that they alone had the combined capacity to create sustained wealth and prosperity. Lee Hsien Loong in stating that Singapore would have to *adapt* to international economic forces well beyond its sovereignty was stating the obvious and appealing to Singaporeans' well-known pragmatism, but in doing so, he was also ceding core PAP political ground. If the PAP did not have full leverage over the newly restructured global city economy at all times, and in fact at crucial times like the 2001 and 2008 recessions the PAP was primarily adapting to global forces beyond its control, how could it continue to claim a monopoly on political power (including complete control over mainstream media and the ability to call elections at short notice with abbreviated campaigns)? Further, if the PAP cabinet members were not the full masters of Singapore's economic destiny, how could they continue to justify their salaries, which are on a scale like no other democratic polity? Indeed, such has been the vocal nature of Singaporean citizens' calls for these salaries to be reined in over the last decade that Lee Kuan Yew and the senior PAP have consistently felt the need to forcefully defend this policy as better than the widespread political corruption seen in other nations (Giam 2010). They have been limited in their ability to quell criticism that the scale of these salaries simply disassociates them from the life of the average Singaporean citizen.

9.4 The Singapore Recession of 2008–2009: The Vulnerability of Being a Global City Exposed

Like national leadership globally, Singapore's PAP never saw the Wall Street financial debacle, the subsequent expansion of events into a full-blown global financial crisis (GFC) and a subsequent collapse in consumer demand in American and European markets (Bhaskaran 2009a, b; Basu 2010; Giam 2010). Singapore's $S248 billion economy, consistently praised for its open exposure to the international economy, scraped in a 1.1 % growth rate for the year 2008, down from a very respectable 7.7 % growth in 2007. It then proceeded to shrink by −14 % in the first quarter of 2009 (Bloomberg in The Australian, various). What shocked most observers more than the scale of the economic downturn was the sheer speed of the decline (Chong 2009, p. 291; see Table 9.2). Multinational and domestic enterprises immediately began reengineering and enacting retrenchments as their export orders evaporated (see Table 9.3). Singapore's Creative Technologies Ltd., a large domestic technology firm often cited by the government as a model of Singaporean enterprise and innovative potential, announced a particularly brutal blow in cuts to its workforce by 2700 in 2008 as international orders dried up.

Whilst the PAP would point to the fact that the origins of the recession lay elsewhere, the quality, depth and sustainability of policy critique aimed at the government regarding Singapore's long-term economic strategy, the almost obsessive pursuit of global city status, highlight the fact that the recession itself simply revealed deeper underlying concerns amongst highly credentialed observers. In this the PAP has only itself to blame. Its failure to promote the development of an indigenous non-state enterprise sector to balance out the predominance of MNEs and state-owned enterprises has been a subject of critique amongst economic policy thinkers for decades to no effect. Lee Kuan Yew's desire to ensure that no independent competing business class, a class of potential political rivals, emerged equally capable to the PAP apparatchik in managing the national economy had been exposed as leaving the city-state vulnerable to the lack of loyalty inherent in highly mobile MNEs. Even at the height of the 2002–2007 economic expansion, some were alarmed at the country's lack of domestically driven enterprise/entrepreneurial activity and the corresponding high level of exposure to global economic fluctuations. Chong (2006. p. 269) stated:

> With a broad lens one can begin to identify the signs of a maturing capitalist economy. Structural unemployment, the disappearance of low-skilled jobs, the economic marginalization of the old and less educated, and the widening income gap between the haves and the have nots, all suggest that the neo-capitalist processes are deeply embedded in the national economy and are, consequently, making the domestic workforce and industries vulnerable to the capricious forces of globalization.

Just prior to the GFC, Singaporean policy thinkers had, at different times, made their concerns clear over the economy's considerable exposure to a US economic downturn. Bhaskaran (2007, p. 27) with considerable insight stated, 'If both business spending and consumer spending in the US go down, then we are in

Table 9.2 Singapore's third quarter 2008 decline into technical recession

Non-oil exports (electronics and pharmaceuticals worst affected)	−8.5 % total −11.4 % manufacturing
Tourism visitor numbers	−6 %
Retail trade (motor vehicles excluded)	2.5 % (compared to 8 % in 2007)
Employment	Over 2000 retrenchments with most in manufacturing and finance
	The Development Bank of Singapore cuts 900 staff
Quarter growth rate	−0.6 %

Source: Chong (2009)

Table 9.3 Singapore sectorial growth rates 2008 year-on-year % change

Total	1.1
Goods-producing industries	−1.0
Manufacturing	−4.1
Construction	20.3
Service-producing industries	4.7
Wholesale and retail trade	2.6
Transport and storage	3.1
Hotels and restaurants	1.2
Information and communications	7.2
Financial services	5.5
Business services	7.4

Ministry of Trade and Industry, Singapore, www.miti.gov.sg

trouble'. The PAP government, on the occasions when it did deem a response necessary, did so with the party line that the PAP knew best. As it was, Bhaskaran's scenario was to play out exactly to Singapore's detriment in 2008–2009. For a society in which the cultural concept of 'face' is so important, the fact that the PAP government had not foreseen the GFC-derived recession, and indeed had publically and forcefully dismissed highly credentialed analysts like Ngiam (2006) and Bhaskaran (2007) in the years immediately prior, struck squarely at its legitimacy (Giam 2010; da Cunda 2012b).

With no signs of meaningful economic recovery in early 2009, PM Lee warned that Singapore would continue to suffer throughout 2009:

> The recession is a global one, and we must expect to see exports and growth remain negative for more months, and perhaps for the whole year. (Asean Affairs 2009)

He and his cabinet responded by introducing a $S20.5 billion ($US13.7 billion) stimulus package equivalent to 8 % of Singapore's GDP, within which his government included $S5.8 billion to spur bank lending, $S5.1 billion to help save jobs, $S2.6 billion in tax measures and grants for business, $S4.4 billion in infrastructure spending and $S2.6 billion for households. Most notably, $S4.9 billion of the package came from government reserves, the first time Singapore's policymakers have ever resorted to such a measure. It could be argued that the amount was not significant when comparing it to Singapore's massive foreign reserves ($S187 billion by year's end 2008), but the symbolism was noted (Asia Wall Street Journal online various). Critics of the stimulus package largely reflected those of CIMB-GK economist Song Seng Wu: it was 'too focused in terms of targeting specific areas, rather than taking a helicopter approach to helping everyone in this kind of worst-case scenario of 5 % contractions'. (http://onlinewsj.com/article/SB123265678165707363.html).

Basu Das (2010) makes the assessment that the stimulus package was crucial in seeing Singapore drag itself out of a dramatic economic decline in the first half of 2009 and return to growth in the second half of 2009 (see Table 9.3) and throughout 2010. Whilst this is unquestionably true, it is equally so that global economic conditions overall were improving at this time. What is beyond dispute is that the PAP's position of holding no public debt, particularly when compared with Europe's Euro area and the United States of America, did provide the island nation with a capital and reputation buffer during the GFC and will continue to provide into the future a distinct competitive advantage for the city-state. How that competitive advantage should be sustained and utilised in the development of Singapore as a global city, one that must have essential global human and capital connections, is the contested political and policy space now being debated within Singaporean elite circles. This paper will now go on to examine two key areas that the PAP has utilised to define Singapore as 'global city' that challenges the PAP to develop policies that incorporate *all* citizens into national progress or cede further ground to its political opponents: state capitalism-global finance and government-MNE engagement policy (Table 9.4).

9.5 State Capitalism Meets Global Finance

Singapore's position as a global city hinges on its current status as an international financial centre. This has not come through liberal market forces as Tan and Lim (2007, p 73) make clear:

> Unlike Hong Kong, Singapore developed as an international financial centre mainly through active government policies... One common policy that both governments share is the view that tight regulation and corporate governance are key elements that contribute to their status as international financial centres.

The state institutions at the heart of the government's management of the financial sector include the Monetary Authority of Singapore (MAS) – concerned with short-term changes in the money market and the stability of the Singapore dollar and the Government Investment Corporation (GIC) – which manages long-term strategic state investments, both locally and internationally. Further, the government has promoted Singapore as a key niche player, offering private banking and wealth management expertise. To achieve this, it has actively imported foreign

Table 9.4 Singapore's 2009 progressive economic performance

1st quarter	−9.4 %
2nd quarter	3.2 %
3rd quarter	0.9 %
4th quarter	3.5

Source: Ministry of Trade and Industry, Singapore, www.miti.gov.sg

talent through a favourable visa and skilled migration scheme, along with a rapid expansion of domestic talent through financial engineering and law courses at local tertiary institutions, most notably Singapore Management University (SMU) (Koh and Mariano 2006; Choy 2010). The Singapore government's success in building the Shenton Way and Marina Bay into international finance hubs is well documented (da Cunda 2010), with the number of foreign financial institutions in Singapore standing at 425 at end-2013 and the growth of the sector as a whole over the last 5 years documented in Table 9.5.

Once the financial crises began to spread beyond Wall Street, in the second half of 2007 and deepened throughout 2008:

> Singapore, closely tied to the global economy, could not escape the impact. Although local banks emerged largely unscathed because of limited exposure to the so-called 'toxic assets', segments of the financial service sector more sensitive to market trends were affected such as the trading stocks, shares and bonds, foreign exchange trading activities, and fund management activities. The local stock-market index has dropped by over 40 percent from the peak of October 2007. (Chong 2009, p. 292)

Having the world's highest levels of capital ratio saving, there was never any real concern as to Singapore's domestic bank ability to survive the GFC turmoil, although not without dramatic reductions in profitability and substantive staff reductions. The Developmental Bank of Singapore (DBS) for instance announced 900 job cuts in early January 2009, in a dramatic turnaround from only six months previously when it was openly recruiting. This was despite the fact that in January 2008, the government had moved to shore up the country's reputation as a well-governed and well-regulated financial entity by strictly applying the new Basel Capital Accord (III). Prior to March 2007, the MAS had actually lowered the tier one capital adequacy ratio (CAR) for local banks from 7 % to 6 % whilst the total CAR requirement remained unchanged at 10 %. Whilst the theoretical aim of these regulatory changes was to free capital for more efficient use in the national economy, in practice, the Singaporean banks were never in any real risk of default as they hold capital ratios well in excess of international requirements. The government was simply determined to highlight Singapore's commitment to international best practice as a global financial city. It was to be the magnitude of state savings investment vehicles under the GIC, TH and other state investment vehicles that cushioned the Singapore Exchange (SGX) from an otherwise far more severe GFC-derived downturn.

The Singapore government also sought to utilise the GFC to gain greater stakes in key international financial sector institutions (along with property and industry

Table 9.5 Total assets and liabilities of financial institutions (year's end)

	2007 ($ mil)	2011 ($ mil)	2012 ($ mil)
Commercial banks	582,859.0	855,811.5	911,767.9
Merchant banks	89,070.2	87,851.0	92,411.0
Asian currency	906,991.0	1,019,336.0	1,093,239.0

To examine trends in the number of financial institutions in Singapore, reference Table 17.7 pages 202–203 with particular attention to the substantial level of fund management institutional growth between 2007 (97) and 2013 (158)
Department of Statistics Singapore. Singapore in Figures 2013. www.singstat.gov.sg
Department of Statistics Singapore. Yearbook of Statistics 2013. www.singstat.gov.sg

investments) as major US and European banks sought capital injections throughout 2008 and 2009 at most favourable terms to the investor. In effect, the Singapore government was attempting to diversify and deepen its portfolio investments in global finance through distress buying. In doing so, it aimed to make them less weighted towards domestic state-owned, or state-linked, enterprises. In doing so, Singapore's elite were following the very same path taken by US and European investors at the time of the Asian financial crisis in 1997–1998. The short-term results, however, opened up a sustained barrage of criticism as the GIC and TH took significant losses resulting from their investments in Western financial firms (and in US property investments). Temasek Holdings suffered a $US2.3 billion dollar short-term loss on its Merrill Lynch investment, or a 31 % reduction in total assets from April to November 2008, leaving it with a then asset base of $US127 billion. The GIC also experienced significant short-term reduction in assets due to poorly timed investments into UBS and Citibank (Crispin 2009). The Singapore government responded, stating that it is unconcerned by immediate losses of any singular investments as collectively they were deemed part of a broader long-term strategic investment in establishing Singapore as a 'global financial city'. As is the case with London and New York, Singapore's aim was to be both a residence for significant fund groups and holder of key worldwide financial assets. Further, both TH and the GIC were more than capable of managing the short-term reductions in value to achieve long-term returns (no one argued with this narrow analysis as the GIC alone at the time held over $US150 billion in its portfolio) (Basu Das 2010).

The stated position of the government has not prevented unprecedented public criticism of the government investment strategy during and post-GFC, as Singaporean citizens openly expressed the view that this was their money and not the PAP's assets and as such any loss over any period was unacceptable. The fact that most of the losses were revealed by the Securities Exchange Commission (SEC) of the United States rather than the Singapore government itself, and no one at senior PAP levels has been held accountable, just added fuel to the domestic critic's calls that the PAP was out of touch with the populace. This dialogue exchange, through a communication medium (blogs and online forums) not controlled by the government, highlights a gap between the PAP leadership and the views of a significant body of Singaporeans who take a keen interest in citizenship and the financial affairs of the state. The fact that these individuals articulated in a highly professional manner a different vision for Singapore as a global financial city, one with far more domestic transparency and with higher levels of direct accountability to that enacted by the government, means that the PAP's policy approach is no longer widely seen in monopoly terms. As a result, since 2008, Singaporeans have found their voice online to forcefully express the view that they think is unacceptable that they need to find out from the *New York Times* rather than the *Straits Times* that their government investment vehicles have lost hundreds of millions of dollars in the United States and that they continued to be denied full transparency in relation to nominally public funds (Giam 2010; da Cunda 2012b).

9.6 Government-Multinational Enterprise (MNE) Engagement Policy

Ngiam (2006, pp. 23 & 194), a respected long-term policymaker and businessman, directed criticisms at Singapore's MNE engagement policy prior to the GFC:

> We have been flying on auto-pilot for too long. The MNCs have contributed a lot to Singapore but they are totally unsentimental people. The moment you're uncompetitive, they just relocate.

He further made plain that Singapore should turn its back on an MNE that is not willing to embrace Singapore and Singaporeans as part of their core innovative processes:

> Knowledge is therefore the key to Singapore's future.

As stated previously, Ngiam assessment of MNE mobility was entirely correct as the once courted electronics sector and others decamped to China and other cheaper localities just 2 years after he wrote the above (also see Table 9.6 for Singapore's manufacturing retrenchment during the 2008–2009 manufacturing downturn).

Table 9.6 Most affected economic sectors in the Singapore recession of 2008–2009

	3Q08	4Q08	1Q09	2Q09	3Q09
Manufacturing	−11.0	−10.7	−24.2	−1.1	6.6
Wholesale and retail trade	4.5	−5.3	−14.8	−13.8	−8.8
Hotels and restaurants	0.0	−0.1	−5.5	−5.9	−2.5
Financial services	5.6	−8.1	−7.6	−4.5	−0.2
Unemployment[a]	2.3	2.5	3.3	3.3	3.4
Visitor arrivals[b] (y-o-y %)	−4.5	−7.7	−13.6	−9.3	0.2
Total trade (y-o-y%)	16.4	−9.6	−27.7	−26.9	−21.4

Ministry of Trade and Industry, Singapore, www.miti.gov.sg

[a]Significantly underestimates retrenchments to the labour force as the sectors most affected have a very high reliance on foreign (mainly Malaysian) labour

[b]Singapore Airlines Inc. and Changi Airport Inc. are absolutely crucial to the health of the broader Singapore economy

Singapore, during the GFC, was hardly alone in witnessing an outwards migration of MNEs, but is significantly different in that it is a global city-state built on free trade absent of any domestic economic hinterland. Before the GFC, when growth was robust, calls for the abandonment of the MNE engagement policy garnered little analytical or policy attention. The PAP throughout the 1990s and 2000s has consistently reminded the Singapore populace that China and India are already providing the island nation with a level of Asian/global competition that it had not had to contend with in previous decades as cities such as Shanghai and Hyderabad became increasingly global geographies. The statistics are stark. China attracted $US50 billion in foreign direct investment (FDI) in 2009, whilst India attracted $US5 billion. So what really shocked the PAP elite and much of the Singapore polity was not the movement of low-medium-skilled manufacturing out of Singapore, as PAP policy since 2001 has aimed for the gradual decline, but the sheer speed of the 2008–2009 GFC-derived MNE electronic/IT manufactures withdrawal. A process they believed could be state-managed over time effectively took place beyond government control in 18 months (2008–2009). Given that much of Singapore's own manufacturing and engineering enterprises exist for the sole purpose of supplying MNE located on the island, the departure of sectorial-specific MNE during the GFC led to an immediate rapid decline in manufacturing output (YoS 2013). The PAP elite, which throughout the 2000s has made clear that future government support will only be extended into the future based on knowledge and innovation investments, has, since 2009, become even more strident in publicly outlining this position in a move to counter political opponents and the vocal critics of MNE engagement policy (da Cunda 2012a, b). Indeed, engagement policy advocates in the cabinet and key state economic bodies strongly stressed that Singapore's economy would suffer had they done so and that the MNE presence on the island was central to the 'global city' vision. That even debating the topic publicly was detrimental to the national interest of Singapore as the leadership of MNE might begin to question the island's low sovereign risk rating. The political inference was clear; any criticism of the MNE engagement policy equated to undermining the national economy and as a result disloyalty to the nation: an unpatriotic act.

With the severe GFC downturn, all this changed. Singaporean MP and entrepreneur, Inderjit Singh (2009, pp. 32–33), openly calling for an end to MNE engagement:

> The MNC (multinational corporation) approach that has been the focus of Singapore's development should no longer be the driver of the economy as it will probably not be feasible for much longer. Developing countries with lower operating costs such as China and India will soon catch up by enhancing their core competencies, making Singapore less viable for many economic activities except for the service industries. Had we focused on the capacity-building of local enterprises, the government would have ensured that they keep moving up the value chain while they internationalise. Local companies will try to make things work and remain in Singapore for the long haul. I fear the time when multinational corporations (MNCs) will move out at a faster rate than we can bring

> newer ones in... As the net flow of MNCs is in an outwards direction, our local companies may not grow fast enough to keep the economy afloat or to create jobs to employ those retrenched by existing MNCs. We must step up our efforts to help local enterprises to become more competitive in a high-cost environment.

He was not alone with the role of MNE in Singapore being fiercely debated by all sides throughout 2008–2011, including the 2011 national election, via online media sources in a manner never seen within the completely state-owned traditional media (Giam 2010; da Cunda 2012a, b). Indeed, despite the PAP leadership's stridency in support, between the GFC 2008–2009 downturn and the 2011 general election, the public intellectual debate (through online sources, blogs, notice boards and the like) about the future nature of Singapore as a global city, including the MNE engagement policy, roared ahead of actual PAP elite thinking and policymaking. It has been a case of political catch-up ever since, and the political repercussion of this cannot be underestimated.

So invested are the PAP in its success, any reduction in Singapore's role as a premier platform for MNEs would undermine the political legitimacy of the PAP governing elite who over decades have invested much political capital in their claimed exclusive ability to entice top-line MNEs to locate core facilities on the island. In speeches delivered prior to, during and after the 2011 election, PM Lee has forcefully stated that those MNEs in Singapore today receive state funding based solely on their willingness to bring leading global innovation to the city-state. That whilst a smaller percentage of the total Singapore workforce will operate in these new areas of advanced manufactures into the future, domestic Singaporean enterprise will benefit greatly through integrating their own developments with these leading-edge enterprises (Lee 2014). This political-economic argument in favour of manufacturing and other MNE state support by the PAP mirrors that given for the presence and support of the international wealth management funds (UBS and others): that economic benefits extrapolate throughout the economy (through taxation, employment, property development and associated costs) brings real benefits to all citizens. Current prominent policies, the courting of private international wealth management firms (UBS and others), the establishment in 2010 of two highly contentious integrated resorts (Sentosa Island IR and Marina Bay Sands IR) and the massive expansion of Jurong Island energy facilities, are in fact the PAP's tacit acknowledgements that Singapore as a 'global city' incorporated a structural weakness of overdependence on high-mobility MNEs. Crucially, none of the above state-supported sectors, international wealth management, integrated resorts and energy processing, can be moved without considerable risk profiles for their investors or not at all (as is the case with the two casino licences). The PAP, in effect, has and continues to move to provide sectorial anchors to shore up both the domestic economy of their global city and their own political legitimacy. The electoral results of the 2011 general election and 2013 Punggol East by-election remind all of the paradigm statement 'the economy is global, politics is local', and the PM states constantly that the PAP stands 'on the side of the people' (Lee 2014).

9.7 Conclusion: The Politics of Creating a Global City

The greatest danger to the PAP, which has been the governing party for the last 40 years, is elitism and complacency (Ngiam 2006, p. 126).

Few question that Singapore is a national economic success story. From 2010 onwards, the national economy did quickly rebound from the GFC economic decline. Political and policy questions previously negated or dismissed by the PAP, however, have been given real political impetus from the GFC downturn having real implications for Singapore's long-term future. The GFC downturn highlighted the fact that even after a decade of unprecedented public investment in sectorial diversification (wealth management, bio-medical technology, advanced manufactures and creative industries, to name a few), the 'global city' project is highly vulnerable to international economic contagion. Whilst Singapore is hardly alone in revealing itself vulnerable to swift global economic shifts, the PAP's proclamation that it alone is uniquely qualified to secure the global city's prosperity (and security) is looking increasingly politically unsustainable. Its constant vigorous refutation of political opponent or non-political analysts alike pre- and post-GFC downturn and the use of state mechanisms (the media, state bodies, the electoral system) to its complete advantage were all targeted during the 2011 general election and the PAP's 2013 Punggol East by-election loss to the Worker's Party effectively by opponents as revealing PAP elite hubris. The PAP's continued use of the state to maintain its apex political position and charge that it exclusively has the strategic capacity to direct the national economy means that it continues to place itself within a paradigm with the Singapore people in which it is held responsible for all aspect of global economic impacts on Singapore's economy, even those global shifts no single political entity within or out of Singapore has sole control over, for example, movements in the international financial system or within the international manufacturing and information technology supply chain systems.

There may in fact not be a viable economic alternative for Singapore's future than one as an uber-global city. But just as Singapore has been a major beneficiary of changes to global finance and services, these very same forces have seen it impacted negatively upon by two economic downturns since 2001, both unforeseen by the government due to their external origins. With the negative global economic shifts beyond the PAP's immediate control, it clearly cannot state that it alone is Singapore's master. The GFC-derived economic downturn in 2008–2009, in particular, has marked a significant change in the balance-of-power equation between the PAP policy elite and its political opponents and policy critics (Koh 2014). Keen policy practitioners and analysts, such as Ngiam (2006), Bhaskaran (2007), Tan (2009a) and Lim (2012), have each called on the PAP to adjust long-term 'global city' strategic thinking, including placing domestic enterprise formation as a first-order economic policy priority and addressing growing polity concerns over equity, urban development, immigration and housing issues.

In a lengthy and wide-ranging interview with the Institute of Policy Studies, Prime Minister Lee (2014) has acknowledged the failure of the PAP to meet these 'heartland' concerns fully and effectively with all citizens and that the PAP itself has no right to expect to govern indefinitely. Equally so, he made clear that the PAP alone had the capacity to 'look beyond the next election' and that Singapore's global city status was not up for negotiation and had to be a developed in a 'stable, predictable and secure way'. No one can question that the PAP has shown itself to be resilient in holding onto power, and with all the political and state assets geared in its favour, it may continue to do so for a long time to come. However, what is clear is that Singaporeans have moved well-past elections obsession with basic growth-in-GDP measures as the central barometer of progress and political legitimacy as witnessed by the fact the PAP's 2011 electoral decline came during a time of robust economic growth (14.8 % in 2010, 5.2 % in 2011) (da Cunda 2012b; YoSS 2013). That as a polity, Singaporeans are increasingly willing to have non-PAP representatives in the parliament who show a clear understanding of the vision they have for their global city: one defined by quality of life, equity, social welfare and environment well-being and not one merely forged by a selective elite. In conclusion, this author finds that the PAP pursuit of the 'global city' status, the opening up of the economy to further international growth, has led to two results that the PAP has been unable to control: greater economic instability and a resulting opportunity for opposition representatives (who themselves qualify for the PAP's own publicly annunciated profile of an idea candidate: highly educated, articulate and connected to their communities) to gain increased levels of electoral support based on policies aimed at forging a more democratic and equitable global city.

References

Asean Affairs: The Voice of Southeast Asia (2009) Singapore: recession may last whole of 2009. Available at www.aseanaffairs.com/singapore_economy_shrinks-125-in-q4. Accessed 25 Jan 2009

Australian Broadcasting Corporation (ABC) (2009) Singapore: downturn and dissent. Saturday Extra. Available at http://www.abc.net.au/rn/saturdayextra/stories/2009/2527911.htm#transcript. Accessed 27 Mar 2009

Basu DS (2010) Road to recovery: Singapore's journey through the global crisis. ISEAS, Singapore

Bhaskaran M (2007) Singapore economy: medium-term outlook. In: Tan TH (ed) Singapore perspectives 2007: a new Singapore. Institute of Policy Studies & World Scientific, Singapore, pp 25–43

Bhaskaran M (2009a) Can Singapore advance as a regional hub? In: Tan TH (ed) Singapore perspectives 2009: the heart of the matter. Institute of Policy Studies and World Scientific, Singapore, pp 83–91

Bhaskaran M (ed) (2009b) The eleventh Singapore economic roundtable. Institute of Policy Studies and The Business Times. Singapore Times Press Reference, Singapore

Chong T (2006) Singapore: globalizing on its own terms. In: Daljit S, Salazar LC (eds) Southeast Asian affairs 2006. Institute of Southeast Asian Studies, Singapore, pp 265–282

Chong T (2009) Singapore in 2008: negotiating domestic issues, confrontations and global challenges, Southeast Asian affairs 2009. Institute of Southeast Asian Studies, Singapore, pp 289–304
Choy KM (2010) Singapore's changing economic model. In: Chong T (ed) Management of success Singapore revisited. Institute of Southeast Asian Studies, Singapore, pp 123–138
Chua HB (2007) Singapore economy: the new and the dual. In: Tan TH (ed) Singapore perspectives 2007: a new Singapore. Institute of Policy Studies & World Scientific, Singapore, pp 7–23
Crispin SW (2009) Cracks appear in Lee's Mantle. Asia Times Online. Available at http://www.atimes.com/atimes/Southeast_Asia/KC20Ae02.html. Accessed 20 Mar 2009
da Cunda D (2010) Singapore places its bets casinos, foreign talent and remaking a city-state. Straits Times Press, Singapore
da Cunda D (2012a) Between nation-state and global city. In: Yahya F (ed) Singapore perspectives 2011 our inclusive society: going forward. Lee Kuan Yew School of Public Policy, Institute of Policy Studies and World Scientific, Singapore, pp 17–23
da Cunda D (2012b) Breakthrough roadmap for Singapore's political future. Lee Kuan Yew School of Public Policy, Institute of Policy Studies and Straits Times Press, Singapore
Department of Statistics Singapore. Year of Statistics Singapore. 2013. Ministry of Trade & Industry, Republic of Singapore. www.singstat.gov.sg
Department of Statistics Singapore (2013a) Singapore in figures 2013. www.singstat.gov.sg. Accessed 20 Jan 2014
Department of Statistics Singapore (2013b) Yearbook of statistics 2013. www.singstat.gov
Ghesquiere H (2007) Singapore's success: engineering economic growth. Thomson, Singapore
Giam G (2010) Singapore version 2.0: alternative proposals for a better Singapore. Available at http://geraldgiam.sg
Koh G (ed) (2014) Singapore perspectives 2013. Institute of Policy Studies and World Scientific, Singapore
Koh WTH, Mariano RS (2006) The economic prospects of Singapore. Pearson, Addison Wesley, Singapore
Lee HL (2014) Dialogue session with Guest-of-Honour, Prime Minister Lee HL. In: Koh G (ed) Singapore perspective 2013. Institute of Policy Studies and World Scientific, Singapore
Lim CY (2009) Transformation in the Singapore economy: course and causes. In: Chai WM, Sng HY (eds) Singapore and Asia in a globalized world: contemporary economic issues and policies. Word Scientific, Singapore, pp 3–24
Lim S (2012) Singapore as a global city: a balancing act. In: Yahya F (ed) Singapore perspectives 2011 our inclusive society: going forward. Lee Kuan Yew School of Public Policy, Institute of Policy Studies and World Scientific, Singapore, pp 25–30
Lim YC, Lee SA (2010) Globalisation state, disappearing nation: the impact of foreign participation in the Singapore economy. In: Chong T (ed) Management of success: Singapore revisited. Institute of Southeast Asian Studies, Singapore, pp 139–158
Mahbubani K (2008) The new Asian hemisphere: the irresistible shift of global power to the east. Public Affairs, New York
Ministry of Trade and Industry Singapore. www.miti.gov.sg. Accessed 2008–2009
Monetary Authority of Singapore. www.mas.gov.sg. Accessed 2008–2009
Murray L (2014) Lost in transition. The Australian Financial Review Magazine, pp 28–32
Neo BS, Chen G (2007) Dynamic governance: embedded culture, capabilities and change in Singapore. World Scientific, Singapore
Ngiam TD with introduction and edited by Tay SSC (2006) A mandarin and the making of public policy: reflections by Ngiam Tong Dow. NUS Press Singapore, Singapore
Ong P (2009) Forging new paths with audacity and vision. In: Tan TH (ed) Singapore perspectives 2009: the heart of the matter. Institute of Policy Studies and World Scientific, Singapore, pp 7–16

Saitharan T (2012) I… Singaporean. In: Yahya F (ed) Singapore perspectives 2011: our inclusive society: going forward. Lee Kuan Yew School of Public Policy, Institute of Policy Studies and World Scientific, Singapore, pp 31–39

Sanyal S (2007) Singapore: the art of building a global city, IPS working paper No. 16. Institute of Policy Studies, Singapore

Seng WK (2012) Keynote address Deputy Prime Minister Mr Wong Kan Seng and Coordinating Minister for National Security. In: Yahya F (ed) Singapore perspectives 2011 our inclusive society: going forward. Lee Kuan Yew School of Public Policy, Institute of Policy Studies and World Scientific, Singapore, pp 5–13

Singapore FTA Network. http://www.fta.gov.sg/accessed. Accessed 2 Apr 2009

Singh I (2009) Magnetic resonance imaging: alternative approach needed for economy. In: Tan TH (ed) Singapore perspectives 2009: the heart of the matter. Institute of Policy Studies and World Scientific, Singapore, pp 23–33

Tan CN (2009a) Reinventing Singapore: global city – from host to home. In: Tan TH (ed) Singapore perspectives 2009: the heart of the matter. Institute of Policy Studies and World Scientific, Singapore, pp 71–81

Tan KS (2009b) Can Singapore preserve its hub status. In: Tan TH (ed) Singapore perspectives 2009: the heart of the matter. Institute of Policy Studies and World Scientific, Singapore, pp 69–70

Turnbull CM (1989) A history of Singapore 1819–1988. Oxford University Press, Singapore

Chapter 10
The Intricacies of the Middle-Income Trap: The Comparative Analysis Between China and Singapore

Young-Chan Kim

Abstract When we talk about the twentieth and the early twenty-first centuries, there were a lot of issues which had relations to the like of war, terrorist attacks and political upheavals, although it may be too early to judge whether the chosen countries meet the given criteria; one salient point of history will be recorded. With 80 % of the world's population moving out of poverty to a middle-class social structure, the Chinese ethnic will be as ever a key player in this transition.

Since 2008 global financial crisis, the mutual trade relationship between the member of ASEAN and China have been enhancing and strengthening through various ways. Especially, sino-diaspora is one of great strengths for Chinese development process. Rivalry in trade between China and its regional neighbours in ASEAN has become a major preoccupation for many regional policymakers.

Regarding Chinese development model, since Xi's 'New Vision', the Singaporean model is an objective which Chinese government and technocrats are going to pursuit for escaping 'middle-income trap'.

Two variants of development models are used, Singaporean model and new frame of Chinese model, which are highly accepted and used in sub-Saharan African countries. The main outcome of this easy will be the similarity and difference between two models and the role of government would be examined.

10.1 Introduction

Global economic growth rates have once again stalled, which has stimulated economists to contemplate a classic and emblematic question regarding the rate of economic growth within the nations that are situated in the Far East of the Asian sector, with China being a specific case study. Is China's economic growth susceptible to the middle-income trap? According to the IMF report in 2013, economic history gives the impression that the contingency of a 'marked fall' in growth in middle-income nations is on average 1.5 times greater than for the advanced

Y.-C. Kim (✉)
Business School, University of Greenwich, London, UK
e-mail: y.kim@greenwich.ac.uk

H.G. Djajadikerta, Z. Zhang (eds.), *A New Paradigm for International Business*,
Springer Proceedings in Business and Economics, DOI 10.1007/978-981-287-499-3_10

economies or for the low-income nations (Regional Economic Outlook: Asia and Pacific, IMF 2013). As a result, this report further concentrates on the economic environment in China.

Typically, countries in the Far East of Asia have demonstrated somewhat breakneck and fruitful economic development phases since the 1970s, which can be correlated to the Japanese rates of growth, which was predominantly influenced by the Korean War (1950–1953). Post the conclusion of the Second World War, the USA released a barrage of trade sanctions and in the process enforced an Asian style Marshall Plan to be initiated in Japan, which in turn served as the catalyst behind Japan's rapid economic growth. During the course of the 1970s, the Four Asian Dragons further demonstrated government-intervened economic development processes and served as the exemplar for less developed nations to emulate. One of the prominent candidates during this period was China.

Post Mao's transformation of Chinese politics, China needed to move forward in terms of her economy which was stagnant at that time. Thus, with the new President, Deng at the helm, China went through a period of expeditious recovery whereby her economy was recovered and various trade links were further established. Deng further utilised economic reform to dislodge his political foes. Since the 'Open Policy: Seek economic truth from the political facts' in 1978, Chinese development has been the most dynamic in the world. More than 10 % growth during the last three decades symbolised a new chapter in the Chinese economy and demonstrated a new frame of the economic growth model in the world, which was known as the Beijing consensus (Ramo 2004). It has commonly been regarded as the comparative economic development model alongside the Washington consensus, which was led by a free trade neo-monetary economic development, contrary to the Beijing consensus, which consists of a government-intervened development system.

Due to the dynamic nature of the economic system, the World Bank conducts theoretical research every 4 years, on the nature of the East Asian economic dynamism, to rehash their exclusive development experiences and the lesson that were learnt in the process and also to identify and expose the challenges which were endured over specific time phases. In the 2007 report, 'An East Asian Renaissance: Ideas for Economic Growth', Gill and Kharas introduced a definition of the 'middle-income trap' and suggested that these nations have 'grown less rapidly than both rich and poor countries'. This is symbolised by the presentation of the South Korean economic situation which was cartooned as a nut in a nutcracker during the course of the 1997 Far East Asian financial crisis.

Further to this, the concept of the 'middle-income trap' is liable for interpretation, as it can be associated with the political, societal and economic environment, with alternate connotations. This paper will examine the intricacies of the 'middle-income trap' in China through the use of the human capital development based on the higher education system. This research further serves as a comparative analysis study between the Singaporean and Chinese higher education systems and the protocol that is required to bypass this trap.

In addition, Sect. 10.2 of the paper reviews various segments of literature that are in tandem with the Chinese middle-income trap and the ways in which it can be averted through human capital development. Next, in Sect. 10.3, the comparison between the Chinese and Singaporean higher education systems will be intricately analysed, and the transition from high school to university via the entrance examinations will further be evaluated. In Sect. 10.3.1, 10.3.2 and 10.3.3, there are three recommendations and theories in which one can avoid the middle-income trap using human capital development. In Sect. 10.4, a conclusion will be put to the matter in question with the most viable and preferred route that one could take.

10.2 Basic Literature of the Middle-Income Trap

According to Aoki (2011), the economic development in East Asia can be divided into five development phases: the Malthusian phase of the poverty trap (M-phase), the government-led development phase (G-phase), the Kuznet process which is primarily accomplished through an structural shift (K-phase), the human capital-based development phase (H-phase) and the post-demographic transition phase (PD-phase). Its theoretical frame was further analysed by Cai who put forward the thesis that

> the division of development phases reveals that the shift from one development phase to another means a jump or breach, or, in other words, while shaking off the poverty trap is an important surpassing step, the shift from middle-income to high-income levels (from the K-phase to H-phase and ultimately the PD-phase) is an equally important, thrilling jump. If the latter is so challenging that some economies have long failed to break through the phase, and the phenomenon is so widespread that it has had statistical significance and entails important theoretical and policy implications, then it is logical for us to use the concept of the middle-income trap. (2012)

When one discusses the intricacies of the Malthusian poverty trap in China, Deng's economic drive plan is perceived as being an integral facet that drove China's economy forward with ease. His policy essentially benefited immensely from the works of his predecessor Mao, who resolved the demographic burden in terms of economic development through the 'Great Leap Forwards Movement' in 1958. The movement resulted in the death of more than 30 million due to famine. In Chinese history, the issues of famine due to the high population were a prominent objective that needed to be overcome. Thus, the depreciation in population meant that they could avoid the Malthusian poverty trap with ease. Furthermore, there was an interesting ideology that was present at that time which stated that '... Why are we (Chinese) so forgetful? The answer my grandmother gave when I asked about 1942 (Henan famine) provides a clue: There are innumerable instances of starvation and cannibalism through Chinese history, and when a people are constantly confronted with death through starvation, how else can they deal with it other than by forgetting?' Liu Zhenyun (2012). Politically and economically, the resolution of famine was one of the prominent targets which the Chinese government had to address and resolve. The movement paved out a route for which the nation could transition to the second phase of the development process, despite the labour shortages.

The open door policy which was initiated and launched by Deng Xiaoping in 1978 had attracted a massive number of foreign direct investment in China, and thus, the Special Enterprises Zone formed a loophole for foreign business to penetrate the Chinese domestic market. At the same time, the structural reform continuously intervened with there being more heated competitions between domestic manufacturers and lower import tariffs for foreign products, which led to the depreciation of the price of the good. The tariff incentive for foreign manufacturers and goods triggered economic tension between state-owned enterprises in China and foreign multinational enterprises. On the other hand, the competition allowed domestic consumers to enjoy better products at diminished prices and essentially dragged the Chinese SOEs to spend more of their budget on R&D and increase both the value and quality of their products. From the open door policy until the end of the millennium period, the Chinese economic system revolved around the government-led development phase (G-phase). Furthermore, the economic transition which Deng desired to enforce was ultimately alike to that of the Japanese and South Korean policies, which managed to develop and enhance their respective economies.

It was the work of external factors which resulted in the Kuznet process, a feat which was achieved through structural shift (K-phase) in China. On 11 December 2001, the membership of the WTO caused China to relax over 7,000 tariffs, quotas and other trade barriers. Although the membership was primarily associated with economic negotiation, there was high demand from the government technocrats to implement 'software' reforms. The open door policy and manufacturing reforms were carried out via the removal of tariffs and attraction of foreign direct investments, which transformed China's economic environment. The competitiveness between manufacturers regarding the quality of their products was greatly heightened which was ultimately beneficial to the general economy. Nevertheless, there have been more regulations imposed and the robustness of government policies for the manufacturing sector has been exemplified.

One of the successful applications of the policy was the government intervention in the city of Shenzhen, which opened its doors in 1980, which altered the system and caused the G-phase and K-phase to occur in unison. The process was emulated from the free economic trade zones within South Korea which started under the reign of President Park Chung-hee.

In addition, the 1997 Asian financial crisis and 2000 dotcom burst stimulated the Chinese economy into becoming a global competitive environment. During the crisis in Far East Asia, China actively acquired research-oriented small and medium enterprises from several countries. Through the successful merger and acquisition procedures, the Chinese state-owned enterprises fortified their external environment as one of great prominence. The membership of the WTO and the global economic crisis allowed the Chinese K-phase to be perceived in a positive light, as it resulted in greater benefits for their economy as a whole.

According to the Asian Development Bank's research report (requoted from the New York Times), the Chinese middle class (defined as those people with daily consumption expenditure between US$ 2 and US$ 20) make up 66 % of the total population and account for 79.2 % of total consumption of China. The Chinese middle class can be divided into three groups: the lower middle class with daily spending between US$ 2 and US$ 4, the mid-middle class with daily spending between US$ 4 and US$ 10 and the higher middle class with daily spending between US$ 10 and US$ 20. Realistically, it is evident that the lower middle class which primarily consists of migrant workers should be expanded and developed in order for them to ascend the social spectrum.

The social and economic environment for the human capital-based development phase (H-phase) is epitomised in the ADB report. However, it is apparent that the wider income inequality between the middle class signals the possibility that the Chinese economy may eventually become the victim of the middle-income trap. To reduce the income inequality between the rural and urban areas, the human capital investment is vital as it provides higher educational opportunities that may bridge the growing gap.

In 2008, the Asian Development Bank warned that such shortages are sufficiently prevalent to pose a risk to growth in China and other parts of emerging Asia. Surveys of employers in China and Asia regularly identify shortages of qualified staff as a prominent business concern. For example, the lack of high-quality human capital helps to explain why Malaysia and Thailand have become synonymous with the middle-income trap. In contrast, the rapid expansion of secondary and then tertiary education helps to explain Korea's successful transition from middle- to high-income status. Whether China can avoid the middle-income trap will presumably depend, in part, on whether it develops an education system that successfully produces graduates with skills that employers require (ADB 2008, requoted from New York Times). In addition, ADB emphasises that the underdevelopment of the service sector in China and other Asian emerging markets is attributable partly to the dominance of traditional low value-added services. It identifies shortage of appropriate human capital as an important explanation for the weakness of modern high value-added service sectors.

Garrett (2004) critically analysed that when rich countries become increasingly affluent because of their accelerating technological advancements, the poorest countries have achieved faster growth in their manufacturing, but those countries in between fail to make headway. In terms of GDP growth and expansion of the domestic market in China, the Chinese government and industries need to be in tandem with one another in order to transform their industrial processes, to cope with this radical change in the global economy.

As Gill and Kharas (2008) pointed out that development strategies and policies that are starkly different from previous ones must be adopted during a country's transition from the middle-income to the high-income phase. Under the obvious phenomenon on demographical changes in China, the economic growth should be slow down. The labour forces are minimised and the absolute quantity of working age decreases; therefore, the economy will no longer benefit from the demographic dividends as a result of having an ample labour supply and a high savings rate. Due to these reasons, the human capital development is important for avoiding middle-income trap in China, and this report is concentrated on higher educational system and its employability in China. According to Cai, the accumulated human capital through education and training is meaningful. Aoki (2011) holds that China has surpassed the K-phase and is shifting to the H-phase that is centred on human capital accumulation. The success of Japan and Korea in overcoming the middle-income phase is also attributable to their smooth shift from that phase. Human capital is also a source of total factor productivity improvement. Kuijs (2009) shows that in the 1978–2009 period, the annual average growth of total factor productivity was approximately 3.0–3.5 %, 0.5 percentage point of which was attributable to improvement in human capital. Whalley and Zhao (2010) also show that human capital plays a role in offsetting the poor performance of total factor productivity (Cai 2012).

As a result, as displayed in the statements above, the Chinese economic growth model essentially emulates the steps and procedures that were taken by their Asian counterparts, namely, Japan and South Korea, and thus is essentially akin to the typical model that most Asian countries opt to follow. The direct intervention of the central government is as demonstrated, vital in paving the way for growth and development of the nation's economy. Henceforth, post the conclusion of the development phase, the income inequality has however increased which has caused great discontent amongst those in the lower echelons of society. Therefore, the only viable route to bridge the gap is via higher education which also is the best manner in which they could avert from the conundrum that is the middle-income trap.

10.3 The Comparative Analysis Between the Chinese and Singaporean Higher Education System

The notion of state capitalism brings forth a 'new dynamic model,' whereby the state plays an 'activist role' in managing the economic system. In Singapore, the Peoples' Action Party (PAP) has, alike to that of the Chinese Communist Party, ruled as a single party and has retained popular legitimacy by delivering inclusive growth which has ultimately increased the standard of living in the nation. The Singaporean model is further state designed and revolves around the notion of utilising investment funds to boost the calibre of the financial and educational service sectors, in order to work for a better tomorrow for the new generation. The government employs various state-owned enterprises to manage the exploitation of resources that they consider to be the states crown jewels in order to create and maintain a large number of jobs. This is a form of capitalism but one in which the state acts as the dominant economic player and uses markets primarily for political gain (Chinese Model) – state-owned enterprises. The human capital development or the higher educational systems from both countries' governments' perceptions also serve as a prominent factor.

Next, the university system of Singapore is meticulously planned by the government to supplement the desires and requirements of the economy in a plethora of ways and forms. Likewise, the Chinese government maintains the state of the higher educational system to ensure that there is a continuous supply of graduates per annum. In 1999, the Chinese government decided to expand the country's higher education system. In 2003, China had 2.12 million university graduates; a decade later, around 6.99 million graduated, expecting on average a salary of around 3,000 yuan ($490) per month, but only 35 % of graduates managed to find a job. This demonstrated a void in which there was a surplus of graduates for the limited amount of jobs that were on offer. The problem was greatly severe that it alerted Xi Jinping the nation's Premier, who met in May 2012, with the college students who were in their concluding years, in Tianjin, encouraging them to take even the most grassroots jobs and to 'issue extraordinary performances in ordinary job situations' (Xinwha report).

The national entrance exam of China, the *Gao Kao*, has been the cause of much debate, due to the arbitrary and somewhat partisan nature of the examination. It is around 16 times easier for a student in Beijing to get a place at the renowned Tsinghua University than it is for a student from the Hunan Province.

A Euromonitor survey (2013) found out that the per capita annual disposable income in China rose by 63.3 % in the 5 years leading to 2012, yet consumer expenditure on education rose by almost 94 %. As a result, the great expectation that the parents of the individual possess, when investing great funds to educate their young, is not sufficiently recouped as due to the inadequate policies of the Chinese government, the employability rates of the next generation is diminutive in comparison to the supply of graduates, and thus it is statistically tougher for the next of kin to become financially stable postgraduation.

Next, a recent survey conducted by the market research company Mintel (2014) found out that nine out of ten children from middle-class backgrounds in China attend fee-charging after-school activities. (One third of the household income is being spent on paying these fees.)

However, for those who go on to do well (0.2 % of top scores), the *Gao Kao* is a life-changing event, and it is a means by which one is able to attain reasonable assurance of eventual high-paying white-collar employment, thereby securing a stable financial future for generations above and below alike. On the contrary, there are various individuals who opt to study abroad to broaden their horizons. Around 400,000 individuals went abroad to study in 2013 and around 330,000 go back to China after they graduate (Fig. 10.1).

To achieve commendable results in the *Gao Kao* examination, the appropriate financial backing of their parents is integral. This is as there are a plethora of costs that are related to sending their children to elementary, middle and high schools where the burden of extracurricular activities drives desperate parents to utilise their life savings to increase the calibre of their offspring via the employment of personal tutors. Thus, their options are fairly limited if their children are not able to

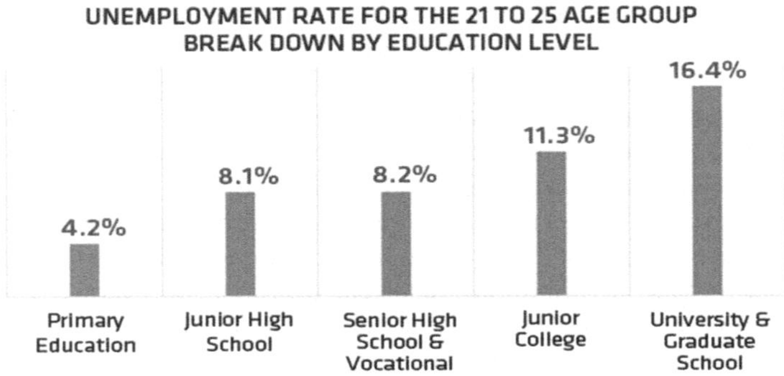

Fig. 10.1 Unemployment rate (*Source*: Mintel report 2014)

find suitable employment post-university to reimburse their parents of their immense investment.

However, unalike to the ability-based scoring system that is active in Singapore, only a minor quantity of students from poorer families earn top grades on the *Gao Kao*, and thus they are shifted to lower-quality universities that have minimal government backing which further hinders their chances of obtaining suitable employment postgraduation. Thus, one can perceive that the merit that the *Gao Kao* once possessed of giving those from poorer families an opportunity to surpass their rich counterparts has greatly diminished and the notion of the examination being a social leveller and a safety valve for talented but poor youths to escape poverty has, in essence, lost its purpose. In line with the statement from an entrance exam coordinator at English First Institution in Guangzhou, the fact that the family income and academic achievement are correlated can be acknowledged. The majority of the examination questions for the English segment require the aid of additional classes and it is evident that those without this backing are unable to answer sufficiently with the knowledge obtained from public institutions.

The *Gao Kao* used to be the only opportunity that one had to alter their social burden and to attain a new life in the city, but in recent times, those from more affluent, urban backgrounds have been favoured. The prominent universities in China are concentrated around the province of Beijing and Shanghai, and it is apparent that they give preference to those from local high schools and are often granting them places, even though they come in with lower exam scores than their rural counterparts. Post the *Gao Kao*, a message regarding the exam was posted on China's popular social networking site *Weibo* which read:

At the Exam (in 2012)

- Write a 400 word essay about the following topic: Two fish are swimming in a river. The older one asks, 'How's the water?' The younger one says, 'I don't know if it's clean or cloudy'.

After the Result

- In Beijing: 'Dad, I got 530 [on the *gaokao*], 53 points higher than the lowest qualifying score for the top-tier universities!' 'Great job, son! Let's go shopping in Shanghai!'
- In Shandong: 'Dad, I got 530, 20 points lower than the lowest qualifying score for the second-tier universities!' 'You're not so bright . . . Don't go [to college]. Get out of here and go and become a migrant worker in Shanghai'.
- In Shanghai: 'Dad, I got 330. Send me abroad'. 'Okay, son. Go get an MBA, then come back and help me. I've got another group of migrant workers coming in from Shandong this year'.
- 'Without gaokao, how can you overcome the children of the rich?'

Furthermore, in comparison with the Singaporean model, the Chinese university system possesses unique tiers for prestige. There have been two government policies for higher education prior to and after the twenty-first century which were known as Project 985 and Project 211. Project 211 was the government's new initiative, which aimed to strengthen 100 universities, and was a national priority for the twenty-first century. The project predominantly aimed to train high-level professional manpower to carry out the national strategy for social and economic development. Furthermore, during the 9th Five-Year Plan period, the government chose 100 institutions of higher learning capability and a group of prominent areas of discipline, which when addressed would greatly improve the quality of education, scientific research, calibre of management and the efficiency of the institution. As a result of the great efforts of the government, the institutions involved in Project 211 will set up national standards in overall quality, with several of the key universities reaching to the standard of advanced international educational institutions in terms of their discipline and the quality of learning that they offer. Adjusting to the regional and sectional development needs further enables these institutions to play integral and often exemplary roles in their respective areas.

Likewise, Project 985 was the brainchild of ex-President Jiang Zemin and was launched on 4 May 1998. At first nine universities were selected, but the number gradually increased to around 40 universities. Unalike to the alternate Project 211, these institutions are globally recognised and consistently achieve excellence in the realm of higher education.

However, in relation to the Singaporean model which alike to the German educational system consists of distinct institutions that are concentrated on specialising in either the job market or in higher education, the Chinese model is greatly vague in the sense that this differentiation is not apparent which could have a daunting effect on the nations job market.

10.3.1 Factor-Drive Education for Labour-Intensive Industries

The breakneck economic growth has transfigured the structure of the labour market in the nation. The double-digit economic growth has created a plethora of job opportunities in an array of alternate fields and has further managed to sustain the growth of aggregated employment within the labour market in China. In addition, the economic paradigm from the agricultural sector to subsequent sectors such as that of manufacturing and further tertiary sectors has resulted in a mass movement of farming labour to urban areas. This has in turn formulated a trend that requires alternate standards of educational qualifications and additional support from the local government in the form of direct intervention. This is required to clarify the typical registration system which goes by the name of *hukou*.

In 2011, the proportion of urban residents in relation to the entire Chinese population, which includes the migrant workers who have dwelled in cities for periods greater than that of 6 months, was around 51.27 % which constituted for just over 680 million out of 1.35 billion (Daily Telegraph, 17 Jan. 2012). According to the report, 690.79 million people were currently living in urban areas, in comparison to the 655.56 million who were residing in the rural regions. In contrast, the proportion of individuals who possess the status of formal urban *hukou* was a mere 36 % of China's total population. This was however beneficial for the cities' dwellers as it permitted them to maintain the flow of migrants and was instrumental in allowing them to control and decrease the labour costs whilst allowing the new urban middle class to retain their entitled privileges. The notion of this registration system was further the subject of great debate; a student who was initially from the Hunan Province but had dwelled in Beijing in order to study was forbidden to reap the benefits of a Beijing citizen for the *Gao Kao* exam. However, upon returning to her home province of Hunan, she found that as she had been in Beijing for an extended period of time, she was again impeded from taking the *Gao Kao*. Thus, she had no option but to take the SAT examination and managed to secure a place at the prestigious Yale University to supplement her desires for a higher education.

In this way, there is frequent 'brain loss' in the Chinese education system, with those who are competent but unfortunate having no option but to continue their studies in foreign institutions (Fig. 10.2).

However, in comparison to the initial generation of migrant workers, the subsequent generations possess a greater deal of intellect and thus have begun to voice their disapproval regarding the tendentious nature of the system, especially the notion of education which prompted political concern. Unalike the previous generation, the standard of education is comparatively superior (as they are more or less middle school graduates) and thus has a thirst to take in more information and become more enhanced and skilled in their respective jobs. Typically, Chinese technical institutions and training programmes related to specific occupations are not sought after as there are minimal opportunities for the individual to transit into higher education. Thus, it is apparent that direct intervention from the government

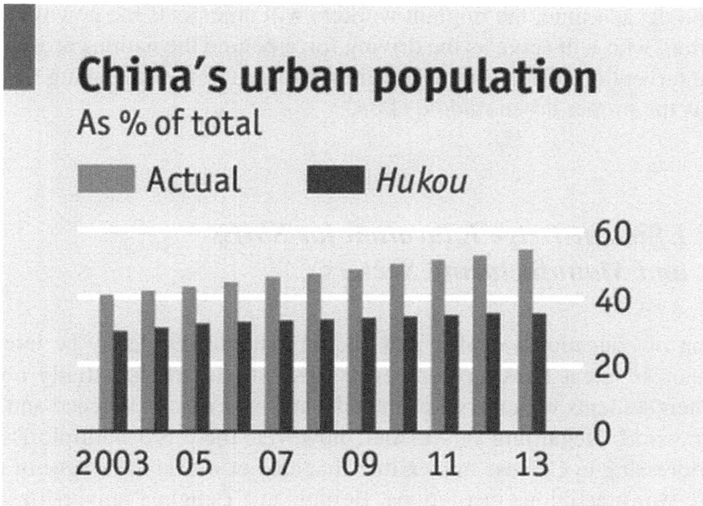

Fig. 10.2 Urban population (*Source*: *The Economist*, 22 March 2014)

is required in a government-led transfiguration that is ultimately the sole way in which one can alter the generic picture of the manufacturing sector and the migration workers.

However, it is due to the fact that migrant and nonuniversity graduates are ultimately more willing and prepared to undertake manufacturing jobs that they are still in great demand. Also, as the Chinese economy is still primarily dependent upon the manpower that the blue-collar jobs bring about, the contribution of the migrant workers is essential. Next, manufacturing, mining and construction make up around 47 % of China's economic output, which is twice their share in the USA, and as the service sector is somewhat less developed, it is apparent that the Chinese economy depends upon this sector. As a result, they must value the services of the migrant workers, and in order for them to establish themselves as the middle class of China, it is vital that the central government takes it upon themselves to amend and reform the *hukou* system in a manner that benefits them.

In addition, a subsequent point of concern from the aspect of the human capital development is that over the next two decades, the nation's labour force will drastically increase from 60 to 160 million people which implies that around 20–50 % of the labour force will be derived from relatively poorer rural areas. Thus, it is apparent that in order to prepare for the massive influx in labour from the rural regions, the urban areas should sufficiently alter their services in order to suit the needs of the new middle class. Factors such as proper social and welfare policies should be implemented in order for them to work in tandem with one another.

However, in order for these policies to become viable, the central government needs to intervene and reform the *hukou* system to bring about further education opportunities for the workers and their next of kin. This is essential in the sense that in around a decade time, the migrant workers will emerge as the new middle class of the nation, who will serve as the driving force behind the nations prosperity, and thus the intervention of the central government is vital in establishing the migrant workers as the proper urban middle class.

10.3.2 Efficient-Drive Education for SMEs and Manufacturing Sectors

The notion of educational quality and quantity should ultimately be interrelated. Post 6 years of great hardship, university institutions are essentially obliged to provide their students with the relevant skills and expertise to succeed and profit in the wider world. Regarding this matter, however, there are multiple issues that require addressing in Chinese universities that are not within the league of the elite. (There are two prestigious institutions, Beijing and Tsinghua universities, and the other C9 universities which are categorised as being tier 1, which are regarded as the jewels of Chinese education, followed by the Project 985 universities and then the lower echelons of the educational ladder which mainly consists of those in the Project 211 league.)

However, there is a conundrum in this scheme that the central government offers fewer opportunities to the migrant workers through the implementation of the *hukou* system, which impedes them from establishing themselves as the urban middle class, whereas the local government increases unemployment rates via the introduction of less prestigious universities results in their being a spanner in the works. This issue ultimately hinders the ‘middle class’ from developing and impedes them from bearing the fruits of prosperity.

The by-product of the dramatic expansion in those opting to continue on to higher education in China (around 6.9 million graduated in 2013) was that there was a great increase in unemployment and there was minimal wage growth for the new graduates as there was a surplus of supply in relation to demand. During the course of the last 5 years, the wage premiums that were paid to higher education graduates stalled by 19 percentage points, whilst unemployment rates amongst those who had freshly graduated have rocketed to over 16.4 %. This was, however, predominantly due to the fact that they opted against taking low prestige blue-collar jobs. The overall supply of higher education graduates has persistently resulted in the depreciation of the average wage levels to 2,125 yuan per calendar month in 2013. As a result, the gap between the migrant workers (1,578 yuan), who are without a college degree to their name, and the graduates is rapidly diminishing.

However, the majority of the university graduates are highly reliant upon the classic office job due to cultural and social implications (China has a Confucian tradition in which educated people are reluctant to engage in manual labour). Within China, working as a government official or holding a managerial position is the highest possible rank one can achieve in comparison to working as an engineer, which is much less sought after, due to aforementioned Confucian traditions.

The initial problem in the Chinese higher education system is the unbalanced nature of the programmes at each university. For instance, more than a half of the total graduates are majoring in humanities and social sciences, but once graduated, the labour market has no place for them to fill and does not bear enough employment opportunities for them. Thus, there is ultimately an overproduction in supply as per the limited demand. Next, a subsequent issue in question is that, especially within the Project 211 league, the skills and expertise that these studies are taught are neither unique nor specialised and thus over half of the graduates from this league are directly fed into the unemployment chain.

However, one can question the reasoning behind the issue. Realistically, one can acknowledge the fact that the social science and humanities departments are essentially sources of 'cheap teaching', as they require minimal sources and solely a minute number of staff. Thus, the local government, who is encouraging the construction of multiple universities, brings forth these programmes in the institutions that are part of the Project 211 and lower in terms of their manner of teaching, which ultimately impedes the chances of prospective employment as the skills that the graduates possess do not suffice.

For instance, Beijing Geely University, a private institution founded in 2000 by Li Shufu, the chairman of the automaker Geely, already has 20,000 students studying a range of subjects, but with an emphasis on engineering and science, particularly auto engineering. Thus, one can acknowledge that these institutions that are not part of the 211 league offer tailor-made lean educational systems with more enhanced employment opportunities upon graduation. Therefore, it is advisory that the local government should adopt these tailored systems and implement them upon the 211 universities and institutions that fall lower than the former in the education chain, in order to improve their calibre and open up a wider world of prospective employment to their respective graduates.

Since 1999, the university expansion scheme permitted the educational institutions below the 4th tier to become higher education providers (a feat which was derived from the educational reforms that were implemented by Mrs Thatcher in 1988 in the UK, whereby all schools are governed by the principle of an 'open environment' and 'local management'). On the contrary, these schemes lay the foundations for wider opportunities for the hungry high school students desperate for an enhanced education. During this expansion, the majority of the quasi-universities chose relatively simplistic subjects in order to attract local and somewhat lower-qualified students fulfilling the demand of their eager parents who longed for their next of kin to obtain a college education. However, although the educational barriers were dissolved, the employment barrier was nevertheless evident. Thus, although they managed to graduate with degrees, the employment opportunities were scarce. Therefore, this resulted in an overproduction of graduates from these programmes (humanities and social sciences) due to the simplistic and relatively cheap nature of them, which triggered the eventual deterioration of the typical office job market in China.

From the local government's point of view, they perceived that getting a greater quantity of individuals into higher education would provide a greater deal of jobs in the local and central economy (mainly due to the double-digit economic development which meant that the economy could take in a greater deal of graduates). However, this phase has passed, and with the alteration in the economic situation of the world, the lucrative employment opportunities that were once open to those from lower-calibre universities have now diminished. Affiliated with local governments or run by private businesses, fourth tier universities and colleges could opt to charge around twice as much as their first tier counterparts, which are owned, operated and subsidised by the central government. Ill-prepared local government's educational reformations and overenthusiastic approaches from farming parents in rural areas produced a surplus of low or non-qualified institutions and graduates that were without the appropriate skills and requirements to enter the wider world. Despite the high fees, the college and universities spent much less teaching each individual student than the first and second tiers universities because they receive so few subsidies from the central government. This fact was further outlined by a multitude of human resource managers who complained that the quality and calibre of new recruits were far lower than the norm, as they were without the appropriate mind-set and the sufficient IT skills (Table 10.1).

Another raising concern is the quality of the university educational process. First of all, the rapid expansion of higher education has outpaced the production of quality-proven teaching staff. The PhD and student ratio has doubled since the expansion began in 1997, and thus there are now wider gaps between the requirement for typical office jobs from a company and the quality of university graduates. According to a recruiting company in Guangzhou, around a fifth of new staff have been allocated into the field of work directly. A greater quantity of graduates enter the field without the basic accounting expertise and the skill to handle statistical data from the global market. Therefore, a vast quantity of firms are opting to re-educate new employees via the use of their own educational systems. ZTE (telecommunications and equipment company based in Shenzhen, China) is a prime example, as they formulated their own university that specialises in installing company-related information to their new recruits and overseas partners. Their recruiting system was initially designed for middle and high school graduates to learn more skills when they would be employed, in future years. However, this scheme has expanded to inform university graduates of the required expertise that are desired in the current market and provides programmes that are closely interlinked with various jobs within a company. It has achieved great success and has proven to result in greater efficiency, and productivity rates have further inclined post the introduction of these educational schemes.

When asked about the facets they consider when faced with possible employment, many job hunters would contemplate the following three questions: 'Does the job align with our major? Does it pay enough? Do we have room to grow?' However, since the economic downturn in China, the space for prospective employment has diminished rapidly.

Table 10.1 The number of graduates from six programmes in Chinese universities

Year	Total no. of graduates	Humanities		Social sciences		Engineering		Medicine		Sciences		Agriculture	
		Graduates	% of total graduates	Graduates	% of total graduates	Graduates	% of total graduates	Graduates	% of total graduates	Graduates	% of total graduates	Graduates	% of total graduates
1978	164,581	18,236	11.1	11,839	7.2	....	....	....	....	....	....	....	....
1985	316,384	38,202	12.1	55,603	17.6	....	....	....	....	....	....	....	....
1990	613,614	67,531	11.0	130,463	21.3	....	....	....	....	....	....	....	....
1995	805,397	178,094	22.1	142,212	17.7	295,839	36.7	100,566	12.5	55,711	6.9	32,975	4.1
2000	949,767	203,626	21.4	203,423	21.4	354,291	37.3	98,200	10.3	59,857	6.3	30,370	3.2
2005	3,067,956	707,309	23.1	832,686	27.1	1,090,986	35.6	164,867	5.4	202,577	6.6	69,531	2.3
2006	3,774,708	859,145	22.8	1,046,179	27.7	1,341,724	35.5	197,231	5.2	253,252	6.7	77,177	2.0
2007	4,477,907	1,001.194	22.3	1,262,801	28.2	1,594.310	35.6	300,389	6.7	230,883	5.2	88,330	2.0
2008	5,119.498	1,291,021	25.2	1,267,833	24.8	1,841,946	36.0	367,491	7.2	253,467	5.0	97,740	1.9

Source: China Statistical Yearbook

Notes: Humanities include philosophy, education, literature and history, social sciences include economics, management and law; Engineering, medicine, science and agriculture combined to account for 135,406 graduates in 1978 (82.3 % of all graduates), 222,579 (70.4 %) in 1985, and 415,620 (67.7 %) in 1990

This problem is acutely well known by the government official, Ye Zhihong, a deputy secretary general of China's Education Ministry who stated that 'There is a structural mismatch – on the one hand, the factories are not eligible to find skilled labour, and, on the other hand, the universities produce students who do not want the jobs available' (Xinwha report July 2013).

To make ends meet, broad employability should be available through various underdeveloped service sectors. Compared to 60 % in Korea, 70 % in Japan and around 80 % in the USA, China has just 43 % of employment in the service sector, occupations which are more compatible for the well-skilled labour force with bachelor degrees.

So what are the barriers to higher education? There are two most prevalent problems. The first may be that China may be a victim of her own success. With rising wages for the typical blue-collar labourer, the opportunity cost of going to higher education has been elevated and is persistently rising, but with little prospectus after graduation. The other is that China has high and rising levels of income inequality, and it is the cause of grave concerns that there will be increasing rates of income inequality in the forthcoming decades, alongside inflated housing prices. Those two reasons will trigger serious social issues within the coming decade.

These problems which are essentially caused by the mishaps of the local and central governments formulate a 'middle-income trap' and hinder the middle class from fulfilling their potential.

10.3.3 Innovation-Drive Education for SOEs and Public Service Sectors

The matter in question is whether China's labour force is apt to acknowledge and accept the challenge of becoming a high-wage, high-skilled workforce.

Based on the statements of a prominent head hunter in the industry, who again persisted on remaining anonymous due to the great controversy of the matter in China, in Shanghai, there is an increasing sense of corruption and bribery that tarnishes one's legitimate transition into the job market.

Throughout the course of the last decade, China quadrupled the number of students enrolled in universities and colleges which greatly boosted the intellectual capacity of the subsequent generation. Nevertheless, its economy is still somewhat dependant and driven by the manufacturing sector, with a plethora of blue-collar jobs outweighing their higher-educated counterparts. Prime Minister Li Keqiang personally led the cabinet meeting, on May 16, that produced the directive for schools, government agencies and state-owned enterprises to hire more graduates, a strategy that has been utilised to increase the frequency in recent years to absorb the jobless but educated youths (Renmin Daily Newspaper 2014).

However, regardless of the feats taken by the Prime Minister in initiating and reforming the employment scheme, there has been solely a minute effect on the job market. This is predominantly due to a multitude of reasons, the most prominent of which is bribery. This is essentially the by-product of political *guanxi* and cash-related bribery which results in an asymmetrical and partisan relationship arising.

There have been numerous instances that have epitomised the tendentious nature of the job market. Through an anonymous source, it was revealed that, recently, a graduate of a mediocre university in Australia went head-to-head with a graduate of Tsinghua University (a major first tier university in China) for a job as an accountant in an American multinational corporation based in Shanghai. The human resource department of the firm initially prioritised those who were of a higher calibre and intellect; but post the introduction of bribery, the conditions were altered to favour those who were familiar with the Western work ethic. As a result, the individual from Australia, who was obliviously of a secondary acumen than the former, was chosen. However, throughout the course of the selection process, it was revealed that the individual had utilised around two million yuan to ensure that the place was secured. These forms of bribery most commonly occur between the middlemen and the applicants, i.e. the head-hunters and recruitment agencies who in their sectarian ways favour those who come with the sufficient financial backing regardless of their competence in their relevant fields. Forms of financially supplemented bribery are a common occurrence within the jobseeking culture in the province of Shanghai and Guangzhou, whereas government-based corruption is prevalent in Beijing.

The notion of innovation is further greatly in demand in recent years, with the government initiating various plans and policies to drive the standard of the nation above and beyond that of its Western counterparts. China's ongoing 5-year plan, through 2015, is concentrating on seven national development priorities, many of them being unadulterated industries that are the trend amongst young and fresh college graduates in the West. They are alternative energy, energy efficiency, environmental protection, biotechnology, advanced information technologies, high-end equipment manufacturing and so-called new energy vehicles, like hybrid and all-electrical cars.

China's objective is to invest up to ten trillion renminbi, or $1.6 trillion, to expand and enhance those industries to represent around 8 % of economic output by the end of the new annum, which is an increase from the 3 % that was recorded in 2010 (Xinwha report 2014).

However, a great deal rests upon whether or not China's authoritarian and autocratic political regime can formulate an educational system that emboldens world-class creativity and innovation that present-day economies are in need of, which can in turn aid in the generation of quality jobs to fit the expertise of modern-day graduates.

Nevertheless, if the nation desires this innovation that'll result in the boosting of her calibre and stature, it is vital that the tarnished political policies are reformed as if left to function in their own ways, and the thriving sources of innovation will undoubtedly be impeded.

Data shows that Peking University's Founder System, which was established on the basis of the Stanford Silicon Valley model in the USA, seeks to accommodate teaching, researching and industrial development to strive for a better future, but is not reaping the benefits that its American counterpart has experienced in recent times. The reasoning behind the conundrum is under much debate, but it is evident that it is a consequence of multiple hidden government regulations, such as taxation matter, which permit the central government to indirectly intervene and assume control. As a result, the crown jewels of China's higher education system, Tsinghua and Beijing University, are left to take a more arduous route to achieve excellence than their Western counterparts.

Due to this, the graduates from overseas and first tier universities aren't granted a fair employability opportunity due to the asymmetrical nature of the industry; and thus, the government needs to formulate a transparent job market to enable the bright minds to expand and flourish and to maximise their potential in their relevant fields. Lately, Xi Jinping's government is steadily dealing with the political side of bribery and corruption in Chinese society, and likewise, similar intervention is required to resolve the issues in employability. As if not dealt accordingly, it will lead to the eventual deterioration of the market as a whole, which may be beyond repair.

Further to this, as Landes predicted, Chinese technology ceased progressing before it could initiate its own Industrial Revolution because of its lack of 'a free market and institutionalised property right' combined with 'totalitarian control over all the activities of social life'. Thus, as displayed by Landes' perceptions, the generic vibe towards innovation is somewhat negative, as without political reform, it merely remains an unfeasible utopia.

10.4 Conclusion

In the June 2014 examination period, there were 9.39 million students taking the *Gao Kao*, the result of 18 years of intense education. 4 % of total GDP had been spent as investment by parents into the education sector with around US$250 billion being spent on improving their children's intellect. On the other hand, there was a national survey on urban residents, released in the winter of 2012, by a Chinese University, which collectively displayed the doom and gloom of unemployment. It further showed that amongst people in their early 1920s, those who possessed a college degree were around four times more unlikely to find any sort of employment than their counterparts who only had an elementary school education to their name.

The Chinese government's inadequate and inefficient education policy serves as the fundamental reasoning behind the lack of prospective employment. The central government of the nation is ultimately underplaying its role in initiating a suitable policy to reform the *Gao Kao* to its former glory as a social leveller. The overall procedures of educational reform are interlinked to the *hukou* system, and thus, it would ultimately be more arduous a procedure in reforming the exam, as it would be far more perplexing than a simplistic alteration of the entrance exam. As a result, the government fails to provide the necessary information regarding the expectations and the consequences that entail higher education in China. On the contrary, due to the dominance of the local government, the quality of higher education in China has swiftly diminished; cheap teaching costs and the high costs of tuition will eventually result in great unemployment rates for graduates.

In addition, the great distortion in the job market results in an abnormal amount of corruption and bribery which tarnishes the employability rate for the graduates. All in all, it is evident that there is a void between the supply and demand for labour forces which results in an imbalance of employment which favours some over the majority.

Next, it is apparent that a great deal rests upon whether or not China's authoritarian political system can formulate an intricate educational structure that emboldens the world-class ingenuity and innovation that is so dearly required in the realm of modern economics, which could further aid in the generation of jobs that are of a high calibre. Nonetheless, as demonstrated by the Korean exemplar in recent times, the greater number of graduates does not necessarily result in entrepreneurial creativity. If China's educational institutions are unable to elucidate the innovation conundrum, the country may face various mishaps in advancing forwards once the fruits of low-cost labour and cheap capital diminish, a feat which could occur sooner than later.

The notion of transition is a lengthy, dynamic and transformative procedure; however, it will imminently be more arduous and convoluted in future years when educational reformation is interlinked to a social aspect. As a result of the various constraints, it is futile to put a name to the notion of reasonable governance, with the boundaries between the central and local governments and the job market due to the vague and ambiguous nature of the matter.

Education reform in Britain that took place under Mr Gove encountered great criticism and was the subject of great debate and was eventually dismissed. Regarding the matter of human capital development, the opportunity that the *Gao Kao* examination brings about should ultimately be impartial and candid, which would satisfy the desires of everyone. The job market should further be transparent for any applicant to readily acknowledge the reasoning behind their decline. On the whole, it is greatly apparent that direct intervention is desperately required from the central government on the matter of human capital development in order for the nation to look forward to a better tomorrow.

According to the World Bank simulation report, moving 1 %, 5 % and 10 % of the labour force out of agriculture and distributing them into the other sectors will, respectively, add 0.7 %, 3.3 % and 6.4 % to China's total GDP (World Development Report 2005). It was testified by Whalley and Zhang (2010) that whilst removing migrant restrictions, wage and income inequality disappears. Abolition of the various institutional obstacles that hinder the development of labour markets will not only enhance migration flows but also make movement rational, by helping to create a development climate and job opportunities suitable for labour mobility, which, in turn, matures the conditions for *hukou* reform.

Acknowledgement I am grateful to Mr Yong-Gyum Kim for taking several interviews and for his field works whilst he was undertaking voluntary social work in Beijing, Jinan, Guangzhou, Shanghai and Shenzhen; his work enhanced the quality and calibre of the project. In addition, I give much thanks to anonymous interviewees in Zhongshan University, Beijing Normal University and Jinan University in Guangzhou which were a great aid in this project.

References

Aoki M (2011) The five-phases of economic development and institutional evolution in China and Japan, ADBI working paper series. Asian Development Bank Institute, Tokyo
Asian Development Bank (ADB) (2008) Development effective review. Asian Development Bank
Bradsher K, Wong S L (2013) Special report: the education revolution. New York Times
Cai F (2012) Is there a "Middle-income Trap"? theories, experiences and relevance to China. China World Econ 20(1):49–61
Daily Telegraph 17 Jan 2012
Euromonitor survey on China (2013)
Fang C (2012) Is there a "Middle-income Trap"? Theories, experiences and relevance to China. China World Econ 20(1):49–61
Garrett G (2004) Globalisation's missing middle. Foreign Aff 83(6):84–96
Gill I, Kharas H (2007) An East Asian renaissance: ideas for economic growth. World Bank, Washington, DC
Gill I, Kharas H (2008) An East Asian renaissance: ideas for economic growth. World Bank, Washington, DC
IMF (2013) Regional economic outlook: Asia and Pacific. IMF, Washington, DC
Kuijs L (2009) China through 2020 – a macroeconomic scenario, World Bank research working paper 9. World Bank China Office, Beijing
Liu Z (2012) Memory, loss. The New York Times Archive
Mintel Market Research on China (2014)
Ramo JC (2004) Beijing consensus. The Foreign Policy Centre, London
Renmin Daily Newspaper, various issues
Several interviewees in Beijing, Jinan, Shanghai, Shenzhen and Guangzhou, whom wish to remain anonymous
The Economist (2014) Urbanisation - moving on up. 22 March 2014
Weibo, various issues
Whalley J, Zhao X (2010) The contribution of human capital to China's economic growth, NBER working paper No. 16592. National Bureau of Economic Research, Cambridge, MA
World Development Report 2005
Xinwha report various issues
Zhang L, Yi H, Luo R, Liu C, Rozelle S (2013) The human capital roots of the middle income trap: the case of China. Agric Econ 44(1):151–162

Chapter 11
Thoughts on Extreme Risk in Indonesia

Roberto Akyuwen, Raymond Boffey, Robert Powell, and Krisna Wijaya

Abstract Portfolios are commonly optimised using return standard deviation. This article explores a variety of alternate methods for optimising the industry mix of Indonesian portfolios. These include value at risk (VaR) and conditional value at risk (CVaR) using both parametric and nonparametric methods. VaR captures risk at a higher threshold than standard deviation, usually at 95 % or 99 % confidence. CVaR captures extreme risks beyond VaR. The study is unique in its application and comparison of both parametric (normally distributed) and nonparametric VaR and CVaR methods to sectoral portfolio optimization. To capture a range of economic circumstances, the data period incorporates the Global Financial Crisis (GFC) as well as pre-GFC and post-GFC years. The study identifies a fairly narrow band of industries that feature as industries of choice in optimised portfolios across our range of metrics, although their optimal proportions differ across metrics. Using these extreme risk optimizers can assist investors in avoiding high-risk stocks and minimising risk for given return levels. Extreme volatility is also an indicator of underlying problems in an industry, and this comprehensive study on sectoral risk provides important information to lenders, regulators, economic policymakers and governments on the performance and risk of the Indonesian sectoral market and in reviewing sector-based investment and economic policies.

11.1 Introduction

Using a dataset from 2005 to 2011, which spanned a range of economic circumstances, Allen et al. (2012) showed that parametric methods appear to work equally as well as nonparametric methods when measuring extreme risk in Indonesian sectors. This is contradictory to most studies in other markets, which generally

R. Akyuwen
Financial Services Authority, Jakarta, Indonesia

R. Boffey • R. Powell (✉)
Edith Cowan University, Perth, WA, Australia
e-mail: r.powell@ecu.edu.au

K. Wijaya
Bank Mandiri, Jakarta, Indonesia

H.G. Djajadikerta, Z. Zhang (eds.), *A New Paradigm for International Business*,
Springer Proceedings in Business and Economics, DOI 10.1007/978-981-287-499-3_11

report that parametric methods do not work well in times of high volatility as they assume a normal distribution which does not capture the high volatility shown in stock returns in periods of high risk such as the Global Financial Crisis (GFC). The authors attribute these somewhat unusual findings to the relatively strong and stable performance of Indonesia during the GFC (arising from factors such as Indonesian banks having strong regulation and not being involved to any great extent in high-risk products such as sub-prime mortgages) and the relatively strong and speedy recovery afterwards. This meant that Indonesian portfolios experienced a more normal distribution of returns over these volatile times than was globally experienced. The interesting question therefore arises as to whether parametric and nonparametric methods work equally as well when extended to the sectoral optimization of Indonesian portfolios. Whilst a nonparametric study has been undertaken on optimising Indonesian portfolios (Akyuwen et al. 2014), using the same dataset as we use in this study, that study provides no comparison to parametric techniques.

Against this background, this article extends the abovementioned studies, by using both parametric and nonparametric VaR and CVaR methods to optimise the industry mix of Indonesian stock portfolios over the same 2005–2011 period used by those studies. Thus a total of four optimising methods (parametric VaR, nonparametric VaR, parametric CVaR and nonparametric CVaR) are used. As far as we are aware, nowhere have both parametric and nonparametric VaR and CVaR methods been applied to sector optimization in Indonesia, making this study a first.

The research question addressed in this study is to determine whether there are any significant differences between the optimal portfolio mix when using each of our four optimization metrics. Significant differences between VaR and CVaR will indicate high risk in the tails of the portfolio mix, which is not captured by the lower risk VaR measure as compared to CVaR. Significant differences between parametric and nonparametric measures will indicate non-normality of distributions. Allied to this research questions is to ascertain whether there are Indonesian industries which consistently feature strongly (or poorly) in an optimal portfolio mix, across each of our four optimization metrics.

Indonesia has the fourth largest population in the world and it is the largest economy in the South East Asian Region. The performance of the Indonesia stock exchange (IDX) has been ranked the world's fifth best in 2010 and second best in 2011 by the World Federation of Exchanges (2011). Yet there is not yet any comprehensive Indonesian study which compares the range of techniques for sectoral optimization which is presented in this article. There are, however, some studies which have investigated Indonesian stock portfolio performance from various other angles, such as use of the single index and constant correlation model (Eko 2008), the impact of macro-variables on the return of a portfolio of Indonesian stocks (Sitinjak 2011) and the use of the momentum investment strategy Wiksuana (2009). There are also non-Indonesian studies using VaR, but not CVaR, such as Weng and Trück (2011) and Jadhav and Ramanathan (2009). There has been very little focus in Indonesia in terms of sectoral optimisation, VaR and CVaR.

Given that this article is the first to undertake a comprehensive comparative analysis in Indonesia between parametric and nonparametric VaR and CVaR as optimizers, the information is of great importance to investors in choosing their portfolio mix and in trying to avoid higher-risk sectors in volatile times as well as to lenders, governments and regulators in understanding which sectors are most vulnerable to downturn times.

The remainder of this paper is structured as follows. Section 11.2 outlines the data used, Sect. 11.3 explains our VaR and CVaR methods and Sect. 11.4 explains construction of the optimal portfolio. Section 11.5 presents the optimal portfolio results, Sect. 11.6 undertakes significance testing for differences between our optimizer methods and Sect. 11.7 concludes.

11.2 Data

We use the same dataset as Allen et al. (2012) and Akyuwen et al. (2014), which is Indonesian stocks which comprise the IDX composite index from 2005 to 2011. This index contains all the stocks listed on the IDX and is thus representative of the IDX as a whole, containing a range of large and small listed stocks. The dataset spans pre-GFC circumstances (2005–2007), GFC (mid-2007–2009) and post-GFC recovery (2010–2011).

We only use companies which have data over the entire period, which is 217 companies with total market cap of Rp. 1,973 trillion (US$205 billion), comprising just over half of all IDX stocks by both number and market cap. We use Global Industry Classification Standard (GICS) sectors, which includes Agriculture, Banks and Insurance, Consumer Discretionary, Consumer Staples, Diversified Financials, Energy and Materials, Industrials, IT and Telecom and Mining and Real Estate. Daily time series data is obtained from Datastream.

11.3 VaR and CVaR Method

VaR is a widely used metric which escalated in popularity since its adoption by the Basel Accords as the primary metric for measuring the market risk of banks. VaR measures the maximum loss over a specified time period at a selected level of confidence. Parametric VaR assumes a normal distribution and is based on the standard deviation (σ) of returns. For example, VaR at the 95 % confidence level is 1.645σ, as obtained from standard normal distribution tables. Of course, such a measure is only useful if returns are expected to be normally distributed, which often is not the case, especially during highly volatile circumstances such as the GFC. Nonparametric, or historical simulation VaR, makes no assumptions about the distribution. It is based on actual past losses, with VaR at the 95 % confidence level being the 95th percentile worst return over the selected time period.

For comparison, we use both methods (parametrical and historical) in this article. For the parametric method, to take account of correlations between the individual entities within each sector, we construct a variance-covariance matrix from which the sector standard deviation and VaR is calculated. For historical VaR, there is no need to construct such a matrix, as we calculate VaR from the weighted average of the historical returns for each sector, because the correlations are naturally embedded in these weighted average returns. Note that in all cases, returns are value weighted according to the market capitalisation of the stock.

Historical simulation VaR does not make any assumption about the distribution, but sorts returns from best to worst, with VaR being the return at the selected level of confidence (e.g. the 95th worst return at a 95 % confidence level).

A downside of VaR is that it says nothing of losses beyond VaR. CVaR addresses this shortfall as it is the average of losses beyond VaR. Therefore, because we measure VaR at the 95 % confidence level in this study, historical CVaR is the average of the worst 5 % of returns and parametric CVaR is the average of those returns exceeding parametric VaR. Because VaR does not address those losses in the extreme tail of the distribution, whilst CVaR does, Allen and Powell (2009, 2011) and Allen, Powell and Singh (2011) have found CVaR to be a superior measure to VaR in downturn times.

11.4 Constructing Our Optimal Portfolio

The construction of an optimal portfolio and efficient frontier using Markowitz (1952) portfolio theory is a well understood theory in finance; hence we will only summarise key differences between the Markowitz approach and our techniques. The Markowitz efficient frontier shows the maximum return level that can be achieved for a given level of risk (with variance or standard deviation being the usual risk measures). Due to correlations between returns, construction of the frontier requires construction of a variance-covariance matrix, and the portfolio is then optimised to obtain the combination of assets which yields the minimum risk for each selected return level. We use exactly the same approach, except instead of variance return, we use VaR return or CVaR return. We set the minimum portfolio weight for each sector to 0 (this can include individual negative return stocks in a sector portfolio). As parametric VaR is just a derivation of standard deviation (1.645σ), the optimal sectoral percentage of a parametric VaR return portfolio is the same as variance return. However, historic VaR return reshapes the frontier as it is based on actual losses. CVaR (both parametric and nonparametric) also reshapes the frontier as it is based on actual losses beyond the VaR measure.

The maximum return point for our portfolio is the highest return that can be generated by any industry sector. The minimum return point is the return associated with the lowest possible VaR (or CVaR). We select eight equidistant points between the maximum possible return and the return associated with the minimum risk (VaR or CVaR), giving a total of 10 return points. We calculate the minimum portfolio VaR and CVaR associated with each point. These VaR return and CVaR return combinations make up the efficient frontier.

11.5 Results

Column 1 of Table 11.1 shows annual returns, with our four optimising metrics (daily figures) in the remaining columns.

Agriculture has the highest return followed by Consumer Discretionary and Diversified Financials, with IT and Telecom the lowest. Mining has the highest volatility. The Agriculture and Mining sectors grew strongly pre-GFC, both falling dramatically in the GFC with falling commodity prices. Agriculture recovered strongly, with Mining's recovery being far more modest. Thus both these industries have high volatility, but Mining has a lower return. Whilst Consumer Discretionary, globally, tends to be a hard hit industry in downturn times due to consumers putting discretionary spending on hold, this is not seen in Indonesia. This is because the GFC was relatively mild and short in Indonesia given they had strong bank regulation with little exposure to sub-prime lending, and the impact was reduced by prompt policy responses by the government and monetary authorities (Siregar et al. 2012). Relatively stable interest rates and property rental prices meant low Real Estate sector volatility. Consumer Staples is traditionally an industry, globally, which is relatively less risky than most during volatile times, as customers continue to purchase essential items, and this is also seen to be the case in Indonesia. The parametric VaR measures (overall 0.0307) are seen to be slightly higher than the historical ones (overall 0.0283), as is also the case with the parametric (0.0475) and

Table 11.1 Return and risk

	Annual returns	Parametric VaR	Parametric CVaR	Historical VaR	Historical CVaR
Agriculture	0.3363	0.0363	0.0596	0.0315	0.0541
Banks and insurance	0.1954	0.0296	0.0429	0.0263	0.0397
Consumer discretionary	0.2869	0.0225	0.0380	0.0187	0.0309
Consumer staples	0.2368	0.0249	0.0395	0.0210	0.0343
Diversified financials	0.2869	0.0366	0.0557	0.0235	0.0435
Energy and materials	0.2097	0.0260	0.0429	0.0260	0.0429
Industrials	0.2023	0.0331	0.0548	0.0365	0.0578
IT and telecom	0.0497	0.0329	0.0464	0.0305	0.0437
Mining	0.2441	0.0455	0.0697	0.0415	0.0663
Real estate	0.2732	0.0254	0.0372	0.0215	0.0327
All sectors	0.2375	0.0307	0.0475	0.0283	0.0435

historical (0.0435) CVaR measures, thus not indicating any fat tails. We now use the above information to generate an optimal portfolio for each of the ten levels of return (as discussed in Sect. 11.4).

We see from Table 11.2 that an investor wishing to maximise returns would invest all their funds in agriculture. As we use the same dataset as the Akyuwen et al. (2014) nonparametric study, the nonparametric (historical) weightings in Table 11.2 align with their study, but the parametric ones are unique to this study. The highest return in Table 11.1 is the same as the highest return for an individual sector in Table 11.2 (Agriculture) as an investor cannot increase return through diversification. An investor wishing to minimise VaR (both parametric and historical, though with slightly different weightings) would have a more diversified portfolio, including large weightings towards Consumer Discretionary, Consumer Staples and Real Estate, which all have relatively low volatility for reasons already discussed. The returns associated with the lowest VaR (CVaR) in Table 11.2 will not equal the lowest return for any individual sector in Table 11.1, as the Table 11.2 VaR (CVaR) figures are correlated as discussed in Sect. 11.4, and an investor can achieve lower risk through diversification. Agriculture's prominence reduces as more conservative returns are sought, due to high volatility. Diversified Financials, Industrials and Mining do not feature as attractive investments from an optimal risk-return perspective. When using CVaR (both parametric and historical), we note that Real Estate becomes much more prominent at the bottom of the tables, due to its relatively lower tail risk.

Figure 11.1 shows how the frontier shifts to the right when using CVaR. There are some differences evident in the historical and parametric frontiers, with parametric measures having slightly overshot the historical measures (as seen by the figures in Table 11.1) due to the low tail risk. To determine if differences in portfolio mix between the different metrics and periods are significant, we will undertake significance testing in Sect. 11.6.

11.6 Significance Testing

Table 11.3 provides a summary of those industries which feature most prominently across our periods from a return, risk and overall perspective. "High return" are those industries which have the highest aggregate percentage representation in the top three return levels of our ten return levels, for each metric (i.e. they are the optimal selection from a risk-return perspective for investors seeking high returns). "Low risk" are those industries which have the highest aggregate percentage representation in the bottom three return levels of the ten return levels for each metric (i.e. they are the optimal selection from a risk-return perspective for investors seeking low risk returns). The "overall" column are those industries which have the highest aggregate percentage representation across all ten return levels in each of our periods, for each metric.

Table 11.2 Optimal portfolios

Parametric VaR and CVaR optimal portfolio											
Returns (%)	Parametric VaR (%)	Agriculture (%)	Banks and insurance (%)	Consumer discretionary (%)	Consumer staples (%)	Diversified financials (%)	Energy and materials (%)	Industrials (%)	IT and telecom (%)	Mining (%)	Real estate (%)
33.63	3.63	100.00	0.00	0.00	0.00	0.00	0.00	0.00	0.00	0.00	0.00
32.68	3.17	80.82	0.00	19.18	0.00	0.00	0.00	0.00	0.00	0.00	0.00
31.73	2.77	61.64	0.00	38.36	0.00	0.00	0.00	0.00	0.00	0.00	0.00
30.79	2.46	43.41	0.00	53.16	0.00	0.00	0.00	0.00	0.00	0.00	3.42
29.84	2.22	27.73	0.00	56.19	0.00	0.03	0.00	0.00	0.00	0.00	16.06
28.89	2.09	14.08	0.00	56.93	2.88	0.62	0.00	0.00	0.00	0.00	25.48
27.94	2.01	6.75	0.00	52.24	14.32	0.26	0.00	0.00	0.00	0.00	26.43
26.99	1.96	1.50	0.00	47.63	20.05	0.00	5.39	0.00	0.00	0.00	25.43
26.04	1.94	0.00	0.00	39.56	23.92	0.00	14.15	0.00	0.21	0.00	22.16
25.10	1.94	0.00	0.00	36.43	23.41	0.00	15.39	0.00	3.99	0.00	20.77
Returns (%)	Parametric CVaR (%)	Agriculture (%)	Banks and insurance (%)	Consumer discretionary (%)	Consumer staples (%)	Diversified financials (%)	Energy and materials (%)	Industrials (%)	IT and telecom (%)	Mining (%)	Real estate (%)
33.63	5.96	100.00	0.00	0.00	0.00	0.00	0.00	0.00	0.00	0.00	0.00
32.51	5.09	77.35	0.00	22.65	0.00	0.00	0.00	0.00	0.00	0.00	0.00
31.39	4.38	55.42	0.00	40.00	0.00	1.96	0.00	0.00	0.00	0.00	2.62
30.27	3.81	37.12	0.00	41.81	0.00	2.70	0.00	0.00	0.00	0.00	18.36
29.15	3.41	18.83	0.00	43.62	0.00	3.45	0.00	0.00	0.00	0.00	34.10
28.03	3.22	7.66	0.00	40.29	10.05	3.15	0.00	0.00	0.00	0.00	38.86
26.91	3.11	0.04	0.00	35.18	21.46	2.39	2.26	0.00	0.00	0.00	38.67
25.79	3.08	0.00	0.00	29.53	23.36	1.10	7.65	0.00	2.74	0.00	35.62
24.67	3.06	0.00	0.00	26.76	22.68	0.54	8.70	0.00	7.36	0.00	33.96
23.55	3.05	0.00	0.00	23.96	22.02	0.00	9.80	0.00	11.96	0.00	32.25

(continued)

Table 11.2 (continued)

Historical VaR and CVaR optimal portfolio

Returns (%)	Historical VaR (%)	Agriculture (%)	Banks and insurance (%)	Consumer discretionary (%)	Consumer staples (%)	Diversified financials (%)	Energy and materials (%)	Industrials (%)	IT and telecom (%)	Mining (%)	Real estate (%)
33.63	3.15	100.00	0.00	0.00	0.00	0.00	0.00	0.00	0.00	0.00	0.00
32.86	2.82	84.40	0.00	15.60	0.00	0.00	0.00	0.00	0.00	0.00	0.00
32.09	2.51	68.81	0.00	31.19	0.00	0.00	0.00	0.00	0.00	0.00	0.00
31.32	2.24	53.21	0.00	46.79	0.00	0.00	0.00	0.00	0.00	0.00	0.00
30.55	2.03	38.69	0.00	57.43	0.00	0.00	0.00	0.00	0.00	0.00	3.88
29.77	1.87	26.00	0.00	59.62	0.00	0.00	0.00	0.00	0.00	0.00	14.38
29.00	1.77	13.44	0.00	61.68	0.18	0.00	0.00	0.00	0.00	0.00	24.70
28.23	1.70	7.62	0.00	57.36	9.66	0.00	0.00	0.00	0.00	0.00	25.36
27.46	1.66	1.80	0.00	53.04	19.13	0.00	0.00	0.00	0.00	0.00	26.03
26.69	1.65	0.00	0.00	45.58	27.54	0.00	1.19	0.00	0.78	0.00	24.91
Returns (%)	Historical CVaR (%)	Agriculture (%)	Banks and insurance (%)	Consumer discretionary (%)	Consumer staples (%)	Diversified financials (%)	Energy and materials (%)	Industrials (%)	IT and telecom (%)	Mining (%)	Real estate (%)
33.63	5.41	100.00	0.00	0.00	0.00	0.00	0.00	0.00	0.00	0.00	0.00
32.74	4.74	81.96	0.00	18.04	0.00	0.00	0.00	0.00	0.00	0.00	0.00
31.85	4.13	63.92	0.00	33.82	0.00	2.26	0.00	0.00	0.00	0.00	0.00
30.96	3.61	45.88	0.00	47.22	0.00	6.90	0.00	0.00	0.00	0.00	0.00
30.06	3.20	30.78	0.00	50.51	0.00	8.09	0.00	0.00	0.00	0.00	10.62
29.17	2.90	16.40	0.00	51.34	0.00	8.46	0.00	0.00	0.00	0.00	23.81
28.28	2.74	5.19	0.00	49.89	4.47	8.33	0.00	0.00	0.00	0.00	32.12
27.39	2.66	0.00	0.00	43.45	17.07	7.01	0.00	0.00	0.00	0.00	32.47
26.50	2.64	0.00	0.00	37.65	22.75	5.60	0.00	0.00	2.62	0.00	31.37
25.60	2.63	0.00	0.00	35.41	22.58	5.06	0.00	0.00	6.47	0.00	30.48

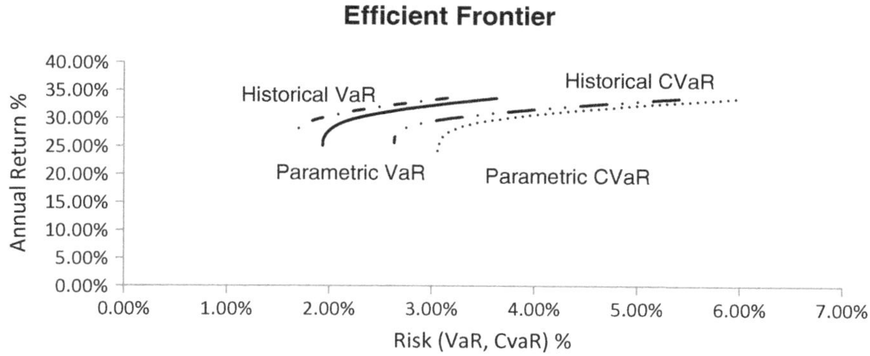

Fig. 11.1 Efficient frontier

Table 11.3 Prominent sectors in the optimal portfolios

Rank	High return	Low risk	Overall
Para VaR			
1	A	CD	CD
2	CD	RE	A
3	RE	CS	RE
Hist VaR			
1	A	CD	CD
2	CD	RE	A
3	RE	CS	RE
Para CVaR			
1	A	RE	CD
2	CD	CD	A
3	RE	CS	RE
Hist CVaR			
1	A	CD	CD
2	CD	RE	A
3	DF	CS	RE

Over the period there are four sectors, i.e. Consumer Discretionary (CD), Agriculture (A), Real Estate (RE) and Consumer Staples (CS), which feature more strongly than other stocks in the optimal portfolios and are thus relatively very attractive stocks for investors to include in their portfolio mix. Agriculture has strong returns with moderate risk levels, Real Estate and Consumer staples have a good balance between risk and return and Consumer Discretionary is strong from both a risk and return perspective.

Although credit risk is not a primary focus of this paper, we mentioned in our introduction that a sector portfolio of stocks which performs poorly from a return or volatility perspective could highlight fundamental problems in that industry which is important information for lenders to those industries. Consistent with this thinking, a Bank for International Settlements (2009) task force reported that market and credit risk are driven by the same underlying forces, which interact significantly in determining asset values and that default may be affected by fluctuations in these asset values. Thus, for completeness, we will briefly address that issue here. To determine whether our four sectors which feature most prominently from an investment perspective would also have less credit risk, we grouped all the stocks from these four sectors into one portfolio (portfolio 1) and all other stocks into another portfolio (portfolio 2) and then tested them for credit risk using a Merton (1974) "distance to default" (DD) model. A detailed explanation of the workings of this model is beyond the scope of this paper, and given that this is a well-known model whose workings are readily available (Bharath and Shumway 2008; Crosbie and Bohn 2003), we will not provide that detail here. Suffice it to say that the model deems the default point of an entity is when asset values fall below outstanding debt. Thus assets, debt and the volatility of asset values form the core components of the model. Portfolio DD is calculated after applying the model to each individual entity, making allowance for correlations between each entity. DD is measured in standard deviations (the number of standard deviations that assets are away from debt, based on volatility in market asset values). Thus a higher DD indicates a lower risk and a DD of zero is the default point.

We see from Table 11.4 that portfolio 1 has a higher DD than portfolio 2. This shows that the four sector portfolio (portfolio 1) outperforms the other sector portfolio from a credit as well as an investment perspective.

We have shown which industries feature in our optimal mix for each of our four metrics. Our research questions require us to determine whether there is significant difference in the mix for each of our four metrics. Thus the final step of our analysis is to undertake significance testing on differences between the optimal portfolios yielded for each of the metrics. For robustness, we will undertake two forms of significance testing, nonparametric and parametric testing. The nonparametric testing will use the Spearman rank correlation coefficient which is based on *ranking* of the sectors in each portfolio rather than proportions. The test is one of *association* or *correlation*, with a high significance meaning that there is similarity in rankings (explanation of the Spearman method can be found in most statistical textbooks and hence will not be explained here). This test will tell us whether it is the same industries which feature most prominently in the different portfolio mixes, but not anything about their proportions. The parametric testing will use chi-square to test for differences in *proportions* between the different optimal portfolios (i.e. does the percentage mix change for the sectors when using different metrics). Contrary to the Spearman test, which tests for *association* (similarity), the proportions test is one of *differences*. For both the parametric and nonparametric tests, we compare each of the ten levels in each of the portfolios against each of the corresponding levels in every other portfolio (e.g. the proportion and ranking of the sectors in the parametric portfolio, at each of the ten levels, significantly similar to the proportion and ranking at each of the ten levels of the nonparametric portfolio and at each of the ten levels of all the other portfolios). We commence with the nonparametric (ranking testing) as shown in Table 11.5.

Table 11.4 Distance to default

	DD
Portfolio 1: (A, CD, CS, RE)	6.84
Portfolio 2: All other sectors	5.30

Table 11.5 Significance testing of rankings

	Parametric VaR	Historical VaR	Parametric CVaR	Historical CVaR
Parametric VaR		**	**	
Historical VaR	**			**
Parametric CVaR	**			**
Historical CVaR		**	**	

** denotes 99 % significance, * denotes 95 % significance and '–'denotes no significance. The shaded areas are where no useful or valid comparison can take place (e.g. parametric VaR and historical VaR can be compared as they are both types of VaR measures, and parametric VaR can be compared to parametric CVaR as they are both parametric measures, but parametric VaR has nothing in common with historical CVaR that would yield a useful comparison). Significance is obtained through use of a Spearman rank correlation test

We note that all of the methods produce significantly similar rankings to each other, i.e. the same industries rank higher in the optimization, no matter what metric is used, as parametric results are similar to nonparametric results and VaR is similar to CVaR. We see this from Table 11.3, where industries such as Agriculture, Consumer Discretionary, Consumer Staples and Real Estate consistently rank highly in the optimised portfolios, across all the metrics. This consistency between metrics indicates a high degree of normality in the Indonesian return distributions, consistent with the Allen et al.'s findings mentioned in Sect. 11.1. We now move to our parametric (proportions) test, with the results presented in Table 11.6.

Here we see a far more mixed result, with highly significant (99 % level) differences between some of the metrics and less significant differences (95 % level) or nonsignificant differences between other metrics. This means that the metrics will consistently tell us which industries are better to include in the portfolio, but yield a different interpretation on the best proportion of each to include. So whilst the ranking tests tended to indicate a high degree of normality in returns, the proportions test (which goes beyond just simple rankings) indicates that there is at least some degree of non-normality in returns which will not necessarily be fully captured by VaR measures (which ignore the tail) or by parametric measures (which assume normality).

Table 11.6 Significance testing of proportions

	Parametric VaR	Historical VaR	Parametric CVaR	Historical CVaR
Parametric VaR		–	*	
Historical VaR	–			**
Parametric CVaR	*			**
Historical CVaR		**	**	

** denotes 99 % significance, * denotes 95 % significance and '–'denotes no significance. The shaded areas are where no useful or valid comparison can take place (e.g. parametric VaR and historical VaR can be compared as they are both types of VaR measures, and parametric VaR can be compared to parametric CVaR as they are both parametric measures, but parametric VaR has nothing in common with historical CVaR that would yield a useful comparison). Significance is obtained through use of a chi-square test for differences in proportions

11.7 Conclusions

Our study explored whether there are any significant differences between the optimal portfolio mix when using each of our four optimization metrics. Significant differences between VaR and CVaR would indicate high risk in the tails of the portfolio mix, which is not captured by the lower risk VaR measure. A number of interesting aspects were noted. There was an extremely high level of association between the metrics when ranking optimal stocks. Those stocks which were found to be the best (worst) to include in the portfolio were consistently the same across all metrics, whether parametrically or historically based and whether using VaR or CVaR. This means that any of these metrics would be as good as each other in ranking (ordering) stocks to include in the portfolio. However, there were significant differences when testing for proportions, meaning that although the metrics chose the same stocks in the same order of preference, they differed in their proportional allocation. Thus a normally distributed parametric approach will not entirely accurately capture the distribution and optimal portfolio mix, and there can also be some significant differences between VaR and CVaR optimised portfolios. The study also provided important information regarding which industries tended to dominate, with Agriculture, Consumer Discretionary, Consumer Staples and Real Estate featuring prominently. This study on the Indonesian sector provides important information to investors in choosing their portfolio mix and optimization methods. The performance of equities can also be useful information to lenders as an indicator of the health or distress of a sector, and in this regard, our study showed some parallels between optimal sectors from an investment perspective and from a default perspective. The identification of sectors which are vulnerable during economic downturns is also important to economic policymakers in formulating policies on industry development and industry support.

Acknowledgements The authors thank Edith Cowan University Faculty of Business and Law Strategic Research Fund for funding assistance.

References

Akyuwen R, Allen DE, Boffey RR, Kramadibrata A, Powell RJ, Singh AK, & Wijaya K (2014) Sectoral risk analysis in Indonesia using extreme metrics: Special focus on primary industries, Working Paper

Allen DE, Powell RJ (2009) Transitional credit modelling and its relationship to market value at risk: an Australian sectoral perspective. Account Financ 49(3):425–444

Allen DE, Powell RJ (2011) Measuring and optimising extreme sectoral risk in Australia. Asia Pac J Econ Bus 15(1):1–14

Allen DE, Powell RJ, Singh AK (2011) Beyond reasonable doubt: multiple tail risk measures applied to European industries. Appl Econ Lett 19(7):671–676

Allen DE, Powell RJ, Boffey RR, Kramadibrata AR, Singh AK (2012) Thumbs up to parametric measures of relative VaR and CVaR in Indonesian sectors. Int J Bus Stud 20(1):27–42

Bank for International Settlements (2009) Findings on the interaction of market and credit risk, wp 0916

Bharath S, Shumway T (2008) Forecasting default with the Merton distance-to-default model. Rev Financ Stud 21(3):1339–1369

Crosbie P, Bohn J (2003) Modelling default risk. www.moodysanalytics.com. Accessed 12 Feb 2014

Eko U (2008) Analisis dan Penilaian Kinerja Portofolio Optimal Saham-Saham LQ-45. Jurnal Ilmu Administrasi dan Organisasi 13(3):178–187

Jadhav D, Ramanathan TV (2009) Parametric and non-parametric estimation of Value-at-Risk. J Risk Model Validation 3(1):51–71

Markowitz H (1952) Portfolio selection. J Financ 7(1):77–91

Merton R (1974) On the pricing of corporate debt: the risk structure of interest rates. J Finane 29:449–470

Siregar H, Hasanah H, Noer AA (2012) Impact of the global financial crisis on the Indonesian economy: further analysis using export and investment channels. Eur J Soc Sci 30(3):438–450

Sitinjak ELM (2011) Faktor Makro Ekonomi (Variabel CRR) pada Return Portofolio Pasar Saham di Indonesia Saat Bullish dan Bearish. Jurnal Organisasi dan Manajemen 7(2):117–139

Weng H, Trück S (2011) Style analysis and Value-at-Risk of Asia-focused hedge funds. Pac Basin Financ J 19(5):491–510

Wiksuana IGB (2009) Kinerja Portofolio Saham Berdasarkan Strategi Investasi Momentum di Pasar Modal Indonesia. Jurnal Manajemen dan Kewirausahaan 11(1):73–84

Chapter 12
Characteristics of Audit Committee and Real Activities Manipulation: Case from Indonesia

I. Putu Sugiartha Sanjaya and Andreas Yudha Mahendra Jati

Abstract The objective of this research is to investigate the impact of characteristics of audit committee on real activities manipulation. This research has a contribution for developing theory on earnings management. The last researches find that audit committee has an impact on accrual earnings management. Because, earnings management are not only using accruals but management can manage earnings through real activities manipulation. Therefore, this study has new angle and perspective to improve studying in relation between audit committee and earnings management. This study collects data from manufacturing industry listed in the Indonesia Stock Exchange on the period 2007–2011. The sum of observations is 125 firm years. The dependent variable of this study is real activities manipulation, and the independent variables are characteristics of audit committee such as the age of audit committee members, gender (the proportion of women on audit committee members), and education of audit committee members. This study uses one proxy for real earnings management such as measuring abnormal operating cash flow. The age, gender, and education of audit committee have no influence on real activities manipulation.

12.1 Introduction

Statement Financial Accounting Concept No. 8 (FASB 2010) suggests that the objective of financial reporting is to provide financial information that is useful to existing and potential investors, lenders, and other creditors. They need this information for making decisions such as buying, selling, or holding equity and debt instruments and providing or settling loans and other forms of credit. Existing and potential lenders and other creditors' decisions depend on the information about the returns that they expect to receive from an investment such as dividends, principal, interest payments, or capital gains, and their decisions about providing or settling loans and other forms of credit depend on the principal and interest payments or other returns that they expect. The expectation of investors, lenders, and other creditors about returns depends on their assessment of the amount, timing, and

I.P.S. Sanjaya (✉) • A.Y.M. Jati
Universitas Atma Jaya Yogyakarta, Yogyakarta, Indonesia
e-mail: siputusugiartha@yahoo.com

H.G. Djajadikerta, Z. Zhang (eds.), *A New Paradigm for International Business*,
Springer Proceedings in Business and Economics, DOI 10.1007/978-981-287-499-3_12

uncertainty of the prospects for future net cash inflows to the entity. To assess prospects of future net cash inflows, investors, lenders, and other creditors need information about the resources of the entity and how efficient and effective the entity's management.

Information about the financial performance will be reflected by changes in the entity's economic resources and claims other than by obtaining additional resources directly from investors and creditor. This information is useful in assessing the entity's past and future ability to generate net cash inflows, which indicates that the entity has increased its available economic resources and its capacity for generating net cash inflows through its operations rather than by obtaining additional resources directly from investors and creditors. Financial reporting is information about financial performance provided by comprehensive income and its components. The comprehensive income will be used by investors, creditors, and others to predict net cash inflows in the future (FASB 2010).

To be more useful for the users, the financial information must be relevant and faithfully represent what it purports to represent. To enhance usefulness, the financial information must be comparable, verifiable, timely, and understandable. These are qualitative characteristics of financial information. The increasing quality of financial information will reduce negative reaction from the market. It means that application of bad corporate governance such as ineffective of audit committee not be able to reduce earnings management. It will impact on negative reaction from capital market. One case of public concern is the financial scandals of Enron. Often investors are misled by the high and low quality of earnings presented in the financial statements.

Earnings are one of valued information for the users. Through the information, users can assess the future performance such as net future cash flow. The information also is used to assess risk of investment or lending. Earnings management is the choice by managers of accounting policies to achieve certain goals. Earnings management is often done by using two methods, accrual earnings management and real activities manipulation. Accrual earnings management is used to reduce or increase reported earnings (Scott 2006). Real activities manipulation is a deviation from the normal operating activities of the company (Roychowdhury 2006). After the Sarbanes-Oxley Act, managers do not like to manage earnings by accrual earnings management. But, they select real activities manipulation. According to Gunny (2005), this shift is caused by several factors. First, accrual manipulation is more often the center of observation or inspection by auditors and regulators rather than decisions about pricing and production. Second, focusing attention only on accrual manipulation is more risky because managers may have limited flexibility to adjust accruals (Graham et al. 2005). Third, real activities manipulation is also likely to be hard to detect by auditors and regulators because managers can make modifications to revenue and expenses.

To maintain the quality of information, listed companies in Indonesia had audit committee since 2001. The audit committee is selected by board of commissioners. Board of commissioners is a unit of the organization structure. This board has a duty to monitor or oversee the board of directors. The audit committee assists the board of commissioners in carrying out their roles and responsibilities of overseeing the fairness of presentation of financial statements in conformity with generally accepted accounting principles, the application of business and financial risk management, the implementation of the company's internal control system, the audit process in accordance with applicable auditing standards, and the implementation of good corporate governance in the management of the company.

On board of commissioners, there are two members such as independent commissioners and commissioners. The head and member of audit committee is the independent commissioner. Audit committee is established based on the board of commissioners' resolution. The establishment will be reported to the shareholders in the general meeting. Based on the audit committee charter, audit committee has to assist the board of commissioners for supervisory duties. The audit committee must communicate effectively together with the board of directors and commissioners with the external and internal auditor.

The provision of Indonesia Capital Market Supervisory Agency on audit committee requires audit committee to consist of at least three members. One of whom is an independent commissioner and who acts as chairman. According to the applicable regulations, the members of audit committee also have the expertise in finance and accounting. The audit committee is composed of chairman (independent commissioner) and two members (independent party).

Audit committee has some duty such as reviewing and monitoring the follow-up on quarterly audited findings. Audit committee also prepares the report for the quarter financial reporting, discusses the annual budget for the next year, and prepares its work agenda for the next year. Its task was expanded to include the areas of risk management, aligning the company's plan to increase the role of risk management in its business operations.

The audit committee held 9 meetings with the attendance of each member. The audit committee has organized its activities and meetings with the directors and other parties. In the meeting they will discuss the quarterly consolidated financial statements, the annual audited consolidated financial statements, and the annual budget for next year with the directors and key employees who oversee the finance and accounting functions.

The existing audit committee's task in the company is to oversee and monitor financial statements. Based on their background in accounting and finance, we expect audit committee to reduce earnings management such real activities manipulation, because real activities manipulation will decrease the quality of financial information. It will have an impact on the users' decision. The users' low-quality financial information will be misleading. Therefore, we will investigate if the characteristics of audit committee can influence real activities manipulation. This study is important because existing audit committee will raise the cost such as wages, incentives, etc., of the companies. The public will appreciate the performance of audit committee that is to protect and maintain the high quality (fairness) of financial reporting. The contributions of this study are for regulators, researchers, and practitioners. The results of this study lead the regulators to improve regulation of selecting the head and members of audit committee from non-controlling shareholders. For researchers, the results of this study help them develop earnings management concepts and audit committee. This study will develop the previous study through replaced discretionary accruals by real activities manipulation. Real activities is one of methods to manage earnings. This study will develop the previous study. For practitioners, the results of our study will give information about performance of the audit committee. This performance is costly or not costly for public.

We have some motivation to study this topic. First, studying audit committee and real activities manipulation is less. Based on our researches, we find only one topic to relate audit committee and real activities manipulation. The purpose of Sun et al.'s (2014) study is to investigate the effectiveness of independent audit committees in constraining real activities manipulation. US firms with stronger incentives to undertake real activities manipulation are selected as sample (Sun et al. 2014). This study also provides further evidence on how audit committee members' additional directorships affect their ability to oversee both accrual and real earnings management. The results suggest that audit committees with high additional directorships are less effective in constraining real activities manipulation. As long as we know based on reading empirical study in Indonesia, we never find studying audit committee and real activities manipulation. Our study is the first to study about audit committee and real activities manipulation in listed company at the Indonesia Stock Exchange. Therefore, our study will give new perspective studying audit committee and real activities manipulation in Indonesia. We will give new empirical evidence audit committee and real acitivities manipulation. We will also give new reference in studying audit committee and real activities manipulation.

The rest of the our paper are as follows. In Sect. 12.2, we relate our work to prior literature and develop our hypotheses relating audit committee characteristics to the real activities manipulation. In Sect. 12.3, we describe the sample selection process and define the variables used in the paper. In Sect. 12.4, we present our empirical results. In Sect. 12.5, we offer some concluding comments.

12.2 Literature Review and Hypothesis Development

12.2.1 Positive Accounting Theory

Positive accounting theory is based on agency theory used to explain and predict accounting choices by managers. Opportunities for the contracting parties can influence accounting choices because accounting numbers are a control mechanism in the agency relationship. Watts and Zimmerman (1986) used positive accounting theory to explain and predict the behavior of management relating to the selection of accounting procedures. Watts and Zimmerman (1986) explained three hypotheses, bonus plan, debt covenant, and political cost.

According to Scott (2006), bonus plan hypothesis asserts that managers of companies with bonus plans are more likely to choose accounting methods that make reported earnings in the current period higher. Debt (equity) hypothesis asserts that the larger the debt to equity ratio of the company, the more likely the company's manager is to choose accounting procedures that shift reported earnings from future period to the current period. In the context of the debt agreement, the manager will manage and regulate the profits that debt obligation that should be completed in a given year may be postponed until next year. For example, managers will delay promotion expense in this year to next year. It is a strategy to increase earnings. It will impact to debt agreement or covenant. It will decrease leverage ratio between total debt to total equity. Under political cost hypothesis, compared to small companies, larger companies tend to choose and use accounting methods that can reduce reported net income more often. This relates to the regulations issued by the government, for example, in the case of taxes taken by the government, the amount corresponding to the percentage of the profits from the company.

12.2.2 Earnings Management

According to Scott (2006), earnings management is the choice by a manager of accounting policies so as to achieve some specific objective. The choice of accounting policies is interpreted quite broadly. It is convenient to divide accounting policy choice into two categories. One is the choice of accounting policies per se, such as straight-line versus declining-balance amortization, or policies for revenue recognition. The other category is discretionary accruals, such as provisions for credit losses, warranty costs, inventory values, and timing and amounts of non-recurring and extraordinary items such as write-offs and provisions for reorganization.

According to Scott (2006), there are some motivations to manage earnings. These are bonus motivation (Healy 1985; Gaver et al. 1995; Holthausen et al. 1995; Guidry et al. 1999), contractual motivation (Sweeney 1994), political motivation (Jones 1991; Cahan 1992; Na'im and Hartono 1996; Key 1997; Navissi 1999), tax motivation (Dopuch and Pincus 1988), changing of CEO motivation (DeFond and Park 1997), and capital market motivation (Perry and Williams 1994; Burgstahler and Dichev 1997; Teoh et al. 1998a, b; Rangan 1998; Erickson and Wang 1999). Earnings are managed to hide the private benefit obtained by controlling shareholder. The benefit is obtained because controlling shareholder is fully entrenched by control rights or exceeding control rights and cash flow rights. Empirically, Haw et al. (2004), Kim and Yi (2006), Ding et al. (2007), and Sanjaya (2010, 2011) find exceeding control rights and cash flow rights will increase earnings management.

Scott (2006) describes four patterns of earnings management as follows:

- Taking a bath

This can occur during periods of stress or reorganization including the placement of a new CEO. If a company had to report a loss, then manager feel better to report greater losses. Manager will more select income decreasing. Because manager can save accrual for next year to increase earnings. In general, this is called "clear the decks." This will lead to higher probability of future earnings. Healy (1985) explains that the manager whose net profit is below the bogey of bonus plan may undertake the action "take a bath" as this will increase the probability of future bonus.

- Income Minimization

This pattern is almost identical to "take a bath" but less extreme. This pattern was chosen to avoid company politically under investigation. Example of policy approaches to minimize the profit is the successful effort for the costs of oil and gas exploration.

- Income Maximization

As in the study of Healy (1985), manager will use to maximize the net income reported for bonus purposes. In addition to the purpose of bonuses, profit maximization is done by a company that violates debt agreements.

- Income Smoothing

The manager has a way of leveling the profit between the bogey and cap. In contrast, earnings may be permanently or temporarily not enough for bonus purposes. Furthermore, if the manager is risk averse, they will choose the reduction of the flow variable bonus.

Earnings management is through real activities manipulation. It is also called real earnings management. Managers also have an incentive to manage earnings by the real activities manipulation. The real activities manipulation affects cash flow and accrual such as a decrease on research and development (Baber et al 1991; Dechow and Sloan 1991; Bartov 1993). Healy and Wahlen (1999), Fudenberg and Tirole (1995), and Dechow and Skinner (2000) focus on accelerating sales, alterations in delivery scheduling, postponement of research and development, and spending restrictions.

Roychowdhury (2006) suggests that the real activities manipulation has two classifications abnormal and normal operational activities. Manipulation of the real activity can be done extensively through price discounts and reductions in discretionary costs to meet earnings targets. Graham et al. (2005) indicate financial executives are more interested in manipulating earnings through the real activity than accruals to meet earnings targets. This has happened because of the following reasons: First, the manipulation of accruals tends to attract auditors or regulators more to supervise than the real decision does. Second, any accrual manipulation causes more risk than the real activities manipulation.

Real activities manipulation can lower the value of the company because this activity has a negative effect on cash flow. Aggressive price discounts to increase sales volume causes customers to expect low prices. It leads to low sales margins. Increase in volume causes an excessive production or overproduction. The result indicates there is an excess inventory that must be sold in subsequent periods. It causes more storage costs of inventory.

Roychowdhury (2006) explains that the real activities manipulation can be done in three (3) ways. First, manipulation of sales is defined as the management efforts to increase sales on a temporary basis in a certain period by offering price discounts or excessive product such as offering lower interest rate or zero percent financing. This strategy can increase sales volume and profit for the year. Second, managers will reduce discretionary expenditures such as research and development expenses and advertising and selling, administrative, and general expenses. Third, overproduction is one strategy to increase earnings. Managers increase production levels. It can lead to lower fixed costs (fixed cost) per unit. This strategy can reduce the cost of goods sold and causes higher operating margins.

12.2.3 Audit Committee

There are two systems in the organization management, single and dual board systems. Indonesia adopts dual board system in its internal organizational structure. There are two separate functions in this system, which is a function of policy making and oversight. Policy-making function is executed by the board of directors, while oversight by the board of commissioners. Commissioners establish audit committees to support their functions. In performing their duties, the audit committees must be an outsider, more expert and experienced, and other qualities. The audit committees should be free from the influence of directors and external auditors. Audit committee is responsible only to the board of commissioners. According to National Committee on Governance in the Code of Good Corporate Governance of Indonesia, understanding of an audit committee is:

> The audit committee is a group of people chosen by the larger group to do a particular job or to perform specific tasks or the number of commissioners responsible corporate clients to assist in maintaining the auditor's independence from management.

The dual board system implemented in Indonesia is shown in Fig. 12.1.

Based on Jakarta Stock Exchange's board of directors, appointment letter No. 315/ BEJ/06200, the audit committee is established and dismissed by the board of commissioners. Audit committees are important to oversee and monitor the board of directors to manage companies. To respond to the importance of the audit committee, the director of the Jakarta Stock Exchange issues appointment letter No.339/BEJ/07-2001 on 20 July 2001. The letter suggests that listed company must have audit committee for the implementation of good corporate governance.

In the letter, the membership of the audit committee consists of at least three members. At least one member of the audit committee has an ability in accounting and finance. Each member of the audit committee must be from independent external, and at least one member shall be designated as chairman of the audit committee. External means outside of a company which are not recorded as commissioners, directors, and employees of listed companies. Independent means outside of a company which does not have a business relationship and affiliation with the listed company commissioners, directors, and major shareholders. They also give a professional opinion in accordance with professional ethics.

The members of the audit committee must be free of any obligation to the listed company. They must not have a particular interest to the listed company or listed company directors or commissioners and free of any circumstances that may cause

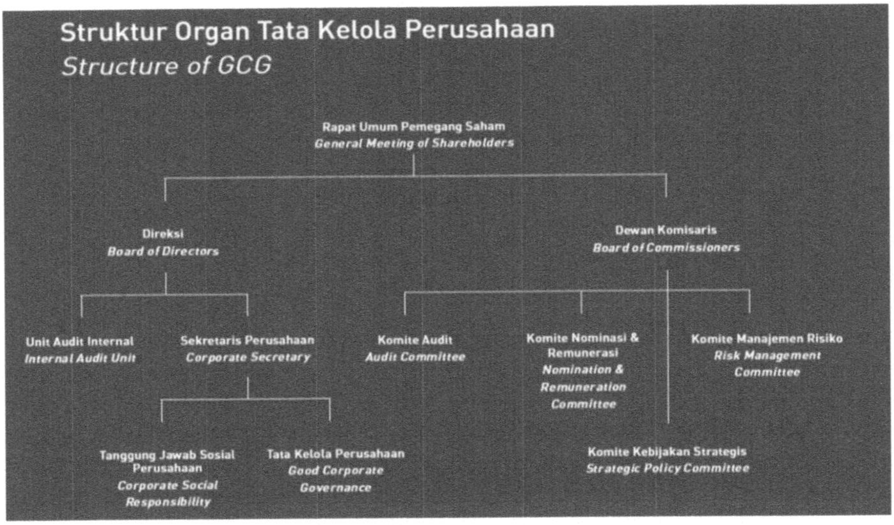

Fig. 12.1 Organization structure of PT Visi Media Asia Tbk

others to doubt the attitude of independence. To maintain independence, there are several external that cannot be members of the audit committee such as a public accountant who worked in public accounting firms that audit the financial statements of listed companies and persons who are not commissioners, directors, or employees of listed companies. They also have the ability to control legal consultant who worked at law firm in the listed companies and employees or commissioners of any other company that has an affiliate relationship with the listed company.

In March 2001, Indonesia Capital Market Supervisory Agency (ICMSA) conducts a press conference about the change of Regulation No. III.A.3; the regulation explains the empowerment of the board of commissioners. The board must establish an audit committee whose function is to assist the commissioner in the operational control (Bapepam 2001). Indonesian Forum for Corporate Governance (2001) also emphasizes the responsibility of the audit committee. There are three areas of responsibilities of the audit committee, (1) the financial statements, (2) the governance, and (3) the control. In financial statements, the audit committees ensure that the financial statements prepared by management must give relevance and faithful representation for the users. They must give a recommendation of the external auditor and assess the accounting policies and decisions.

In corporate governance, the audit committees have to ensure the company's operations in compliance with laws and regulations, ethics, and litigation. In control, the audit committees must oversee the company with regard to understanding and monitoring the issues and matters with potential risks, the internal control systems, and the process of supervision by the internal auditors. The scope of internal audit should include the assessment of the adequacy and effectiveness of internal control systems.

According to Fleming (2002), the audit committees should have three primary responsibilities. These are to monitor the risk of the company, to evaluate the effectiveness of the internal controls, and to oversee the financial statement process. According to Wilkinson et al. (2000), the role of the audit committees is to review audit status and findings and to maintain direct communication between board members, management, and external and internal auditors. They also should review the audited financial statements with the internal auditors and the board of commissioners, the operation of the internal audit department, the management performance, and the compliance with applicable laws and regulations.

To increase audit committee functions, they must be independent, have experience and knowledge of accounting and finance, and have joined meetings with management and internal audit. These are documented empirically by Kalbers and Fogarty (1993), McMullen and Raghunandan (1996), Abbott and Parker (2000), Carcello and Neal (2000), Beasley and Salterio (2001), DeZoort and Salterio (2001), Raghunandan et al. (2001), Klein (2002a), and Fleming (2002).

12.2.3.1 Independence of Audit Committees

Kalbers and Fogarty (1993) indicated that the issue of whether the audit committees actually do their responsibilities remains insufficiently understood. In this study, Kalbers and Fogarty (1993) examine the nature and extent of the audit committees' task. The results indicate a factor of legitimacy and independence of audit committee members required by the audit committee to do their duties. McMullen and Raghunandan (1996) examine whether the audit committees work effectively. The research was conducted by a survey of 51 companies with financial reporting problems. This is the implementation of SEC regulations and reporting of quarterly earnings. McMullen and Raghunandan (1996) find that for companies which have financial distress, the composition of the audit committee members is only 67 % of the external. Meanwhile, for companies which have no financial distress, the composition of the audit committee members is 86 % of the external. The results suggest that more independent audit committee is more ability to monitor board of directors for more efficient to manage company. Independent audit committee is more effective to monitor board of director because it has not conflict of interest. It has good impact for company.

Abbott and Parker (2000) examine the relationship between characteristic audit committees such as independent members and has experience in public accounting firm. This public accounting firm has specialized industries. It indicates audit committee has good experience to be effective audit committee to monitor board of director. They distribute questionnaires about the issues in the election of the auditor for the 500 companies listed on the NYSE, AMEX, or NASDAQ. In this study, the sample firms are randomly selected from a list of firms with financial auditor data available in COMPUSTAT for 1994–1995, and proxy statements for

1994 are available in the database of the S & P Corporate Text. Abbott and Parker (2000) suggest that the active and independent audit committee correlates positively with the selection of a public accounting firm that has industry specialization.

DeZoort and Salterio (2001) examine a sample of 68 audit committee members who resolve accounting policy dispute case. DeZoort and Salterio (2001) find that audit committee members with independent director experience and audit knowledge tend to support the auditors when there is accounting policy dispute, whereas those members with current experience as executive directors are less likely do. Klein (2002a) examines whether SEC rules should be implemented by the company. He tests the economic determinants behind differences in audit committee independence for a sample of more than 400 major US corporations that were traded publicly during 1991–1993. Klein (2002a) finds that independent audit committee is positively associated with independent board of directors.

Fleming (2002) argues that there are five specific ways to improve the effectiveness of the audit committee. First, tasks, duties, and responsibilities of the audit committee should specifically be defined by SEC. Second, the presence of an audit committee demonstrates compliance with standards through the submission of annual compliance reports with the SEC and other independent agencies. Third, the audit committee service should be recognized as a separate profession and individuals who will be members of the audit committee must meet the specific criteria before they are selected. Fourth, the period of the appointment of the audit committees should be limited to 3–5 years and the chairman of the audit committee should have limited tenure. Fifth, the SEC or another independent body should evaluate the independence of audit committee members.

12.2.3.2 Experience and Knowledge of Accounting and Finance

To improve the oversight of the quality of financial statements, accounting and financial knowledge is a must for members of the audit committee. In this case, members of the audit committee should receive training in accounting and finance. Raghunandan et al. (2001) explain the need for an audit committee member who has a background in accounting and finance. Kalbers and Fogarty (1993) found that audit committee effectiveness was associated with organizational and personal bases of audit committee power. Audit committee members should have expertise in accounting and auditing.

To improve the effectiveness of the audit committee, they must review the internal audit proposals related to the program, plan, and coordinate with the external auditors. The audit committees are also reviewing the results of the internal audit as it relates to financial reporting, internal controls, and compliance with the law (Raghunandan et al. 2001). The purpose of the review is to ensure the implementation of the internal control system can be done in an effective enterprise (Raghunandan et al. 2001). According to Fleming (2002), the responsibility of the audit committee must ensure that financial reporting is free from manipulations. Therefore, they must have financial reporting knowledge and experience.

12.2.3.3 Meeting with Management and Internal Audit

The audit committees should communicate their duties and responsibilities to the management and the internal auditors. Therefore, they understand the roles and responsibilities of committee members in the company. According to Kalbers and Fogarty (1993), there is a significant difference between the effectiveness of the audit committee members and the internal auditors since audit committees communicate more than the internal auditors. This is means for internal audit in the process of control.

McMullen and Raghunandan (1996) describe the need for relatively frequent meetings between the audit committee and management and internal and external auditors. Effectively audit committees will conduct regular meetings with the internal auditors and management to ensure the financial reporting process. McMullen and Raghunandan (1996) show that there are only 23 % of companies with problems in its financial statements in a scheduled meeting of the audit committee conducted for at least three or more times in a year and 40% of companies that have no financial statement problem. Scheduling time for audit committee meetings is important. The audit committee should have a dialogue with the independent and external auditors and management before they conduct the inspection.

According to Fleming (2002), the member of the audit committee should conduct a meeting. The meeting should not be limited to only three to four times in a year. This meeting should depend on the size of the risk in the company. Committee members are expected to provide 100–300 h a year. The committee should also be responsive to listen and pay attention to the external auditors.

12.2.4 Audit Committees and Earnings Management

Empirically audit committee can reduce accrual earnings management. Chtourou et al. (2001) conduct a study to investigate the effect of governance practices of the company (board of directors and audit committee) to the accrual earnings management. The sample of this study is in COMPUSTAT 1996. Chtourou et al. (2001) find that earnings management is significantly associated with several governance practices of corporate management (audit committee and board of directors). The audit committee with independent members can reduce earnings management practices.

Xie et al. (2001) test the role of the board of directors, audit committee, and the executive committee in preventing earnings management. Xie et al. (2001) use the sample of the S & P 500 that were registered in June for each of 1992, 1994, and 1996. Samples are 282 companies. Xie et al. (2001) find that independent board and audit committees are active and knowledgeable about finance which is an important factor to prevent the tendency of managers to manage earnings.

Klein (2002b) examines whether the characteristics of the audit committee and board of directors are related to earnings management. Klein (2002b) uses 692 large companies in the USA publicly traded and listed in the S & P 500 March 31, 1992 and 1993, with the annual meeting of shareholders held between July 1, 1991, and June 30, 1993. Klein (2002b) finds a negative correlation between the independent audit committee and earnings management. Less independence of audit committee will increase earnings management.

12.2.5 Hypothesis

The age of members of the audit committee is a proxy indicating the experience and resistance to risk taking and change. Audit committee members who are older will be more conservative in selecting the external auditor, more preventive against collision between external auditors and managers, and more experience than the young auditor (Qi and Tian 2012). Based on this explanation, the hypothesis is formulated as follows:

H1 The age of audit committee members has a negative effect on real activities manipulation.

Women are more trustworthy than men. Men have more possibilities to manipulate earnings. The conservative women have a higher level of ethics than the audit committee men. Qi and Tian (2012) find that gender differences in leadership can positively impact on profitability. They argue that gender differences may lead to differences of opinion. It can lead to excellence from one company to another company. The alternative hypotheses can be formulated as follows:

H2 The proportion of female audit committee members has negative effect on real activities manipulation.

Qi and Tian (2012) explain that education level can reflect a person's abilities and skills. Executives with higher levels of education can make better decisions based on their cognitive abilities to better process and analyze the information and problems in the company. Researchers believe that the educational level of audit committee members negatively affects real activities manipulation. The alternative hypotheses can be formulated as follows:

H3 The level of education of the members of the audit committee has negative effect on real activities manipulation.

12.3 Research Methods

The population in this study is all manufacturing companies listed on the Indonesia Stock Exchange. We select all manufacturing companies listed on the period 2007–2011 (Table 12.1).

12.3.1 Variables

The dependent variable in this study is real activities manipulation. It is proxied by abnormal cash flow operating activities. We measure real activity manipulation using a residual model of Roychowdhury (2006) as follows:

$$CFO_{it}/A_{it-1} = \alpha_0 + \alpha_1(1/A_{it-1}) + \beta_1(S_{it}/A_{it-1}) + \beta_2(\Delta S_{it}/A_{it-1}) + \varepsilon_t \quad (12.1)$$

where

(a)

$$CFO_{it}/A_{it-1} \quad : \frac{\text{cash flow from operation firm i period t}}{\text{total assets in beginning year}}$$

(b)

$$(S_{it}/A_{it-1}) \quad : \frac{\text{sales firm i period t}}{\text{total assets in beginning year}}$$

$$(\Delta S_{it}/A_{it-1}) \quad : \frac{\text{changes sales firm i period t}}{\text{total assets in beginning year}}$$

(c)

ε_t : regression residual (proxy *REM*)

Table 12.1 Process of selected samples

	2007	2008	2009	2010	2011
Manufacturing companies listed on period 2007–2011	142	152	146	147	150
No annual report on the IDX's website	(32)	(29)	(37)	(31)	(34)
No complete data for audit committee	(79)	(86)	(80)	(72)	(70)
No complete data on financial statement to measure research variables on IDX's website	(16)	(19)	(12)	(5)	(10)
Total samples	15	18	17	39	36

Data sources

We use secondary data such as data collected from records or databases. Source of data used is secondary data from company financial statements obtained through the Indonesian Capital Market Directory (ICMD), www.idx.co.id, Corner Exchange at Universitas Atma Jaya Yogyakarta

The independent variables in this study are the personal characteristics of the audit committee. They are the age, the proportion of women, and the education level. Control variables in this study are the size of the company and leverage.

12.3.2 Empirical Model

$$REM_{it} = \alpha + \beta_1 AGE_{it} + \beta_2 GEN_{it} + \beta_3 EDU_{it} + \beta_4 SIZE_{it} + \beta_5 LEV_{it} + \varepsilon_i \quad (12.2)$$

where

(a) REM_{it}: real activities manipulation firm i period t
(b) AGE_{it}: the age of audit committee members firm i period t
(c) GEN_{it}: gender of audit committee members firm i period t
(d) EDU_{it}: level of education of audit committee members firm i period t
(e) $SIZE_{it}$: ln-asset of total assets firm i period t
(f) LEV_{it}: total liabilities to total assets firm i period t

12.4 Results

Table 12.2 presents descriptive statistics.

The results of descriptive statistics are the minimum *REM* −3.16 and maximum 1.54. The mean of real activity manipulation is −0.4976 and standard deviation is 0.67741. The minimum value of *AGE* is 3.47 and the maximum value 4.28. The mean value of *AGE* is 3.9316 and standard deviation is 0.17843. The minimum value of *EDU* is 0.67 and the maximum value 2.33. The mean of *EDU* is 1.4220 and standard deviation is 0.40199. The minimum value of *SIZE* is 23.19 and maximum value of *SIZE* is 31.47. The mean value of *SIZE* is 27.7233 and standard deviation is 0.25441.

Table 12.2 Descriptive statistics

	N	Minimum	Maximum	Mean	Std. deviation
REM	125	−3.16	1.54	−0.4976	0.67741
AGE	125	3.47	4.28	3.9316	0.17843
GEN	125	0.00	0.67	0.1380	0.18577
EDU	125	0.67	2.33	1.4220	0.40199
SIZE	125	23.19	31.47	27.7233	1.60890
LEV	125	0.01	1.45	0.4632	0.25441

12.4.1 Test of Hypothesis

Multiple regression analysis is used to test the hypothesis.

The results of multiple regression analysis in Table 12.3 showed that the age of the audit committee (*AGE*) does not have a negative influence on abnormal operating cash flow (real activities manipulation). The results are consistent according to Wardhani and Joseph (2010). They stated that the age of the audit committee does not have any effect on the real activity manipulation. The results showed that the senior audit committee does not guarantee that a person can detect and anticipate real activities manipulation. Experience in accounting is one of the things that cause a more senior audit committee to detect real activities manipulation. Although more senior but does not have adequate experience in accounting and finance, a person will have a difficulty in detecting the occurrence of real activities manipulation.

The results of multiple regression analysis show that the proportion of women members of the audit committee (*GEN*) has a negative and significant influence on abnormal operating cash flow (real activities manipulation). Based on the results, hypothesis two is not supported. It means that more proportion of women in audit committees has no negative influence on real activities manipulation. These results suggest that more women in audit committee will increase real activities manipulation. These results are not consistent with Qi and Tian (2012) finding that proportion of women in audit committee has negative influence on real activities manipulation. Based on the results, women in audit committee cannot reduce real activities manipulation.

Based on the results, the education level of audit committee does not have an impact on real activity manipulation, because the level of education cannot reflect personal characteristics of audit committee. Existing audit committees in listed companies have many levels of education such as from senior high school until PhD with many backgrounds. Audit committees are not only from accounting and finance, but they are from many backgrounds (disciplines). If audit committees have with minimum knowledge in accounting and finance, they also have less knowledge about earnings management. Therefore, audit committees with highest

Table 12.3 Test of hypothesis

		Unstandardized coefficients		Standardized coefficients	T	Sig.
Model		B	Std. error	Beta	B	Std. error
1	(Constant)	3.730	1.351		2.761	0.007
	AGE	−0.448	0.360	−0.118	−1.244	0.216
	GEN	−0.930	0.306	−0.255	−3.041	0.003
	EDU	−0.114	0.138	−0.068	−0.827	0.410
	SIZE	−0.086	0.039	−0.205	−2.202	0.030
	LEV	0.469	0.225	0.176	2.082	0.039

level of education will have weakness to detect and reduce real activities manipulation, because they do not have knowledge in accounting and finance.

We also have some argument why the results of characteristics of audit committee are not consistent with our expectation. First, the audit committees are established by the board of commissioners. In the board of commissioners, there are independent commissioners. They represent the interest of public or non-controlling shareholders. The selected independent commissioners are conducted in general meeting of shareholders. Decisions in general meeting of shareholders are mostly determined by the majority or controlling shareholders. It means whether independent commissioner is independent in fact or in appearance. Because independent commissioner is selected by controlling shareholder in general meeting shareholders. Therefore, independent commissioner is in appearance. The independent is a serious problem for commissioner because independent commissioner is represent non-controlling shareholders. Independence is a serious problem for independent commissioners.

Second, if independence of board commissioner is independent in appearance so selected audit committees conducted by board of commissioners will be a problem in independence. Because selected process of the audit committees by the board of commissioners is also a big problem. Based on the selected process, there are two arguments: (1) whether audit committees have good quality to protect non-controlling shareholders and (2) whether audit committees can assure the high quality of financial information. This argument is based on Cleassens and Fan (2002) that conventional corporate governance mechanism such as takeovers and audit committee is not enough to reduce agency problem in Asia. This is one reasoning why audit committee cannot reduce real activities manipulation. Third argument is whether members of audit committee actually understand and know current issues in accounting and finance. How can a member who is not from accounting understand and know the current problem in accounting? It is also a problem causing why audit committee cannot prevent real activity manipulation. The competency and ability of the members of audit committee will have an impact on the effectiveness of audit committee in their duty.

12.5 Conclusion

This study concludes the age of audit committee members has no influence on real activities manipulation. Second, the proportion of women in audit committee has negative influence on abnormal operating cash flow. It means women tend to support real activity manipulation. Third, the education level of audit committee members does not have an impact on real activities manipulation. The implication of this study is that Financial Services Authority in Indonesia is expected to renew the regulation of the proportion of audit committee members. The audit committees are unit in company assuring the quality of the financial statements. They are expected to have the capacity to detect and prevent real activities manipulation.

The expected number of audit committee members who are knowledgeable in accounting and finance is not only one person, but at least 2/3 of the total number of audit committee members. They will make decisions not only based on a subjective judgment but based on the knowledge and competence.

We have difficulty in processing the data especially in terms of samples. The number of samples used in the research lacks data sources. We have limitation to access data because not all annual report in IDX's database and not all the companies publishing the annual report include a detailed description of the audit committee. We have some suggestion for next researchers who may test other variables such as educational background and financial accounting as well as courses and training in accounting and finance, because they can support the ability of the audit committee to prevent and reduce manipulation in financial statements.

References

Abbott LJ, Parker S (2000) Auditor selection and audit committee characteristics. Audit J Pract Theory 19:48–66

Baber WR, Fairfield PM, Haggard JA (1991) The effect of concern about reported income on discretionary spending decision: the case of research and development. Account Rev 73:305–333

Bapepam (2001) Perubahan peraturan Bapepam. Jakarta

Bartov E (1993) The timing of asset sales and earnings manipulation. Account Rev 68:840–855

Beasley MS, Salterio SE (2001) The relationship between board characteristics and voluntary improvements in audit committee composition and experience. Contemp Account Res 18:539–570

Burgstahler D, Dichev I (1997) Earnings management to avoid earning decrease and losses. J Account Econ 24:99–126

Cahan SF (1992) The effect of antitrust investigations on discretionary accruals: a refined test of the political-cost hypothesis. Account Rev 67:77–95

Carcello JV, Neal TL (2000) Audit committee composition and auditor reporting. Account Rev 75:453–467

Chtourou SM, Jen B, Lucie C (2001) Corporate governance and earnings management. Working paper. University Laval, Canada

Cleassens S, Fan JPH (2002) Corporate governance in Asia: a survey. Int Rev Financ 3:71–103

Dechow PM, Skinner DJ (2000) Earnings management: reconciling the views of accounting academics, practitioners and regulators. Account Horiz 14:235–250

Dechow PM, Sloan R (1991) Executive Incentives and the horizon problem: an empirical investigation. J Account Econ 14:51–89

DeFond ML, Park CW (1997) Smoothing income in anticipation of future earnings. J Account Econ 23:115–139

DeZoort FT, Salterio SE (2001) The effects of corporate governance experience and financial-reporting and audit knowledge on audit committee Members' judgments. Audit J Pract Theory 20:31–47

Ding Y, Zhang H, Zhang J (2007) Private vs. State ownership and earnings management: evidence from Chinese listed companies. Corp Gov 15:223–238

Dopuch N, Pincus M (1988) Evidence on the choice of inventory accounting methods: LIFO versus FIFO. In: Ray B, Kothari SP (eds) Financial statement analysis. McGraw-Hill/Hal, New York, pp 269–300

Erickson M, Wang SW (1999) Earnings management by acquiring firms in stock for stock mergers. J Account Econ 27:149–176
FASB (2010) Conceptual framework: statement of financial accounting concepts no. 8, Financial Accounting Foundation, Connecticut
Fleming JM (2002) Audit committees: roles, responsibilities, and performance. Pa CPA J:29–32
Forum for Corporate Governance in Indonesia (2001) Peranan Dewan Komisaris dan Komite Audit dalam Pelaksanaan corporate governance (Tata Kelola Perusahaan). Jakarta
Fudenberg D, Tirole J (1995) A theory of income and dividend smoothing based on incumbency rents. J Polit Econ 103:75–93
Gaver JJ, Kenneth MG, Jeffrey RA (1995) Additional evidence on bonus plans and income management. J Account Econ 19:3–28
Graham JR, Harvey CR, Rajgopal S (2005) The economic implication of corporate financial reporting. J Account Econ 40:3–73
Guidry F, Andrew JL, Steve R (1999) Earnings based bonus plans and earnings management by business unit managers. J Account Econ 26:113–142
Gunny K (2005) The relation between earnings management using real activities manipulation and future performance from meeting earnings benchmarks. Thesis, University of Colorado
Haw IM, Hu B, Hwang LS, Wu W (2004) Ultimate ownership, income management, and legal and extra-legal institutions. J Account Res 42:423–462
Healy PM (1985) The effect of bonus on accounting decisions. J Account Econ 7:85–107
Healy PM, Wahlen JM (1999) A review of the earnings management literature and its implications for standard setting. Account Horiz 13:365–383
Holthausen RW, David FL, Sloan RG (1995) Annual bonus schemes and the manipulation of earnings. J Account Econ 19:29–74
Jones JJ (1991) Earnings management during import relief investigations. J Account Res 29:193–228
Kalbers LP, Fogarty TJ (1993) Audit committee effectiveness: an empirical investigation of the contribution of power. Audit J Pract Theory 12:24–47
Key KG (1997) Political cost incentives for earnings management in the cable television industry. J Account Econ 23:309–337
Kim NB, Yi CH (2006) Ownership structure, business group affiliation, listing status, and earnings management: evidence from Korea. Contemp Account Res 23:427–464
Klein A (2002a) Economic determinants of audit committee independence. Account Rev 77:435–452
Klein A (2002b) Audit committee, board of director characteristics, and earnings management. J Account Econ 32:375–400
McMullen DA, Raghunandan K (1996) Enhancing audit committee effectiveness. J Account 182 (2):79–81
Na'im A, Hartono J (1996) The effect of antitrust investigations on the management of earnings: a further empirical test of political cost hypothesis. KELOLA 13:126–142
Navissi F (1999) Earnings management under price regulation. Contemp Account Res 16:281–304
Perry SE, Williams TH (1994) Earnings management pricing management buyout offers. J Account Econ 18:157–179
Qi B, Tian G (2012) The impact of audit committees' personal characteristics on earnings management: evidence from China. J Appl Bus Res 28:1331–1344
Raghunandan K, William JR, Dasaratha VR (2001) Audit committee composition, "gray directors", and interaction with internal auditing. Account Horiz 15:105–118
Rangan S (1998) Earnings management and the performance of seasoned equity offerings. J Financ Econ 50:101–122
Roychowdhury S (2006) Earnings management through riel activities manipulation. J Account Econ 42:335–370
Sanjaya IPS (2010) Entrenchment and alignment effect on earnings management. Indones J Account Res 13(3):247–264

Sanjaya IPS (2011) The influence of ultimate ownership on earnings management: evidence from Indonesia. Glob J Bus Res 5:61–69

Scott WR (2006) Financial accounting theory, vol 4. Prentice Hall, Scarborough

Sun J, Lan G, Liu G (2014) Independent audit committee characteristics and real earnings management. Manag Audit J 29:153–172

Sweeney AP (1994) Debt covenant violations and Managers' accounting responses. J Account Econ 17:281–308

Teoh SW, Welch I, Wong TJ (1998a) Earnings management and the long-Run market performance of initial public offerings. J Finance 6:1935–1974

Teoh SW, Welch I, Wong TJ (1998b) Earnings management and the underperformance of seasoned equity offerings. J Financ Econ 50:63–99

Wardhani R, Joseph H (2010) Karakteristik Pribadi Komite Audit dan Praktik Manajemen Laba. Simposium Nasional Akuntansi XIII

Watts RL, Zimmerman JL (1986) Positive accounting theory. Prentice-Hall, Englewood Cliffs

Wilkinson JW, Cerullo MJ, Raval V, Wong-on-Wing B (2000) Accounting information system: essential concepts and applications, 4th edn. Wiley, New York

Xie B, Davidson III WN, Dadalt PJ (2001) Earnings management and corporate governance: the role of board and the audit committee. Working paper. Southern Illinois University, Carbondale.

Chapter 13
The Influence of Monitoring Mechanisms and Opportunistic Behaviors Toward Earnings Management

Aziani Idris, Zuraidah Mohd Sanusi, and Mohd Taufik Mohd Suffian

Abstract Corporate collapse which resulted from financial scandals keeps increasing in numbers. This study examines the influence of monitoring mechanisms and opportunistic behaviors toward earnings management (EM). Discretionary accrual is a proxy of EM in this study. Monitoring behaviors are proxied by two variables named leverage and dividend. Opportunistic behaviors are proxied by free cash flow (FCF) and profitability (ROA). 481 companies listed in Bursa Malaysia were collected, while another 401 public companies were collected from the Australian Stock Exchange. Several statistical analyses were carried out to examine the influence of monitoring mechanisms (leverage and dividend) and opportunistic behaviors (free cash flow and profitability) toward EM. The findings of this study revealed that only opportunistic behaviors have significant influence on EM in Malaysia. However, for Australia, the result indicated that only one determinant of monitoring mechanisms (dividend) has significant relationship with EM. The same goes to opportunistic behaviors, which indicated that only FCF has significant relationship with EM. For pool data countries, the result revealed that the hypotheses were also partially supported by both monitoring mechanisms and opportunistic behaviors toward EM.

13.1 Introduction

The collapse of Enron in 2001 has become the hottest debates in the accounting world and followed by other companies such as WorldCom in 2002, Tyco in 2002, HealthSouth in 2003, Freddie Mac in 2003, American Insurance Group in 2005, and

A. Idris
Universiti Teknologi Mara (UiTM) & Accounting Research Institute (ARI), Shah Alam, Malaysia

Z. Mohd Sanusi
Accounting Research Institute (ARI) & Universiti Teknologi Mara (UiTM), Shah Alam, Malaysia

M.T. Mohd Suffian (✉)
Universiti Teknologi Mara (UiTM) & Accounting Research Institute (ARI), Perak, Malaysia
e-mail: taufik815@perak.uitm.edu.my

H.G. Djajadikerta, Z. Zhang (eds.), *A New Paradigm for International Business*, Springer Proceedings in Business and Economics, DOI 10.1007/978-981-287-499-3_13

Lehman Brothers in 2008, to name a few. These financial scandals were brought to the limelight of the regulators, professionals, academicians, and also practitioners (Sun and Rath 2009). The main question would be why such thing happens. This is where the earnings management is analyzed and more research is done by the researchers to provide their outlook on the earnings management itself. Primarily, the term earnings management itself is considered as the act of the managers within their capability and judgment in misleading the stakeholders about the economic performance of the organization or manipulating the financial statements (Healey and Wahlen 1999).

Earnings management is employed when there are opportunistic behaviors of the managers to maintain the performance and profitability of the company. In practice, the opportunistic actions to manage earnings often occur among the companies which have high surplus free cash flow (Bukit and Iskandar 2009). Moreover, companies with high surplus free cash flow are said to be a strong reason for the opportunist managers to play their role (Bukit and Iskandar 2009). According to previous studies, it was proved that the companies face major agency problems when there is high surplus free cash flow (Chung et al. 2005). Moreover, the agency problems are also critical when there are low investment opportunities but the free cash flow is high, which triggers the managers to manipulate earnings (Gul 2001). Therefore, free cash flow and agency problem will be the driver for the earnings management to happen.

When there is a need to maintain the performance and profitability of the company, the opportunist managers may use discretionary accruals for earnings management and come out with consistent dividend payout policy (Kato et al. 2001, 2002). The managers grab the opportunity to give a good picture on the company's performance by using surplus FCF for dividend payment and not for the profitable investment or expansion of the company. It is because the dividend payout policy is seen as a benchmark for a company's performance (Wang et al. 1993).

Earnings management might differ between countries because of the difference in the standard use, practice, culture, regulation, and many more. For example, in Malaysia, abnormal items are strictly treated as exceptional items, while in Australia, the Australian Accounting Standard Board (AASB), 1995, required companies to classify materially abnormal items in order to distinguish them from "normal" earnings. The ambiguity of AASB 1018 gives flexibility to Australian firms whether to classify an item as an ordinary item or abnormal item. This shows that even with a different accounting practice, regulation, and culture, earnings management is still continuously carried out by managers either opportunistically or in a good way. This study extends the earnings management literature by comparing the monitoring mechanisms and opportunistic behaviors of Malaysia and Australia.

In 2002, the Australian Securities and Investments Commission (ASIC) decided to increase its corporate surveillance activities in response to the accounting scandals that happened in the USA. ASIC pointed out their concern on the perception of possible abuses and earnings quality in Australia (Buffini 2002). This is because the corporation's financial health and reliability of reported earnings are major factors of the earnings quality's notion (Beaver et al. 1968; Bernard 1995; Feltham and Ohlson 1995; Green and Segal 1996).

Hence, it is important to conduct a comparison study of earnings management in Malaysia and Australia as it can present the result for both countries which have different capital market, industrial stocks, accounting standard, institutional structure, and corporate governance. The awareness on social and cultural influences toward accounting is increasing among researchers and standard setters (Hussein 1996). Additionally, there are few studies done on the comparison of earnings management between countries. Different countries might have different standards, systems, and also culture. Thus, it would be interesting to see the result of the study done between developing and developed countries which are Malaysia and Australia.

Normally, investors will think that the company is well performed if they pay constant dividend even when they are not. There is also evidence that small-sized firms and low-profitability firms are aggressively involve in earnings management as companies with scarce operating cash flow would anyway involve in earnings management in order to fulfill the requirements of dividend payout (Sun and Rath 2009). Hence, this study is to examine the importance of monitoring mechanisms and opportunistic behaviors of Malaysian and Australian companies in managing earnings.

This study provides empirical evidence regarding the factors that contribute to the level of earnings management which are the monitoring mechanisms and the opportunistic behaviors of the managers. Furthermore, despite Australia being a developed country which has a larger economy-wide context as compared to Malaysia, the developing country also could give a shed to the regulators in setting the most favorable level of management and accounting discretion for companies. This study also investigates how monitoring mechanisms and opportunistic behaviors of managers give effect to the level of earnings management for both countries.

13.2 Literature Review and Hypotheses Development

13.2.1 Agency Theory and Earnings Management

The main concern of the agency theory is on the agency problem when the principal (shareholder) and agent (management) come up with different objectives and divisions of labor (Jensen and Meckling 1976). The crucial notion in the concept of agency theory is whether an agent who is engaged by the principal as their representative to make the best decision has a consistent interest with the principal or the agent has a conflict of interest when carrying out their obligation. In the case of separation of ownership and control of the company, the agent (management) might have incentives to gain their personal benefit rather than to maximize the wealth of the principal.

The beauty of accounting is that there are many choices of accounting methods available which give opportunity to the managers to manage a company's earnings. The flexibility in the accounting principles provides opportunity for managers to manage earnings in order to gain personal benefit such as rewards and promotions or it could be to avoid managers' retrenchment (Davidson et al. 2004).

Earnings management is an amendment in the timing and structure of an operating, investing, and finance activity to influence earnings (Graham et al. 2005; Gunny 2005; Roychowdhury 2006 and Zang 2007). It can be said that most firms are engaged in earnings management, and it is because of either market pressure or the managers' opportunistic behavior. According to Bukit and Iskandar (2009), there are two types of earnings manipulation which can be categorized as earnings fraud and earnings management. As stated in MIA (2002), fraudulent financial reporting is intentionally omitting or misstating the disclosures of a financial statement, whereas earnings management relates to the misapplication of accounting principles or methods that is done intentionally or/and the intentional manipulation or omission of accounting records.

The managers will make sure the consistency of a company's performance and to impress the stakeholders, so that they will get rewards from them (Bukit and Iskandar 2009). This performance-based incentive with the addition of surplus free cash flow creates serious agency problem (Chung et al. 2005).

The company showed poor long-run performance as compared to the pre-listing period (Ku Ismail et al. 1993) because they require a big chunk of equity capital to finance the company's investment. The manipulated earnings give the stability picture of the company that investors or future investors are looking for. During the initial public offering (IPO), the opportunistic managers are using income-increasing accruals to manage earnings upward in order to enjoy high proceeds from the offering (Chen et al. 2005; DuCharme et al. 2001, 2004; Roosenboom et al. 2003; Teoh et al. 1998a). The level of EM can be reduced through monitoring by an audit committee and independent board of directors (Davidson et al. 2005; Peasnell et al. 2000).

Normally, in companies with FCF, managers may decide to invest in low-return projects or even projects with negative net present value (NPV) if there is deficiency of effective monitoring and punitive actions by stakeholders (Chung, et al. 2005). The managers involve themselves in this opportunistic behavior in order to enjoy their self-perquisite. Engaging in nonprofitable activities and projects somehow creates the agency cost in which the shareholders need to bear.

Discretionary accounting choices are referred as "informational perspectives" where the flexibility in GAAP is being utilized to boost the reported accounting information as they view discretionary accruals that are done by managers as a medium to cloak the factual underlying economic performance of the company to increase the privilege of the managers at the expense of the shareholders (Badertscher et al. 2012; Jensen 2005; Teoh et al. 1998a, b; Dechow and Skinner 2000; Beneish 2001; Nelson et al. 2002; Hribar and Jenkins 2004; Revsine et al. 2005; Badertscher 2011).

13.2.2 Monitoring Mechanisms

Monitoring mechanisms can be in terms of internal monitoring and also external monitoring. According to the research done by Van de Poel and Vanstraelen (2007), Dutch listed companies have a lower level of abnormal accruals resulting from their adequate and effective internal control.

Leverage could be a form of mechanism to avoid earnings management or it could harm the corporation. The management's ability to exploit the company's asset and use it for personal benefits can be constrained with the existence of external lenders (Bilimoria and Huse 1997). As lenders are very concerned on the debt repayment by the company, they will ensure that the management will make use of the cash available on the profitable investment. A previous study found that less long-term emoluments are paid to the chief executive officer (CEO) of highly leveraged firm. That means there is no room for the management to expropriate the company's cash flow if there is a presence of a lender's monitoring. Past studies also indicated that monitoring by lenders contribute to the profitability and growth of the company (Cable 1985 and Nibler 1995); however, it is inconsistent with Cable (1985) and Nibler (1995) and Chirinko and Elson (1996).

According to Uwuigbe et al. (2012), dividend decision and policy in a company provide information regarding the performance of a company to the stakeholders. For the investors, the determination of funds that flow to them and funds retained by the company for investment is based upon the dividend decision (Ross et al. 2002) and must be equally good to the investors and corporation. This is because future earnings and future potential dividends are determined by the firm investment and it also influences the cost of capital (Foong et al. 2007). It is said that institutional investors are an effective monitoring mechanism in order to ensure the managers meet the dividend payment and not harming the shareholders' interest and thus decrease the agency problem (Shah et al. 2010).

13.2.3 Opportunistic Behaviors

In this study, the opportunistic behaviors of the managers are discussed in terms of free cash flow and the profitability of the company. Initially, FCF is a surplus or extra cash flow which is readily available to be used to finance any project that can give positive net present value (Jensen 1986). Agency problem will occur if FCF in a company is wrongly invested or expensed in a way that the manager disregards to maximize the shareholders' wealth (Jensen 1986). Ironically, it is in the hand of the manager either to invest in a profitable investment or low-return investment.

Normally, earnings management used by companies with surplus free flow can be connected to discretionary accruals (DAC) whereby high surplus free cash flow is being the reason of high discretionary accruals and the manager tends to use income-increasing accruals to boost the reported earnings (Chung et al. 2005).

Firms with high free cash flow and have low growth opportunity are associated with the agency problem (Chung et al. 2005; Gul and Tsui 1998). Managers of company having declined profitability are motivated to smooth earnings (White 1970). Two of the strong incentives by managers to manipulate earnings are severe fluctuated income and declined profitability in a company (Ashaari et al. 1994).

Dechow et al. (1995) investigate performance related to discretionary accruals and found that the null hypothesis of no earnings management at rates exceeding the specified test levels is applied to samples of firms with extreme financial performance and is rejected by all models used in that study. However, it is inconsistent with Guay et al. (1996).

13.2.4 Hypotheses Development

According to Jensen (1986), when debt financing took place in a company, the lender will monitor the company's activities and the management spending is restricted, subject to the lender prescription. This is to ensure the company commits with the debt repayment, and the commitment will reduce the company's cash and consequently can avoid the management to misuse the cash (Jensen 1986; Maloney et al. 1993; Stulz 1990).

The debt commitment should be taken seriously by the company as they have to use the free cash flow to pay their debt, and that means less cash left for the management to spend. The monitoring activities by the lenders have showed to increase in the value of shareholders' wealth resulting from a decrease in managerial discretion on investment decision and leveraged recapitalization firms.

There is a similarity between leverage and dividends because these two will lessen the cash available in the company and hence reduce the likelihood of earnings management to happen (Ling et al. 2008). As an institutional investor, they can act as a strong mechanism to force the management to pay out dividends, but if they pay high dividend, it may reduce the cash available for the debt repayment later on (Li and Huang 2007; Shah et al. 2010). Hence, based on the above arguments, the first hypothesis developed is as follows:

H1: Monitoring mechanisms is negatively related to earnings management.

Free cash flow in a company should be used or managed in an appropriate way by the managers in a way that it maximizes the wealth of the investors and increases the company's future earnings. However, if the free cash flow is not spent as to what the managers are obliged to do, then it raises agency problems (Jensen 1986).

Activities that are carried out based on the managers' personal interest can be obscured by manipulating accounting number and reporting minimal disclosure to the shareholders as they do not have access to the inside information. During the disclosure to the shareholders, the underlying assumptions of the investment and the investment cash flows are presented inadequately.

The opportunist managers may attempt to miss out some of the preparation of the projected cash flow and profit forecast. They took a wrong decision in investing the company's cash flow which could negatively affect the company's future earnings. The managers may discretely increase the reported earnings by employing accounting numbers. Therefore, the second hypothesis is:

H2: Opportunistic behaviors are positively related to earnings management.

13.3 Research Methodology

13.3.1 Sample Collection

The samples of this study are from Malaysian and Australian public listed companies. It consists of 888 companies listed in Bursa Malaysia and 1,614 companies listed in the Australian Stock exchange. The sample is collected for 3 years from year 2010–2012. In this study, 481 of the listed Malaysian companies and 401 - Australian listed companies had been chosen. All listed companies are chosen for both countries except from the financial institutions. In addition, the reduced Australian sample which was more than 50 % might be because of the dividend payment where companies usually announce their dividend payment in the next financial year, or it might be that they do not pay dividend at all. As shown in Table 13.1, after excluding companies from the banking and financial sector, the total of both companies from Malaysia and Australia is 882 cases. The data collected for both Malaysia and Australia are extracted from Thomson Datastream.

13.3.2 Earnings Management

The dependent variable in this study is the earnings management which can be determined based on the discretionary accounting accruals employed by the managers (see, e.g., Teoh et al. 1998b). The total accrual consists of both discretionary and non-discretionary accruals, so non-discretionary accrual must be separated from the total accrual. Based on the prior research, total accruals (Healy 1985); modified Jones abnormal accruals (Jones 1991; Dechow et al. 1995); and discretionary accruals (Kothari et al. 2005) are used to measure the earnings management. In measuring total accruals (TAC), this study follows the model used by Kothari et al. (2005) as it is the latest model which has been measured, predicted, as well as monitored by the researchers (Cooper and Schindler 2008).

In order to attain a better comparison of performance matching and to generate the normal and non-discretionary proxy, Kothari et al. (2005) insist to expand the modified Jones model by including a performance measure in the accruals regression which is ROA_{it} or ROA_{it-1}.

Table 13.1 Selection for 2010, 2011, and 2012

	Sample data	Missing/unavailable	Final sample
Malaysia	888	407	481
Australia	1,614	1,214	401
Total	2,502	1,620	882

The equation is as follows:

$$\begin{aligned} \mathrm{TAC}_{it} &= \beta_0 + \beta_1(1/\mathrm{ASSETS}_{\mathrm{it-1}}) + \beta_2(\Delta\mathrm{SALES}_{it}) + \beta_3\mathrm{PPE}_{it} \\ &+ \beta_4\mathrm{ROA}_{it(\mathrm{or\ it-1})} + \varepsilon_{it}\ ; \quad \text{and} \end{aligned}$$

where

TAC = total accruals
ASSETS = total assets
Δ SALES = change in sales revenue
PPE = property, plant, and equipment
$\mathrm{ROA}_{it(\mathrm{or\ it-1})}$ = net income in the current year (or previous year) divided by total assets in the current year; all other variables are as previously defined
ε_{it} = unspecified random factors

The model proposed by Kothari et al. (2005) for total accruals is based on their performance-matched discretionary accrual approach which is as follows:

$$\mathrm{TAC}_{it} = \big[(\Delta \text{ non-cash current asset}_{it}) - \big(\Delta \text{ current liabilities}_{it} \text{ excluding the current portion of long-term debt}\big) - (\text{Depreciation and amortization}_{it})\big]/\text{total assets}_{\mathrm{it-1}}.$$

Hence, the discretionary accrual (DAC) is the residual (ε_{it}) from the regression above.

TAC is presumed as the total increase from discretionary and non-discretionary accruals. Therefore, the equation for the sum up of discretionary accruals and non-discretionary accruals are:

$$\mathrm{TAC} = \mathrm{DAC} + \mathrm{NDAC}$$

In this study, DAC is extracted from the difference between TAC and non-DAC. It is assumed to be the outcome of managers' opportunistic behavior of choices of accounting methods which is consistent with the previous studies.

13.3.3 Independent Variables

This study examines the effect of the monitoring action by lenders and shareholders on the earnings management. Leverage is measured by calculating the ratio of long-term debt to the book value of equity (Givoly et al. 1992; Jelinek 2007). The measurement used for dividend in this study is in accordance with Schooley and Barney (1994) where they use the dividend yield by dividing the dividend per share with the closing market price per share.

In determining the opportunistic behavior, the company's free cash flow and profitability are tested in this study. The measurement for free cash flow used by Lehn and Poulsen (1989) is employed in this study and is done by deducting expenses such as tax expense, interest expense, and dividend from the operating income before depreciation. According to Lie and Li (2005), this study used return on asset (ROA_t) to measure the profitability of the company. ROA_t is defined as operating income divided by the cash-adjusted total asset (i.e., total assets minus cash and cash equivalents). In addition, the ROA used in this study is from the current year because according to Kothari et al. (2005), ROA_t is better matched which produced less misspecified tests.

Total assets are used in this study to control the influence of monitoring mechanism and opportunistic behavior on the earnings management. The measurement used is a log transformation of total assets (LOG_TA) as used by (Jones and Sharma 2001).

13.4 Findings

13.4.1 Descriptive Statistic: Malaysia

Table 13.2 presents the descriptive analysis for the dependent variable, independent variables, and also the control variable used in this study within the context of the Malaysian public listed companies.

The results for skewness for all variables are within the range of the standard where the lowest is for DAC valued at −0.003 and the highest is for DIV valued at 0.56. Meanwhile, for kurtosis, all variables have negative values but still in the range of −2 to +2 where the lowest value is −0.494 for LEV. In addition, FCF, ROA, and LOG_TA have the highest value for kurtosis. Thus, the result for skewness and kurtosis for Malaysian sample does not violate the normality assumption as previously stated by De Vaus (2002).

13.4.2 Correlation Analysis: Malaysia

Table 13.3 summarizes the result of Pearson correlation for all variables of public listed companies in Malaysia. According to the table, the coefficient correlation ranges between −0.123 and 0.492. The result shows that the highest correlation is

Table 13.2 Descriptive statistic for Malaysian sample (2010–2012)

	Mean	Mean (after Van Der Waerden)	Minimum	Maximum	Std. deviation	Skewness	Kurtosis
DAC (ABS)	0.155	0.00292	−3.19974	3.19974	0.99716	−0.003	−0.076
LEV	20.6865	0.02354	−1.2694	3.1978	0.94109	0.318	−0.494
DIV	2.7131	0.04413	−0.9112	3.1978	0.89456	0.56	−0.487
FCF	0.0564	0.00000	−3.1978	3.1978	0.99595	0.000	−0.074
ROA	5.1288	0.00000	−3.1978	3.1978	0.99595	0.000	−0.074
LOG_TA	5.8000	0.00000	−3.1978	3.1978	0.99595	0.000	−0.074

Notes: *DAC* discretionary accruals, *LEV* leverage ratio, *DIV* dividend yield, *FCF* free cash flow, *ROA* return on asset, *LOG_TA* log of total assets

Table 13.3 Pearson correlation test result for Malaysia (2010–2012)

	DAC (ABS)	LEV	DIV	FCF	ROA	LOG_TA
DAC (ABS)	1					
LEV	−0.001	1				
DIV	−0.009	−.123**	1			
FCF	−0.044	−.115**	0.297**	1		
ROA	0.054*	−.094**	0.411**	0.492**	1	
LOG_TA	0.076**	0.389**	0.208**	0.107**	0.267**	1

*Correlation is significant at the 0.05 level (two tailed)
**Correlation is significant at the 0.01 level (two tailed)

between ROA and FCF at $r = 0.492$, $p < 0.01$. Therefore, it indicates that ROA and FCF have a strong positive correlation.

In addition, discretionary accrual (DAC) has a positive relationship with ROA at $r = 0.054$, $p < 0.05$, and LOG_TA at $r = 0.076$, $p < 0.01$, but they are not highly correlated to each other. Meanwhile, leverage (LEV) is negatively correlated with dividend (DIV) at $r = -0.123$, $p < 0.01$, and free cash flow (FCF) at $r = -0.115$, $p < 0.01$. Moreover, the correlation between LEV and LOG_TA has a positive correlation at $r = 0.389$, $p < 0.01$. It shows that DIV is positively correlated with FCF, ROA, and LOG_TA at $r = 0.297$, 0.411, and 0.298, $p < 0.01$. Finally, LOG_TA is positively correlated with FCF at $r = 0.107$, $p < 0.01$, and ROA at $r = 0.267$, $p < 0.01$.

13.4.3 Multiple Regression Analysis: Malaysia

Table 13.4 shows the regression result and adjusted R^2 which indicated the value of 0.012. In other words, it explains that 1.2 % of the variation in earnings management is explained by leverage, dividend, free cash flow, and return on asset, while the rest cannot be explained by monitoring mechanisms and opportunistic behaviors. Meanwhile, the F-test result indicated the significant value at 4.621 ($p < 0.05$). From the result above, both independent variables (FCF and ROA) and LOG_TA were statistically significant at the $p < 0.05$ level.

Following the coefficient result in Table 13.4, it is indicated that both leverage and dividend (monitoring mechanisms) are not significant with the values of −1.444 and −1.408, respectively. Therefore, H1 is rejected.

The result indicates the significant values of −2.95 and 2.683 ($p < 0.05$), respectively, for both FCF and ROA (opportunistic behaviors). To be precise, there is significant negative relationship between FCF and EM, whereas for ROA it shows a positive relationship with EM. Therefore, H2 is supported and there is significant relationship between opportunistic behaviors and earnings management.

According to the tolerance and VIF results in Table 13.4, the tolerance value was more than 0.1 for all variables. It indicates that the multicollinearity assumption

Table 13.4 Multiple linear regression for Malaysia (2010–2012)

Model	B	Std. error	Beta	t	Sig.	Tolerance	VIF
(Constant)	0.006	0.026		0.23	0.818		
LEV	−0.045	0.031	−0.043	−1.444	0.149	0.785	1.275
DIV	−0.046	0.033	0.041	1.408	0.159	0.79	1.266
FCF	−0.09	0.03	−0.09	−2.95	0.003*	0.744	1.345
ROA	0.088	0.033	0.087	2.683	0.007*	0.645	1.551
LOG_TA	0.088	0.031	0.088	2.881	0.004*	0.735	1.361
R^2	0.016						
Adjusted R^2	0.012						
F-value	4.621						
df	5						
N	1,443						

was not violated. Conversely, the VIF results were between 1.266 and 1.551 which were below the ceiling value of 10. Hence, all variables used in this study were correlated among them and did not create multicollinearity problems.

13.4.4 Descriptive Statistic: Australia

Table 13.5 shows the descriptive statistic for public listed companies in Australia. For the descriptive analysis of Australian public listed companies, discretionary accruals, FCF, ROA, and LOG_TA have the largest dispersion, while leverage and dividend have a slightly lower dispersion.

The results for skewness for all variables are within the range of the standard. Meanwhile, for kurtosis, all variables have negative values except for DIV but still in the range of −2 to +2. Thus, the result for skewness and kurtosis for Australian sample does not violate the normality assumption as previously stated by De Vaus (2002).

13.4.5 Correlation Analysis: Australia

Table 13.6 summarizes the result of Pearson correlation for all variables of public listed companies in Australia. According to the table above, ROA and FCF have the highest and strongest positive relationship at $r = 0.727$, $p < 0.01$, as well as LOG_TA which also has a relatively strong positive correlation with LEV, DIV, FCF, and ROA which ranges between 0.505 and 0.562. In addition, DIV also seems to have a strong positive correlation between FCF and ROA at $r = 0.504$ and 0.495, $p < 0.01$, respectively. Moreover, DIV, FCF, and ROA show a positive correlation with LEV which ranges between $r = 0.471$ and $r = 0.314$, $p < 0.01$. Finally, the

Table 13.5 Descriptive statistic for Australian sample (2010–2012)

	Mean	Mean (after Van Der Waerden)	Minimum	Maximum	Std. deviation	Skewness	Kurtosis
DAC (ABS)	16.7079	0.000	−3.145	3.145	0.9953	0.000	−0.0827
LEV	23.9625	0.0536	−0.7747	3.145	0.8695	0.6908	−0.4141
DIV	2.0617	0.0722	−0.5	3.145	0.8006	1.097	0.1331
FCF	0.8664	0.000	−3.145	3.145	0.9953	0.000	−0.0827
ROA	−8.509	0.000	−3.145	3.145	0.9953	0.000	−0.0827
LOG_TA	5.007	0.000	−3.145	3.145	0.9953	0.001	−0.0827

Table 13.6 Pearson correlation test result for Australia (2010–2012)

	LEV	DIV	FCF	ROA	LOG_TA
DAC (ABS)					
LEV	1				
DIV	0.471**	1			
FCF	0.361**	0.504**	1		
ROA	0.314**	0.495**	0.727**	1	
LOG_TA	0.562**	0.529**	0.519**	0.505**	1

*Correlation is significant at the 0.05 level (two tailed)
**Correlation is significant at the 0.01 level (two tailed)

DAC variable of Australian sample also shows a negative correlation between LEV, DIV, and LOG_TA at a value of $r = 0.077$ t0 $r = 0.105$, $p < 0.01$.

13.4.6 Multiple Regression Analysis: Australia

Table 13.7 explains the results for the multiple regression of the relationship between monitoring mechanisms (LEV and DIV), opportunistic behaviors (FCF and ROA), and EM for public listed companies in Australia. It explains that 1.9 % of the variation in earnings management is explained by leverage, dividend, FCF, and ROA, while the balance cannot be explained by monitoring mechanisms and opportunistic behaviors. Meanwhile, the F-test result indicated the significant value at 5.552 ($p < 0.05$); therefore, this model is significant to explain the relationship.

From the result above, only dividend (DIV) for monitoring mechanism was statistically significant at −2.122, $p < 0.05$ level. There is a significant relationship between dividend (DIV) and earnings management only; meanwhile, for leverage (LEV) and EM, the relationship was insignificant. The result did indicate the significant value only for free cash flow (FCF) variable for opportunistic behaviors at a value of 2.801 ($p < 0.05$). Therefore, H2 is partially supported only for FCF but not for ROA. Hence, there is a significant relationship between FCF and earnings management, meaning that the context of opportunistic behaviors is not wholly significant but partially for FCF.

According to the tolerance and VIF results in Table 13.7, the tolerance value was more than 0.1 for all variables. Thus, it indicates that the multicollinearity assumption was not violated. Oppositely, the VIF results were between 1.564 and 2,337 which were below the ceiling value of 10. Hence, all variables used in this study were correlated among them and did not create multicollinearity problems.

Table 13.7 Multiple linear regression for Australia (2010–2012)

Model	B	Std. error	Beta	t	Sig.	Tolerance	VIF
(Constant)	0.007	0.029		0.251	0.802		
LEV	−0.021	0.041	−0.018	−0.515	0.606	0.639	1.564
DIV	−0.098	0.046	−0.078	−2.122	0.034*	0.598	1.673
FCF	0.122	0.044	0.122	2.801	0.005*	0.428	2.337
ROA	0.002	0.043	0.002	0.053	0.958	0.437	2.287
LOG_TA	−0.118	0.039	−0.118	−2.992	0.003*	0.523	1.911
R^2	0.023						
Adjusted R^2	0.019						
F-value	5.552						
df	5						
N	1,203						

*Correlation is significant at the 0.05 level (two tailed)
**Correlation is significant at the 0.01 level (two tailed)

13.4.7 Malaysia and Australia (Pool Data)

13.4.7.1 Descriptive Statistic

Table 13.8 shows the descriptive statistic for public listed companies in Malaysia and Australia from 2010 to 2012. The result shows the mean for the discretionary accruals of both countries at 0.0016. The minimum value for DAC was −3.1997, whereas the maximum value was 3.1997. The standard deviation of DAC was reported at 0.9966.

The first independent variable is the leverage ratio. The mean score for the LEV was 0.0382, while the minimum and maximum values were −1.2694 and 3.1978, respectively. In average, the public listed companies in Malaysia and Australia have an average of 3.82 % of long-term debt financing as compared to the equity financing. The standard deviation of LEV has a value of 0.9091.

The following variable is dividend yield ratio (DIV), which reported mean, minimum, and maximum values of 0.0569, −0.9112, and 3.1978, respectively. Moreover, the standard deviation for DIV was 0.8531. Hence, it can describe that the minimum dividend payable over the share price for public listed companies in Malaysia and Australia was 5.69 %.

The FCF, ROA, and LOG_TA have reported the same scores of the minimum and maximum of descriptive statistic which are valued at −3.1978 and 3.1978, respectively. In contrast, the mean score for FCF was 0.0003, for ROA was 0.0005, and for LOG_TA was 0.0000. Lastly, the standard deviations for the FCF, ROA, and LOG_TA were valued at 0.9960, 0.9959, and 0.9955, respectively.

For the descriptive analysis of public listed companies in Malaysia and Australia, DAC, FCF, ROA, and LOG_TA have the largest dispersion as to their standard deviation, while leverage and dividend have a slightly lower dispersion. The results for skewness for all variables are within the range of the standard of −2 to +2 where the lowest is for DAC, FCF, and ROA which is valued at −0.001 and the highest is for DIV valued at 0.758. Meanwhile, for kurtosis, all variables have

Table 13.8 Descriptive statistic for pool data (Malaysia and Australia)

	Mean	Mean (after Van Der Waerden)	Minimum	Maximum	Std. deviation	Skewness	Kurtosis
DAC (ABS)	0.155	0.0016	−3.1997	3.1997	0.9966	−0.001	−0.084
LEV	20.6865	0.0382	−1.2694	3.1978	0.9091	0.462	−0.44
DIV	2.7131	0.0569	−0.9112	3.1978	0.8531	0.758	−0.232
FCF	0.0564	0.0003	−3.1978	3.1978	0.996	−0.001	−0.083
ROA	5.1288	0.0005	−3.1978	3.1978	0.9959	−0.001	−0.081
LOG_TA	5.3195	0.0000	−3.1978	3.1978	0.9955	0	−0.083

negative values and in the range of −2 to +2. The lowest value is −0.440 for LEV, while the highest value of kurtosis for Malaysian and Australian public listed companies is −0.081. Thus, all the values of skewness and kurtosis for Malaysia and Australia are within the standard range.

13.4.7.2 Correlation Analysis

Table 13.9 summarizes the result of Pearson correlation for all variables of public listed companies in Malaysia and Australia for 2010 to 2012. According to the table above, ROA and FCF have the highest and strongest positive relationship at $r = 0.599$, $p < 0.01$. LOG_TA has a relatively strong positive correlation with LEV valued at $r = 0.464$ as well as ROA and DIV at $r = 0.446$. In addition, DIV also seems to have a medium and positive correlation between FCF and LOG_TA at $r = 0.385$ and 0.345, $p < 0.01$, respectively. ROA also has medium correlation with LOG_TA at $r = 0.375$. Moreover, DAC and DIV showed a negative correlation at $r = -0.042$. Finally, the LEV variable of these two countries showed a significant relationship with DIV, FCF, and ROA which range between $r = 0.083$ and $r = 0.12$.

Table 13.10 shows the regression result and adjusted R^2 which indicated the value of 0.004. It explains that 0.4 % of the variation in earnings management is explained by leverage, dividend, FCF, ROA, and LOG_TA, while the rest cannot be explained by monitoring mechanisms and opportunistic behaviors. Meanwhile, the F-test result indicated the significant value at 3.128 ($p < 0.05$); thus, this model is significant to explain the relationship.

From the result above, only dividend (DIV) for the monitoring mechanism was statistically significant at 2.668, $p < 0.05$ level. Another monitoring mechanism which is leverage (LEV) was not significant. Hypothesis one (H1) for this study which stated earlier that there is a significant relationship between monitoring mechanisms and earnings management was partially supported by the result in Table 13.11. Thus, there is a significant relationship between dividend (DIV) and

Table 13.9 Pearson correlation test result for pool data (Malaysia and Australia)

	DAC (ABS)	LEV	DIV	FCF	ROA	LOG_TA
DAC (ABS)	1					
LEV	−0.034	1				
DIV	−0.042*	0.120**	1			
FCF	−0.017	0.092**	0.385**	1		
ROA	0.023	0.083**	0.446**	0.599**	1	
LOG_TA	−0.006	0.464**	0.345**	0.295**	0.375**	1

*Correlation is significant at the 0.05 level (two tailed)
**Correlation is significant at the 0.01 level (two tailed)

Table 13.10 Multiple linear regression for pool data (Malaysia and Australia)

Model	B	Std. error	Beta	T	Sig.	Tolerance	VIF
(Constant)	0.007	0.019		0.345	0.73		
LEV	−0.041	0.024	−0.037	−1.682	0.093	0.775	1.29
DIV	−0.07	0.026	−0.06	−2.668	.008*	0.748	1.338
FCF	−0.036	0.025	−0.036	−1.476	0.14	0.622	1.608
ROA	0.069	0.026	0.069	2.648	.008*	0.559	1.789
LOG_TA	0.017	0.024	0.017	0.684	0.494	0.644	1.552
R^2	0.006						
Adjusted R^2	0.004						
F-value	3.128						
df	5						
N	2,646						

earnings management only; meanwhile, for leverage (LEV) and earnings management, the relationship was insignificant.

Hypothesis two (H2) of the current study stated that there is a significant relationship between opportunistic behaviors and earnings management. Hence, the result did indicate the significant value only for the return on asset (ROA) variable for opportunistic behaviors at a value of 2.648 ($p < 0.05$). Therefore, hypothesis two is partially supported only for ROA but not for FCF. Hence, there is a significant relationship between ROA and earnings management, meaning that the context of opportunistic behaviors is not wholly significant but partially between ROA and earnings management.

According to the tolerance and VIF results in Table 13.10, it indicates that the multicollinearity assumption was not violated. On the other hand, the VIF results were between 1.29 and 1.789 which are below the ceiling value of 10. Hence, all variables used in this study were correlated among them and did not create multicollinearity problems.

Table 13.11 Independent *t*-test between Malaysia and Australia

	Country	N	Mean	Std. deviation
DAC (ABS)	Malaysia	1,443	0.0029	0.9972
	Australia	1,203	0.0000	0.9986
LEV	Malaysia	1,443	0.0235	0.9411
	Australia	1,203	0.0558	0.8691
DIV	Malaysia	1,443	0.0441	0.8946
	Australia	1,203	0.0722	0.8006
FCF	Malaysia	1,443	0.0000	0.9960
	Australia	1,203	0.0007	0.9964
ROA	Malaysia	1,443	0.0000	0.9959
	Australia	1,203	0.0011	0.9962
LOG_TA	Malaysia	1,443	0.2905	0.7791
	Australia	1,203	−0.3485	1.1130

	F	Sig.	T	Sig. (two tailed)	Mean difference
DAC (ABS)	0.000	0.9937	0.098	0.922	0.0029
LEV	2.328	0.1272	−0.909	0.363	−0.0323
DIV	7.462	0.0063	−0.851	0.400	−0.0281
FCF	0.002	0.9682	−0.018	0.986	−0.0007
ROA	0.000	0.9822	−0.028	0.977	−0.0011
LOG_TA	0.003	0.0000	0.007	0.995	0.6390

13.4.8 Further Analysis

Independent *t*-test is intended to examine whether there is a significant difference in the means for leverage (LEV), dividend (DIV), free cash flow (FCF), return on assets (ROA), and log total assets (LOG_TA) between Malaysia and Australia. Hence, independent *t*-test is executed to compare the difference in means for the variables examined in both countries. This is to capture the changes in variables examined in Malaysia and also Australia.

For the DAC variable, Malaysia has a mean value of 0.0029, while Australia has 0.0000. In addition, standard deviation is stated at 0.9972 for Malaysia while for Australia 0.9986, and the mean difference is 0.0292. The p-value for DAC is 0.9937 which is more than 0.05; hence, there is no statistically significant difference in the means for DAC between Malaysia and Australia.

For the LEV variable, Malaysia has a mean value of 0.0235, while Australia has 0.0558. In addition, standard deviation is stated at 0.9411 for Malaysia while for Australia 0.8691, and the mean difference is −0.0323. The p-value for LEV is 0.1272 which is more than 0.05; hence, there is no statistically significant difference in the means for LEV between Malaysia and Australia.

The mean for Malaysia's DIV showed the value of 0.0441, while for Australia the value was 0.0722. The mean difference between these two countries was −0.0281. On top of that, the standard deviations were 0.8946 and 0.8006, respectively. DIV showed $p = 0.063$ which means more than 0.05; thus, there is no significant difference in the mean for DIV between Malaysia and Australia.

As per Table 13.11, FCF has a mean value of 0.0000 for Malaysia and 0.0007 for Australia, while the mean difference between these two countries was −0.0007. Meanwhile, the standard deviation indicated the values of 0.9960 and 0.9964, respectively, for Malaysia and Australia. FCF showed $p = 0.9682$ which means more than 0.05; thus, there is no significant difference in the means for FCF between Malaysia and Australia.

The next variable is ROA which stated the mean value of 0.0000 for Malaysia and 0.0011 for Australia, whereas the mean difference between these countries was −0.0011. Meanwhile, the standard deviations for both countries are valued at 0.9959 and 0.9962, respectively. ROA showed $p = 0.9822$ which means more than 0.05; thus, there is no significant difference in the means for ROA between Malaysia and Australia.

Finally, for the log total assets variable, the means for Malaysia and Australia stated the values of 0.2905 and −0.3485, respectively, while the mean difference is stated at 0.6390. On the other hand, the standard deviations for Malaysia and Australia were 0.7791 and 1.1130, respectively. Therefore, there is a significant difference in the mean between Malaysia and Australia since $p = 0.000$ which is below 0.05.

Overall, the result from the independent *t*-test analysis indicated that there is no significant mean difference for all the variables tested for Malaysian and Australian public listed companies except for the log total assets (LOG_TA) variable.

13.5 Conclusion

This study is carried out to scrutinize the relationship between monitoring mechanisms and opportunistic behaviors with earnings management. To be precise, this study examines the relationship between leverage, dividend, free cash flow, profitability, and earnings management for Malaysian and Australian listed companies. This study was empirically conducted based on the sample of Malaysian and Australian listed companies for the year 2010 to 2012. The proxy for earnings management is discretionary accruals (DAC). In addition, leverage (LEV) and dividend (DIV) were used as determinants of monitoring mechanisms while for opportunistic behaviors were free cash flow (FCF) and profitability (ROA).

During data analysis, it was found that there is no relationship between monitoring behaviors and EM in Malaysian listed companies. Thus, H1 for the Malaysian context is not supported. Meanwhile, there is a significant negative relationship between FCF and EM in Malaysian public listed companies. It is consistent with Jones and Sharma (2001) where he found that firms with a low level of cash flow associated with high cash flow in the new economy sector. Then, in this study, ROA was found to have a significant positive relationship with EM for Malaysia. This finding is consistent with Healy (1985) which previously stated that when performance is abnormally high, the tendency for managers to manage reported earnings is also high. Therefore, H2 for the Malaysian context is supported, and there is a significant relationship between opportunistic behaviors and earnings management.

The results for Australian listed companies showed that only dividend (DIV) has a significant relationship with EM. Leverage was found to have no relationship with EM in the Australian context. The negative relationship is not consistent with Kasanen et al. (1996) which showed the positive relationship between dividend and EM. Hence, H2 is partially supported in terms of DIV and EM. While for FCF and EM, the result showed a significant positive relationship between those variables consistent with Jones and Sharma (2001) and Bukit and Iskandar (2009). The result showed that ROA is not associated with EM in Australian public listed companies. Hence, H2 for the Australian context is partially supported.

For the pool countries (Australia and Malaysia), leverage (LEV) was found to have no relationship with EM, while DIV has a significantly negative association with EM consistent with the study done by Haider et al. (2012). Thus, H1 is partially supported in terms of DIV as monitoring mechanisms. This gives the indication that the increment in dividend payment resulted to lower earnings management practices. H2 also is partially supported in the context of ROA and EM where the result shows a significant positive relationship between these two variables consistent with Healy (1985). Meanwhile, FCF was found to have no significant relationship with EM.

The findings of this study may assist regulators and policy makers to make some improvement on the basis of monitoring mechanism to govern the management action. Consequently, if the monitoring mechanisms are effective and efficient, these could limit the opportunistic behaviors of the managers to manage earnings. Hence, this will enable investors, future investors, board of directors, and other stakeholders to make better decision in assessing financial reports which are more reliable, accountable, and transparent.

Several limitations in conducting this research give initiatives for future research. This study is not conducted based on specific industries or firm size. This is due to the time constraints explained previously. On the other hand, the huge reduction in Australian sample because of missing and unavailable data also affects this study. If specific industries or firm size is used in this study as well as the larger sample for Australia, then the research findings might be different. This reason makes sense because different industries and different firm sizes experienced different levels of earnings management. The magnitude and composition of the variable used also might differ between industries and firm sizes. Thus, the variables examined in this study would produce more extensive and conclusive findings. All the limitations give some insight for future research.

There are various possible areas that could be explored in the future with more extensions of time and sample. Future research in this area may be extended to the classification of companies for each industries and sectors. The extension of sample period also should be considered in order to observe the trends of earnings management. On top of that, future research should conduct a comparison study of earnings management for more countries as it could give more comprehensive outlook on earnings management between countries.

Acknowledgment We would like to thank the Accounting Research Institute (ARI) and the Research Management Institute (RMI), Universiti Teknologi MARA (UiTM), in collaboration with the Ministry of Education Malaysia (MoE), for providing support for this research project. We are indeed very grateful for the grant; without which, we would not be able to carry out the research.

References

Ashari N, Koh HC, Tan SL, Wong WH (1994) Factors affecting income smoothing among listed companies in Singapore. Account Bus Res 24:291–301

Badertscher B (2011) Overvaluation and the choice of alternative earnings management mechanisms. Account Rev 86:1491–1518

Badertscher BA, Collins DW, Lys TZ (2012) Discretionary accounting choices and the predictive ability of accruals with respect to future cash flows. J Account Econ 53:330–352

Beaver W, Kennelly J, Voss W (1968) Predictive ability as a criterion for the evaluation of accounting data. Account Rev 43:675–683

Beneish M (2001) Earnings management: a perspective. Manag Financ 27:3–17

Bernard V (1995) Feltham-Ohlson framework: implications for empiricists. Contemp Account Res 11:733–747

Bilimoria D, Huse M (1997) A qualitative comparison of the boardroom experiences of U.S and Norwegian women corporate directors. Int Rev Women Leadersh 3(2):63–73

Buffini F (2002) Chairman Heed ASIC's Wake-up Call, Australian Financial Review, September 25. John Fairfax Group, Sydney

Bukit RB, Iskandar TM (2009) Surplus free cash flow, earnings management and audit committee. Int J Econ Manag 3(1):204–223

Cable J (1985) Capital market information and industrial performance: the role of West German Q&nki. Econ J 95:118–132

Chen KY, Lin K, Zhou J (2005) Audit quality and earnings management for Taiwan IPO firms. Manag Audit J 20(1):86–104

Chirinko RS, Elston JA (1996) Banking relationships in Germany: empirical results and policy implications, working paper, Emory University, May 1996

Chung R, Firth M, Kim JB (2005) Earnings management, surplus free cash flow, and external monitoring. J Bus Res 58:766–776

Cooper DR, Schindler PS (2008) Business research method, 10th edn. McGraw-Hill, Singapore

Davidson WN III, Jiraporn P, Kim YS, Nemec C (2004) Earnings management following duality-creating successions: ethnostatistics, impression management, and agency theory. Acad Manag J 2:267–275

Davidson R, GoodwinS J, Kent P (2005) Internal governance structures and earnings management. Account Finance 45(2):241–267

De Vaus D (2002) Surveys in social research, 5th edn. Routledge. Ch, London

Dechow P, Skinner D (2000) Earnings management: reconciling the views of accounting academics, practitioners, and regulators. Account Horiz 14:232–250

Dechow PM, Sloan RG, Sweeney AP (1995) Detecting earnings management. Account Rev 70:193–225

DuCharme LL, Malatesta PH, Sefcik SE (2001) Earnings management, IPO valuation and subsequent performance. J Account Audit Financ 16:369–396

DuCharme LL, Malatesta PH, Sefcik SE (2004) Earnings management, stock issues and shareholders lawsuits. J Financ Econ 71:27–49
Feltham G, Ohlson J (1995) Valuation and clean surplus accounting for operating and financial activities. Contemp Account Res 11:689–732
Foong SS, Zakaria NB, Tan HB (2007) Firm performance and dividend- related factors: the case of Malaysia. Labuan Bulletin Int Bus Financ 5:97–111
Givoly D, Hayn C, Ofer AR, Sarig O (1992) Taxes and capital structure: evidence from firms' response to the Tax Reform Act of 1986. Rev Financ Stud 5(2):331–355
Graham JR, Harvey CR, Rajgopal S (2005) The economic implications of corporate financial reporting. J Account Econ 40:3–73
Green D, Segal J (1996) The predictive power of first-quarter earnings reports: a replication. J Account Res 4:21–36
Guay WR, Kothari SP, Watts RL (1996) A market-based evaluation of discretionary accrual models. J Account Res 34:83–105
Gul FA (2001) Free cash flow, debt monitoring and Managers' LIFO/FIFO policy choice. J Corp Financ 13:475–492
Gul FA, Tsui SL (1998) A test of the free cash flow and debt monitoring hypothesis: evidence from audit pricing. J Account Econ 24:219–237
Gunny K (2005) What are the consequences of real earnings management? Working paper: University of Colorado at Boulder
Haider J, Ali A, Sadiq T (2012) Earning management and dividend policy: empirical evidence from Pakistani listed companies. Eur J Bus Manag 4(1):83–90
Healy PM (1985) The effect of bonus schemes on acccounting decisions. J Account Econ 7(1):85–107
Healy PM, Wahlen JM (1999) A review of the earnings management literature and its implications for standard setting. Account Horiz 13(4):365–383
Hribar P, Jenkins N (2004) The effect of accounting restatements on earnings revisions and the estimated cost of capital. Rev Acc Stud 9:337–356
Hussein ME (1996) A comparative study of cultural influences on financial reporting in the US and The Netherlands. Int J Account 31:95–120
Jelinek K (2007) The effect of leverage increases on earnings management. J Bus Econ Stud 3 (2):24–46
Jensen MC (1986) Agency costs of free cash flow, corporate finance and takeovers. Am Econ Rev 76:323–329
Jensen M (2005) Agency costs of overvalued equity. Financ Manag 34(1):5–19
Jensen MC, Meckling WH (1976) Theory of the firm: managerial behavior, agency costs and ownership structure. J Financ Econ 3(4):305–360
Jones JJ (1991) Earnings management during import relief investigations. J Account Res 29 (2):193–228
Jones S, Sharma R (2001) The impact of free cash flow, financial leverage and accounting regulation on earnings management in Australia's 'Old' and 'New' economics. Manag Financ 27:18–38
Kasanen E, Kinnunen J, Niskanen J (1996) Dividend-based earnings management: empirical evidence from Finland. J Account Econ 22:283–312
Kato K, Kunimura M, Yoshida Y (2001) Banks' earnings management before potential violation of dividend regulation in Japan. Working paper: Osaka University of Economics, Nagoya City University and Sumitomo-Life Research Institute Inc
Kato K, Kunimura M, Yoshida Y (2002) Dividend behavior and pure accrual management of Japanese Banks. Working paper: Osaka University of Economics, Nagoya City University and Sumitomo-Life Research Institute Inc
Kothari SP, Leone AJ, Wasley CE (2005) Performance matched discretionary accrual measures. J Account Econ 39(1):163–197

Ku Ismail et al. (1993) Performance of new stock issues on the KLSE, Capital markets review, KLSE and RIIAM publications 1(5): 81–95
Lehn K, Poulsen A (1989) Free cash flow and stockholder gains in going private transactions. J Financ 44:771–787
Lie E, Li W (2005) Dividend changes and catering incentives. J Financ Econ 80:293–308
Li Q, Huang G (2007) Influence of institutional ownership on cash dividend policy of China listed companies. The sixth Wuhan international conference on E-business – international finance track, pp 1876–1880
Ling FS, Abdul Mutalip ML, Shahrin AR, Othman MS (2008) Dividend policy: evidence from public listed companies in Malaysia. Int Rev Bus Res Pap 4(4):208–222
Maloney MT, McCormick RE, Mitchell ML (1993) Managerial decision making and capital structure. J Bus 66(2):189–217
MIA (2002) Malaysian approved standards on quality control, auditing, review, other assurance and related services (Part 1). www.mia.org.my/handbook/guide/MASA/MASAPart1.pdf
Nelson M, Elliott J, Tarpley R (2002) Evidence from auditors about managers' and auditors' earnings management decisions. Account Rev 77:175–202
Nibler M (1995) Bank control and corporate performance in Germany: the evidence. Working paper No. 48, St. John's College, Cambridge, June 1995
Peasnell KV, Pope PF, Young S (2000) Detecting earnings management using cross-sectional abnormal accruals models. Account Bus Res 30(4):313–326
Revsine L, Collins D, Johnson W (2005) Financial reporting and analysis, 3rd edn. Pearson Prentice Hall, New Jersey
Ross SA, Westerfield RW, Jaffe J (2002) Corporate finance, 6th edn. McGraw-Hill, Boston
Roosenboom P, Van der Goot T, Mertens G (2003) Earnings management and initial public offerings: evidence from the Netherlands. Int J Account 38:243–266
Roychowdhury S (2006) Earnings management through real activities manipulation. J Account Econ 42(3):335–370
Schooley DK, Barney LD Jr (1994) Using dividend policy and managerial ownership to reduce agency costs. J Financ Res 17(3):363–373
Stulz RM (1990) Managerial discretion and optimal financing policies. J Financ Econ 26(1):3–27
Sun L, Rath S (2009) An empirical analysis of earnings management in Australia. Int J Soc Educ Econ Manag Eng 3(7):295–311
Teoh S, Welch I, Wong T (1998a) Earnings management and the long-run market performance of initial public offerings. J Finance 50:1935–1974
Teoh S, Welch I, Wong T (1998b) Earnings management and the underperformance of seasoned equity offerings. J Financ Econ 50:63–99
Uwuigbe U, Jafaru J, Ajayi A (2012) Dividend policy and firm performance: a study of listed firms in Nigeria. Account Manag Inf Syst 11(3):442–454
Van de Poel K, Vanstraelen A (2007) Management reporting on internal control and earnings quality: Insights from a "low cost" internal control regime. Proceedings of the European Accounting Association, Lisbon, Apr 2007, pp 25–27
Wang KJ, Erickson G, Gau W (1993) Dividend policies and dividend announcement effects for real estate investment trust. J Am Real Estate Urban Econ Assoc 21(2):185–201
White GE (1970) Discretionary accounting decisions and income normalization. J Account Res 8:260–273
Zang AY (2007) Evidence on the tradeoff between real manipulation and accrual manipulation, working paper: University of Rochester
Shah SZA, Yuan H, Zafar N (2010) Earnings management and dividend policy: an empirical comparison between Paskitani listed companies & Chinese listed companies. Int Res J Finance Econ 35:51–60. ISSN 1450–2887

Chapter 14
Can Market Orientation Sustain Management of Microfinance Institutions? The Case Study of Amanah Ikhtiar Malaysia (AIM)

Soheil Kazemian, Rashidah Abdul Rahman, Zuraidah Mohd Sanusi, and Adewale Abideen Aedyemi

Abstract This paper aims at providing insights into how the three dimensions of market orientation, namely, customer orientation, competitor orientation, and inter-function coordination, affect the management sustainability of Amanah Ikhtiar Malaysia (AIM) as the largest microfinance institution in Southeast Asia. In a cross-sectional survey, Partial Least Squares (PLS) was used to test the hypotheses on a convenience sample of 67 % of AIM's top management level. In addition, 400 customers and 300 employees from various branches based on their customers' number were also chosen randomly. The results provided empirical evidences that indicate management sustainability is influenced by customer orientation and inter-function coordination significantly. In contrast, competitor orientation has insignificant effects on management sustainability of AIM. The result of the paper enhanced further the literature in understanding the long-term sustainable social performance-based market orientation.

14.1 Introduction

In response to the need by the international community to design a comprehensive and full-supportive financial package for helping the poor, Muhammad Yunus developed the Grameen Bank model (microcredit and microfinance that provides

S. Kazemian (✉) • Z. Mohd Sanusi
Accounting Research Institute (ARI), Universiti Teknologi Mara (UiTM), Shah Alam, Malaysia
e-mail: soheil.kazemian@yahoo.com

R. Abdul Rahman
Faculty of Economics and Administration, King Abdul Aziz University (KAU), Jeddah, Kingdom of Saudi Arabia

A.A. Aedyemi
Accounting Research Institute (ARI), International Islamic University Malaysia (IIUM), Gombak, Selangor, Malaysia

H.G. Djajadikerta, Z. Zhang (eds.), *A New Paradigm for International Business*, Springer Proceedings in Business and Economics, DOI 10.1007/978-981-287-499-3_14

small loans to poor entrepreneurs) in Bangladesh, in 1976 (Li and Rouyih 2007). The Grameen Bank model has flourished in the past four decades all over the world. Likewise, in Malaysia, the Amanah Ikhtiar Malaysia (AIM) was established in September 1987, using the Grameen Bank model with some modifications. AIM as one of the biggest Grameen Bank replications in Asia, plays a very significant role in reducing poverty in Malaysia (Ramli 2001).

Although microfinance business has a great market in Malaysia, still one of the most remarkable issues of microfinance institutions (MFIs) in Malaysia is their unsustainability which makes lack of outreach and, finally, diminishing poverty alleviation. MFIs in Malaysia are mostly not able to manage themselves financially and are severely dependent on governmental grants (Ahmad 2003). It could be the reason for the low number of microfinance providers despite the high demand for the microfinance services.

Although sustainability has got the same meaning in all markets, it has been defined specifically in each business, in particular. According to Cheney et al. (2004) and Fontaine et al. (2006) and based on the stakeholder theory, sustainability as a general definition is a complex and multifaceted concept, covering a broad spectrum of areas and topics from habitat conservation, to energy consumption, to stakeholder satisfaction and financial results. The original or literal meaning of the term is equivalent to permanence and implies the notion of durability, stability, and eternalness. On the other hand, sustainability in microfinance business means achieving sustainable financial and social performance (Qayyum and Ahmad 2006).

Therefore, the sustainability of MFIs and the issue of outreach and sustainable financial performance are strongly linked. Furthermore, from another perspective, accountability in MFIs is about achieving these two main organizational objectives (outreach and sustainable financial performance). Consequently, it seems necessary for MFIs to sustain current clients and attract more new ones as their financial and social resources in order to reach sustainability and meet accountability objectives.

Thus, in order to achieve this goal, MFIs need to follow a valid and reliable plan, which contains guidelines in attracting and saving clients, taking proper decisions in confrontation to competitors, and finally taking proper internal interaction, enhancing the organization in the market.

Kohli and Jaworski (1990, p. 6) defines market orientation as "the organization wide generation of market intelligence pertaining to current and future customer needs, dissemination of the intelligence across departments, and organization wide responsiveness to it." This concept totally focuses on its three dimensions, namely, customer orientation, competitor orientation, and inter-function coordination, which are constructed from three major factors that include intelligence generation, intelligence dissemination, and responsiveness, based on the importance of sustaining and attracting customers (Kohli and Jaworski 1990).

In general, this study aims to address one gap in "sustainable performance-based market orientation research" in microfinance business, clarifying whether the nature of market orientation can affect the management sustainability of MFIs or otherwise, applying the concept of sustainability at the microlevel of the organization in the microfinance business.

The current study determines the influences of market orientation on management sustainability of AIM, as the oldest and biggest microfinance provider in Malaysia, to clarify how management sustainability of AIM is affected by the three dimensions of market orientation. Further, two control variables, namely, sustainability of customer and employee, are used to determine the relationship between independent and dependent variables.

14.2 Theoretical Background

14.2.1 Sustainability of Microfinance Institutions

According to Sebhatu (2009), having long-term financial and social performance is the most important characteristic of sustainable organizations. Nevertheless, changing managers in organizations in some conditions may be considered as normal, but these changes must not affect the main objectives of the organizations. The management's main goals in sustainable corporations are reaching the highest possible level of efficiency via creating added value for their main stakeholders and integrating the efficiency, social, and financial performance of their organization. Despite the any changes in management level, this objective should be followed by the organizations. Thus, sustainable organizations are measured by, first, their sustainable management through some items like whether they have fixed management strategies despite the change of managers, whether the time given to the manager to accomplish his/her goals is enough, whether the corporation is driven by predetermined strategies and not by managers' feelings, whether the managers' turnover rate in the corporation is high, etc.

Further, the relationship between top management attitude in terms of saving clients and sustainability of the organization could be affected by some more variables like having sustainable customers and employees. As it is clear, customers play the main role in the survival of each business, so saving current customers and attracting more new ones is a very important objective for all organizations. In addition, saving and training employees could make corporations more efficient and sustainable. Thus, the relationship between independent and dependent variables in this study (dimensions of market orientation and management sustainability of MFIs) could be affected by two control variables, namely, sustainability of customer and employee (Qayyum and Ahmad 2006).

14.2.2 Microfinance in Malaysia

Despite the World Bank classifying Malaysia as an upper middle-income country, it has got one of the fastest economic growths among Asian countries. According to the World Economic Outlook (2012), Malaysia increased its GDP growth rate from

0.5 % in 2001 to 7.2 % in 2010. In addition, the World Bank (2012) confirmed that the poverty rate in Malaysia has also been reduced; the proportion of people whose income is below USD1.25 (RM4) per day decreased from 2.1 %in 1995 to 0.5 % in 2004. Furthermore, based on SME (2011), in 2010, small and medium enterprises (SMEs), as the main users of microfinance services, comprise of 80 % microenterprises, 18 % small enterprises, and 2 % medium enterprises. The SMEs constitute 99.2 % or 548,247 of total business establishments and contribute about 32 % of GDP, 59 % of total employment, and 19 % of total exports. Nevertheless, Malaysia is still challenged by the problem of poverty. In 1997, there were 10.9 % of households in rural areas of which 56,000 were under the poverty line. Despite reducing the poverty rate, because of the worldwide economic slowdown and declining commodity prices, the percentage of people in poverty increased in recent years (Li and Rouyih 2007). The poverty rate in Malaysia in 2010 was 3.8 %, and almost 34 % of 1.4 million workers earned below the poverty line of RM720 monthly (BNM 2011).

14.2.3 Background of AIM

Amanah Ikhtiar Malaysia was the first microfinance institution in Malaysia and the largest Grameen Bank replication outside Bangladesh McGuire et al. (1998). It was developed in 1988, under the Trustee Incorporation Act 258 (revised 1981) (Chamhuri and Quinones 2000). AIM is a poverty-oriented microfinance institution that provides loans only to the poor. Selangor, in Peninsular Malaysia, was the site of the pilot project of the Grameen Bank concept, known as "Project Ikhtiar." The pilot project was conducted by two social scientists, Dr. David Gibbons and Professor Sukor Kasim from the Universiti Sains Malaysia. "Project Ikhtiar" was successful and showed that a group-lending system similar to the Grameen Bank model can be applied in Malaysia. AIM's micro-lending services have been widely offered throughout Malaysia.

14.3 Theoretical Framework and Hypothesis of Study

Based on previous literature, market orientation appears as an important factor in leading organizations to the main objectives of sustainability (superior long-term social and financial performance) (Bhuian and Habib 2005). Market-oriented firms are likely to achieve long-term profit by providing superior value to the customers by identifying their current and future needs, knowing the strengths and plans of competitors, showing coordinated and just-in-time reactions, and presenting new services in order to affect the market environment (Narver and Slater 1990). Several studies have been conducted, examining the capabilities of market-oriented organizations in reaching superior long-term performance (Jaworski and Kohli 1993;

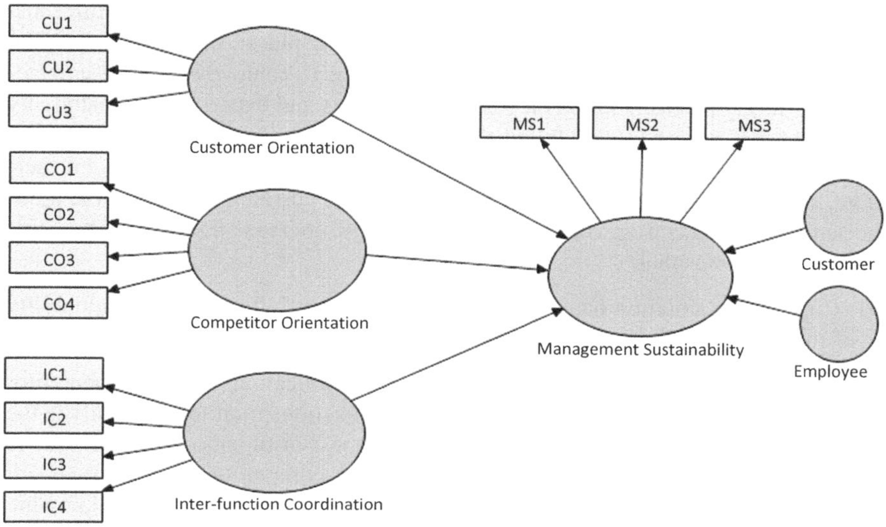

Fig. 14.1 Research model

Narver and Slater 1990; Ruekert 1992). Based on this positive linkage between market orientation and institutional sustainability in various industries, the proposed model emphasizes on the role of market orientation for achieving high performance by microfinance providers. In addition, two more control variables, namely, having sustainable customers and employees, are considered as effective factors on the relationship between dimensions of market orientation and aspects of sustainability. Figure 14.1 shows the key components of the framework. As can be seen, the framework posits market orientation of a firm as an independent variable and its management sustainability as a dependent variable.

Based on previous body of literature, it is expected that following market orientation's strategies enables organizations to reach superior social and financial performance that may cause rise to management sustainability. This argument is fully supported by the "stakeholder theory." According to Freeman et al. (2004), using market orientation strategies in order to create superior value for customers, supporting customer failures, and adherence to social responsibilities can help MFIs to attract more customers and stay sustainable, socially and financially, and consequently positively affect the sustainability of management.

As mentioned above, market orientation has three dimensions: customer orientation, competitor orientation, and inter-function coordination. Customer orientation means driving corporations based on the current and future needs of customers, which requires knowledge of the customer target market (CU1), knowing and analyzing their current demands and predicting future demands (CU2), and creating customer superior value by focusing on meeting their needs in order to make them satisfied (CU3). According to Singh and Ranchhod (2004), organizations are able to attain competitive advantages and reach superior organizational performance, through creating superior customer value and analyzing current and future customer's needs. In addition, since market orientation places the customer at the center of all the activities of an organization, it aims to achieve customer satisfaction by offering products based on customer's desires and expectations. A study by Reichheld and Sasser (1990) found that firms can improve profits from 25 % to 85 % by making an improvement of only 5 % in their customer retention. Furthermore, they have found that if 2–5 % of the additional customers are retained, it has the same effect as cutting costs by 10 % which will increase the profit. Thus, this study hypothesizes that:

H1: Customer orientation has a positive and significant influence on sustainability of management of microfinance institutions.

The second characteristic of market-oriented organizations is being competitor oriented. By definition, competitor-oriented organizations monitor and analyze the actions and capabilities of competitors for making just-in-time decisions in order to show the best reactions (Narver and Slater 1990). A competitor-oriented organization firstly should be informed about the level of competitive intensity by knowing the competitive environment (CO1). It should be able to evaluate its own ability and power as well as that of its competitors. This organization should have a systematic procedure for gathering all the relevant data (CO2) and transferring this information from the competitors to top management (CO3) for making suitable and just-in-time decisions (CO4) (Armstrong and Collopy 1996; Kohli and Jaworski 1990; Tortosa et al. 2009). Some studies suggest that competitor-oriented firms, which continuously monitor progress about rivals, gain opportunities by creating products or marketing programs that are differentiated from those of competitors (Im and Workman Jr 2004) or by adopting an effective "second-but-better" approach, which assists them to gain long-term performance (Frambach et al. 2003). Similarly, according to the mentioned literature, the current study hypothesizes that:

H2: Competitor orientation has a positive and significant influence on sustainability of management of microfinance institutions.

Inter-function coordination is reflecting level of interactions and communications that assists organizations to provide better quality of services (Grinstein 2008). Generally, market-oriented organizations should have something new for presenting such as innovations to impress the market and customers in order to persuade them to stand by the organization. Inter-function coordination is directly related to the top management attitude of whether they want to be the best in the market or otherwise (IC1). If so, how much is their risk tolerance (IC2)? Alternatively, do they have the capability for being innovative (Gresham et al. 2006)? On the other hand, "too much" collaboration and information sharing, innovation, and risk-taking, however, often have a negative effect (Szymanski and Henard 2001). Still, at the heart of inter-functional coordination lies the sharing of market information that is crucial for new product development, and that is why internal connectedness (IC3) and conflicts (IC4) may have remarkable effects (Im and Workman Jr 2004). Similarly to other dimensions of market orientation, the following hypothesis is considered:

H3: Inter-function coordination has a positive and significant influence on sustainability of management of microfinance institutions.

Further, the current research measures management sustainability of microfinance institutions through its definition (Crittenden et al. 2011; Sebhatu 2009). Generally speaking, management sustainability is driving the organization based on customers' demands and not by managers' personal feelings. Management sustainability of microfinance providers is about managers' management duration (MS1) and stability of organization's managerial guideline regardless of the changing of managers (MS2) and whether turnover of managers is something normal or not (MS3).

14.4 Research Method

The main objective of the current study is to empirically test the level of influences of the three dimensions of market orientation as independent variables on sustainability of AIM as the dependent variable similar to the approach used by Narver and Slater (1990a). For measuring the level of a firm's market orientation, the 14-item MKTOR scale developed by Narver and Slater (1990a) and the 32-item scale of market orientation originally developed by Jaworski and Kohli (1993) were used. The Narver and Slater's (1990) measurement scale (MKTOR) has been used extensively in studies on market orientation and has been widely recognized for its validity and reliability (Ngai and Ellis 1998; Ngansathil 2001; Pelham and Wilson 1995). The reported reliability coefficient of the scale has been reported to be above the 0.7 threshold as recommended by Nunnally (1978).

14.4.1 Data Collection

The study was based on a survey of the biggest Islamic microfinance provider in Malaysia, Amanah Ikhtiar Malaysia (AIM). The survey field work started in August 2012 and continued to July February 2013. Questionnaire protocol was used as the primary means for data collection. Data were gathered from three distributed types of questionnaires. The first category of questionnaires was distributed among AIM's top management level. In this particular category, all respondents were decision makers and have influences on the organization's strategies. These managers responded to measurements related to the independent variables (three dimensions of market orientation) and dependent variables (measurements of organization's sustainability). Data was collected from 30 respondents out of 45 questionnaires that constitute 67 % of AIM's top management level at the monthly center meeting in the main branch.

The second and third types of questionnaires were distributed among employees and customers to get data about the sustainability of employees and customers in AIM, respectively. For these last two respondent categories, two branches were chosen randomly, one branch with more than 5,000 customers and another one with less than 5,000 customers. The questionnaires were distributed and collected during the branches' weekly center meeting. In total, 400 customers and 300 employees responded to the related questionnaires which, according to Israel (1992), are reliable. This study adopts PLS-SEM as the statistical method to assess the research model.

14.4.2 Hypothesis Testing

Next we proceeded with the path analysis to test the six hypotheses generated. Figure 14.2 and Table 14.1 illustrate the results. The R^2 value for management sustainability was 0.483, suggesting that 48.3 % of the variance in extent of *management sustainability* can be explained by customer orientation, competitor orientation, and inter-function coordination. As Hair et al. (2011, 2012) point out, each path coefficient greater than 0.2 reflects significant relationship between two respected variables. Therefore, a close look shows that customer orientation was positively related to extent of management sustainability ($\beta = 0.317$, $p < 0.01$) and so was inter-function coordination positively related to management sustainability ($\beta = 0.485$, $p < 0.01$), whereas competitor orientation was not a significant predictor of extent of management sustainability ($\beta = 0.126$, $p < 0.01$). Therefore, H1 and H3 of this study were supported, whereas H2 did not receive statistical support. In this study it was found that inter-function coordination was the most significant predictor of extent of sustainability followed by customer orientation. The higher the extent of inter-function coordination, the better is the microfinance institution's management sustainability.

14.5 Discussion

The sustainability literature has focused on the notion that a proper implementation of market orientation leads to superior sustainable performance. Yet to date, a limitation of this mentioned fact is the lack of research about the relationship between market orientation's dimensions and management sustainability of organizations (O'Cass and Ngo 2007). Two main objectives of accountability in MFIs are, first, to reach more clients in the poorer strata of the population (outreach or social performance) and, second, financial sustainability (Mersland and Øystein Strøm 2009). Furthermore, based on the stakeholder theory, managing stakeholders is about creating as much value as possible for stakeholders, without resorting to trade-offs (Freeman et al. 2004). Thus, the top management of each organization

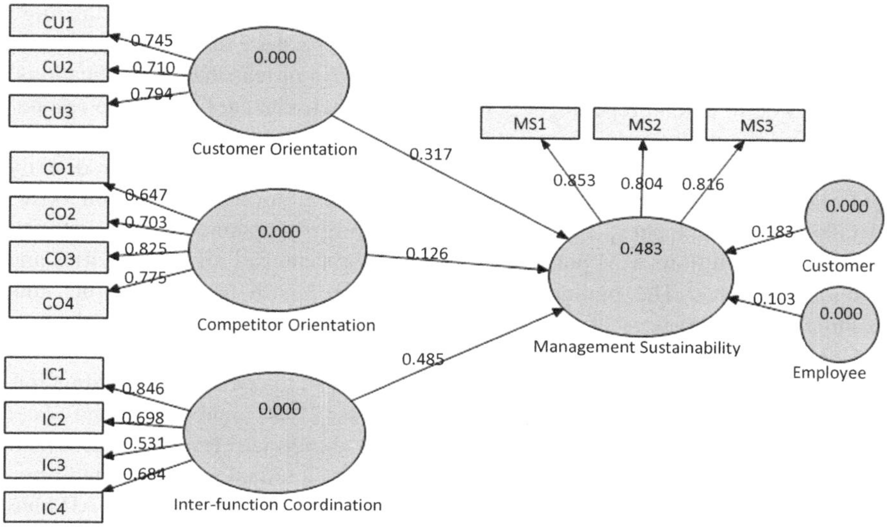

Fig. 14.2 Results of path analysis

Table 14.1 Coefficients and hypothesis testing

Hypothesis	Relationship	Coefficient	t value	Supported
H1	CusOri → ManSus	0.317	3.471	YES
H2	ComOri → ManSus	0.126	1.105	NO
H3	Int → ManSus	0.485	4.612	YES

should pay attention to every appropriate guideline for improving the organization's financial and social performance in order to create as much financial benefits as possible for the stakeholders.

The central argument of this research is that microfinance is known as an efficient tool for poverty alleviation, but in order to maximize its efficiency, MFIs need to increase their sustainable performance through sustaining management. In addition, organizations with a strong established investment should be aware that for making financial benefit, in addition to producing high-quality products or services, organization's ability to save current clients and attract more new ones and to be innovative in creating superior customer value is also required. This proposition has been corroborated by the empirical findings of this study in which customer orientation and inter-function coordination have positive impacts on organization's sustainable performance of management. In addition, unlike the previous body of literature, in this study sustainability is investigated at the microlevel, like sustainability of management.

By definition, AIM got a high level in customer orientation. Based on the results of the current study, AIM has got high ability in providing new services based on the clients' preferences and their future demands by analyzing their current needs.

In addition, AIM emphasized on keeping the clients satisfied through creating more added value for them. Some of taken actions in this regard are the following: failure customers (those couldnt meet their liabilities because of reasonable justifications) are welcome to extend repayment period, each branch manager should be responsible to the clients' complaints, unsatisfied clients even can talk to top management level, R&D department is responsible to measure clients' satisfaction level, directly and frequently, clients can contact top management through suggestion boxes installed in all branches, and so on. Totally, fully adoptable to the customer orientation definition, AIM places the clients at the center of all the activities and provided services. The findings are fully consistent with previous studies that examined the influences of customer orientation on sustainable performance of organizations (Ghani and Mahmood 2011; Megicks et al. 2005; Ruekert 1992).

On the other hand, AIM also has got a high level in inter-function coordination. Similar to Gresham et al. (2006), Kohli and Jaworski (1990), and Narver and Slater (1990), the results of this study also proved that appropriate level of interorganizational interactions and communications made AIM a united and integrated organization and may give rise to sustainability of management. What's more, AIM has several advisors in deferent aspects and areas, including Shariah. For instance, they got shariah panel as internal and Bank Islam as external shariah advisors. These valuable characteristics can assist each MFI's decision maker to become more innovative and competitive by providing new services with the lowest possible risk.

However, regarding the insignificant relationship between competitor orientation and sustainability in AIM, this fact indicates that AIM is the biggest microfinance provider as compared to other microfinance institutions in Malaysia. Thus, AIM is not used to having any serious competitors. From a moral point of view, AIM's management prefers to focus on their own activities rather than concern with the activities carried out by the other microfinance institutions. These findings are totally inconsistent with some other conducted studies (Armstrong and Collopy 1996; Deshpandé and Farley 1998; Narver and Slater 1990).

Based on the results of this study, it is claimed that market orientation clearly affects management sustainability of AIM which is directly responsible for the long-term social and financial performance of the organization. The findings of the current study can be classified into three different categories. First, the positive impact of customer orientation on sustainable management replicates previous researches that found a positive relationship between market orientation and performance at the macrolevel (Jaworski and Kohli 1993; Matsuno and Mentzer 2000). In other terms, based on the findings, creating superior customer value, analyzing customers' current and future demands, and identifying customer target market affect sustainable management performance (management sustainability) of AIM significantly.

Second, the results have shown that there is a conflicting theoretical perspective in this part. Nevertheless, as discussed above because of noncompetitive market in the microfinance business in Malaysia, competitor orientation does not affect management sustainability of AIM significantly; however, according to previous studies, it is revealed that in normal markets (with more competitive atmosphere), sustainability of organizations could be affected by competitor orientation (Armstrong and Collopy 1996; Jaworski and Kohli 1993).

Third, the results provide empirical validation that AIM's long-term management sustainability is significantly affected by inter-function coordination. Meaning, top management emphasis, top management risk tolerance, interdepartmental connectedness, avoiding interdepartmental conflicts, and having innovations in the business in order to affect the market and clients have a significant influence on sustainability of AIM.

14.6 Conclusion

This empirical study advances past theories such as the stakeholder theory, or marketing-based theories like adaptive structuration theory and agency theory, about market orientation and organizational sustainability. From both theoretical and empirical standpoints, the current study attempted to address one gap in the "sustainable performance-based market orientation research" in microfinance business: employing market orientation at the microlevel such as sustainability of management. In addition, the results also indicated that there is a conflicting theoretical perspective on the nature of market orientation (dimensions of market orientation). This study addressed this gap by empirically determining:

- The effects of each dimension of market orientation on management sustainability
- The effects of two major control variables (sustainability of customers and employees) on sustainable management and financial sustainable performance (simultaneously with dimensions of market orientation)

Remarkably, these fundamental issues have not been addressed in any empirical study to date.

To sum up, the current study provided some empirical evidences that following customer orientation and inter-function coordination influence management sustainability of AIM significantly. On the other hand, competitor orientation has no significant impacts on management sustainability of AIM.

References

Ahmad I (2003) Current situation of microfinance in Malaysia and its issues. Agriculture Bank of Malaysia, Kuala Lumpur

Armstrong S, Collopy F (1996) Competitor orientation: effects of objectives and information on managerial decisions and profitability. J Mark Res 33(2):385–394

Bhuian SN, Habib M (2005) The relationship between entrepreneurship, market orientation and performance: a test in Saudi Arabia. J Transl Manag 10(1):79–98

Bank Negara Malaysia (2011) The annual report. Retrieved on Aug2013 from: http://www.bnm.gov.my/index.php?ch=en_publication_catalogue&pg=en_publication_bnmar&ac=89&yr=2011
Chamhuri S, Quinones B (2000) Microfinance in Malaysia: aiming at success. Microfinance and poverty alleviation: 180–199
Cheney H, Nheu N, Vecellio L (2004) Sustainability as social change: values and power in sustainability discourse. Sustainability and social science: Roundtable proceedings: 225–246
Crittenden VL, Crittenden WF, Ferrell LK, Ferrell O, Pinney CC (2011) Market-oriented sustainability: a conceptual framework and propositions. J Acad Mark Sci 39(1):71–85
Deshpandé R, Farley JU (1998) Measuring market orientation: generalization and synthesis. J Mark Focus Manag 2(3):213–232
Fontaine C, Haarman A, Schmid S (2006) The Stakeholder Theory. dalam http://www.edalys.fr/documents/Stakeholders%20theory.pdf. Accessed 11 Nov 2011
Frambach RT, Prabhu J, Verhallen TM (2003) The influence of business strategy on new product activity: the role of market orientation. Int j res mark 20(4):377–397
Freeman RE, Wicks AC, Parmar B (2004) Stakeholder theory and "the corporate objective revisited". Organ Sci 15(3):364–369
Ghani U, Mahmood Z (2011) Factors influencing performance of microfinance firms in Pakistan: focus on market orientation. Int J Acad Res 3(5):125–132
Gresham G, Hafer J, Markowski E (2006) Inter-functional market orientation between marketing departments and technical departments in the management of the new product development. Process J Behav Appl Manage 8(1):43–65
Grinstein A (2008) The effect of market orientation and its components on innovation consequences: a meta-analysis. J Acad Mark Sci 36(2):166–173
Hair JF, Ringle CM, Sarstedt M (2011) PLS-SEM: indeed a silver bullet. J Mark Theory Pract 19 (2):139–152
Hair JF, Sarstedt M, Ringle CM, Mena JA (2012) An assessment of the use of partial least squares structural equation modeling in marketing research. J Acad Mark Sci 40(3):414–433
Im S, Workman JP Jr (2004) Market orientation, creativity, and new product performance in high-technology firms. J Mark 68:114–132
Israel GD (1992) Determining sample size: University of Florida Cooperative Extension Service, Institute of Food and Agriculture Sciences, EDIS
Jaworski B, Kohli A (1993) Market orientation: Antecedents and consequences. J Mark 57:53–70
Kohli AK, Jaworski BJ (1990) Market orientation: the construct, research propositions, and managerial implications. J Mark 54:1–18
Li PJ, Rouyih H (2007) Microfinance In Malaysia. In: Mun HW (ed) Malaysian economic development issues and debates. Malaysian Economics Development, Malaysia, pp 133–143
Matsuno K, Mentzer JT (2000) The effects of strategy type on the market orientation-performance relationship. J Mark 64(4):1–16
McGuire PB, Conroy JD, Thapa GB (1998) Getting the framework right: policy and regulation for microfinance in Asia: Foundation for Development Cooperation Brisbane
Megicks P, Mishra A, Lean J (2005) Enhancing microfinance outreach through market-oriented new service development in Indian regional rural banks. Int J Bank Mark 23(1):107–125
Mersland R, Øystein Strøm R (2009) Performance and governance in microfinance institutions. J Bank Financ 33(4):662–669
Narver JC, Slater SF (1990) The effect of a market orientation on business profitability. J Mark 54:20–35
Ngai JCH, Ellis P (1998) Market orientation and business performance: some evidence from Hong Kong. Int Mark Rev 15(2):119–139
Ngansathil W (2001) Market orientation and business performance: empirical evidence from Thailand. The University of Melbourne
Nunnally J (1978) Psychometric methods. McGraw-Hill, New York
O'Cass A, Ngo LV (2007) Market orientation versus innovative culture: two routes to superior brand performance. Eur J Mark 41(7/8):868–887

Outlook WE (2012) Malaysia – Real GDP growth: World Data Atlas. http://knoema.com/atlas/Malaysia/GDP-growth

Pelham AM, Wilson DT (1995) A longitudinal study of the impact of market structure, firm structure, strategy, and market orientation culture on dimensions of small-firm performance. J Acad Mark Sci 24(1):27–43

Qayyum A, Ahmad M (2006) Efficiency and sustainability of Micro Finance Institutions in South Asia. South Asian Network of Economic Research Institutes (SANEI)

Ramli M (2001) Amanah Ikhtiar Malaysia: the Oldest GB Replication. Source: http://www.grameen-info.org/dialogue/dialogue47/crMalaysia.html. Accessed 21 Sept 2013

Reichheld FF, Sasser WE (1990) Zero defections: quality comes to services. Harv Bus Rev 68 (5):105–111

Ruekert RW (1992) Developing a market orientation: an organizational strategy perspective. Int j res mark 9(3):225–245

Sebhatu SP (2009) Sustainability performance measurement for sustainable organizations: beyond compliance and reporting. Karlstad University, Karlstad

Singh S, Ranchhod A (2004) Market orientation and customer satisfaction: evidence from British machine tool industry. Ind Mark Manag 33(2):135–144

SME (2011) SME annual report. In: D. SME (ed) Census 2011

Szymanski DM, Henard DH (2001) Customer satisfaction: a meta-analysis of the empirical evidence. J Acad Mark Sci 29(1):16–35

The World Bank (2012) Poverty and inequality statistics. World Data Atlas. http://knoema.com/atlas/Malaysia/Poverty-level (Vol Mar 12)

Tortosa V, Moliner MA, Sánchez J (2009) Internal market orientation and its influence on organisational performance. Eur J Mark 43(11/12):1435–1456

Chapter 15
Mitigating Money Laundering: The Role of Designated Non-financial Businesses and Professions in Southeast Asian Countries

Normah Omar, Razana Juhaida Johari, Muhammad Asri Mohamed Azam, and NurulAini Othmanul Hakim

Abstract Money laundering (ML) is a process to make "dirty money" appear to be clean. The Asia/Pacific Group on Money Laundering (APG) was established in Bangkok, Thailand, in 1997 through an initiative by the "Financial Action Task Force (FATF) Asia Secretariat" in 1995. Its primary objective was to obtain wide regional commitment to implement anti-money laundering (AML) policies and initiatives and secure agreement to establish a more permanent regional anti-money laundering body. The role of APG is to combat money laundering and the financing of terrorism in the Asia/Pacific region. This paper examines the compliance to FATF Recommendations into national legislation of ten Southeast Asian countries in relation to the role of professionals such as accountants, lawyers and company secretaries. These professionals are known as "designated non-financial businesses and professions" (DNFBPs). The paper suggests some recommendations that are considered vital in combating money laundering activity.

15.1 Introduction

Money laundering is a predicate offence. It involves the whole facet of processes to "cleanse" dirty money so that it can be used for normal business transactions (He 2010). Money laundering activities affect not only the criminal justice systems but they also have the capacity to destabilise financial institutions and financial systems. In contrast to most other types of crime, money laundering is notable for the diversity of its form, participants and settings. The Asia Pacific Group on Money Laundering (APG 1997) in cooperation with an international body, Financial Action Task Force (FATF 1989), works collaboratively to consolidate support for anti-money laundering measures. At its Asia/Pacific Money Laundering Symposium in February 1997, the APG has been officially established by specific "terms of reference" as an autonomous regional anti-money laundering body. At the same

N. Omar (✉) • R.J. Johari • M.A.M. Azam • N.O. Hakim
Accounting Research Institute, Universiti Teknologi MARA, Shah Alam, Malaysia
e-mail: normah645@salam.uitm.edu.my

H.G. Djajadikerta, Z. Zhang (eds.), *A New Paradigm for International Business*, Springer Proceedings in Business and Economics, DOI 10.1007/978-981-287-499-3_15

time, an "APG Secretariat" was established to be located in, and financially supported by, Australia.

In essence, APG promotes a forum in which regional issues can be discussed. Member countries are also encouraged to share their experiences and to engage in operational cooperation. In addition, APG facilitates the adoption and implementation by members of internationally accepted measures to combat money laundering and terrorism financing. FATF issues recommendations known as "40 + 9" that member countries need to comply. Whilst 40 Recommendations deal with anti-money laundering standards, there are also nine Special Recommendations that represent standards to mitigate terrorism financing activities.

The designated non-financial businesses and professions (DNFBPs) is a "specialised" reporting institution. Comprised mainly of lawyers, accountants, company secretaries and precious stones dealers, the DNFBPs have important roles in mitigating money laundering and terrorism financing activities. Among their basic responsibilities include (i) conducting due diligence on their clients, (ii) reporting suspicious transactions and (iii) maintaining full records of transactions over a specified period of time. In complying with these responsibilities, there are a lot of issues faced by the APG members in Southeast Asian countries. The ten countries analysed for this paper are Malaysia, Thailand, Indonesia, Myanmar, Philippines, Vietnam, Brunei, Lao People's Democratic Republic (LPDR), Singapore and Timor-Leste. Money laundering methods and techniques have changed over the years in response to countries' developing new countermeasures. Donato (2004) highlighted the increasing use of legal persons (lawyers) to disguise the true ownership and control of illegal proceeds. He further noted the use of professionals such as accountants and company secretaries to set up new businesses through which the illegal proceeds are channelled.

15.2 FATF Recommendations Related to DNFBPs

In 2003, FATF introduced "40 + 9" Recommendations which set minimum standards of action for member countries to implement the details according to their particular circumstances and legislative frameworks. In view of aggressive actions taken by FATF in monitoring money laundering within financial institutions, many countries have seen a significant shift in laundering activities from the traditional banking sector to nonbank financial sector (e.g. money changers and remittance financial services) and nonfinancial businesses and professions. Money launderers resorted to the nonfinancial sector to try to conceal laundered proceeds and revenues of crimes. As indicated earlier on, designated non-financial businesses and professions "DNFBPs" are comprised of casinos, real estate agents, dealers in precious stones, lawyers, notaries, independent legal professionals, accountants and trust and company service providers (see Remo 2012; Santha 2007; Smith and walker 2010).

The involvement and the participation of DNFBPs to mitigate money laundering and terrorism financing activities will ensure continued successful assessment of

Table 15.1 FATF Recommendations for DNFBPs

Recommendation 12 (DNFBP: customer due diligence)
R. 5 – Customer due diligence
R. 6 – Politically exposed persons
R. 8 – New technologies and non-face-to-face business
R. 9 – Third parties and introducers
R. 10 – Record keeping
R. 11 – Unusual transactions
Recommendation 16 (DNFBP: suspicious transaction reporting)
R. 13 – Suspicious transaction reporting
R. 14 – Protection and no tipping-off
R. 15 – Internal controls, compliance and audit
R. 21 – Special attention for higher-risk countries
Recommendation 24
DNFBP – Regulation, supervision and monitoring
Recommendation 25
DNFBP – Guidelines

FATF standards globally (Susan 2010; Tan 2007). Table 15.1 shows FATF Recommendations related to the DNFBPs.

15.2.1 Recommendation 12 (DNFBPs: Customer Due Diligence)

Under this recommendation, reporting institutions (in this case DNFBPs) should pay special attention to all complex, unusual large transactions and all unusual patterns of transactions, which have no apparent economics or visible lawful purpose. That means, DNFBPs need to know their clients (know your client). Recommendation 12 also includes the need for DNFBPs to conduct customer due diligence and maintain proper record keeping of their clients and related business transactions.

The customer due diligence and record-keeping requirements for DNFBPs are further detailed out by Recommendations 5, 6, 8, 9, 10 and 11 as follows:

- Casino –when customers engage in financial transactions equal to or above the applicable designated threshold
- Real estate agents – when they are involved in transactions for their client concerning the buying and selling of real estate
- Dealers in precious metals and stones – when they engage in any cash transaction with a customer equal to or above the applicable designated threshold
- Lawyers, notaries, other independent legal professionals and accountants – when they prepare for or carry out transactions for their client concerning the

following activities such as buying and selling of real estate; managing of client money, securities or other assets; management of bank, savings or securities accounts; organisation of contributions for the creation, operation or management of companies; creation, operation or management of legal persons or arrangements; and buying and selling of business entities
- Trust and company service providers – when they prepare for or carry out transactions for a client concerning the activities listed in the definition in the Glossary of the FATF Recommendations

15.2.2 Recommendation 16 (DNFBP: Suspicious Transaction Reporting)

Recommendation 16 states that financial institutions should develop programmes against money laundering and terrorist financing. These programmes should include the development of internal policies, procedures and controls and adequate screening procedures to ensure high standards when hiring employees as well as ongoing employee training programmes. That means designated non-financial businesses and professions need to report any suspicious transactions that involve their clients to the competent authority. The requirements set out in Recommendations 13–15 and 21 apply to all DNFBPs subject to the following qualifications: Lawyers, notaries, other independent legal professionals and accountants should be required to report suspicious transactions when, on behalf of or for a client, they engage in a financial transaction in relation to the activities described in Recommendation 12.

Dealers in precious metals and dealers in precious stones should be required to report suspicious transactions when they engage in any cash transaction with a customer equal to or above the applicable designated threshold. Trust and company service providers should be required to report suspicious transactions for a client when, on behalf of or for a client, they engage in a transaction in relation to the activities referred to in Recommendation 12. Lawyers, notaries, other independent legal professionals and accountants acting as independent legal professionals are not required to report their suspicions if the relevant information was obtained in circumstances where they are subject to professional secrecy or legal professional privilege.

15.2.3 Recommendation 24 (DNFBP: Regulation, Supervision and Monitoring)

DNFBPs should be subjected to regulatory and supervisory measures. For example casinos should be subjected to a comprehensive regulatory and supervisory regime that ensures that they have effectively implemented the necessary anti-money laundering and terrorist-financing measures.

- Casinos should be licensed.
- Competent authorities should take the necessary legal or regulatory measures to prevent criminals from holding or controlling interest or being an operator of a casino.
- Competent authorities should ensure that casinos are effectively supervised.

Countries should ensure that the other categories of DNFBPs are subjected to effective systems for monitoring and ensuring their compliance with requirements to combat money laundering and terrorist financing. This may be performed by a government authority or by an appropriate self-regulatory organisation.

15.2.4 Recommendation 25 (DNFBP: Guidelines)

The competent authorities (in most countries, this is represented by their Financial Intelligence Unit or FIU) should establish guidelines and provide feedback which will assist financial institutions and designated non-financial businesses and professions in applying national measures to combat money laundering and terrorist financing and, in particular, in detecting and reporting suspicious transactions.

15.3 Analysis of Countries' Compliance on FATF Recommendations Related to DNFBPs

Table 15.2 provides a summary of APG's evaluations of ten Southeast Asian countries. Essentially the FATF evaluation is categorised into four ratings: full compliant (C), largely compliant (LC), partial compliant (PC) and noncompliant (NC).

15.4 Summary of Compliance on FATF Recommendations Related to DNFBPs

15.4.1 Evaluations on R.12 (DNFBP: R.5, 6, 8–11)

Based on the Mutual Evaluation Report, eight out of ten countries including Singapore and Brunei which are categorised as developed countries were rated as "noncompliant (NC)". Most countries do not have implementation of customer due diligence (CDD) procedures and other obligations as required under the FATF

Table 15.2 Countries' rating based on the latest Mutual Evaluation Report (MER)

Countries	Latest MER	R.12	R.16	R.24	R.25
Malaysia	2007	PC	PC	PC	LC
Thailand	2007	NC	NC	NC	PC
Indonesia	2008	NC	NC	NC	PC
Myanmar	2008	NC	PC	NC	NC
Philippines	2009	NC	NC	NC	PC
Vietnam	2009	NC	NC	NC	NC
Brunei	2010	NC	NC	NC	PC
Lao PDR	2011	NC	NC	NC	NC
Singapore	2011	NC	PC	NC	LC
Timor-Leste	2012	PC	PC	NC	NC

Recommendation 12 (Koker 2006). Countries also do not have specific requirements to DNFBPs pertaining to these Recommendations. There are some countries that only recognised a few professions or businesses as DNFBP, for example, in Brunei, only registered agents and trustees as DNFBPs are included in the AML/CFT regime. For Singapore, real estate agents, dealers in precious metals and stones, accountants and trust service providers (other than trust companies) and company service providers do not have any AML/CFT obligations pertaining to Recommendation 12.

Malaysia and Timor-Leste were the only two countries rated "partially compliant (PC)". Among the reasons these two countries were able to obtain better rating scores compared to their counterparts are firstly, the regulations on anti-money laundering and anti-terrorism financing are already legislated. Secondly, efforts to monitor FATF compliance among DNFBPs are still at their infancy level, hence it was impossible for the assessors to establish their effectiveness. For the other countries such as Thailand, Indonesia, Vietnam and Lao PDR, the scores were mostly at "non-compliant (NC)" level. This implicates that there are no anti-money laundering and anti-terrorism financing legislation that are enforceable on DNFBPs in in these countries.

15.4.2 Evaluations on R.16 (DNFBP: R.13–15 and 21)

DNFBPs basically have reliable and strong knowledge in the business environment considering their job descriptions as an accountant, auditor, tax consultants and business consultants as well as lawyer. These professional-based entities have the main role that understands the business environment and look for the daily activities of their client and customer. In other words, they have knowledge and ability to monitor if any suspicious transaction and business activities. Therefore they have the obligation to submit Suspicious Transaction Reports (STR) to the authorities based on their capacity as reporting institution.

Based on the finding in the Mutual Evaluation Report, it shows that Brunei is one of the developed countries which appeared to have a lack of knowledge on their obligation to response on any suspicious activities or transactions in their client or customers' business. As such, DNFBPs in Brunei have appeared not obligated to do such, and even their legislations are not extended to all DNFBPs. Among the DNFBPs, only Trust and Company Service Providers (TCSPs) are subjected to STR reporting, tipping-off, safe harbour and internal control obligations. Effective implementation of these obligations by TCSPs has not been established by monitoring and supervision. Singapore, Malaysia, Timor Leste and Myanmar have been rated as "PC" for this Recommendation whilst the rest of the six countries have been rated "NC". Nevertheless, DNFBPs in Singapore also have lack of understanding of their obligations to report STRs. The limitations identified under Recommendation 14 with respect to the tipping-off provision also affect compliance with Recommendation 16. The measures to implement Recommendation 13 suffer from the deficiency as the reporting obligation is not implemented effectively (lack of understanding about the reporting obligation and low numbers of reports being filed even though the requirements have been in place for 4 years).

Malaysia and Timor-Leste have little knowledge on their obligations to STRs for DNFBPs. Even though Malaysia has Anti-Money Laundering and Anti-Terrorism Financing Act (AMLATFA 2001) in place, there were initially no explicit obligations for DNFBPs to report any suspicious transaction. It was only after the amendments were made in 2008, that accountants and lawyers are named as reporting institutions "RIs". In other developing countries such as the Philippines, Vietnam and Thailand, DNFBPs were not obligated to report STRs. For example, in Thailand, DNFBPs are not required to develop programmes against ML and TF. They also are not required to give special attention to business relationships and transactions with countries that do not or insufficiently apply the FATF Recommendations as required by Recommendation 2.

As for the finding analysis, there are countries that have insufficient knowledge on combating money laundering. Either the government failed to highlight the role and obligations of DNFBPs or there is lack of awareness on DNFBPs' part towards their obligations. It is vital for DNFBPs to be well-aware so that the main objective to combat against money laundering can be achieved.

15.4.3 Evaluations on R.24 (DNFBP: Regulation, Supervision and Monitoring)

Nine out of ten countries of Southeast Asia are noncompliant (NC) with Recommendation 24 which is regulation and supervision of DNFBPs. Thailand, Indonesia, Myanmar, Philippines, Vietnam, Brunei, Lao PDR, Singapore and Timor-Leste are the countries that do not implement the anti-money laundering and terrorism financing regulation and supervision that have been recommended by FATF. For example in Timor-Leste, there is no assigned body responsible for supervision of AML/CFT purposes, and DNFBPs are not yet subjected to any AML/CFT supervision. Same goes to the Philippines in which there are no effective regulation and supervision of casinos for AML/CFT purposes. This is because casino and gaming operators are not covered institutions in AMLA (Anti-Money Laundering Act).

Out of ten countries in Southeast Asia, Malaysia is the only country that has been rated as "PC" which means partially compliant. In Malaysia, the Bank Negara Malaysia (BNM – FIU) is responsible for monitoring and ensuring the DNFBPs' compliance with AML/CFT requirements under the AMLA and has adequate supervisory powers over DNFBPs. However, Malaysia still has weaknesses in the effectiveness of compliance monitoring and absence of on-site examinations and has inadequate resources for effective supervision of entities under the responsibility of BNM Financial Intelligent Units.

15.4.4 Evaluations on R.25 (DNFBP: Guidelines)

Under R.25, countries are required to establish guidelines and provide feedback in order to combat money laundering and terrorist financing and also in detecting and reporting suspicious transactions. "LC", "PC" and "NC" have been rated to Malaysia, Thailand, Indonesia, Myanmar, Philippines, Vietnam, Brunei, Lao PDR, Singapore and Timor-Leste. Only Malaysia and Singapore have been rated as "LC" which is largely compliant. For example, in Malaysia, the BNM has conducted ongoing consultation in the course of preparing AMLA requirements and in seeking to ensure the guidance issued by BNM is appropriate to the scope of that sector's business. Moreover, the Companies Commission of Malaysia also takes part in assisting BNM in the development of guidelines in relation to DNFBP.

Thailand, Indonesia, Philippines and Brunei are rated as partially compliant. This is because in most of these countries, their competent authorities have not yet provided DNFBPs with guidelines to assist them to implement and comply with their respective AML/CFT requirements. Countries that have been rated as "NC" indicate that no guidelines have been established for the implementation and compliance with AML/CFT provisions.

15.5 Conclusion

Based on the analysis rating above, Malaysia is the best country among other Southeast Asian countries such as Thailand, Indonesia, Myanmar, Philippines, Vietnam, Brunei, Lao PDR, Singapore and Timor-Leste. With one LC rating (R25) and three PC ratings, Malaysia stood to be "the best" compliant country. The legislation on DNFBPs has been made available, and this group of business and profession has to comply with the requirements. Nevertheless, it was mentioned in the APG report that the legislation was only newly introduced in 2006, i.e. 1 year prior to the APG evaluation in 2007. As such, the implementation of FATF standards in terms of customer due diligence, suspicious transaction reporting, regulation, supervision, monitoring and guidelines are still at their infancy stage.

Many other Southeast Asian countries have not yet put in place relevant legislation for the DNFBPs. There are several factors that contribute to the "lack of compliance" in these countries. One very important factor involves "structural issue". Many countries in Asia consist of developing economies characterised by relatively low institutional capacities and political and economic instability. Some countries are also perceived to have a high level of corruption. Therefore, it creates forces for both demand and opportunity for money laundering. An effective domestic AML/CFT regime requires the existence of certain structures, such as a robust regulatory framework, the rule of law, government effectiveness, a culture of compliance and an effective judicial system. Some Asian economies do not have these structural elements or have significant weaknesses or shortcomings that impair the implementation of an effective AML/CFT framework. Government policies on taxes, currency controls and trade restrictions can also encourage individuals to circumvent formal financial channels and drive the demand for money laundering (The Nation 2013).

Second factor relates to high level of criminal activity. Certain criminal activities in Southeast Asia generate illegal proceeds that create a demand for money laundering. Southeast Asian countries are "surrounded" by other countries that are well-known as major centres of narcotics manufacturing. Revenues from the drug trade are moved out from these areas and laundered or reallocated to other areas of production using these countries as "transit" points. The last factors that contribute to the demand for money laundering activities and make it more difficult to enforce AML/CFT regulations are social, cultural and legal norms. Strong confidentiality rules and privacy laws in a number of jurisdictions in certain Southeast Asian countries prevent the availability and accessibility of information on suspicious transactions to regulators and other authorities. In addition, it reduces transparency and makes it difficult to enforce "know your customer" requirements.

Acknowledgement The research was supported by the Ministry of Education Malaysia through Accounting Research Institute (ARI), Universiti Teknologi MARA. We also acknowledged the assistance rendered to us by the Research Management Institute of UiTM. In collecting our data, we thank Bursa Malaysia officers who helped us gather the appropriate financial data for the study.

References

Anti-Money Laundering and Anti-Terrorism Financing Act (2001) Act 613, the Commissioner of Law revision, Malaysia under the Authority of the Revision of Laws Act 1968

Asia-Pacific Group on Money Laundering (APG) (1997) www.apgml.org. Accessed 31 Oct 2013

Asia-Pacific Group on Money Laundering (2013) APG annual report 2012–2013

Donato M (2004) Combating black money: money laundering and terrorism finance, international cooperation and the G8 role. Universita di Lecce economics working paper No 56/26. Available at SRRN: http://srrn.com/abstract=561183
Financial Action Task Force (FATF) (1989) www.fatf-gafi.org. Accessed 10 Nov 2013
He P (2010) A typological study on *money laundering*. J Money Launder Control 13(1):15–32
Koker D (2006) Money laundering and suppression of financing of terrorism: some thoughts on the impact of customer due diligence measures on financial exclusion. J Financ Crime 13(1):26–50
Remo VM (2012) Why do many go to pawnshops more than banks? Philippine Daily Inquirer. http://business.inquirer.net/96065/why-do-many-go-to-pawnshops-more-than-banks. Accessed 15 Nov 2013
Santha VM (2007) Factors affecting money laundering: lesson for developing countries. J Money Launder Control 10(3):352–366
Smith RG, Walker J (2010) The illegal movement of cash and bearer negotiable instruments: typologies and regulatory responses. Trends Issues Crime Crim Justice 402:1–6
Susan D (2010) Implementation of anti-money laundering standards in Asia. Retrieved from Country Analysis Unit. www.frbsf.org. Accessed Oct 2013
Tan S (2007) Singapore guidance notes on money laundering for solicitors. J Money Launder Control 2(4):372–374
The Nation (2013) Factors combined to encouraged illegal casinos. http://www.nationmultimedia.com/opinion/Factors-combine-to-encourage-illegal-casinos-30202924.html. Accessed 16 Nov 2013

Chapter 16
Money Laundering and Terrorist Financing: Real Global Cases, Behavioural Theories and Internal Control Mechanism

Normah Omar, Razana Juhaida Johari, Siti Suharti Bt Sukir, and Jamaliah Said

Abstract Money laundering is a process to make 'dirty money' appear to be clean. The money laundering activities affect not only the criminal justice systems, but they also have the capacity to destabilise financial institutions and financial systems. While illustrating the five real global cases which are involved in money laundering and terrorist financing, this paper also discusses the criminal behavioural causation theories as to reasonably analyse the behavioural aspect of the perpetrators. Notably, the main cause for the recent hike in money laundering and terrorist financing offences is due to leakages in internal control. Thus, a few possible weaknesses from the internal control mechanisms are highlighted as to give a clearer picture on this issue. Finally, this paper also includes some discussions on the proposed mitigation risk mechanisms as to improve effectiveness and good governance towards the implementation of policies and regulation on money laundering and to counter the terrorist financing.

16.1 Introduction

Money laundering is a special type of financial crime that has generated increasing global concerns in this modern age. The crime, commonly known as a 'crime of concealment', usually involves large sums of illegal money being mobilised in many economies through the financial system. The complete process of money laundering consists of placement stage, layering stage and integration stage. The wave of globalisation and liberalisation, privatisation, free-trade zones, offshore banking centres, electronic financial transfers, smart cards and cyber-banking has made it available to launder millions of dollars in illegal activities each day (Ping He 2010). In other words, money laundering serves the purpose of concealing the illegal proceeds of crime by distinguishing them as lawful earnings (http://www.un.org/ga/20special/featur/launder.htm).

N. Omar (✉) • R.J. Johari • S.S.B. Sukir • J. Said
Accounting Research Institute, Universiti Teknologi MARA, Shah Alam, Malaysia
e-mail: normah645@salam.uitm.edu.my

H.G. Djajadikerta, Z. Zhang (eds.), *A New Paradigm for International Business*, Springer Proceedings in Business and Economics, DOI 10.1007/978-981-287-499-3_16

Criminal organisations increasingly subcontract the task of money laundering to specialised professionals because the methods required to circumvent law enforcement officials are becoming ever more complex. Professionals are used not only to conceal the origin of the source of the proceeds but to manage the subsequent investment into legitimate real estate and other assets. Money launderers constantly seek new ways to circumvent regulation and seizure of assets. Yet, along with sophisticated schemes, considerable amounts of money are still smuggled as bulk cash.

Notably, there were various researches that have been conducted in examining global money laundering and terrorist financing occurrences. Among all, previous studies reported money laundering through banking and insurance institutions, lottery businesses and realty. There are also studies which highlight international trade-based money laundering through professionals such as lawyers and accountants as well as discusses on the offences, preventive mechanisms and regulations. On the other hand, by taking into considerations the previous studies on money laundering and terrorist financing occurrences, this paper illustrates the five real global cases of money laundering that took place in various organisations as to observe the money laundering activities and to reasonably analyse the actions of the perpetrators through the behavioural theories. In addition, this paper also highlighted the leakages in internal control and proposed mitigation risk assessment as well as the role of Designated Non-Financial Businesses and Professions ('DNFBPs') in helping the nation to curb the money laundering activities.

16.2 Five Global Cases of Money Laundering

Below are the selected related cases which translated the 'dirty' money into legitimate money or other assets through the stages of placement, layering and integration. Placement is the first stage that involves the movement of cash from the location of acquisition as to avoid detection from the authorities and to then transform the monies into other asset forms. This could be done by placing the monies into the financial system circulation or smuggle them out of the country. The second stage, layering is to make more difficult for the authorities to detect and uncover laundering activities. In this stage, the perpetrators will create complex layers of financial transactions such as converting the monies into monetary instruments or buying material assets as to cover the audit trail and provide anonymity. Finally, integration is the final stage at which the monies are integrated into the legitimate economic and financial system and are assimilated with all other assets in the system. This could be done through the method such as property dealing, false import/export invoices, foreign bank complicity, etc. By this stage, it is very difficult for the authorities to distinguish between legal and illegal wealth.

16.2.1 *Money Laundering Through Banking Institutions and Companies*

16.2.1.1 Case One

Franklin Jurado, a Harvard-educated Colombian economist, pleaded guilty of money laundering in a New York federal court in April 1996 and was sentenced to seven and a half years in prison. He moved $36 million in profits from US cocaine sales for the late Colombian druglord Jose Santacruz-Londono in and out of banks and companies in an effort to make the assets appear to be of legitimate origin. He layers the illegal money out of Panama through the offices of Merrill Lynch and other financial institutions to Europe. In 3 years, he opened more than 100 accounts in 68 banks in 9 countries: Austria, Denmark, the United Kingdom, France, Germany, Hungary, Italy, Luxembourg and Monaco. Some of the accounts were opened in the names of Santacruz's mistresses and relatives, others under assumed European-sounding names. Keeping balances below $10,000 to avoid investigation, Jurado shifted the funds between the various accounts. He established European front companies with the eventual aim of transferring the 'clean' money back to Colombia, to be integrated and invested in Santacruz's restaurants, construction companies, pharmacies and real estate holdings. The scheme was interrupted when a bank failure in Monaco exposed several accounts linked to Jurado (Ping He 2010).

16.2.1.2 Case Two

Marco Manuel Luis, a San Diego real estate agent, was sentenced to 48 months in prison and ordered to pay more than $500,000 in compensation to banks on 27 August 2012. Luis pleaded guilty to two counts of conspiracy to launder money related to the purchase of a Rancho Santa Fe residence exceeding $2,000,000 and to conspiracy to launder money related to the purchase of the Palomar Mountain property and residence. Luis admitted that he was the real estate agent for convicted drug trafficker Joshua Hester, and he submitted and facilitated the false loan applications in the name of nominee purchasers, verification documents and financial documents for Hester. He intentionally assists co-conspirators in completing the loan application for the Rancho Santa Fe property, knowing that Hester was the true owner of the property from December 2006 to 30 September 2009. Luis also admitted that he intentionally falsified the loan application, in the name of Kelsey Wiedenhoefer, including her alleged annual income, her employment history and the source of down payments for the Rancho Santa Fe property, to secure the loan. Luis knew that the monthly mortgage payments were made with criminally derived proceeds. Luis confessed that he prepared a fraudulent loan application for the Palomar Mountain property and residence in the name of Jay Hansen for convicted drug trafficker Joshua Hester. Luis misrepresented Hansen's income as $150,000 and his employment history and arranged for a false verification of rent form (http://www.irs.gov/uac/2012).

16.2.1.3 Case Three

In June 1997, Nachum Goldberg was sentenced a 5-year jail for evasion of $20 million in tax. The authority would forfeit their family home under a reimbursement agreement to pay $15 million to the Australian Taxation Office. He also loses $200,000 in cash that was recovered at the time of his arrest. The two sons also lose half the equity in their homes. And all will probably be bankrupted. He had also laundered money from a sale of illegal imported diamonds into Australia. Illegal proceeds will later be deposited to the overseas suppliers via his United Charity account. This avoided millions of dollars in sales tax on the stones and yet more millions of dollars in income tax on the profits. He had moved about $90 million in dirty money out of Australia to Israel via a special account which the ANZ Banks manager had provided for him in the name of United Charity. United Charity did not exist. It was not a registered charity, nor a registered company, nor even a business name. The fact that the ANZ branch designated the United Charity account a special 'manager account' minimised official scrutiny. And more important still, the branch's willingness to accept Goldberg's transfers to Israel in 200 false names meant that AUSTRAC's computers failed to detect any pattern to the payments.

A newly appointed manager in ANZ Banks noticed that huge amounts of cash were going through it and notified the National Crime Authority. In September 1995, the investigation was handed over to Operation Flange, a joint task force of the Australian Taxation Office, NCA and AFP. Four banks in Jerusalem and Tel Aviv were used to receive the money that Goldberg sent offshore, but the bulk went to Bank Leumi in Jerusalem, of which Goldberg's brother David was the manager. Telephone intercepts allowed Australian police to identify numbered accounts at Bank Leumi, Israel Discount Bank, United Mizrahi Bank and the Republic National Bank in Geneva, as well as two coded accounts, referred to by Goldberg as the 'Rabbi Sapir' account and the 'Uncle George' account.

16.2.2 Money Laundering Through Professionals Such as Lawyer

There are also money laundering cases which were executed through professional services such as lawyers. For example, in May 2010, Mr Rondos, 43, was charged by the Supreme Court in New York with money laundering, grand larceny and scheme to defraud. He was sentenced to an indeterminate term of 5–15 years in state prison and ordered to pay approximately $2.8 million in restitution. He had been appointed as guardian and stole about $4 million from 23 people who are mentally and physically disable. Later, he placed and layered the illegal proceeds through personal expenses covering the mortgage on his home in Ridgewood, New Jersey, kitchen renovations, landscaping and a home theatre. In some instances, prosecutors said, Mr Rondos continued to steal money from victims' estates after they had died. This case was reported by 'good Samaritan' regarding Mr Rondos' activities. The assets he controlled in the cases covered in the indictment total between $20 million and $30 million. Guardians in New York are appointed by judges to manage the affairs of people who cannot handle their own because of physical or mental problems. Judges must also assign examiners to ensure that a guardian is handling the finances appropriately. Guardians must present examiners an annual summary to show what, if anything, has been done with an account's assets. Mr Rondos often did not file the summaries, and the examiners often did not report that failure to judges. It appears that the examiners may have been too friendly with him and turned their heads to the fact that he had not been filing his summaries (http://law.justia.com/cases/new-york/other-courts/2013).

16.2.3 Money Laundering Through Non-profit Organisation

The 'dirty' money could also be laundered through non-profit organisation. For instance, on 1 May 2007, Aruran Vinayagamoorthy and Sivarajah Yathavan were charged with three indictable offences under Criminal Code Act 1995 (Vinayagamoorthy and Anor v DPP (C'th) (2007) VSC 265 (17 July 2007). They are the members of a terrorist organisation, the Liberation Tamil Tigers of Eelam (LTTE) by making funds available to a terrorist organisation and providing support or resources to a terrorist organisation. There was evidence that pieces of equipment had been purchased by Vinayagamoorthy in Australia similar to equipment said to have been used by the LTTE in Sri Lanka. Similarly, he bought software from a Western Australian company used to design the hulls of small high-speed boats and hydraulic steering equipment for such vessels. As far as financial dealings were concerned, the movement of money allegedly from Mr Vinayagamoorthy's bank accounts was initially en-routed to Malaysia before they were channelled and submitted to LTTE account in Sri Lanka. The purported crime however was only proved by inference and not by direct evidence. LTTE has been declared to be a terrorist organisation by a number of other countries and by the UN, although the relevance of these declarations on the issues in this case may be a matter of considerable debate.

16.3 Behavioural Criminal Causation Theories

A big challenge for any countries during a period of significant reform and fiscal consolidation is to ensure that any major business change is delivered within a viable risk management and control framework. Risk in money laundering and terrorist financing is always an important issue, but in a period of considerable financial pressure, the risk of it may increase for a number of reasons including:

- Job losses and the fear of redundancy can lead people to commit money laundering and terrorist financing.
- People are more likely to disregard internal control or engage in unethical business practices.
- Economic pressures may have a direct effect on people's ability to rationalise fraudulent actions.
- Staff reductions may mean fewer resources being spent on internal controls.
- Risk, compliance and assurance systems can be impacted by diminished investment.
- Revised or new programmes may not have taken account of the risk of money laundering and terrorist financing.

The criminal behavioural causation theories can be used to explain on the possible reason of why people committed offence in money laundering and terrorist financing. Under the learning theories, criminal behaviour is believed to be learned via interactions with other persons in a process of communication. The principal part of the learning of criminal behaviour that occurs within intimate personal groups includes techniques of crime commission, motives and drives, rationalisations and attitudes. The specific direction of motives and drives is learned from definitions of the legal code as favourable or unfavourable. A person becomes delinquent because of an excess of definitions favourable to violation of law over definitions unfavourable to violation of law (Byrne 2010). Miller (1958) argues that participation in youth gang often provides a training ground for future organised crime participants. He identified toughness and smartness as important values necessary for such development. He also suggests that the crime-community nexus integrates the individual desires into a general group interest as well as developing capacity for intimate and persistence interaction.

Criminal behaviour is learned from association with others. The strength of association will influence the act of crime. Deprivation and exposure to success innovative model like drug dealer or gambler may affect susceptibility to criminal behaviour. This theory can relate to the case of Franklin Jurado and Marco Manuel Luis which they might have learned from their group which was involved in drug smuggling, and then the illegal proceeds that they obtained are being hidden by doing the stage of placement, layering and integration to avoid being caught by the police. Besides that, this theory can also relate to the case of Aruran Vinayagamoorthy and Sivarajah Yathavan which they learned from his organisation in Sri Lanka in fighting against other groups in Tamil Nadu wars.

While the cultural deviance theories assume that the criminals act against the law because they belong to a unique subculture associated with alternative language and culture that exist in lower-class area. They are characterised as being tough, taking care of one's own affair and rejecting any kind of governmental authority. The role models are normally a drug dealer and thief (Micheal and Potter 2007). For the court case of Franklin Jurado and Marco Manuel Luis, they can be categorised under these theories where their similar country of origin is from the South America group and mostly their main illegal business culture in selling, smuggling drug and human trafficking. The cultural relationship bound between them is the key motivation of committing the crime.

The other related behavioural causation theories is the rational choice theories. These theories are referring to people who commit crime which they choose to do so after considering the risk of detection and punishment for the crime (risk assessment) as well as the rewards either for personal or financial benefits of completing it successfully (Micheal and Potter 2007). It can be related through the case of Steven Rondos, where he was an educated person and having a good successful career as a lawyer. His intelligence and ego thus reflected that he had recognised the possible advantages and disadvantages of his decision before he chose to continue to commit the crime by misusing and misconducting on his client's property and money. His belief with his intelligence and skills would not cause his illegal activities to be detected by the authorities.

Last but not least is the theory of psychological traits and criminality. These behaviour criminal causation theories tell about the correlation between the psychological traits and likelihood of crime. A person's personality trait is important in daily decision-making process. For example, anxiety, conduct disorder, depression and short attention span have been identified. Such traits tend to make people susceptible to problems such as substance abuse, promiscuity, violence and sociopath (psychopathic) (Micheal and Potter 2007). This is related with the Nachum Goldberg court case. Based on judge statement on his case, it is clearly mentioned that Nachum Goldberg did the predicate offences not because of his greed but to get his satisfaction and reputation by helping other rich people and himself in avoiding the tax. Besides that, he feels happy that he has the special ability to disguise against the strict rule and orthodox of his Jewish ethnic (The Sydney Morning Herald (Sydney, Saturday, 14 Oct 2000)).

16.4 Leakages in Internal Control

Good governance in internal control is very crucial, and in the case of money laundering and terrorist financing, the role of internal control is observed by two separate institutions which are (i) competent authority and (ii) reporting institutions. Both of these institutions are the authorised and responsible institutions in handling and governing the internal control in managing the money laundering and terrorist financing.

16.4.1 *Competent Authority*

A competent authority is any person or organisation that has the legally delegated or invested authority, capacity or power to perform a designated function. Similarly, once an authority is delegated to perform a certain act, only the competent authority is entitled to take accounts therefrom and no one else. Usually, the competent authority for every country falls under the responsibility of the central bank of that country. For example, based on the real case, Franklin Jurado who is the Colombian economist had helped the drug cartel to launder the money from Panama. He was able to layer the illegal proceeds by opening 100 bank accounts in 68 bank institutions in 9 countries which are Austria, Denmark, the United Kingdom, France, German, Hungary, Italy, Luxembourg and Monaco. He successfully manipulated the banking institutions by using the name of mistress and relatives and a fake European name. He makes sure that every account balance was maintained below $10,000, so that banks deal with it without suspicion. Finally, he opened a few upfront companies in Europe to integrate and clean the money before it was transferred back to Colombia in the form of investment money in restaurant and other legal businesses. In addition, in another case, Aruran Vinayagamoorthy and Sivarajah Yathavan were charged with three indictable offences under Criminal Code Act 1995. Both are the members of a terrorist organisation, the Liberation Tamil Tigers of Eelam (LTTE), making funds available to LTTE which was related as a terrorist organisation and providing support or resources to a terrorist organisation.

16.4.1.1 Possible Weaknesses in Internal Control

In the light of the rapid growth of this phenomenon and the use of most banking and financial forms, as the technical development, the diversity of financial and banking means and tools, the growing phenomenon of financial liberalisation and the growing link of financial and banking systems have a significant impact to the growth of such phenomenon and its complexity.

The concern in the phenomenon of money laundering and the risks to the most important economic sectors would affect the reputation of the competent authority and may lead to the confiscation of its money. Control regulations on the administration and governance of the money laundering policies and regulation through the role of Office of Foreign Asset Control ('OFAC') compliance are inadequate. In some of these cases, the bank self-identified the issues and is engaged in remediation. In some cases, the bank's internal control mechanisms to mitigate and detect money laundering activities are still not "up-to-par" with the required standards. As stipulated by Reem (2012), key internal control systems, including filtering process and independent testing remain inadequate and insufficient for early detection to combat money laundering.

Ineffective control mechanism especially on the suitability of policies and procedures, supporting the function of the competent authority through its tasks to evaluate and examine the anti-money laundering programme and reporting procedure, leads to the loopholes in money laundering controls. Competent authority may also have a lack of awareness and coordination programme to the reporting institutions regarding the money laundering and terrorist financing issues. The establishment of the relevant law on money laundering and terrorist financing itself would mean nothing without thorough governance on it. The absence of good governance in combating such problems reflected on lower assurance level about the overall effectiveness of the anti-money laundering and terrorist financing measures established by the organisation.

16.4.2 Reporting Institution

Reporting institution could include financial and nonfinancial institutions. The Designated Non-Financial Businesses and Professions (DNFBPs) are attractive venues for criminals. DNFBPs are consistently targeted by criminals for criminal influence and criminal exploitation. Criminals attempt to infiltrate or influence both the financial industries and DNFBPs to facilitate theft, fraud, money laundering and other crimes. DNFBPs can be categorised as casinos, real estate agents, dealers in precious metals, dealers in precious stones, lawyers, company secretaries, accountants and other independent legal professionals. For instance, Steven Rondos (20 March 2013) is a legal appointed guardian who has good relations with the court examiner. Along the way, he did not file the client's financial summary, and the court examiner had failed due diligence because he did not report it to the judge. Rondos stole the client's asset and used them for personal expenses such as home mortgage in Ridgewood New Jersey, kitchen renovation, landscaping and home theatre. In some cases, he even stole the victim's real estate after they died.

While in the case of Mr Marco Manuel Luis (19 March 2012), he was the real estate agent. He had been involved in falsifying the loan document on behalf of the drug cartel to buy the home mortgage. The false information was related to annual income, employment history and down payment source of income. He also knew that the down payment and monthly mortgage payment are from 'criminally derived proceeds'. In addition, the case of Nanchum Goldberg [2001] is also related where it was operated via a centralised digital currency service. He opened an account in the name of United Charity and transferred money from Australia to Israel. The United Charity was found as a fictitious entity that had no legal basis and had not been registered as a charity organisation or company. The account was used solely to launder the illegal cash proceeds from an Australian business activity that had not been disclosed to the Australian Taxation Office.

16.4.2.1 Possible Weaknesses in Internal Control

In this study, it could be said that the bank institution has failed to adopt and implement a compliance programme that adequately covers the required Bank Secrecy Act (BSA)/Anti-Money Laundering (AML) programme elements due to an inadequate system of internal control and an ineffective independent testing. The bank institutions also do not have enterprise-wide policies and procedures to ensure that foreign branch suspicious activity involving customers of other bank branches is effectively communicated to other affected branch locations and applicable AML operation staff. Also, to ensure that on a risk basis, customer transactions at foreign branch locations can be assessed, aggregated and monitored.

Apart from that, the banks did not develop adequate due diligence on customers, particularly in the Commercial and Business Banking Unit, a repeat problem, and failed to file all necessary suspicious activity reports (SARs) related to suspicious customer activity, significant shortcomings in SAR decision-making protocols and an ineffective method for ensuring that referrals and alert are properly documented, tracked and resolved.

16.5 Proposed Risk Mitigation Measurement

With legislation such as the USA Patriot Act (2001) and Sarbanes-Oxley Act (2002) that shape the way financial and nonfinancial institutions, so-called reporting institution, do their business, internal controls are not just an accounting issue, but a key management concern. Competent authority has to ensure that all reporting institutions are taking necessary steps to strengthen its compliance especially through effective internal control including the creation of a written oversight plan, setting aside adequate funding for compliance personnel and steps to improve reporting mechanism.

A system of strong internal controls can ensure that the goals, objectives and profitability targets of a financial and nonfinancial institution are met while maintaining reliable financial and managerial reporting. With an established, tested set of internal controls, the financial and nonfinancial institutions can also ensure that they are in compliance with the legislation and regulations and mitigate the risk of unexpected losses or mistakes that could damage their entity's reputation. Establishing effective internal controls is a multistep process that includes the input of the board of directors and/or audit committee, chief financial officer and chief operating officer, among others (Hasselt and Sparshott 2013).

The role of the Financial Intelligent Unit (FIU) should serve as similar as the function of the audit committee to check the adequacy and effectiveness of internal control systems for the purpose of combatting money laundering and countering terrorist financing (Financial Intelligence 2011). The basic role is to verify the adequacy of the internal control system and its effective implementation and make recommendations to all reporting institutions on how they would activate the system and its development so as to achieve the purposes of the system in the fight against money laundering and protect the countries from the risks of money laundering. This can be done by avoiding particularly the risk of damage to the reputation of the entity or the risk of non-continuity of the activity as the FIU has the right, without any restrictions, to access all information, policies and procedures for fighting against money laundering. The audit committee is considered as an assistant body emanating from the reporting institutions that helps their entity's management in the implementation of its responsibilities relating to financial and accounting policies, internal control procedures and the detection of the reporting institutions' commitment to develop internal control system of their entity to achieve the goal of protecting the entity from the money laundering operations.

Either financial or nonfinancial institution like the Designated Non-Financial Businesses and Professions (DNFBPs) should develop and implement a framework of internal controls (e.g. policies, procedures and processes) for all operating divisions and departments reasonably designed to safeguard operations against money laundering and terrorist financing. The internal control on anti-money laundering (AML)/counterterrorist financing (CTF) needs to cover all related activities and programmes such as suspicious activity reporting, currency transaction reporting (where required), customer identification and DNFBP's record-keeping, record retention and compliance. Internal controls should also include account opening and documentation procedures and management information or monitoring systems adequate to detect and report suspicious activity in a timely manner to authorities. In addition, internal controls should mitigate the inherent risk of any high-risk account, customer, product or service as well as transactions to or from a high-risk country (e.g. sanctioned country, noncooperative nation) that could be misused for money laundering or terrorist financing. In assessing of how to mitigate potential risks and provide audit committees with assurance that controls are in place to mitigate risk, the reporting institutions should perform adequately these relevant mechanisms:

- Look at the business in terms of business operation processes. Within each business operation process, consider the major risks. What could go wrong? Where? Consider highly complex or subjective areas included in the process, and identify the risks associated with those areas.
- Determine the high-risk area. To control the risk, has the board developed policies and procedures with respect to high-risk areas? If so, is there a system in place to periodically test those procedures to ensure that the processes are operational and in compliance with board-approved policies and procedures?
- Identify and document a control structure to mitigate identified risks. Identify a set of clear, concise, well-organised procedures that control risk and identify weaknesses and inefficiencies within the internal control system. Evaluate the controls based on the products and services the entity offers, and assign a risk rating to each of those areas.

- Perform a periodic assessment. Establish an internal audit function to ascertain internal control effectiveness and ensure that procedures are in place to address all risk areas. If resources are not available internally, outsource the assessment. Have internal audits performed annually. For example, public banks should ensure that two separate firms perform the internal and external audits if they outsource the internal audit.
- Correctional programmes that include doling out punishment for acts or crimes committed are another way in improving the weaknesses in internal control. One important goal embodied in the very particular corrections is the reduction of the likelihood an offender will continue to engage in his (criminal) behaviour. This goal may be pursued through punitive sanctions intended to deter future acts from a specific offender or through rehabilitative/improvement programmes designed to facilitate positive change (http://www.sanctionswiki.org/Lessons_Learned).

Development of an ongoing employee training programme for an appropriate personnel is one crucial aspect. Nevertheless, the role of the compliance officer is also important and is not limited to provide the financial and nonfinancial institutions with guidance on Patriot Act compliance. Compliance officer and other appropriate staff should have timely access to customer identification data and other customer due diligence (CDD) information, transaction records and other relevant information. The compliance officer is responsible for the implementation of an ongoing training programme for the entity. It is recommended that the compliance officer's responsibilities also include identifying and undertaking appropriate action on matters of money laundering and terrorist financing concerns that are identified as part of the risk assessment process. A compliance officer can also provide the reporting institutions with input on adherence to rules and regulations, while making good economic decisions and business sense. With state and national charter amendments, new regulations and federal legislation, the landscape of the financial and nonfinancial institutions is changing daily. By adapting effective internal controls and assessing them on a periodic basis, the reporting institutions can more effectively mitigate risk and meet the goals of the organisation (Anderson and Pulsipher 2003).

16.6 Conclusion

The infiltration and sometimes saturation of dirty money into legitimate financial sectors and national accounts can threaten the economic and political stability. Money laundering and terrorist financing impact on financial behaviour and macroeconomic performance in a variety of ways including policy mistakes due to measurement errors in national account statistics and volatility in exchange and interest rates due to unanticipated cross-border transfers of funds. In spite of that, such crime also provide the threat of monetary instability due to unsound asset structures, effects on tax collection and public expenditure allocation due to misreporting of income, misallocation of resources due to distortions in asset and commodity prices and contamination effects on legal transactions due to the perceived possibility of being associated with crime.

Growing cases in money laundering and terrorist financing through the financial institutions and DNFBPs are very concerning. Despite having tight policies and regulation on money laundering and terrorist financing, it seems to not give any impact to gauge with such crimes. Organised crimes are likely to use the services and consultancy from the DNFBPs especially those in accounting and legal professions. Their knowledge and skills especially on the possible opportunities to disguise the illegal proceeds and legal backgrounds are the main criteria of their function to avoid those illegal activities being detected by the authorities. It is important to 'clean' the money, and somehow, they even can ensure that it also could generate possible profits from such reinvestment of illegal activities. Of all the above-mentioned role of DNFBPs, it is clear that serious action has to be taken on improving the policies and regulation on them. Wide awareness and continuous monitoring programmes have to be emphasised to ensure governance of ethics and conduct of DNFBPs.

The perpetrators' behaviour especially related with the five real global cases discussed earlier can be predicted by various researches done previously. The criminal behavioural causation theories are able to explain the influential factors towards the perpetrator's behaviour specifically on money laundering and terrorist financing offences. The understanding of the perpetrators' common behaviour could highlight the possible environment which directly affects their decision in committing the offences. Some of the identified criminal behavioural causation theories are the learning theories, cultural deviance theories, rational choice theories and psychological traits and criminality theories.

Finally, the role of effective internal control has always been the key issue for effective and good governance of the policies and regulation on money laundering and terrorist financing. It is very crucial to identify the possible weaknesses in internal control as it will enable the competent authority and also reporting institutions to enhance the possible leakages in internal control and provide a better control mechanism. Correctional programmes have to be imposed to all participated criminals especially those involving the reporting institutions. Continuous review on the current practice of policies and regulation in fighting the crime against money laundering and terrorist financing will reflect good governance and serious commitment of assurance on the countries.

Acknowledgement We wish to thank the Accounting Research Institute, Universiti Teknologi MARA (UiTM), Malaysia, and the Ministry of Education, Malaysia, for providing the support for this project. In fact, this paper constitutes a small component of a bigger research project on the role of DNFBPs in mitigating money laundering and terrorist financing in the market place. In particular, we express our gratitude to the researchers of the AML/CFT research cluster at the Accounting Research Institute of UiTM.

References

Anderson B, Pulsipher J (2003) Mitigating risk through effective, comprehensive internal controls. Publication & Resources on Corporate Governance, www.wib.org

Byrne J (2010) An overview of psychological theories of crime causation. Lecture graduate criminology seminar, Northwestern University

Financial Intelligence Unit (2011) Belize Anti-Money Laundering & Combating the Financing of Terrorism (AML/CFT) Guidelines for Designated Non-Financial Business Professions (DNFBP), pp 1–10

Hasselt CV, Sparshott J (2013) U.S. Cites Bank of montreal for money-laundering weakness. http://online.wsj.com. Accessed 17 May 2013

Michael DL, Potter GW (2007) Theories of organized criminal behaviour in Organized Crime, 4th edn. Pearson Education International Prentice Hall: Kentucky, USA

Miller WB (1958) Lower class culture as a generating milieu of gang delinquency. J Soc Issues 14:5–19

Ping He (2010) A typological study on money laundering. J Money Laundering Contr 13(1):15–32

Reem O (2012) The role of the audit committee in raising the efficiency of the internal control system to combat money laundering in Jordanian Banks. Int Res J Financ Econ, Al-Balqa University, SSN 1450–2887 Issue 88

The Sydney Morning Herald (Sydney, Saturday, October 14, 2000)

Vinayagamoorthy, Anor v DPP (C'th) (2007) VSC 265 (17 Jul 2007) Last Updated: 23 Jul 2007 (in the supreme court of Victoria)

Chapter 17
Structure of Marketing Program for Islamic Microfinance Institutions

Soheil Kazemian, Rashidah Abdul Rahman, Zuraidah Mohd Sanusi, and Zuraeda Ibrahim

Abstract This paper attempts to show that how employing a comprehensive marketing program will assist Islamic microfinance institutions (MFIs) in improving their overall performance. Islamic microfinance institutions just like other Islamic organizations should follow Islamic rules (Shariah) in all aspects of business. Then a suitable marketing program for Islamic microfinance institutions should include predefined marketing concepts relying on the Islamic values. Similar to other organizations, the main purpose of the marketing program of the Islamic microfinance institutions is to retain existing customers and attract new ones. Other than this, the efficient marketing program should contain some specifications emphasizing on the nature of the market and institution itself, competitors, developing the marketing plan, and the clients' preferences. In fact, there are some significant differences between conventional Islamic types of microfinance that need to be highlighted in the marketing plan, like avoiding predetermined rate of interest, emphasizing on sharing risks of investments between both sides of each transaction (not only the borrowers) and so on. The paper highlights the major characteristics of an appropriate marketing program of Islamic microfinance institutions, specifically. In addition, differences between marketing programs of conventional and Islamic type of microfinance institutions are also indicated.

17.1 Introduction

Saving by households is widely regarded as a good habit to cultivate and has become a global phenomenon over the past three decades. People from every social and financial level, rich or poor, are interested in saving their money in order to meet future consumption, accumulate some funds for investment, or protect

S. Kazemian (✉) • Z. Mohd Sanusi • Z. Ibrahim
Accounting Research Institute (ARI), Universiti Teknologi Mara (UiTM), Shah Alam, Malaysia
e-mail: soheil.kazemian@yahoo.com

R. Abdul Rahman
Faculty of Economics and Administration, King Abdul Aziz University (KAU), Jeddah, Kingdom Saudi Arabia

H.G. Djajadikerta, Z. Zhang (eds.), *A New Paradigm for International Business*, Springer Proceedings in Business and Economics, DOI 10.1007/978-981-287-499-3_17

themselves against unforeseen circumstances, among other purposes (Brafu and Ahiakpor 2011; Kohli and Jaworski 1990). However, it is quite difficult for poor societies to obtain access to formal financial services like credit and saving facilities (Cravens 1991) because the terms and conditions applied are complicated. For that reason, microfinance has become a significant source of funding for such societies, and subsequently, these microenterprises play a very important role in poverty alleviation.

Microfinance refers to financial transactions involving small monetary amounts among financial providers and young and poor entrepreneurs, poor households, and micro-businesses. The activities include group guarantees, character-based lending, and short-term repeat loans (Brafu and Ahiakpor 2011). The United Nations (2009, p. 8) has defined microfinance as "the offer of small financial services and the management of small amounts of financial resources through an array of financial products and a system of intermediary function that are targeted at low income earners."

In recent years, the number of customers of Islamic and conventional microfinance institutions has shown a dramatic increase. Many Islamic and conventional microfinance institutions have been established in response to the increase in people's knowledge about the benefits of using microfinance services. Microfinance has proved its effectiveness in helping the poor to create significant changes in their livelihoods and make strides toward increasing their living standards, reducing their vulnerability, and creating the financial ability to pay for their children's education and basic health care (Hudson and Mutesasira 2002). As a result, the market players have become extremely competitive, and clients have an ever-expanding choice of financial service providers to choose from (Wright et al. 2003). However, microfinance products also have some disadvantages and limitations.

Loans in conventional microfinance are based on a predetermined rate of interest. In this case, the borrowers, especially the poor ones, are burdened with a high cost of borrowing. The higher repayment scheme is due to the amount of loans owed plus the interest sum (El-Komi and Croson 2007). This predetermined interest, also known as *riba* or usury, is prohibited by Islamic law and forbidden by Judaism and Christianity. Furthermore, in conventional microfinance, the loan borrowers bear all the risks.

In contrast to conventional microfinance, financial part of Islamic rules (*Shariah*) applied to Islamic microfinance emphasizes that in each transaction, risks and profits or losses should be shared (Obaidullah 2008). Based on Islamic concepts, if every person in an Islamic society carries out their duties well, the incidence of poverty will decline. Carrying out one's duties involves concepts like "brotherhood" and "Al-Adl," which mean that every Muslim must be responsible for the conditions of others as a way of pleasing Allah, which is the most important aim. As a result, the majority of low-income Muslims would prefer to deal with *Shariah*-compliant products offered by Islamic financial institutions than to deal with conventional products (Wilson 2007).

Due to the problems associated with conventional microfinance and the growing desire among Muslim societies to deal only with *Shariah*-compliant products, conventional microfinance has been seen as a less attractive and less competitive option. It is unable to attract many potential clients, specifically among Muslims.

Furthermore, it has been estimated that one-third of the world's poor are Muslims (The Economist 2008), and therefore conventional microfinance providers are likely to experience a reduced demand from this group of people.

To retain existing customers and attract new ones is often regarded as difficult for microfinance providers, particularly so for Islamic MFIs as they are new in the market. This is due to the fact that in the microfinance provider's market, the majority of MFIs are limited to short-term products. Therefore, their clients can easily decide to leave their current microfinance service provider at the end of the loan cycle (Wright 2000).

As a consequence, retaining existing customers and attracting new ones as sustainable financial resources has been one of the most serious challenges faced by MFIs, particularly for Islamic MFIs during recent years. Therefore, when introducing services and facilities, microfinance providers should be aware of the latest marketing strategies. Although there is an extensive literature on Islamic microfinance studies, a study on the marketing strategies of Islamic microfinance institutions in Malaysia seems to be an unexplored research setting. As such, it is important that this paper first identifies which marketing approach is the most suitable to be applied by the Islamic microfinance service providers in order to be sustainable and to remain important and relevant institutions for the poor.

The remainder of this paper is organized as follows: Sect. 17.2 reviews the literature related to the marketing program for Islamic MFIs, and Sect. 17.3, the final section, draws conclusions from this review.

17.2 Literature Review

Much has been written about microfinance providers, and matters concerning these topics have been widely debated by academics, government agencies, practicing accountants, and investors. However, many issues remain unresolved. A large body of literature exists on marketing strategies, microfinance, and Islamic microfinance providers.

This section presents a general concept of marketing. Section 17.2.1 defines marketing and describes various marketing approaches applied in the microfinance market. A discussion of a marketing program for Islamic MFIs is presented in Sect. 17.2.2, and marketing strategies for Islamic MFIs are discussed in Sect. 17.2.3.

17.2.1 Marketing in Microfinance

The term "marketing" is usually associated with promotional, advertising, and public relations activities to increase the level of selling of a service, product, or concept. In a broader perspective, marketing can be defined as a program encompassing a collection of activities including market segment, position strategy, demand and consumer analysis, promotion, and competitive analysis. Marketing has become significant for MFIs during recent years because of environmental and internal aspects like enhanced competition in MFI markets, declining growth rate in certain MFIs, increasing client dissatisfaction, and a growing recognition that MFIs should be more customer oriented/client led (Grant 2000).

For most MFIs, marketing means responding to the market in terms of developing new products based on customers' needs (Wright et al. 2003), but marketing strategies have a deeper implication in the microfinance market. Marketing strategies for microfinance include corporate branding and identification as well as product delivery systems and customer service strategies, in addition to the product strategies. These strategies can lead the Islamic microfinance institutions (IMFs) to achieve a sustainable performance, enhance customer loyalty, and subsequently increase profitability (Churchill and Halpern 2001). Generally speaking, marketing for MFIs can be defined as an analytical tool for investigating and realizing clients' needs. It could guide IMFs to understand their target market (which clients should the IMF target?); how many clients does it have? And how many clients should it expect to capture (market share)? Because of increasing desertion by clients, increasing competition in some microfinance markets, and growing recognition that MFIs need to be more customer oriented, the concept of marketing in microfinance has become very relevant in recent years (Grant 2000).

Furthermore, because of the "Islamic" label, marketing in Islamic microfinance business should have some special characteristics in comparison with other microfinance providers. When a microfinance provider claims that it follows Islamic *Shariah* financial rules, it is supposed to exhibit Islamic behavior in all aspects, not only in financial matters (Khan et al. 2007). Islam is like a package which is based on obtaining Allah's satisfaction by helping each other and being responsible for others' financial and social conditions. For instance, an Islamic institution should consider its competitors' condition, its customers' financial situation, and other matters in order to help them whenever they need assistance. This is because, in addition to attracting new customers and achieving more financial benefits, the main objective of such an institution is to follow Islamic behavioral and cultural rules for getting Allah's blessing and satisfaction (Shirazi 2008).

The microfinance industry is beginning to mature, and with this maturity comes change (Costa et al. 2011). In recent years, commercial banks have started to downscale their services to the traditional clientele of MFIs, and furthermore, in Islamic countries, they have started to provide some Islamic services for their Muslim clients (Chowdhry 2006). In addition, some institutions have become formalized financial institutions, and microfinance institutions are eager to enter the market. Meanwhile, customers have become more sensitized and sophisticated about the quality of services and types of products. In conclusion, the IMFs need to focus on retaining current customers and identifying new clients interested in the financial services they offer in order to achieve financial stability and sustainable performance. To achieve this goal, every MFIs, whether Islamic or conventional, should be concerned with maximizing their return on investment (profitability)

Table 17.1 External and internal factors affecting profitability through appropriate marketing strategies

Determinant of profitability	Effects/benefits of marketing
Internal factors	
Increase portfolio size	A market and demand analysis can identify potential target markets for the institution's product
	A positioning strategy can assist the institution in better defining how clients perceive the product and how it is delivered
	Promotional activities can raise client awareness of the product
Reduced client loss	A marketing program allows the institution to monitor and analyze customer behavior so that it can anticipate potential problems and proactively address them before clients actually leave. In order to retain current customers by solving their future problems based on Islamic concept of "brotherhood"
Improved repayment rates	Consumer analysis can help an institution identify the causes for low repayment rates – i.e., inappropriate product design, external shocks, poor delivery – so that the appropriate solutions can be put in place
External factors	
Competition	A marketing program allows the institution to monitor the competition and analyze its effects on clients so that the Islamic MFI can keep up with or stay ahead of the competition
Economic environment	Market research can highlight factors affecting the local economy (weather, religious holidays, etc.) that could affect either clients' demand for financial products or their ability to repay
Political/regulatory environment	Market research can pinpoint policies and regulations that could affect the charges rate an institution should charge, the level of capitalization, etc.
External shocks	A marketing program allows the institution to analyze any potential shift in product demand because of catastrophic changes, such as floods, war, economic crises, etc.

Sources: Adopted from Tran (2000). Innovations in microfinance, p. 2

(Grant 2000). Table 17.1 illustrates the external and internal factors which can affect profitability that can be addressed through a marketing program (El-Komi and Croson 2007; Grant 2000).

Similar to conventional MFIs, the external and internal factors affecting profitability through appropriate marketing programs and strategies also apply to IMF. For example, the internal factors which include *increasing portfolio size* can increase the Islamic MFIs' market share by attracting more Muslim or even non-Muslim customers based on promoting Islamic financial values like interest-free loans. *Reducing client loss* can clearly show one of the significant Islamic concepts, namely, "brotherhood," and attract more clients by helping them to solve any potential problems. *Improving repayment rate* is one of the strategies of Islamic MFIs which do care about solving its client's problem. In addition, external factors include *analyzing competition*, which can help Islamic IMFs in showing appropriate reactions to competitor's actions and learn from them, by monitoring their actions. *Economic environment* is also considered as another marketing strategy. For example, an Islamic MFI can share information on local economic situation that may affect the client's financial position. *Political/regulatory environment* is also an important factor to be considered in the microfinance business. A marketing strategy must also consider *external shocks* that may affect product demand.

The appropriate marketing programs and strategies for Islamic MFIs are discussed in the following section.

17.2.2 Marketing Programs for Islamic MFIs

The use of the word Islamic to describe a company's operations has huge implications, starting from how the services or products are developed and ending with how it is handled after the final use. Islamic is not just a name; it is an entire business philosophy that incorporates every single aspect of the business (Alserhan 2011). From the marketing point of view, each Islamic MFI that wants to grow and reach a sustainable financial and social performance should have an efficient and comprehensive predetermined marketing program which can present all of the useful data related to the organization, including understanding the nature of the market and institutions and its competitors and developing the marketing plan (Sebhatu 2009).

17.2.2.1 Market and Institution Analysis

The first step of a marketing program for an Islamic IMF provider is defining the Islamic market and the characteristics (nature) which an Islamic market should have; then, a comprehensive analysis about the nature of the market and the nature of the institution should be defined. This step provides a general overview of the market for financial services and the current and potential situations faced by the institution (Grant 2000).

Nature of the Market In Islam, a market is held wherever and whenever an exchange takes place between buyers and sellers under mutually agreed terms and conditions. In general, the Islamic market is where the target consumer is a Muslim and non-Muslim; this definition includes Muslim countries as well as Muslim and non-Muslim communities in non-Muslim countries (Alserhan 2011). Market has a very important situation in Islam; making money through the training and tacking trade as a profession are strongly recommended in *Shariah*. "O ye who believe! Squander not your wealth among yourselves in vanity except it be a trade by mutual consent" (Quran 4:29). Prophet Muhammad also says: "the man who brings merchandise to our market is like the one who fights in Allah's cause."

Knowing which market the Islamic MFI wants to be successful in and its characteristics (nature of the market) can help the organization to make appropriate decisions in various situations. After that, MFIs should identify their nature as well, in order to estimate how much they can adopt themselves with the marked environment's changes. They should know what they are looking for, what are their objectives specifically, and what external and internal factors can impress them in achieving their goals. There are three kinds of markets for Islamic microfinance institutions to consider (Grant 2000; Karim et al. 2008): new markets, developing markets, and developed market.

New markets include a situation in which there are few financial service providers and little effective demand for financial services.

Developing markets are markets where effective demands for financial services have started to increase, but microfinance providers cannot meet those demands. In this case, the institutional focus is on developing institutions to meet those demands.

Developed markets have three characteristics: every kind of financial service is available, clients can easily choose their favored Islamic microfinance provider, and competition among the service providers is developing (Grant 2000; Zeller 2006).

Hence, the Islamic microfinance needs to identify the nature of their market, so that they can plan the marketing program which suits the market that they are in.

Nature of Institutions Islamic microfinance providers can be categorized into different groups based on their characteristics in several aspects.

Institutional Type Generally speaking, there are many kinds of legal microfinance providers, including both Islamic and conventional types such as commercial or Islamic banks, NGOs, village-based organizations, and credit unions. Each of these types may have its own target market, goals, and level of development. Some of them, like commercial banks, usually undertake very careful market analysis to prepare an organized marketing program in order to enter the microfinance market. On the other hand, some of them, like small NGOs or village-based microfinance providers who focus on credit delivery to the very poor, may not have professional financial staff. They are neither motivated nor trained to develop and follow a marketing program.

Institutional Objectives All Islamic MFIs are focused on poverty alleviation. Some of them are nonprofit seeking, which means their main goal is to help the poor rather than to be a profitable corporation. These include small NGOs and village-based financial providers. On the other hand, the main focus of commercial banks is their profitability and financial performance.

Development Level A developed (mature) Islamic microfinance provider should have characteristics such as a larger portfolio size, a greater number of clients, and a more formalized client monitoring system to show progress on the path to sustainability.

Financial Resources The level of financial resources depends directly on the development level. For young Islamic MFIs, the first and most significant issue is obtaining access to Islamic financial resources to meet the demands of borrowers. Only after solving the problem of financial resources by accessing loan funds will they focus on marketing. However, matured Islamic MFIs try to create a stronger marketing culture within the institution and then extend it to the market to attract new customers (Zeller 2006; Grant 2000; Hiatt and Woodworth 2006).

17.2.2.2 Competitor Analysis

A successful marketing program should also analyze the competitive environment in order to estimate the level of flexibility of the market when one of the competitors does something new. Competitors in Islamic and conventional microfinance business mean other choices for the customers. In other words, normally customers are attracted to the IMF institution that has provided their needs better than other IMF institutions (Wilson 2007). Therefore, the IMFs should monitor others' actions and competitive environment to respond to any action or changing of conditions which can threaten their benefits or attract the customers in the target market. The Islamic MFIs can also attract other competitor's clients; for example, they can attract the competitors' failed clients, identifying their disadvantages and helping them to improve and giving another chance based on the "brotherhood" concept in *Shariah*. That is why competitor analysis is very important in sustaining the marketing program.

17.2.2.3 Marketing Plan

After identifying the nature of the market and institutions and analyzing the competitors, the next step is to look at the organization's marketing plan. A marketing plan is a comprehensive plan which outlines an organization's overall marketing efforts (Tahir and Umar 2008). In other words, a marketing plan is just like a road map for an institution, which means it shows the current position of the organization and identifies where it wants to be and how it should get there, as well (Grant 2000). For Islamic MFIs, a marketing plan can be realized by the organization's marketing philosophy. Adding the word "Islam" or "Islamic" in the concept of market, marketing, or any kind of businesses will be understood to mean *Shariah*-compliant practices, adhering to the teachings of Islam regarding all facets of trade, applying Islamic business ethics, and observing the market manners as detected by the religion of Islam (Alserhan 2011). These concepts have characterized the maturation of most industries over time, and they are also clearly discernible in the Islamic microfinance industry. This process of maturation is usually linear, which means the organization should pass through each phase before moving to the next. The concepts relevant for Islamic microfinance activities are identified in Fig. 17.1.

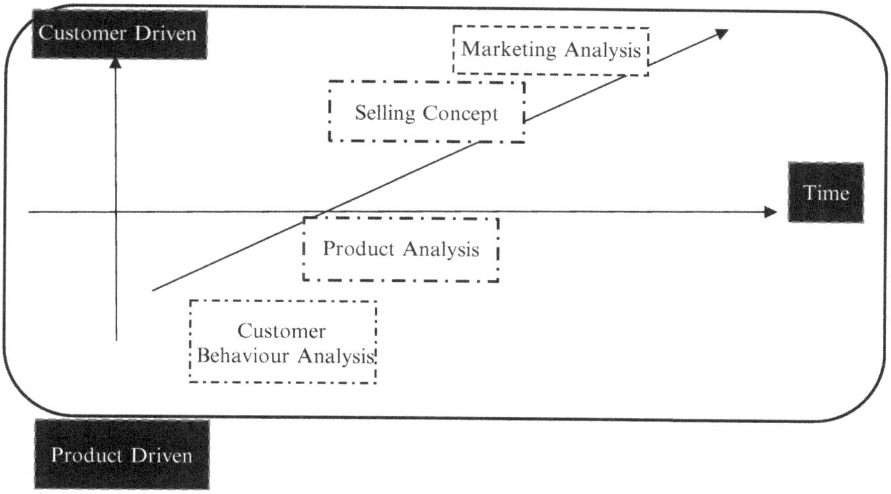

Fig. 17.1 Development of a marketing plan (Sources: Adopted from Grant (2000) and Wright et al. (2003))

Figure 17.1 depicts the process of becoming from a product-driven organization to a customer-driven organization and its required instruments in a specific period.

(a) *Customer behavior analysis:* focuses on analyzing the customers' needs (for providing services, based on customers' reasons for desertion) and developing new products according to clients' need and preferences (Grant 2000). To achieve this goal, Islamic MFIs can consult with experts in Islamic financial rules when introducing new *Shariah*-compliant microfinance services (Wilson 2007).

(b) *Product analysis:* in this stage, the Islamic MFIs should produce services based on customer behavior analysis in a cost-efficient and profitable way with a minimum level of risk; in terms of Islamic microfinance, all the services and products should be Islamic. In this case, it could include some activities that reduce the cost of services in order to reduce charges, for example, to extend repayment time period to help the poor or how they can use other potential aspects of Islamic financial rules for introducing some other *Shariah*-compliant services like *Tawaro* and *Qardolhasan* in order to provide interest-free loans as stated in *Shariah* (El-Gamal 2002).

(c) *Promoting and selling the products:* this includes persuading potential customers to use the services provided (Wright 2000). This can be achieved in several ways, such as introducing new services to the clients and increasing client awareness about the organization and overall product offerings (Grant 2000). As an Islamic organization, the Islamic MFI following this concept should avoid criticizing competitors to clients or even discussing the disadvantages of competitors' services. It should only introduce the services that it provides (Shirazi 2008).

(d) *Marketing analysis*: as the last stage of becoming a customer-driven organization, Islamic MFI should consider and analyze all the internal and external factors which can impress the market environment. For instance, it should focus on some special dates, which are important for its target customers. If customer target are farmers, Islamic MFIs should consider that in some special months per year, their ability for repayment will decrease and in these months, they need more money, so the Islamic MFIs can plan to meet their needs. After this last stage, Islamic MFIs can become a customer-driven organization from being a product-driven one.

17.2.3 Marketing Strategies for Islamic MFIs

As mentioned earlier, marketing is a comprehensive field aimed at strengthening the institution by maintaining focus on the client. As argued by Philip Kotler et al. (2003),

> Marketing attempts to understand the needs of the client and to adapt operations in order to meet those needs and achieve greater sustainability. It addresses the issues of new product development, pricing, the location of operations and the promotion of the institution and its products. In doing so, it creates exchanges that satisfy individual and organizational goals.

Hence, it is vital for Islamic microfinance organizations to recognize the important role of marketing strategy; Hudson and Mutesasira (2002) believed that "the importance of formal planning in association with strategy development and particularly implementation. Plans serve as the road map to delivering against strategic objectives and optimize process consistency, timing, co-ordination, momentum and overall control." Furthermore, discussing the departments which are engaged in marketing within each organization, Kholi and Jawarski (1990) stated that several departments should be involved in activities to meet the customer target market. One or more departments should focus on understanding the customer's current and future needs, specifically, and the gathered data should be shared. According to Robinson (1994), a blend of motives which can be met with a blend of saving products determines the demand for deposit facilities. In addition, there are three factors which can affect the pricing policy of microfinance institutions, namely, demand, cost structure, and competitors' price. Furthermore, there are some other pricing options open to microfinance institutions based on these three major considerations. Alternatives include breakeven and profit impact target pricing, cost and pricing, relationship pricing, skimming pricing, penetration pricing, market rate pricing, and value-in-use pricing.

Further, P. Kotler (1994) mentioned that one of the most important points in a marketing program is realizing differences between a marketing program and marketing strategies. In the current context, marketing strategies are linked to marketing approaches or programs adopted by microfinance institutions, directly. In addition, achieving the marketing objective of a microfinance provider will be difficult unless marketing strategies are translated into marketing programs.

Organizations that need to attract Muslim customers should align their marketing strategies with Islamic values and standard guidelines. Muslims believe that Islam provides ways and suggestions for a better life at both organizational and personal levels. Then, Islamic firm's customers should feel that these firms are trying to develop *Shariah* advises for making their lifestyle better. Therefore, it is highly recommended to these organizations to pose that they are *Shariah* followers in all aspects. The first and most important stage for achieving this goal is following Islamic marketing strategies, like using religion as a brand and making products fully Islamic (Alserhan 2011). According to Cravens (1991), marketing approaches are defined as planning and implementing of specific actions in the market place. The specific actions include pricing policing, product policing, marketing communication, delivering and distribution policies, and service policies.

Grönroos (1990) stressed that the most visible aspect in marketing strategies of microfinance institutions is marketing communication. The marketing communication methods for MFIs can be categorized as follows:

(a) Advertising: for instance, mass media like radio, TV, press, and outdoor and transport media to reach large audiences.
(b) Sales promotion, which is related to short-term objectives. This includes giving away consumer appliances of various values in return for different levels of deposits.
(c) Personal selling or face-to-face marketing.
(d) Public relations: this involves creating a good image for the microfinance provider in the minds of potential customers or indirect marketing.

Wright et al. (2003) provided a comprehensive and complete summary of the marketing strategies for microfinance institutions. According to them, marketing strategies for microfinance institutions comprise three distinct categories: corporate brand strategies, product strategies and product delivery, and customer service strategies.

Corporate Brand Strategies As defined by Philip Kotler et al. (2003), these include "a name, term, symbol or design (or a combination of them) which is intended to signify the goods and services of one seller or group of sellers and to differentiate them from those of competitors." Some of the most notable responsibilities of the marketing team of each microfinance institution are the development of brand attributes and positioning statement based on branding communication plan, internally and externally, in order to achieve some of the marketing objectives like corporate identity and corporate communications and public relations. Furthermore, for Islamic organization like Islamic MFIs, using religious brands like *Halal* can capture a craving for purity that goes beyond duty of their faithful adherents. At first look, brand is how customers can distinguish Islamic and non-Islamic organizations. Therefore, for Islamic MFIs who target Muslim customers, using religion as a brand is very important. Islamic branding can be defined in three ways: by religion, by origin, and by customers.

First is by *religion*, which means the microfinance organizations are strictly based on *Shariah* compliance. For instance, everybody, when they see the *Halal* brand on foods, realizes that this product is *Shariah* compliant; similarly, when people see the brand of an MFI includes Islamic signs like *Qardolhasan* or *No-Riba*, they will understand that this MFI is an Islamic MFI. Second is by *origin*, which means that these firms are known as Islamic because they originate from Islamic countries. However, they do not promote themselves as *Shariah* compliant since some of them are completely noncompliant, like the Emirates Airlines, which is known as Islamic but serves alcohol that is clearly prohibited in Islam. Similarly, the Grameen bank in Bangladesh looks Islamic because it is working in an Islamic country, but it is not *Shariah* compliant because it operates with a predetermined interest. Third is by *customers*; this type of brands is using organizations in non-Muslim countries targeting Muslim customers; for example, a microfinance provider in a non-Muslim country which produces financial services only for Muslims is known as an Islamic institution (Alserhan 2011).

Product Strategies A product strategy is a strategic approach to developing and enhancing products to fit the needs of the market and going about activities to optimize sustainable sales of the product in the most profitable manner. The first step for product strategies is the *development and differentiation* of products, which is a process of continually and systematically assessing the needs of the market and its different segments in order to support product development and innovation that caters for those needs in the most feasible and profitable manner. In particular, MFIs will be looking for opportunities that are not oversupplied from a competitive perspective. *Brands and tagline* are another part of product strategies that focuses on influencing potential clients to use the microfinance services provided. There are some tools that can assist the microfinance institutions to reach its goals, such as designing a brand which can transmit a feeling of confidence and loyalty to visitors and creating a short sentence which can modify the MFIs' objectives and appeal to the audience as a tagline. The last part of product strategies is the *sales strategy*. In the final analysis, an MFI's sales strategy will depend on its products and its target market. These will dictate the balance between pull-based and push-based strategies to sell the products. A pull-based strategy involves large sums of money spent on advertising and promotion to increase demand. This pulls the customers to demand the product on the basis of advertising, public relations, sales promotions, and direct marketing (Wright et al. 2003). On the other hand, a push-based strategy uses a sales force to push the product through personal selling and direct marketing. From the Islamic perspective, naming an organization Islamic is not possible, while its products and services are not *Shariah* compliant (Shirazi 2008). So Islamic MFIs should adopt their services to Islamic financial rules in terms of giving free interest-based loans. As mentioned earlier, Islamic financial rules still have a lot of potential for introducing new *Shariah*-compliant services based on products, like *Qardolhasan*, *Tawaro*, and so on.

In selling the products or services, the sales structure of the sales strategy can be shown graphically as in Fig. 17.2.

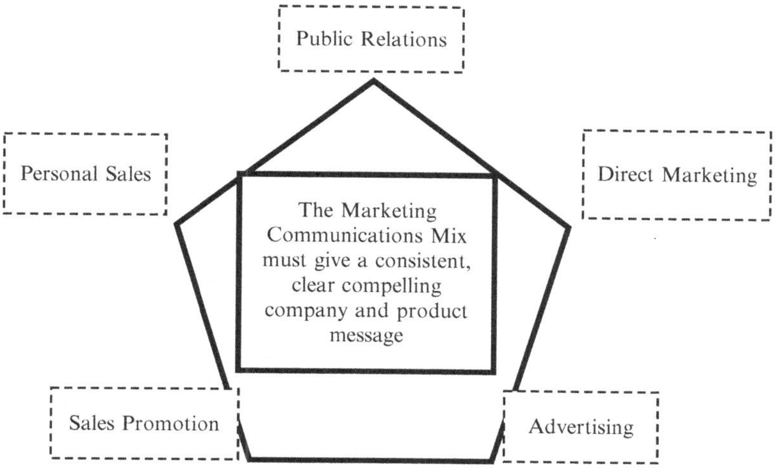

Fig. 17.2 The selling structure (Source: Adopted from Wright et al. (2003))

In this strategy:

Advertising generates demand for the Islamic MFI's products and not only through face-to-face communication channels. It can be very comprehensive and complicated, like using mass media and other channels.

Public relations: means promoting the Islamic microfinance-provided services indirectly to potential clients.

Sale promotion: involves making some special offers like waived fees or reducing opening balances to motivate potential clients to start using the Islamic microfinance services.

Direct marketing: one of the selling forms which creates a linkage between Islamic MFI and its prospects, directly. For instance, kiosk marketing in busy places, distribution of leaflets, and direct mail.

Personal selling: staff move out in cities, villages, or towns meeting people one-on-one, trying to motivate clients to use the provided services.

Product Delivery and Customer Service Strategy This is defined as ways to deliver the services provided and sold to the customers and to obtain their feedback in order to increase customer satisfaction and create enhanced customer value. The cheapest and fastest way for delivering products is *personal training* or delivering by employees. For more matured Islamic MFIs, because of the large number of clients, this method does not work. These institutions follow the *delivery process development*, which includes setting up of a specific department to meet the Islamic MFI's goals. For instance, such strategies are practiced by most MFIs in developed countries. In recent years, MFIs have been using the *technology strategy* for delivering products, such as by using clients' Internet bank accounts.

17.3 Conclusion

Microfinance as a comprehensive financial package is known to be an effective tool for poverty alleviation. Due to some conflicts between conventional microfinance and the financial part of Islamic rules (*Shariah*), conventional microfinance may not be able to provide products and services acceptable to Muslim societies. Thus, there is a need for an Islamic microfinance that adopts Islamic financial rules such as avoiding the imposition of predetermined interest rates and sharing risk and benefits or losses between the lender and the borrower. With a growing demand for Islamic microfinance services among Muslim countries, the number of Islamic microfinance institutions has increased. This has led to greater competition among Islamic MFIs and between them and conventional microfinance institutions. Currently, the main focus of attention is on the best approach for each microfinance institution to adopt in order to achieve sustainable performance and profitability and to retain its current customers, as well as attracting new customers. That is why the concept of marketing was introduced in the microfinance industry. Marketing in microfinance differs in some respects from marketing in other industries, because MFIs are faced with poor customers who expect the MFIs to rescue them. In addition, in the microfinance industry, retaining customers is much more difficult than in other industries; because of the short-term financial services provided, customers can decide to stay with a particular MFI or leave for another one. Furthermore, some aspects of the marketing concept have a different meaning for Islamic MFIs because, as Islamic institutions, earning financial gains should not be their most significant objective. They provide Islamic financial services in order to please God and to help the poor to improve their livelihood. Thus, they are required to follow Islamic behavior and culture in all aspects of their business, especially in marketing and using marketing strategies. These include, for instance, attracting new clients, promoting the services they provide, reacting to their competitors' actions, designing Islamic brands and taglines, delivering *Shariah*-compliant products to clients and obtaining their feedback, and caring for their clients' situation after using their products. While it is not intended to suggest that conventional microfinance institutions do not incorporate these aspects in their marketing, following these strategies should be highlighted in Islamic microfinance institutions.

References

Alserhan BA (2011) The principles of Islamic marketing. Gower Publishing Limited, England

Brafu WG, Ahiakpor F (2011) Understanding the marketing strategies of microfinance institutions within the Accra metropolis of Ghana: case of selected institutions. Afr J Mark Manag 3 (2):45–55

Chowdhry S (2006) Creating an Islamic microfinance model – the missing dimension, Bangladesh

Churchill C, Halpern S (2001) Building customer loyalty: a practical guide for microfinance institutions. Microfinance Network, Washington, DC, pp 22–39

Costa MFd, Silva WC, Paula TS (2011) Social marketing and nonprofit organizations. World Acad Sci Eng Technol 77:287–292

Cravens D (1991) Strategic Marketing, 3rd edn. Richard D. Irwin, Homewood

El-Gamal MA (2002) "Interest" and the paradox of contemporary Islamic law and finance. Rice University in Houston, pp 1–33

El-Komi M, Croson R (2007) Experiments in Islamic microfinance. University of Texas, Dallas

Grant W (2000) Marketing in microfinance institutions. Paper presented at the Advancing Microfinance in Rural West Africa, Bamako

Grönroos C (1990) Service management and marketing: managing the moments of truth in service competition. D.C. Health Lexington Books, Lexington

Hiatt SR, Woodworth WP (2006) Alleviating poverty through microfinance: village banking outcomes in central America. Soc Sci J 43:471–477

Hudson R, Mutesasira L (2002) A review of MFI marketing strategies and activities. MicroSave, Nairobi

Karim N et al (2008) Islamic microfinance: an emerging market niche, Focus Note 49. CGAP, Washington, DC

Khan T, Hassan M, Ahmed H, Abdulaziz Slaoui (2007) Framework and strategies for development of Islamic microfinance services. Paper presented at the Islamic Microfinance Development: Challenges and Initiatives, Dakar

Kohli AK, Jaworski BJ (1990) Market orientation: the construct, research propositions and managerial implications. J Mark 54:1–18

Kotler P (1994) Marketing management: analysis, planning, implementation and control, 8th edn. Paper presented at the Prentice-Hall, New Jersey

Kotler P, Littlefield E, Morduch J, Hashemi S (2003) Is microfinance an effective strategy to reach the Millennium development goals? CGAP Focus Note 32

Obaidullah M (2008) Introduction to Islamic microfinance. International Institute of Islamic Business and Finance, IBF Education and Charitable Trust

Robinson M (1994) Savings mobilization and micro-enterprise finance; the Indonesian experience. Paper presented at the Indonesian experience in the new World of micro-enterprise finances, Maria, Elizabeth Rhyne

Sebhatu SP (2009) Sustainability performance measurement for sustainable organizations: beyond compliance and reporting. Service Research Centre Karlstad University, Karlstad

Shirazi SSH (2008) Islamic Law handbook of Islamic rulings on Muslim's duties and practices. Imam Shirazi World Foundation, fountain books, Washington, DC

Tahir M, Umar M (2008) Marketing strategy for Islamic banking sector in Pakistan. (M. Sc. In Business administration Final Thesis), Blekinge Tekniska Hogskola, Sweden

The Economist (2008) Poverty: the bottom 1.4 billion. The Economist. Retrived 20 Feb 2014 from http://www.economist.com/node/12010733

The United Nation (2009) United Nations millennium development goals. http://www.un.org/millenniumgoals/

Tran N-A (2000) Innovations in microfinance; Marketing in microfinance institutions. "Advancing Microfinance in Rural West Africa", Conference Bamako, Mali, February 2000. TECHNICAL NOTE NO. 2 Released 10/2000

Wilson R (2007) Making development assistance sustainable through Islamic microfinance. IIUM J Econ Manag 15(2):197–217

Wright G (2000) MicroFinance systems: designing quality financial services for the poor. University Press Limited Dhaka, and Zed Books, London/New York

Wright G, et al (2003) Strategic marketing for microFinance institutions. MicroSave – Market-led solutions for financial services, Nairobi, pp 2–31

Zeller M (2006) A comparative review of major types of rural microfinance institutions in developing countries. Agric Financ Rev 66(2):195–213

Chapter 18
Myanmar's Experience in Regional Integration: Implications for Trade, FDI, and Sustainable Development

Shwe Zin Ko

Abstract Through Myanmar's transition into the ASEAN Economic Community and becoming a democratic system, the country is embarking to upgrade its status to a developing country with equitable and harmonized development. Undoubtedly, economic openness and regional integration speed up Myanmar's developmental progresses; however, disparity among the states and regions is occurring at the same time. This paper attempts to review whether Myanmar's states and regions have equality of opportunity from economic development, specifically from the improvement in international trade and foreign direct investment (FDI) liberalization measures, during its regional integration period because the high disparity in the country can lead to disruption in the long-term sustainable development.

18.1 Introduction

Myanmar was a wealthy country in Southeast Asia before the World War II. However, after its independence in 1948, Myanmar was isolated from the world economy for half of a century because of political instabilities, civil unrests, and economic sanctions. As a result of these disruptions, Myanmar became one of the least developed and lowest-income countries. In February 2011, Myanmar transitioned into a democratic political system and reconnected with the world. Following democratization, four economic policy objectives were set together with a series of reform measures under the Framework for Economic and Social Reform (FESR)[1] (2012–2015) and long-term National Comprehensive Development Plan (NCDP) (2011–2031) (The President's Office 2014). In addition, Myanmar Comprehensive Development Vision (MCDV) was also laid down, with growth strategies that provide the foundation for a comprehensive and consistent set of economic

[1] FESR is "policy priorities for 2012–2015 towards the long-term goals of the National Comprehensive Development Plan" (Framework for Economic and Social Reforms 2012).

S.Z. Ko (✉)
Edith Cowan University, Perth, WA, Australia
e-mail: szko@our.ecu.edu.au

H.G. Djajadikerta, Z. Zhang (eds.), *A New Paradigm for International Business*,
Springer Proceedings in Business and Economics, DOI 10.1007/978-981-287-499-3_18

policies, infrastructure, and human resource development plans. Even though the democratic government has many institutional constraints, the reform measures are being implemented across sectors since 2011.

How has Myanmar progressed in this development process? This paper consists of a review from the aspect of Myanmar's international trade and investment liberalization measures, with an expression of concern about whether they have equality of opportunity for its citizens. The reason for this concern is that unequal distribution of economic development can lead to political and social unrest and national disintegration, which can generate a danger to long-term sustainable development (The Asian Development Bank 2011, p. 4). This paper firstly presents Myanmar's engagement[2] in the Association of Southeast Asian Nations (ASEAN) toward the establishment of the ASEAN Economic Community (AEC). Then, this paper reviews Myanmar's developmental trend and estimates inequalities by the states and regions. Finally, this paper provides the suggestions that should have improved as the fast track to adjust inequalities and to integrate into regional community in expeditious manner. Although this paper uses up-to-date international trade and FDI data, the estimation of inequalities by the states and regions is based on the household level data[3] of 2009–2010 fiscal year[4] (hereafter FY) and also the ADB's 2014 estimation for Myanmar.

18.2 Myanmar's Engagement in ASEAN

Possessing a strategic location, and resources, and recognizing the strength of regional integration, Myanmar became a member of ASEAN in 1997. Since then, Myanmar has been fulfilling the requirements toward the integration of the ASEAN Economic Community (AEC). Up to this moment of the fourth and final phase of implementation (2014–2015), 9,500 tariff lines out of 9,558 had been reduced 0–5 % under the tariff reduction scheme of ASEAN Trade in Goods Agreement (ATIGA).[5] Of which, 80 % were already set up as 0 % tariff rate since 2012 and it must have to extend to 93 % in 2015, and after that, all of the 9,500 tariff lines should remove tariff rate by 2018 Ministry of National Planning and Economic Development (MNPED) (2013).

In addition to the tariff reduction, Myanmar has been trying to liberalize barriers that previously prevent the free flow of goods, services, investment, and movement of persons. International trade restriction measures from the previous government regime are being eased significantly, including facilitation of export/import

[2] Myanmar's engagement in ASEAN is the most significant regional integration effort.

[3] The Integrated Household Living Conditions Survey in Myanmar was conducted in 2010 from 18,660 households throughout the nation.

[4] Myanmar's fiscal year (FY) is from 1st April to 31st March.

[5] The remaining 58 tariff lines out of 9,558 include 51 lines from General Exclusion List (GEL) and 7 lines from Sensitive List (SL).

licensing procedures, permission to export of previously restricted agricultural commodities,[6] and exemption of commercial tax on the export of agricultural products, fishery products, livestock products, and value-added forestry products (The Ministry of Commerce 2014).

Furthermore, Myanmar Customs Department has been implementing Myanmar Automated Cargo Clearance System (MACCS) based on the successful experience of Japan with the assistance of Japanese Grant Aid. Through its National Single Window, Myanmar is going to establish ASEAN Single Window to save time and cost of trading among ASEAN member states. Participation in the pilot project 1 under ASEAN-wide self-certification system will be Myanmar's further step toward reducing trading costs and accelerating the movement of goods across borders Ministry of National Planning and Economic Development (MNPED) (2013).

Similar to the trade facilitation endeavors, Myanmar has been working on four pillars of investment to comply with the ASEAN Comprehensive Investment Agreement (ACIA), namely, promotion, protection, facilitation, and liberalization. The Foreign Direct Investment (FDI) law promulgated in 2012 and the new regulations reinforced in 2013 have introduced several liberalized measures, such as the removal of some previously restricted sectors; the permission of fully foreign ownership in unrestricted activities and 80 % ownership in restricted activities; tax incentives including a 5-year tax holiday; nontax incentives for other favored industries; and the right to lease land from the government or authorized parties for a period of 50 years with extensions for another 20 years in 10-year installments (The Asian Development Bank 2014, p. 96). Under the Directorate of Investment and Company Administration (DICA), one-stop services are being provided both for the foreign and citizen investors in five different cities of Myanmar, namely, Yangon, Mandalay, Nay Pyi Taw, Mawlamyine, and Taunggyi (2014).

There have been many trade and investment liberalization measures during Myanmar's regional integration period under the AEC pillar of ASEAN community. These measures are meant to establish a single market and production base and to have equitable economic development among ASEAN member states. But at what cost for Myanmar? To figure out this question, this paper looks at the economic development and socioeconomic development of Myanmar from 2005 to the present.

18.3 Economic Development Trend of Myanmar

18.3.1 Country with Rich Natural and Human Resources

Holding vast fertile land in three principal agroecological zones and natural resources, Myanmar is geographically located between two nations with emerging

[6] In the past, the exportation of rice and rice products, peanuts, peanut oil, red sesame, brown sesame, and sesame oil was prohibited in Myanmar.

markets: India and China. Myanmar's 135 national races are living in 7 states and 7 regions across the country (Appendix). Ayeyarwady Region, Yangon Region, Bago Region, Mon State, Tanintharyi Region, and Rakhine State are located in delta and coastal areas. Mandalay Region, Sagaing Region, and Magway Region are situated in dry zones. Chin State, Kayin State, Kayah State, Shan State, and Kachin State are positioned in hilly regions. Among the states and regions, Yangon Region and Mandalay Region are major economic areas. Ayeyarwady Region, Sagaing Region, Magway Region, and Mandalay Region are known as major agricultural zones. Shan State, Kayin State, Chin State, and Tanintharyi Division are well known for their horticulture and border trade routes with neighboring countries.

Myanmar has vast potential for natural resources exploration and processing industries. According to the Asian Development Bank (ADB)'s estimate, there are "7.8 trillion cubic feet of proven natural gas reserves, 3.2 billion barrels of oil reserves, 19,000 cubic meters per capita per year of renewable water resources, 100,000 MW of hydropower, 50 % of forest cover land area and 90 % of world's rubies" (2014, p. x).

In addition, Myanmar has a large labor force at 31 million people with 1.3 % annual increased rate. Of which, youth labor force accounts for 40 % of total force with an equal gender participation rate (The ADB 2014, p. 124). Therefore, Myanmar has also a huge potential for labor-intensive industries such as agriculture, manufacturing, and hotel and tourism. And also, Myanmar has the great potential for Myanmar's new products and a renewed competitiveness in near future (The OECD 2014, p. 42).

18.3.2 GDP and International Trade

From 2005 to the present, Myanmar's real gross domestic product (GDP) growth rate has been experiencing an upward trend though it went down to the lowest points between 2006 and 2008 due to the global financial crisis (Central Statistical Organization [CSO] 2012; The ADB 2014). However, Myanmar's urbanization rate is merely 33 % in 2014 because over 50 % of the population is still employed in the agricultural sector, although it only accounts for 31 % of GDP (The World Bank Database 2014). From this composition, this study can estimate the inefficient and less diversification pattern of Myanmar's agricultural sector. At the same time, the industry sector accounts for about 32 %, and services sector contributes 38 % in GDP. According to the ADB's projections, "there will be a significant shift from the agricultural sector to the services sector by 2030 in Myanmar. At 7 % annual GDP growth rate, the contribution of services sector will be 53 % and industry sector will be 17 %" (2014, p. 126).

The dominance of agricultural sector reflects on the small-sized and medium-sized enterprises (SMEs) and on Myanmar's exports. The ADB estimates that 63 % of Myanmar SMEs are engaging in the food and beverages production sector, which use agricultural inputs. At the same time, 86 % of Myanmar's exports are still from primary industries whereas Myanmar's trade volume has significantly increased from USD 5,541 million in 2005–2006 FY to USD 20,375 million in 2013–2014 FY. While the exports of agricultural products rose distinctively from 15 % to 22.5 %, the CSO states that the exports of manufacturing products gradually increased from 38 % to 40.5 % within the same periods. One of the reasons for the increased in Myanmar's agricultural and manufacturing export is due to the trade preferences such as duty- and quota-free market access under the EU's Generalized System of Preferences (GSP) for least developed countries and the Certificate of Origin (CO) under the preferential tariff treatment scheme.

However, due to less economic diversification, Myanmar's trading partners are still limited. As of 2013–2014 FY, Thailand absorbed 48 % of Myanmar's export, followed by India (13 %), Singapore (8 %), and Japan (6 %) (Ministry of Commerce 2014). This situation is very marginal and vulnerable for Myanmar exporters and producers, especially if the demand from these countries becomes less or if the global commodity prices fall in future.

In addition, Myanmar's less economic diversification also limited the opportunities for primary producers and local SMEs, to directly engage in the international and regional trade. As most of the local producers are operating their businesses informally with limited market knowledge, they cannot meet the requirements to have an official trading right with overseas. Therefore, Myanmar's export sector is almost dominated by registered trading companies and manufacturers.

Since Myanmar has liberalized in international trade and FDI sectors, the country has started experiencing trade deficit issue since 2012–2013 FY as shown in Fig. 18.1. Between 2005–2006 FY and 2013–2014 FY, the importation of capital goods for investment increased significantly from 33 % to 44 %. Similarly, the

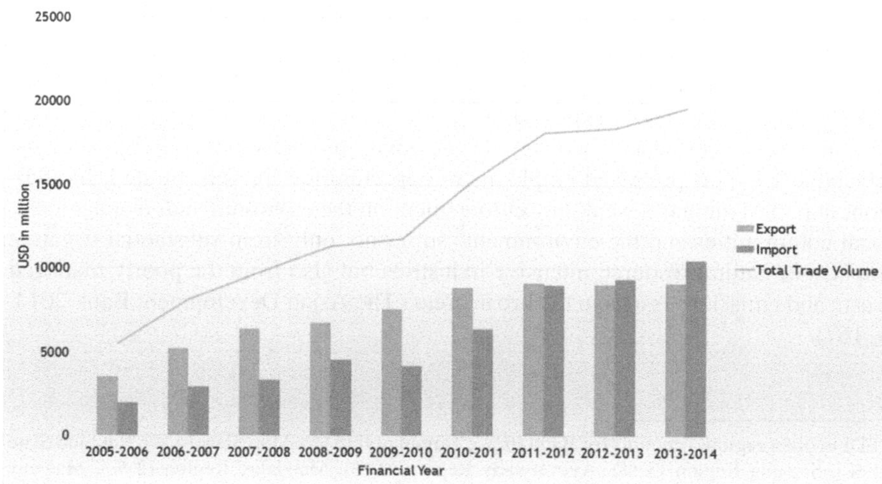

Fig. 18.1 Volume of Myanmar's international trade (from 2005–2006 FY to 2013–2014 FY) (Source: The Ministry of Commerce (2014))

importation of industrial raw materials increased slightly from 38 % to 39 %. However, the importation of personal goods largely declined from 29 % to 17 % due to the increased production of substitutable goods in the country.

18.3.3 Inflow of Foreign Direct Investment

Parallel with international trade, the country has received substantial amount of FDI year on year as shown in Fig. 18.2. The inward flow of FDI has increased significantly from USD 6,065 million in 2005–2006 FY to USD 42,951 million in 2013–2014 FY. According to DICA data (2014), as of September 2014, the hydropower sector occupied the largest share of cumulative FDI at 39 %, followed by the oil and gas sector (30 %), manufacturing sector (9 %), the transport and communication sector (6 %), mining sector (6 %), hotels and tourism sector (4 %), industrial estate (3 %), livestock and fisheries sector (0.88 %), agriculture sector (0.46 %), construction sector (0.08 %), and other sectors (0.31 %). The inflow of FDI was mainly from China (42.17 %), followed by Thailand (20.46 %), Singapore (13.92 %), the United Kingdom (6.77 %), the Republic of Korea (6.19 %), Malaysia (3.31 %), and Vietnam (1.03 %).

Although Myanmar has received a significant increase in FDI at union level, there is a large gap in FDI inflow across the country between 2009–2010 FY and 2014–2015 FY (Fig. 18.3). Along with FDI promotion and liberalization measures, the amount of FDI inflow into manufacturing sector increased significantly in recent years. From this trend, this study can imply that Myanmar is developing its labor-intensive industries, mainly concentrating in the urban areas where the industrial zones are located.

As of September 2014, Yangon Region received the largest share of FDI in manufacturing sector at 68 %[7] (Fig. 18.4). Apart from this region, the other states and regions with persistent high poverty rates still received limited FDI inflow, mostly in natural resource exploitation sector. As the majority of extracted natural resources are exported as raw materials or primary products to the foreign markets, Myanmar's export price and employment opportunities are very limited. In addition, due to Myanmar's weak law enforcement on the environmental management, local communities and the environment[8] suffer not only from substantial negative impacts of natural resource-intensive industries but also from the poorly managed waste and emissions issues in the urban areas (The Asian Development Bank 2014, p. 167).

[7] FDI in other regions accounts for Bago (6 %), Tanintharyi (5 %), Mon State (4 %), Rakhine State (4 %), Sagaing Region (3 %), Ayeyarwady Region (2 %), Mandalay Region (2 %), Magway Region (2 %), Shan State (1 %), and Kachin State (1 %).

[8] Myanmar ranks the lowest in 58 natural resource-rich economies (Resource Governance Index 2014).

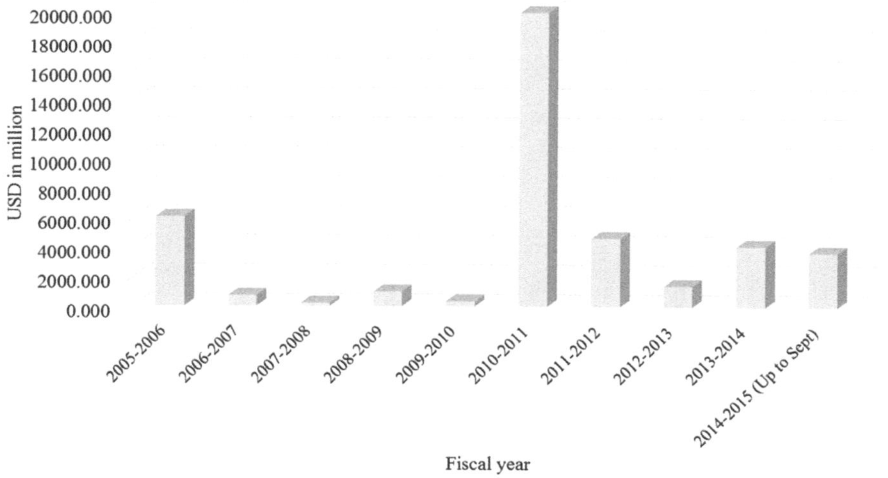

Fig. 18.2 The inflow of FDI into Myanmar (from 2005–2006 FY to 2014–2015 FY [up to September]) (Source: DICA (2014))

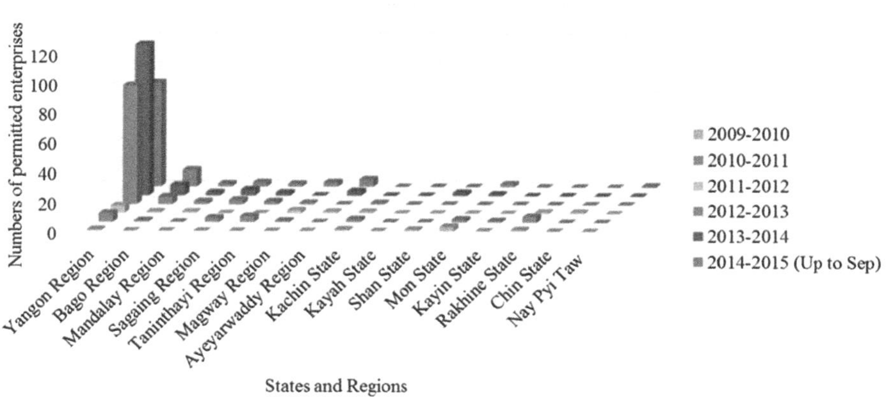

Fig. 18.3 Number of active FDI enterprises by the states and regions (from 2009–2010 FY to 2014–2015 FY [up to September]) (Source: DICA (2014))

18.3.4 Situation of Myanmar's SMEs

As well-performed SMEs are the major veins of equitable economic development of a country by creating employment opportunities and by utilizing resources efficiently, this study explores the situation of Myanmar's SMEs. According to the recent survey of Masato Abe and Dutta, there are 127,000 registered enterprises and 620,000 unregistered businesses in Myanmar as of 2014. Among the registered enterprises, 99.4 % can be classified as SMEs (2014, p. 11). Compared to other

Fig. 18.4 Number of FDI enterprises by sectors by the states and regions as of September 2014 (Source: DICA (2014))

developing countries and least developed countries, Myanmar has only 2.6 SMEs per 1,000 people, and on average one Myanmar SME firm hired 20 workers between 2009 and 2010. Another survey by Chipchase et al. also points out that Myanmar SMEs are falling behind in competitive advantage with SMEs from ASEAN member states in terms of design, technology, price, quality, quantity, and distribution channels under the influx of imported commodities (Chipchase et al. 2014, p. 140).

In addition, during the regional integration period, Myanmar SMEs still cannot directly get engaged in either international trade or supply chain network with foreign investors because of their unregistered business practices and influence of informal business culture. This situation is confirmed by the survey results of Masato Abe and Dutta (2014) and Chipchase et al. (2014). Furthermore, these surveys indirectly reveal the necessity to improve corporation between the public and private institutions. This situation is a burden for the government with limited institutional capacity. As a consequence, Myanmar's SME institutional framework is only in an infancy stage, and Myanmar SMEs are having limited support services that prevent them to improve productivity and efficiency to get engage in ASEAN's goal of establishing single market and production base. Accordingly, Myanmar SMEs cannot enjoy fruitful results from regional integration. Having this paradox is confirmed in the Myanmar SMEs Policy Index produced by ASEAN SME Policy Index (2014, p. 209).

18.3.5 Constraints of Economic Activities

There are two core factors that hinder the inflow of FDI into the states and regions in Myanmar. The first core factor is peace and stability because there are still frequent religious and ethnic conflicts in some states and regions. The second core factor is infrastructural constraints. Among various infrastructural constraints, the most significant issues are shortage of electricity, inefficient transportation system, and underdeveloped information and communication technology (ICT) (The Asian Development Bank 2014, p. 143). These constraints are also confirmed as parts of 10 major business environment constraints for Myanmar SMEs as shown in Fig. 18.5 (2014).

18.3.6 Socioeconomic Development of Myanmar

During the years of Myanmar's movement toward AEC, there have been significant improvements in some social statistics such as health indicators at union level (Fig. 18.6) (The ADB 2014). Some statistics also show that Myanmar poverty rate[9] has declined from 32 % in 2005 (The UNDP 2012) to 25.6 % in 2014 (The ADB 2014). Therefore, this study estimates the present situation whether these improvements occurred in each state and region harmoniously. To estimate the socioeconomic development in each state and region, this study uses the Integrated Household Living Conditions Survey (IHLCS) of 2009–2010 FY by assuming the similar situation in 2014. There are two aspects that confirm the existence of similar situation among the states and regions between 2009–2010 FY and the present. The first aspect is having slight differences in an urbanization rate, from 31 % in 2010 to 33 % in 2014, according to the The World Bank Database (2014). The second aspect is based on persistent inflow of FDI into the states and regions. To estimate education and health data, this study takes the ADB's 2014 estimate for Myanmar.

18.3.7 Unemployment and Underemployment

The IHLCS indicates that "one in every four Myanmar citizens is considered poor in Myanmar" by proving the existence of high poverty gap ratio[10] between urban and rural areas (Fig. 18.7). Much more wide spreading poverty rate in rural areas than in urban areas, the occurrence of the highest poverty gap ratio (84 %) is found in Chin State and Rakhine State, which are isolated from major economic activities due to their geographical location, frequent outbreak of natural hazards and conflicts, and having very poor infrastructure (The MNPED 2011). Furthermore, FDI projects in those states are only in natural resource exploration industry, and thus,

[9] Myanmar's poverty reduction target is to reduce by half to 16 % between 2005 and 2015 (The UNDP 2012).

[10] This poverty gap ratio describes "the average shortfall of the poor from the poverty line multiplied by the poverty incidence. It is a measure of the depth and incidence of poverty" (Ministry of National Planning and Economic Development 2011, p. 6).

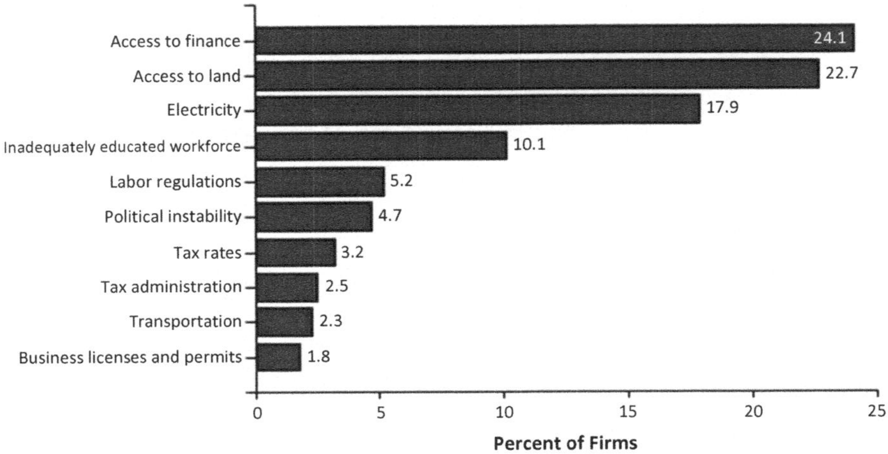

Fig. 18.5 Business environment constraints of Myanmar firms in 2014 (Source: The World Bank Groups Enterprise Surveys (2014))

Health Indicator	1995	2000	2005	Latest Year	Average of 7 ASEAN countries
Life expectancy at birth, female (years)	62.6	64.2	65.6	66.9	74.5
Life expectancy at birth, male (years)	58.3	60.0	61.5	62.8	68.9
Maternal mortality ratio (modeled estimate, per 100,000 live births)	380	300	230	200	168
Mortality rate, infant (per 1,000 live births)	66.9	58.5	50.7	41.1	24.9
Mortality rate, under-5 (per 1,000)	92.0	78.8	66.6	52.3	31.0

ASEAN = Association of Southeast Asian Nations.

Notes: Latest year is 2011 for life expectancy at birth, 2010 for the maternal mortality ratio, and 2012 for child and infant mortality rates. The seven ASEAN countries in the average figure are Cambodia, Indonesia, the Lao People's Democratic Republic, Malaysia, the Philippines, Thailand, and Viet Nam.

Source: World Bank, World Development Indicators (accessed March 2014).

Fig. 18.6 Health indicators in Myanmar and selected ASEAN countries, 1995–latest year (Source: The ADB (2014, p. 105))

the majority of people from these areas have been living in chronic poverty for decades.

Next, this paper looks at unemployment rate and underemployment rate (Fig. 18.8). While the unemployment rate in Myanmar is at around 4 % since 2010, underemployment has been on the rise, "climbing 3.6 % points from 2005 to 2010," according to the survey of IHLCS cited by ADB (2014, p. 128). More than a

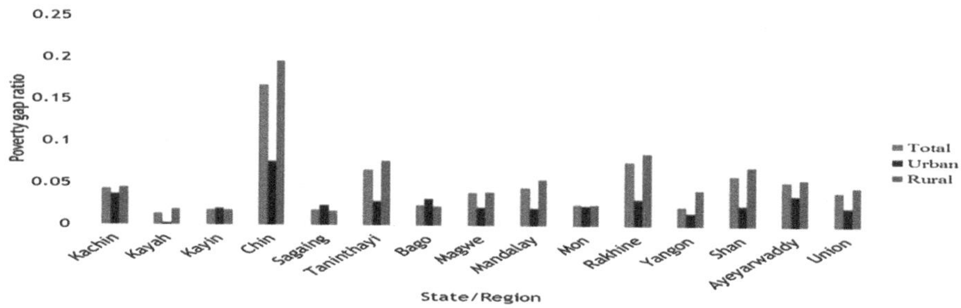

Fig. 18.7 Poverty gap ratio in Myanmar (2009–2010) (Source: The MNPED (2011))

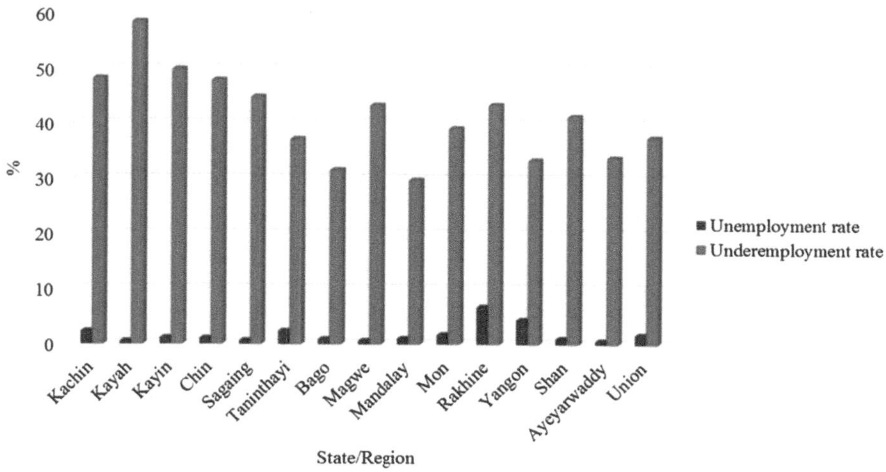

Fig. 18.8 Unemployment rate and underemployment rate by states and regions (2009–2010) (Source: The MNPED (2011))

third of the workforce (38 %) are working less than 44 h per week (41 % for women). The possible reason can be due to the influence of informal working culture in Myanmar. "Some 41 % of the workforce can be classified as own-account workers, while 15 % are contributing family members and 18 % casual workers. Together, 74 % of the workforce can be categorized as informal" (The MNPED 2011).

As a consequence of insufficient formal employment opportunities, many Myanmar youth workers have been seeking employment in other countries. "Although the number of officially registered migrant workers is about 1.6 million, the estimates of the actual number run as high as 4.7 million, almost 8 % of the population" (Win and Naing 2012).

18.3.8 Consumption and Healthcare

Due to the development gap among the states and regions, Myanmar has large consumption gap between urban and rural, which is 525,929 Kyat at union level, 736,008 Kyat at urban, and 415,457 Kyat at rural (Ministry of National Planning and Economic Development 2011). The largest gap between the rich and the poor is found in the areas where major economic activities are operating (Yangon Region, Mandalay Region, Magway Region) and where major agricultural activities are taken place (Kayin State, Sagaing Region, Shan State, and Ayeyarwady Region) (Fig. 18.9).

Then, this study looks at the health indicators, such as antenatal care and low birth weight by states and regions (Fig. 18.10), because a healthy life for children can provide opportunities to pursue education to survive from impoverishment (The ADB 2014). Compared to other states and regions, the areas that have the highest poverty gap (Shan State and Chin State) receive the least antenatal care, followed by Sagaing Region, Magway Region, and Kayin State. Because low consumption and less antenatal care can cause low birth weight, Shan State has the highest low birth weight rate, followed by Kayin State and Ayeyarwady Region. Besides, Mon State, Rakhine State, and Kachin State have a similar level of high underweight birth rate.

18.3.9 Education

In addition, this study also looks at the enrolment rate of colleges and technical and vocational education and training (TVET) because supporting proper education to

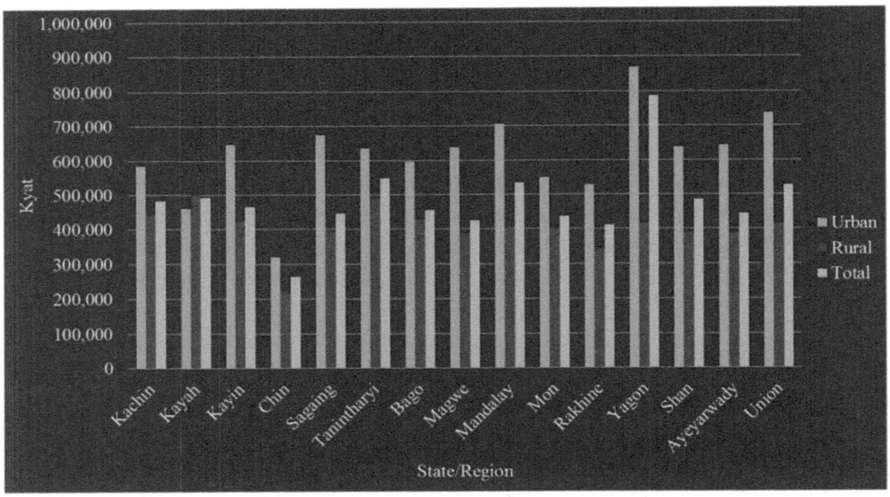

Fig. 18.9 Consumption gap between the richest and the poorest 20 % by states and regions (2009–2010) (Source: MNPED (2011))

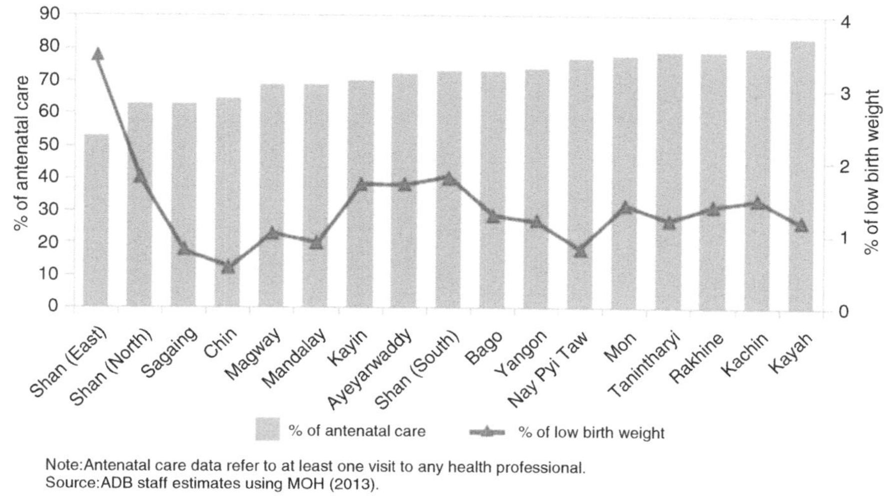

Fig. 18.10 Antenatal care and low birth weight by states and regions (2011) (Source: The ADB (2014, p. 110))

the citizen is the core factor to survive from poverty and to attract more FDI into each state and region (Figs. 18.11 and 18.12). To narrow the disparities in the educational outcomes among different levels and groups of society, genders, and rural and urban is essential to have more inclusive outcomes. It is observed that two thirds of the college enrolment rate and 80 % of TVET enrolment rate are from urban areas. Similarly, 80 % of those who enrolled in colleges and TVET are also classified as rich (The ADB 2014).

18.3.10 Other Indexes and Scores

Other indexes and scores also confirm the existence of disparity in Myanmar. The Sustainable Society Index (SSI)[11] reports that Myanmar was ranked 88 out of 151 countries, pertaining to these areas: 123 in the human well-being (HW) index[12], 36 in environmental well-being (EW) index[13], and 103 in the economic well-being (EcW) index[14] (2012). These scores indicate the necessity for the country to have a well-balanced society in harmony with its surroundings.

[11] The SSI measures "the level of sustainability of a country and to monitor progress to sustainability" (Sustainable Society Index 2012).

[12] HW: Basic needs, health, personal, and social development

[13] EW: Nature and environment, natural resources, climate, and energy

[14] EcW: Economy

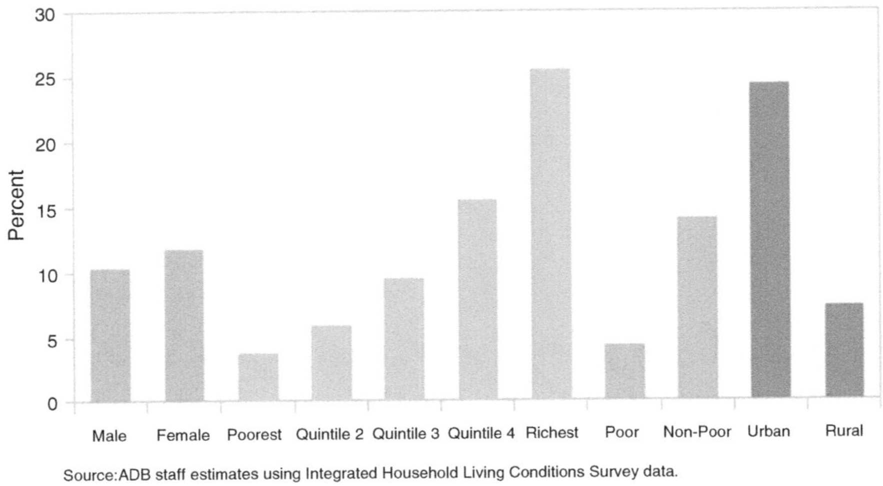

Fig. 18.11 College enrolment rates among 17–20 years old (Source: The ADB (2014, p. 120))

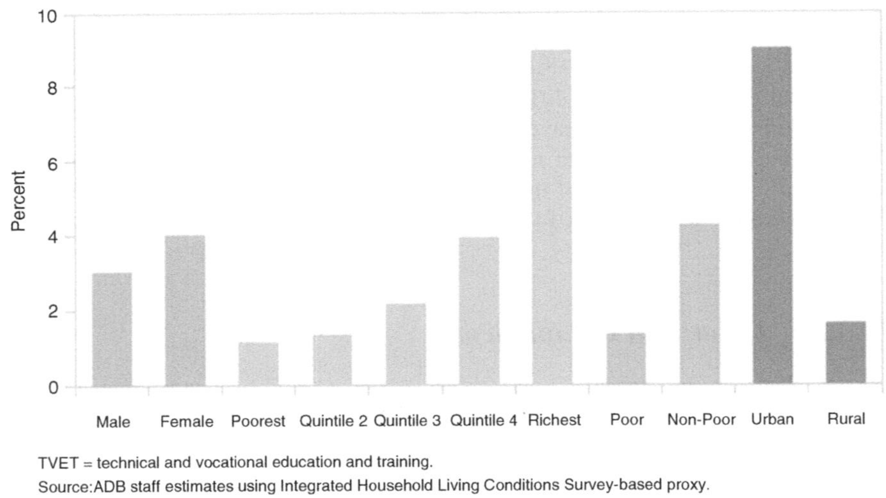

Fig. 18.12 TVET participation rates among working-age adults (Source: The ADB (2014, p. 120))

Likewise, "Myanmar achieves a Happy Planet Index Score (HPI)[15] of 44.2 and ranks 61 of all the 151 countries analyzed. It reflects a 'middling' life expectancy,

[15] The Happy Planet Index (HPI) measures "how well nations are doing in terms of supporting their inhabitants to live good lives now, while ensuring that others can do the same in the future" (Happy Planet Index 2012).

'middling' levels of experienced wellbeing, and a moderate ecological footprint" (2012). A further assessment of Myanmar's human development index (HDI)[16] for 2012 showed that Myanmar was ranked 149 out of 187 countries, with a HDI value of 0.498; therefore, Myanmar's HDI ranking was classified and considered as low human development (The United Nations Development Programme 2013).

Based on these indexes and social statistics, the disparity among the states and regions is more distinctive across Myanmar. Narrowing disparity in health and education sector and creating employment opportunities in each state and region shall have to include as policy priorities and to implement immediately because those are the most efficient ways for the present and future generation to achieve fruitful results from regional integration.

18.4 Implications

Establishing AEC in 2015 is just at the beginning of stepping into one of the regional integrations involved by Myanmar. Myanmar may experience new opportunities and more challenges when it moves forward to achieve "Post-2015 Vision," that is, "to realize a community that is politically cohesive, economically integrated, socially responsible and a truly people-oriented, people-centered and rules-based ASEAN" (2014, pp. 35–36).

Undoubtedly, an increased in international trade and FDI inflow can support Myanmar to achieve its developmental goals quickly. However, even during the regional integration period, Myanmar's economic growth created significant inequalities and environmental and social challenges, and thus, the developmental trend seems unsustainable. In addition, Myanmar's business environment is still influenced by the informal practices of closed economy from the past, which not only hinders its economic diversification and production capacity of Myanmar's firms but also limits the direct participation of local producers to engage in international trade and to establish national, regional, and global supply chain.

To counter the current situation, the government should urgently have to conduct the real ground level survey to determine the intensity of development gap and environmental damages in each state and region. Based on the survey result, the government should have to formulate and implement the specific strategy addressing each region and state, in which the following points should have to include and implement as the fast track:

- To enforce effective environmental management mechanism
- To improve basic infrastructure, specifically electricity, transportation, and ICT
- To support proper training to the local workforce to get engaged in economic activities and employed in formal working places

[16] "The HDI is a composite statistic of life expectancy, education, and income indices used to rank countries into four tiers of human development" (Wikipedia 2014).

- To improve healthcare services
- To upgrade education sector
- To encourage SMEs to get involve in formal business environment and to develop their capacity and productivity
- To provide policy and physical supports to SMEs to establish in national, regional, and global supply chain
- To invite FDI projects in other sectors rather than natural resources exploration
- To attract FDI projects in other states and regions rather than major economic regions

Appendix

States and Regions of Myanmar (Source: www.oxfordburmaalliance.org (2014))

References

Abe M, Dutta MK (2014) A new policy framework for Myanmar's SME. 142:1–53 http://artnet.unescap.org/pub/AWP-142-Masato-Abe.pdf, UNESCAP, Bangkok
Central Statistical Organization (CSO) (2012) Statistical yearbook 2011, CSO, Nay Pyi Taw
Chipchase J, Serota L, Tay V, Mon S, Ko AK, Oo YY, Oo YL (2014) Afford two, eat one. In: Scanlon MG (ed) Financial inclusion in rural Myanmar. Institute of Money, Technology and Financial Inclusion, University of California, Irvine
Directorate of Investment and Company Administration (DICA) (2014) DICA, Yangon
Framework for Economic and Social Reforms (FESR) (2012) (63)
Happy Planet Index (2012) http://www.happyplanetindex.org/countries/myanmar/. Accessed 2 Apr 2014
Ministry of National Planning and Economic Development (MNPED) (2013) Framework for economic and social reforms: policy priorities for 2012–2015 towards the long-term goals of the National Comprehensive Development Plan. Nay Pyi Taw
Oxford Burma Alliance (2014) http://www.oxfordburmaalliance.org/ethnic-groups.html. Accessed 8 Dec 2014
Revenue Watch Institute (2014) The 2013 Resource Governance Index. http://www.resourcegovernance.org/sites/default/files/rgi_2013_Eng.pdf
Sustainable Society Index (2012) http://www.ssfindex.com/. Accessed 31 Aug 2014
The Asian Development Bank (ADB) (2011) Framework for inclusive growth indicators. Key Indicators for Asia and the Pacific 2011: Special Supplement
The Asian Development Bank (ADB) (2014) Unlocking the potential, Myanmar, pp 1–216
The Association of Southeast Asian Nations (2014) Thinking globally, prospering regionally ASEAN economic community 2015. The ASEAN Secretariat, Jakarta
The Economic Research Institute for ASEAN and East Asia (ERIA), The Organization for Economic Co-operation and Development (OECD) (2014) ASEAN SME policy index 2014. In: E S R W Group (ed) Economic Research Institute for ASEAN and East Asia, Jakarta
The Ministry of Commerce (2014) MoC, Nay Pyi Taw
The Ministry of National Planning and Economic Development (2011) Integrated household living conditions survey in Myanmar (2009–2010): MDG data report. SiDA, UNICEF and UNDP
The Organisation for Economic Co-operation and Development (OECD) (2014) OECD investment policy reviews. OECD Publishing, Myanmar
The President Office (2014) http://www.president-office.gov.mm/en/. Accessed 31 Aug 2014
The United Nations Development Programme (2012) UNDP country programme for Myanmar (2013–2015). http://www.asia-pacific.undp.org/content/dam/rbap/docs/programme-documents/BU-CP-2013-2015.pdf
The United Nations Development Programme (UNDP) (2013) Human Development Report: The Rise of the South: Human Progress in a Diverse World, New York
The World Bank Database (2014), Urban population (% of total), http://data.worldbank.org/indicator/SP.URB.TOTL.IN.ZS. Accessed 15 Nov 2014
The World Bank Groups Enterprise Surveys (2014) http://www.enterprisesurveys.org/Data/ExploreEconomies/2014/myanmar. Accessed 22 Oct 2014
Wikipedia (2014) http://en.wikipedia.org/wiki/Sustainable_Society_Index. Accessed 22 Oct 2014
Win M, Naing K (2012) Job creation and skill development by border area development between Myanmar and Thailand. Presentation to ILO/JICA Workshop on Skills Development in the Thailand Myanmar Border Areas

Chapter 19
Why Is Sri Lanka a New Investment Darling in Asia?

Dilhani Kapu Arachchilage

Abstract Sri Lanka remains one of the most attractive investment destinations in the Asia-Pacific region, especially after ending elongated terrorism in 2009 by the present government of Sri Lanka. As stated in Development Policy Framework released by the government of Sri Lanka in 2010 in 'Mahinda Chinthana – Vision for the Future', it is expected to position Sri Lanka to be the Emerging Wonder of Asia. In achieving this aspiration, investment is welcomed by the government in virtually all sectors of the economy in order to expand, diversify and upgrade the industrial and export base of the country. In this milieu, the paper introduces economic background of the country while highlighting the reasons for investing in Sri Lanka together with main strategic perspectives and current challenges.

19.1 Introduction

Sri Lanka (formerly Ceylon) is an island about the size of Tasmania in the Indian Ocean, lying east of the southern tip of the Indian subcontinent from which it is separated by the Palk Strait. The population of Sri Lanka as at the end of 2013 was 20.48 million, with 2.3 million people living in the capital city of Colombo. Sri Lanka seemed like an attractive destination for investments and business due to open-market reforms introduced in 1977, good geographical location, a democratic parliamentary system of governance, capable bureaucracy, sound basic education of the workforce and the list goes on (Wijesinha 2014). However, from mid-1983 Sri Lanka was afflicted by a serious civil conflict between the government forces and the Liberation Tigers of Tamil Eelam (LTTE). When the war was intensifying in the country, another battle was being fought – the battle for the Sri Lankan economy.

As a result of prolonged war for nearly 30 years and recent global economic crisis, the country's economy was hit badly by 2009. Money from Sri Lankan securities flew out, exports were collapsing and the Central Bank of Sri Lanka intervened heavily to stem the steep depreciation of the rupee. While the civil war

D.K. Arachchilage (✉)
Edith Cowan University, Perth, WA, Australia
e-mail: d.kapuarachchilage@ecu.edu.au

H.G. Djajadikerta, Z. Zhang (eds.), *A New Paradigm for International Business*,
Springer Proceedings in Business and Economics, DOI 10.1007/978-981-287-499-3_19

had reached its peak in the early part of 2009, Sri Lanka was haemorrhaging foreign reserves threatening the financial stability of the country. By February and March that year, the Sri Lankan government acknowledged that Sri Lanka's balance of payments was in crisis as the country had foreign reserves to finance only a few weeks of exports while having precarious levels of dollar debt financing (as percentage of official reserves) when facing a hostile global economic climate.

On 18 May 2009, the Sri Lankan government formally announced its military victory over the LTTE and its regaining of complete territorial control over Sri Lanka. On 19 May 2009, Sri Lankan President His Excellency Mahinda Rajapaksa delivered a victory speech to Parliament. Over the course of the 26-year conflict, hundreds of thousands of people were displaced by the fighting, and several thousands of people were killed. After ending the civil war in 2009, 5 years on, the Sri Lankan economy is in a very different place and considered as a new investment darling in Asia.

19.2 Overview of Sri Lankan Economy

Sri Lanka began economic liberalisation by introducing open-market system in 1977 while moving away from socialism. Sri Lanka's export-oriented policies have seen a shift from a reliance on agricultural exports to an increasing emphasis on the services and manufacturing sectors. The services sector accounts for almost 60 % of GDP. Manufacturing, the fastest-growing sector accounting for almost 30 % of GDP, is dominated by the garment industry. The agriculture sector, though decreasing in its importance to the economy, nevertheless accounts for around 11 % of national output and employs more than one-third of the workforce. The public sector remains large, with the state continuing to dominate in the financial, utilities, health and education sectors. Sri Lanka is also characterised by high levels of literacy (91 %) and life expectancy (75 years) and a low rate of infant mortality (14 per 1,000 live births), figures comparable to those of developed countries.

In early 2009, the economy was hit by a balance of payment crisis. Persistent high budget deficits forced the Sri Lankan government to rely on short-term financing from international markets. The global financial crisis resulted in a sudden stop to this financing. Capital outflows and intervention by the central bank to prevent the exchange rate from depreciating – exacerbated by a decline in demand for Sri Lanka's exports – resulted in a significant loss of international reserves which remained low. On 24 July 2009, the IMF Executive Board approved Sri Lanka's request for a standby arrangement (SBA) in an amount equivalent to US $2.6 billion to support the country's economic reform programme.

Remarkably, Sri Lanka's success in generating economic growth has been improving since the end of the civil war in 2009. The IMF SBA was successfully concluded by July 2012, just 3 years since it began. Sri Lanka's foreign reserves are back on solid footing and according to recent indications are up to an all-time high of US$8.5 billion, sufficient to support 6 months of imports. GDP growth has picked up from an average of 5.5 % during the 2000–2009 period to 7.5 % in the post-war period and is estimated to exceed 7 % in 2014 as well. From having to seek exceptional external assistance from the IMF then, Sri Lanka is now managing to borrow on its own in international capital markets at interest rates. Poverty rates have fallen from 22.7 % in 2002 to 6.5 % in 2012. An impressive and far-ranging public infrastructure drive continues apace and is strengthening the country's prospects for attracting a new wave of foreign investment and for becoming a strong regional economic hub.

19.3 Why Invest in Sri Lanka?

As per the 'Development Policy Framework' released by the government of Sri Lanka in 2010 in 'Mahinda Chinthana – Vision for the Future', the government has successfully designed and implemented plans to position Sri Lanka as the Emerging Wonder of Asia (Fig. 19.1).

According to Mahinda Chinthana – Vision for the Future (2010), the core objective of the government is to transform Sri Lanka into a strategically important economic centre of the world by transforming Sri Lanka to be the Pearl of the Asian Silk Route once again, in modern terms. Using the country's strategic geographical location effectively, it is expected to develop Sri Lanka as a naval, aviation, commercial, energy and knowledge hub, serving as a key link between the East and the West (Mahinda Chinthana – Vision for the Future 2010, p. 11.)

In order to achieve the aforesaid vision, the important role that investments should play in economic growth is well established. Sri Lanka has set itself an ambitious medium-term growth target of 8 %+, and this would be key to satisfy the rising aspirations of post-war Sri Lanka population. To achieve this level of growth, the country needs around 35 % investment as a share of GDP (at current levels of capital efficiency). Investment needs of a country are often constrained by the available domestic savings, and in Sri Lanka this is very low – 17 % (around 24 % when savings remitted by migrant workers are added). So the country is seeking foreign investment sources to bridge the savings-investment gap which is around 10 % of GDP.

In the immediate period following the end of the war, it was possible to see a noticeable bump in private sector activity. All major banks aggressively expanded their branch network. All major consumer durables and retail firms opened up outlets and showrooms in new regions. And the construction sector enjoyed a significant impetus. This trend has certainly manifested in the tourism and property development arena too. For instance, the Altair Tower by Indocean Developers coming up opposite the Beira Lake is set to be Sri Lanka's tallest building and is designed by Moshe Safdie, famous for being the architect of the Marina Bay Sands in Singapore. Meanwhile, marking Sri Lanka's biggest domestic private sector investment, the John Keells Holdings Group is setting up a US$600+ million mixed-used development – the Waterfront Project – in the heart of the city. Other

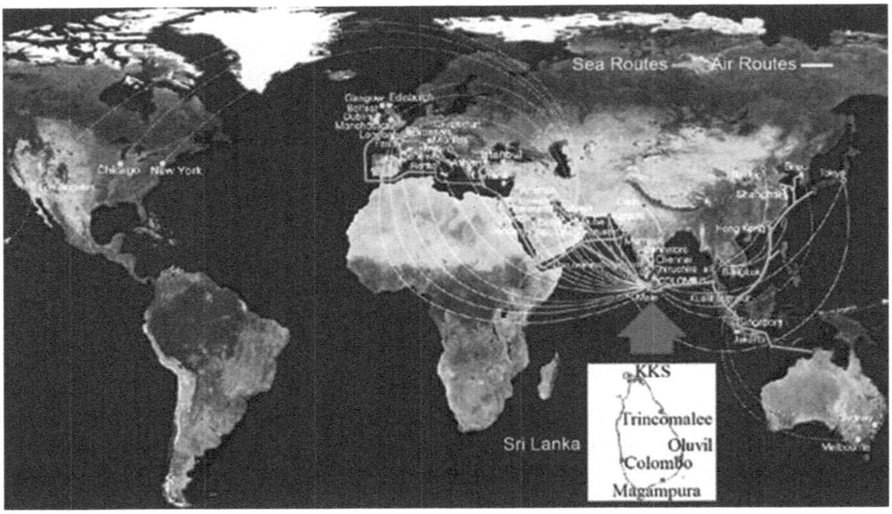

Fig. 19.1 Sri Lanka: a dynamic global hub (Source: Mahinda Chinthana – Vision for the Future, development policy framework 2010, p. 11)

projects include the five-star Shangri-La Hotel, Crown Colombo Resort and ITC Hotel in Galle Face. All these are property development projects, and in this new post-war phase, Sri Lanka is touting its achievements and attracting global players not only in mega real estate but also in the technology, finance, supply chain and manufacturing categories.

Two of the set of elements of a good investment climate are infrastructure and macroeconomic stability – both of which are now in impressive territory in Sri Lanka, compared to 5 years ago. The ongoing infrastructure drive – mainly in connective infrastructure like new ports, highways and roads – is unparalleled since the Accelerated Mahaweli Development Programme. Meanwhile, policies to ensure a stable macroeconomic environment have paid dividends – inflation in single digits (compared to over 20 % in 2008), low and stable interest rates and the budget deficit being steadily reigned in. So these should certainly be encouraging signs for investors.

19.4 Current Investment Strategy of the Sri Lankan Government

The Sri Lankan government offers a wide range of incentives for investors. These incentives are available to both foreign and domestic investors.

Over two decades, successive governments have pursued a policy of economic liberalisation with the emphasis on private sector investment. The pro-business policy environment includes total foreign ownership across almost all areas of the economy; a constitutional guarantee on the safety of foreign investment; investment laws which are transparent and automatic; a sophisticated legal and regulatory framework covering areas such as intellectual property, settlement of disputes, generous fiscal incentives and concessions; an open economic system permitting free transfer of fees, profits, capital earnings and foreign exchange transactions on current account payments; and double taxation relief agreements with 29 countries and investment protection agreements with 23 countries.

The government envisages foreign investment playing an important role in bringing investment and technology into Sri Lanka. During the past decade, Sri Lanka benefited disproportionately from direct investment inflows which were on average equivalent to 1.5 % of GDP. The government projects to double the level of inflows during the current decade, particularly in the areas of tourism, urban development, IT/BPO services, pharmaceutical and renewable energy.

The private investment of around 18–20 % of GDP is targeted to rise to around 22–24 % of GDP. This includes the foreign direct investments (FDI) of around 2 % of GDP at present which is expected to be progressively increased to 5 % of GDP within a 6-year timeframe to sustain economic growth in excess of 8 %. The incentives for investment will shift from an overdependence on tax and duty concessions to genuine business opportunities that will emerge and evolve in an environment of peace, availability of quality infrastructure, stable financial environment and the optimization of the use of educated and skilled workforce.

Incentives offered for foreign investors fall under two classes or 'regimes', and the investor may be eligible for inducements provided by either of these regimes. They are:

- BOI incentives under Sect. 17 of the BOI law
- General incentives under the 'normal laws' of the country

When an investment agreement is signed with the BOI, the incentives granted and commitments made cannot be changed by successive governments. The grant of incentives depends on the type of the project proposed. Enterprises which meet specific criteria qualify for incentives under Sect. 17 of the BOI law; the incentives include (a) tax holidays from 5 to 20 years, (b) concessionary tax at 15 % after expiry of tax holiday, (c) import duty exemption from capital goods, (d) import duty exemption on raw materials if utilised for export, (e) exemption from exchange controls, (f) no restriction on repatriation of dividends and profits, (f) free transferability of shares, (g) the right to 100 % foreign ownership in almost all sectors of the economy and (h) concessionary taxation on expatriate income.

The Board of Investment (BOI) is positioned to be the premier investment promotion agency profiling the bigger opportunities that exist in partnership with line agencies, obtaining necessary clearances of forecasting investment requirements to facilitate speedier investment approvals and implementation. Strategic investment promotion is mainly focused on the following aspects and sectors:

Information Technology/Business Process Outsourcing Sector (IT/BPO) With the educated pool of talent available in the country and the expansion of IT education in all parts of the country, the IT/BPO sector which currently exports services to the value of US$300 million is targeted to increase to a billion-dollar industry in 5 years' time. This sector will absorb a talent pool in excess of 25,000. High-profile international BPO operators will be attracted in addition to the few that are already present in the country. IT training is recognised for skills developments and in education to support this thrust sector.

Urban Township Development The city of Colombo and the principal cities of the country are identified for development. The Urban Development Authority, Tourism, Ports and the Board of Investment will work together to attract suitable investors for the development of hotels and mixed development for housing, shopping and other public services.

Leisure and Tourism Tourism, which has already shown an upsurge, is planned to be increased to 2.5 million tourists and positioned as a US$2–3 billion economic activity. In order to accommodate and increase diversified numbers, hotels and other facilities such as air and road linkages, infrastructure and other leisure-related activities are being made available for potential investors, preserving biodiversity and unique destinations for a range of investments in ecotourism, wildlife, business, sea, mountains and culture.

Import Replacement Industries With the expansion of the construction and services sectors, there is an increased demand for ceramic ware, furniture, steel, cement, etc. It is aimed to expand Sri Lanka's industry base to further strengthen the country's capability by bringing these industries to international standards so that in the longer term, in addition to serving the domestic industry initially, great potential in textiles, leather, pharmaceutical, fertiliser, cement and renewable energy and food processing exists for import replacement.

High Value-Added Exports The US$3.5 billion apparel industry is expected to be a strong value-added industry becoming US$4.5 billion with backward and vertical integration and favouring up-market products. Value-added Sri Lankan branded tea, rubber products, cinnamon and spices, gems and jewellery and ceramics are projected to be over a billion US$ industry each.

Agriculture and Agro-farms The Livestock and Dairy sector covering eight farms in North Central, North Western and Southern Provinces with a land area of 1,750 ha has been put into productive use through partnership arrangements in order to support the national drive for self-sufficiency in milk. This, together with addressing other constraints such as the quality of the cattle stock, quality of animal feed as well as modern techniques and know-how, will also be for new investment opportunities which will be profiled for potential investors.

Industrial Zones The 12 BOI zones have been transformed within a 3-year timeframe into model zones depicting the country's expectations for standards in regard to environment, infrastructure, employee relations and technology improvements. New dedicated zones will also be established with private investments in IT parks and knowledge-based service centres, to generate exports and technology, as well as knowledge-based economic activities. These zones will be linked for skills development, advanced research activities, high-value product creation and other commercial operations. The unutilized space in these industry zones, an extent of two acres, provides new investments in well over 40 factories which have been made available to potential investors.

19.5 Bilateral Relationships Between Sri Lanka and Australia

Supporting Sri Lankan economic growth and reducing regional inequalities are in Australia's national interest. Australia has good bilateral relations with Sri Lanka, underpinned by trade and investment flows, education, immigration, strong people-to-people links and development cooperation. Australia's Sri Lankan community has a population of approximately 110,000 people.

Australia is committed to assisting the economic and social development of Sri Lanka. As the political and economic situation in the country improves, Australia has shifted focus from short-term humanitarian support in conflict-affected areas during the war period to long-term development assistance.

In 2012–2013, Australia provided $42.6 million in development assistance to Sri Lanka for demining and reconstruction of schools and houses damaged during the civil conflict, while it is expected to spend $42.8 million in 2014–2015. Funding also helped disadvantaged people find work, start a business or restart sustainable farming or fishing activities.

In 2012–2013, a two-way merchandise trade between Australia and Sri Lanka was $340 million with exports to Sri Lanka totalling $244 million. Vegetables, dairy products and wheat were the main merchandise exports. Tea, clothing and rubber tyres were Australia's main imports from Sri Lanka.

Education plays a significant role in the relationship, with Australia the most popular study destination for Sri Lankan students. About 4,500 Sri Lankan students are currently enrolled at Australian universities. A number of Australian tertiary providers operate distance education facilities in Sri Lanka including Monash College, an affiliate of Monash University, and the Australian College of Business and Technology, an affiliate of Edith Cowan University. The University of Southern Queensland provides a distance learning programme in Sri Lanka, which is offered by the Institute of Chartered Accountants of Sri Lanka.

Among the largest Australian investments is Ansell's Ansell Lanka rubber products plant in Biyagama, which is one of the largest foreign investments in an industrial plant in Sri Lanka.

19.6 Current Challenges

Sri Lanka is fighting with many other Asian countries to secure 'mindshare' among international investors. As Athukorala and Jayasuriya (2012) state, Sri Lanka 'is now forced to compete for foreign investment and export markets with the giant labour rich economies of China and India as well as with other Asian Countries such as Vietnam and Bangladesh' (p. 22).

Due to strong pressures from special interests and domestic lobbies, administrative feasibility, competing political imperatives and cultural factors, it is also not easy for the government to create some policy reforms to attract more FDIs. For instance, in 2013, the government could do very little to negotiate misplaced public protests regarding alleged toxic effluents from a rubber gloves factory and instead forced its closure and relocation. The factory was a leading exporter of value-added rubber gloves and owned by one of Sri Lanka's oldest blue-chip companies. Another example is Sri Lankan government's rejection to allow casinos at three superluxury resorts planned in the capital city of the country valuing US$1.3 billion by James Packer from Australia (Crown Sri Lanka Resort), by local conglomerate John Keells Holdings ($US650 million development) and by a local businessman Dhammika Perera ($US300 million project) as the opponents highly criticised the plan by emphasising that they would lead to prostitution which is highly rejected by Sri Lankan Buddhist culture. Following the incident Packer said 'Sri Lanka's ambitious tourism targets are only achievable with the right tourism infrastructure and attractions' and cited the success of Singapore in turning around its performance as a tourism destination with the development of two casino resorts (Cummins 2014).

Further, some other policies on private sector development have sent unfavourable signals and got investors worried. In 2011, the government introduced a controversial bill that expropriated 37 private enterprises which it described as 'underperforming and underutilised assets'. It included seven companies with foreign capital participation like the stock exchange-listed Hotel Developers Lanka PLC, which owns the five-star Hilton Colombo Hotel building and a waterfront convention centre owned in part by a Singaporean firm. Meanwhile, new policies regarding foreign ownership of land were introduced which bans sale of land to foreign nationals and instead imposes very high tax requirements on foreigners leasing land, creating disincentives for foreign investment. Also, on the trade side, Sri Lanka has regressed into greater protectionism (measured by tariff and para-tariffs imposed on imports) in the last 10 years, as reported by Pursell and Ahsan (2011). Thus, undertaking bold and fundamental reforms to policy and governance structures in the country will be key to becoming and staying an attractive investment location and promote growth.

It is important for Sri Lankan government to understand from other post-war contexts that reform in a short period *is* possible. In Georgia, for instance, post-war government reforms helped take it from 112th of 183 countries in the world in the ease of doing business to the top 20th easiest countries in the world, between 2006 and 2011. Policy reforms based on research findings steered the Georgian government towards deregulation of the economy. The number of licences and permission needed to start or run a business was reduced. The effect of these reforms on FDI flows was seen early. By 2007 itself, FDI inflows amounted to around 18 % of GDP (it was just 8 % in 2003). Meanwhile, fiscal policy reforms helped boost tax revenue, from under 10 % of GDP in 2004 to nearly 25 % in 2012 (Attygalle 2013).

19.7 Concluding Remarks

Sri Lanka is having a resilient economy with inherent dynamism. Even during the height of the war, Sri Lanka grew at between 5 % and 6 %, and Sri Lanka is currently aspiring to achieve, and indeed breach, the 8 % growth level and sustain it over a long period. Sri Lanka needs a sustainable growth in order to cater to the rising and evolving socioeconomic aspirations of a post-war populace. In order to realise these socioeconomic aspirations, the government requires to introduce and maintain bold and coherent economic policies in spite of pressures coming from foreign and domestic lobbying groups to attract investors as that would help the country to consolidate the post-war gains and build a prosperous future for *all* its people.

References

Annual Reports (2003–2013) Central Bank of Sri Lanka, Sri Lanka

Athukorala P, Jayasuriya S (2012) Economic policy shifts in Sri Lanka: the post- conflict development challenge. Working Paper No. 2012/15, Australian National University, Canberra

Attygalle K (2013) Reforming a post-war economy in four years? talking economics digest, July–December, Institute of Policy Studies of Sri Lanka, Colombo

Cummins C (2014) James Packer's Sri Lanka casino bid stumbles over prostitution claim, Sydney Morning Herald (28 Apr 2014)

Department of National Planning (2010) Development policy framework 2010: Mahinda Chinthana- vision for the future, Sri Lanka, Colombo

Household Income and Expenditure Surveys (2006–2013) Department of Census, Sri Lanka

Indraratna A D V de S, Vidanagama S, Wijesinha A (2014) Way forward for sustained growth. Sri Lanka Economic Association, Colombo

Pursell G, Ahsan FMZ (2011) Sri Lanka's trade policies: back to Protectionism. Australia South Asia Research Centre Working Paper 2011/03, Australian National University, Canberra

Wijesinha A (2014) Post-war economic progress: investment, positioning, and reforms in a New Sri Lankan economy. Ground Views: Journalism for Citizens available. http://groundviews.org/2014/05/18/post-war-economic-progress-investment-positioning-and-reforms-in-a-new-sri-lankan-economy/. Accessed 19 Oct 2014

Wijesinha A, Ekanayake R, Mahendra G (2013) Incentivizing foreign investment in Sri Lanka and the role of tax incentives, research studies: working paper series no. 17 (April 2013), Institute of Policy Studies of Sri Lanka, Colombo

World Bank World Development Indicators. http://data.worldbank.org/indicator/. Retrieved 20 Oct 2014